MW01253397

VARIORUM COLLECTED STUDIES SERIES

Perception, Conscience and Will
in Ancient Philosophy

Richard Sorabji

Richard Sorabji

Perception, Conscience and Will
in Ancient Philosophy

ASHGATE
VARIORUM

Published in the Variorum Collected Studies Series by

Ashgate Publishing Limited
Wey Court East
Union Road
Farnham, Surrey
GU9 7PT
England

Ashgate Publishing Company
Suite 3–1
110 Cherry Street
Burlington, VT 05401–3818
USA

www.ashgate.com

ISBN 9781409446699

British Library Cataloguing in Publication Data
A catalogue record for this book is available from the British Library.

The Library of Congress has cataloged the printed edition as follows: 2013930753

VARIORUM COLLECTED STUDIES SERIES CS1030

The paper used in this publication meets the minimum requirements of the American National Standard for Information Sciences – Permanence of Paper for Printed Library Materials, ANSI Z39.48–1984. ∞ ™

MIX
Paper from
responsible sources
FSC
www.fsc.org
FSC® C013056

Printed and bound in Great Britain by
TJ International Ltd, Padstow, Cornwall.

CONTENTS

This volume contains xxxiv + 288 pages

INTRODUCTION

This book is about the human mind with a focus on sense perception, but it finishes with chapters on moral conscience and will. Sense perception raises the further questions of the mind-body relation, of self-awareness, of infinite divisibility and the continuum, of the capacities of animals and children and of the relation between perception and reason. On all topics the introduction interconnects the papers and presents fresh material to fill out the picture. For the topic that has proved most popular, the physiological process in sense perception, a bibliography is provided as well as latest thoughts. On the final two topics, a view of moral conscience and the will is argued that provides an alternative to other interpretations. The picture of the main topics shows that each continued to develop into a richer and richer account throughout the 1200 year course of Ancient Greek Philosophy up to 600 CE, and, in such subjects as self-awareness or the approach to intentional objects, into an increasingly sophisticated one.

The Mind-Body Relation, Chapters I–II

The first two chapters are about the mind-body relation, the first in Aristotle, the second in Plato and in late Greek Aristotelians and Platonists. In Chapter XIII below, I shall sometimes have to distinguish soul from mind in ancient discussions, but for the present I am using the term 'mind' as the term most familiar in current usage. Concerning Aristotle I argued that his account of the mind-body relation is interestingly different from modern accounts. About the late Greeks my theme is that in a variety of ingenious ways they revolted from materialistic accounts, such as that found in Galen. In between the original publication of Chapters I and II, there appeared a pioneering article about the period intervening between Aristotle and Galen by Victor Caston, from whom first as a pupil and then as a colleague I have often learnt.[1] To defend a very small difference between us on the post-Galen part of the story, I owe a clarification.

Aristotle's greatest defender and interpreter to a later age was Alexander of Aphrodisias, who lived five hundred years after Aristotle and held

---

[1] Victor Caston, 'Epiphenomenalisms, ancient and modern', *The Philosophical Review* 106, 1997, pp. 309–63.

the Aristotelian chair in Athens around 205 CE. There is only limited agreement now with the verdict of an earlier leading scholar of Alexander, who emphatically described him as a materialist both in philosophy of mind and more generally.[2] I side with the current majority against a materialistic interpretation. As Chapter 2 explains, Alexander disagreed with his older contemporary, the great doctor-philosopher Galen (c. 129–199 CE), who held that that the soul, apart from Plato's immortal soul if there was such a thing (36,12–16), was simply the chemical blend of the body (a view rejected in Plato's *Phaedo* along with its equivalent that the soul was simply the attunement of the body), and that capacities of the mind simply *followed* the blend of the body. Galen congratulated the early Aristotelian Andronicus for saying that the soul either was the blend of the body or followed the blend of the body, but himself insisted on its actually *being* the blend.[3] Alexander repeatedly denied that the soul was the blend or attunement of the body, and insisted instead that it was, as Aristotle thought, a capacity that *supervened* (*epiginesthai*, sometimes just *epi*) on the blend of the body. The clarification I must introduce is that 'supervene', though a literal translation of the Greek, does not carry the same meaning that it has been given in modern analytic philosophy. In Alexander, to say that the soul supervenes on the blend tells us no more as yet than that the blend is a necessary prerequisite for there being a soul. In modern analytic philosophy by contrast supervenience implies co-variation. Same bodily state – same psychological state. That would be closer to materialism than Alexander's view.

Alexander's use of the term 'supervene' may be illuminated by the sixth century Christian scholar of Neoplatonism, Philoponus, who repeated Alexander's term later, with the difference that he transferred it from the soul to the soul's capacities, and said that they *supervene* on the blend. Philoponus contrasted with supervening both Galen's *'following'* the blend as a necessary accompaniment and being its *result* (*apotelesma*). The blend is merely a necessary prerequisite and the soul's capacities neither follow necessarily from it, nor result from it.[4] Nonetheless, colours are treated differently from capacities of the soul. Although a colour merely *supervenes* on the suitability

[2] Paul Moraux, *Alexandre d'Aphrodise, Exégète de la Noétique d'Aristote*, Les Belles Lettres, Paris 1942, pp. xviii; 10–11; 32–3; 49; 167–9. Marwan Rashed cites 6 more recent opponents, himself included, in his *Essentialisme, Alexandre d'Aphrodise entre logique, physique et cosmologie*, de Gruyter, Berlin 2007, p. 30, nn. 92; 94: Donini, Thillet, Accattino, Sharples and Gottschalk. On the other hand, William Charlton, has an unpublished paper, 'Physicalism in Alexander's De Anima', which argues for a certain materialism and also for a mechanistic tendency.

[3] Galen, *Quod animi mores* 44, 12–20.

[4] Philoponus, *Commentary on Aristotle On the Soul* 51,13–52,1;

of the blend, and is not a *result* of it,[5] it is allowed to *follow* (169,17; 170,28) the suitability of a blend. Philoponus often followed Alexander closely, and indeed, the same differentiation between capacities of the soul and colours is found earlier in Alexander. In two texts, talking of white, Alexander allows that it both supervenes on *and* follows from the blend of the body.[6] But with the soul Alexander repeatedly confines himself in his treatise *On the Soul* to saying that it is a capacity that '*supervenes*' on the blend.[7] That 'supervene' does not automatically imply 'follow' becomes clear at 66,6–8, where, talking of the soul in a different context, he says that its more perfect capacities supervene on (*epi*) the lower ones, reason on perception. Here he could not add 'follow', which implies necessarily accompanying, because lower animals, in his view, have perception without reason.

The situation in Alexander, then, seems to be that supervening does not automatically imply following. It is allowed to be compatible with following a blend in the case of properties like white, but he does not countenance the idea that the soul follows the blend of the body. The only exception is found in the supplement to his *On the Soul*, a work called *Mantissa*, which starts with a summary of his views and includes some stretches that are clearly incompatible with his other work. *Mantissa* 104,28–34, has not been particularly suspected of inauthenticity, but it has no parallel in *On the Soul* when it says that different types of soul in different animals *follow* from different types of blend. I don't know whether this represents a change of view, or rather a change of subject from speaking of when we find any soul at all, to discussing when we find different *types* of soul. Certainly the first (the presence of any soul at all) has not been allowed to *follow* from the blend. That would again have brought us somewhat closer to materialism, so it is important to see that Alexander avoids it.

To turn to Philoponus' own innovations, and to different aspects of the mind-body relation, I mention one of them only briefly in Chapter II: mutual interaction between mind and body. By philosophising one can change one's emotional disposition. Attending philosophy lectures can reduce irascibility. But the causal interaction between mind and body works in two directions. Attending philosophy lectures can make one leaner and drier, and it is this in turn that reduces irascibility. The passage adds another influence of mind on body: the student's understanding of the lecture is shown by physiological changes reflected in the face, and this guides the lecturer. This is the only

---

[5] Philoponus, *On Aristotle On coming to be and passing away* 169,24–7; 170,12–35.

[6] Alexander, *On the Soul* 24,10; *Commentary on Aristotle's Topics* 50,19–23 and 51,3.

[7] Alexander, *On the Soul* 24,18–23; 25,3–9; 26,20–22.

contribution I mentioned to knowledge of other minds. But there are others in other authors and I have discussed some of them elsewhere.[8]

Plato thought of the soul as making *spatial* movements which accounted for some mind-body interactions. Later Platonists preferred to relate soul to body non-spatially. This view is found especially in Porphyry, although I should have warned that there is controversy about the identification of one of the texts ascribed to him.[9]

Another big aspect of mind-body relations that I have discussed only elsewhere is the Platonist theory of reincarnation whether in human or in animal form. This raised questions as to whether Plato believed literally in reincarnation in animal form, and if so, whether the animal is animated only by remote control or by some non-spatial relationship, of which some are discussed in Chapter II. It also raises questions about incarnation as a human. What role is played in forming the body by the parents, including the mother, what by the soul that is waiting to be incarnated and what by Plato's World Soul? If the parents play a large role, what directs the waiting soul to a suitable body? Is it the World Soul, or does the waiting soul create its own body? Since I wrote about this,[10] an important treatise by Porphyry has been translated, *Porphyry to Gaurus On how embryos are ensouled*,[11] and the translator is now writing about the development of the subject after Porphyry.

So far I have spoken chiefly about Chapter II. As regards Chapter I, I did not intend, as two good colleagues suggested, to imply that Aristotle endorsed another modern theory, functionalism.[12] My intention was rather to show that his view about the mind-body relation differed from *all* current views. My denial that Aristotle's theory contains Brentano's idea of an intentional object of perception is more fully discussed in Chapter IV, where I trace the intervening reinterpretations which I think were required before Brentano

---

[8] *The Philosophy of the Commentators 200–600 AD, a Sourcebook*, vol. 1, Psychology, Duckworth, London, and Cornell University Press 2005, Bloomsbury, London, 2011, Ch. 9, 'Knowledge of other minds', pp. 242–4.

[9] John Rist doubts if the whole of the passage cited from Nemesius is a quotation from Porphyry, and from his *Summikta Zetemata*, 'Pseudo-Ammonius and the soul/body problem in some Platonic texts of late antiquity' *American Journal of Philology* 109, 1988, pp. 402–15.

[10] Richard Sorabji, *Animal Minds and Human Morals*, Duckworth and Cornell 1993, Bloomsbury 2011, Ch. 13; *The Philosophy of the Commentators 200–600 AD, a Sourcebook*, vol. 1, Psychology, Duckworth, London, and Cornell University Press 2005, Bloomsbury, London, 2011, Ch. 6(d), pp. 213–16. The subject is taken much further by James Wilberding, *Porphyry to Gaurus*.

[11] *Porphyry to Gaurus On how embryos are ensouled*, translated by James Wilberding, Bloomsbury, London 2011.

[12] Kathy Wilkes, *Physicalism*, Routledge, London 1978; Myles Burnyeat also took me this way in our earlier discussions.

could read his idea into Aristotle. As regards the passage where Aristotle says that what rules out *seeing* that one sees is not lack of coloration in the eye, my early interpretation is corrected in Ch. III, p. 213, and Ch. XI, pp. 132–3, below. These explain that this is a dialectical move and does not imply that one is self-aware of seeing by *perceiving* as well as *receiving* coloration in the eye jelly. The dialectical move should be clearer still from the fuller treatment in my book *Self*, Oxford and Chicago University Presses 2006, pp. 206–9.

Chapters III–V, physiological process and intentional object in perception

Chapter III (defended in Chapter V) discusses both the physiology of perception and its cognitive aspect. It thus both links with the preceding topic of mind-body relations and paves the way for Chapter IV, which concerns the centuries of reinterpretations leading up to Franz Brentano's. He found in Aristotle his idea, seminal for modern philosophy of mind, of perception and all mental activities as being directed to non-physical 'intentional objects', as they are called.

Chapter III examines first the *formal* cause of perception in Aristotle. He thought it a kind of discrimination. But since he differs from his teacher Plato in denying *reason* to animals other than humans, he has to explain how other animals cope in the world by expanding dramatically in comparison with Plato what *perception* can do. The sense of smell, for example, enables them to perceive not just an odour, as in Plato, but an odour as lying in a certain direction and as belonging to a deer. They can thus combine the idea of an odour with various predicates, or predicate certain things of it. But perception requires also a *material* cause, a physiological process. I argue that in seeing, for example, the physiological process is the eye jelly's borrowing colour patches from the scene perceived.

This physiological interpretation is presented (pp. 211, 220, 224–5 of the original) as a preliminary to the discussion of Franz Brentano in Chapter IV. Brentano lay at the far end of a long tradition of commentary on Aristotle, when in 1874 he cited Aristotle's 'reception of form without matter' in perception and thought as already referring to his own distinctive idea, that perception and thought are directed to 'intentional', rather than real objects. The object of my visual experiences or of my hopes and fears does not have to exist in reality in order to be their object. It need only have what Brentano calls 'intentional inexistence', and this he considered a characterising feature of mental as opposed to physical activity.

Victor Caston has argued, and will document more fully in a book in preparation, that ideas of intentional objects and attitudes are to be found also

xii INTRODUCTION

in the Stoics and in Augustine,[13] although the route of commentary on Aristotle was, I think, the one that influenced Brentano. In my view, in order to see how Brentano could understand Aristotle to be talking about something so non-physical as an intentional object, we need to trace the series of reinterpretations through late antiquity and the Islamic and Latin-speaking Middle Ages. It was in order to free Aristotle from various difficulties in the *physical* side of his theory of perception that the late Greek commentators increasingly understood his ideas in a *non-physical* way. Their aim was not to give the most straightforward reading of Aristotle's text, but to give Aristotle the most defensible view. This might be called simply a distortion of his actual view, but I see it as a heuristically fruitful transformation of his view that finishes up by giving us the concept of an intentional object. If my interpretation of Aristotle's original view is right, we shall miss the transformation and the way the history of philosophy works, if we do not see what the original view was. But my interpretation is still a matter of controversy.

The controversy about physiology between myself and my one-time sparring partner, Myles Burnyeat, first published in 1992, has proved very popular. For most of 1970 to 1978, Burnyeat and I lectured together to London philosophy students, one delivering the lecture and the other making objections. An appendix will provide a list, kindly assembled by others,[14] of 37 publications on the subject between 1992 and 2012. But I also cite in Chapter III many agreements and disagreements with my interpretation from before 1992. On my view, Aristotle thought that seeing, for example, involved the physiological process of the eye jelly borrowing colours from the scene observed. On his, Aristotle postulated no physiological process at all. Caston's masterly attempt to adjudicate[15] has not convinced the protagonists entirely, but it has changed the terminology of the debate as being one between followers of the *spirit* and of the *letter* in interpreting Aristotle's idea that the organ becomes like the sense object.

In 1992, Burnyeat very interestingly showed that Philoponus understood Aristotle's idea that in seeing we receive matter without form in his way and differently from me.[16] In text 9 of my Chapter III,[17] Philoponus says that the

---

[13] Victor Caston, 'Something and Nothing: The Stoics on Concepts and Universals' *Oxford Studies in Ancient Philosophy*, vol. 17, 1999, 145–213.

[14] 31 items were assembled by Joachim Aufderheide, and I drew others from Peter Lautner, Roberto Grasso, Kunio Qatanabe and from my own awareness.

[15] Victor Caston, 'The spirit and the letter: Aristotle on perception', in R. Salles, ed., *Metaphysics, Soul and Ethics. Themes from the Work of Richard Sorabji,* Oxford University Press, pp. 245–320.

[16] Myles Burnyeat, 'Is an Aristotelian Philosophy of mind still credible?', 1992. see appendix.

[17] Philoponus, *On Aristotle On the Soul*, pp. 432, 32 – 433,11; 438,6–15.

sense organ does not become coloured or odorous. The organ of sight, for example, does not contain a liquid, but the gas *pneuma*, and this is the basic organ for all five senses. It would not be a suitable material for taking on colours. Philoponus' interpretation is that receiving form without matter does not involve, as I thought, receiving coloration without particles. Rather, form is received only cognitively (*gnôstikôs*). The only exception is the sensing by touch of hot, cold, fluid or dry, which inevitably involves, in addition to the cognitive effect, the sense organ being affected materially (*hulikôs*) by these four qualities.

On the other hand, there have been two recent new pieces of evidence thanks to a finding by Peter Lautner, whose relevance we both noticed. An 11th century codex of Philoponus' commentary *On Aristotle On the Soul* includes a passage that is printed by Hayduck at the foot of p. 293 of his edition.[18] The author appears to be Philoponus and in the first 13 lines, he repeatedly says that perception is nothing but the discrimination of the effect (*pathos*) produced in the sense organ by the object of sense. So there is a physiological process as well as the cognitive activity. This claim is compatible with Philoponus' denial that the sense organ becomes coloured or odorous, as emerges from more recent work by Lautner. The physiological change received by the organs of sight, hearing and other sensitive powers, as he explains in a new paper in preparation,[19] is rather compression or expansion in the *pneuma* which they contain. I leave it to Lautner to provide the evidence.

Chapter V seeks to present some other chapters of Aristotle's *On the Soul* as offering no counter-evidence about physiological processes, and finishes by finding Brentano's idea of an intentional object absent from Aristotle's theory of thinking.

Chapter VI, demarcating the five senses

Book 2, chapters 3, 4 and 6 of Aristotle's *On the Soul* make clear that the five senses and other perceptual powers should be defined by reference to the properties that they perceive. Each is the perception of such objects, and this, with one exception, is the programme of definitions carried out in the ensuing chapters. The description in 2.6 of these properties as intrinsic (*kath' hauta*) objects of the senses may actually mean that they define the senses, as I

---

[18] *Commentaria in Aristotelem Graeca* vol. 15. Peter Lautner, 'Methods in examining sense-perception: John Philoponus and ps-Simplicius', *Laval Théologique et philosophique*, vol. 64, 2008, pp, 651–61, at p. 654.

[19] Peter Lautner, '*Gnôstikôs* and/or *hulikôs*: Philoponus' account of the material aspects of sense perception'.

suggested. But I also warned that Aristotle recognises more than one meaning of the expression and that the case does not rest on this. Colour, sound and flavour are named as intrinsic objects of their respective senses, but shape and size are also intrinsic objects, evidently to what is sometimes elsewhere called the common sense, because they are later said to be merely accidental objects of the five senses, 3.1, 425a15.

2.6 makes a second distinction, or perhaps double distinction: colour, unlike shape, is a peculiar or proper (*idion*) object of sight, because it is perceived *only* by sight, and he adds about proper objects that *hearing*, for example, cannot be deceived that there is *sound*. This second claim would be justified if he intended the further point that *whenever* we hear, we hear sound. This is not to deny that *sight* might be deceived that there was sound, which could be why he weakens the 'cannot', when he later switches from hearing to *perception*, and says that *perception* is *minimally* deceived about a proper object, 3.3, 428b19.

The exception is the sense of touch, which Aristotle defines differently, partly, no doubt, because it perceives so many different kinds of property. He defines it not by the numerous objects it perceives, but by the fact that it operates by direct contact. Contact, however, is equally a feature of the sense of taste, which was not by ordinary Greeks thought of as a form of touch any more than it is by us. Plato had a solution. He had defined touch in his *Timaeus* as the sense which does not depend on a localised organ, because many parts of the body can exercise it. This makes it unlike taste. This is the second case in which Aristotle's contact criterion causes him difficulty. Another, highlighted by the work of John Ellis, was discussed in Chapter IV. If touch and taste are the only senses that operate by direct contact, will not the fragrance of an apple have to detach itself from any apple particles, rather than the particles directly contacting the organ of smell? But Aristotle's logic denies that a particular apple's fragrance can detach itself from the apple's particles. If Aristotle counters that what detaches itself and is received by the organ is not the fragrance, but some effect of the fragrance, will that that fit with his idea that in perception sensible forms are received?

Chapters VII–IX, the physics of senses and sense-objects

Chapter VII, intermediate colours

Chapters VII–IX move to the physics of perception and perceptibles, the subject of Aristotle's *On Sense Perception*. Chapter VII treats Aristotle's view in *On Sense Perception*, Chapters 3, 4 and 7 that other shades of colour are mixtures of the darkest, the black of pure earth, with the brightest, the white of pure fire. The most pleasant of the other colours are produced by ratios of black to white which are numerically simple, and similarly for flavours and odours. This would transfer to other sensibles the Pythagorean discovery that the pleasing consonant pairs of notes are produced by mathematically simple differences of string length in the ratios 1:4, 1:3, 1:2, 2:3, and 3:4. Goethe backed Aristotle against Newton as understanding the painter's colours. They both noticed that the sun is variously coloured by a cloudy or sooty atmosphere and Goethe thought that this was how varnishes changed the colour of paintings. Aristotle knew of theories about the combination of black and white ingredients, but he substituted in place of the idea that they are juxtaposed or superimposed, his own idea that they are blended into a chemical mixture.

It is interesting that Aristotle, despite important oversights in his theory, is more mathematical in intent here than Plato, contrary to a very common stereotype. For Plato had said in *Timaeus* 68B and D that no one could know the ratios of his own theory of colour and no human could test them. A very limited testability is suggested for Aristotle's Pythagoreanising theory.

Chapter VIII, borrowed colour and light, minimum perceptibles

The next subjects are discussed in Aristotle *On Sense Perception*, Chapters 3, 6 and 7. Every body, Aristotle thinks, contains the transparent elements air and water, and therefore has some degree of transparency, however low, throughout. The seat of colour in a body is its transparency, and, more precisely, the outer surface of its transparency, which coincides with the outer surface of the body. But as to which colour appears at the surface, the mixture of dark and bright colour at the surface, discussed in Aristotle's Chapter 3, does not apply to *borrowed* colour. The borrowed colour of the sea depends on the viewer's distance and angle of viewing. But Aristotle does not ascribe this borrowed colour to reflection, even though he knows that what is reflected also depends on the viewer's angle of vision. Implausibly, he speaks as if the variation of colour depends only on the sea's movements. As to how borrowed colour differs from illumination or light, the latter (light) makes the sea seeable-*through*, the former makes it seeable. Moreover, light penetrates beyond the surface.

Light is defined as the property of being *actually* seeable-through because of the presence in the transparent medium of fire or fire-like substance. Because light is the product of mere *presence*, it does not have to travel, part way before whole, and in this it is like some qualities, such as a pond's being frozen. Freezing can also 'leap', without travelling part way before whole. But the acceptance of mere *presence* prevents Aristotle from explaining the directionality of light, why it does not easily go round corners, but allows shadows and night. He is nonetheless very aware of its directionality, and he uses the common talk of rays. But he prefers to speak of the directionality not of light, but of the influence of colour. Moreover, this is talk of the direction of causal *influence*, not of travel, part way before whole. Philoponus was later to extend the directionality of causal influence to the case of light. Aristotle is aware, unlike Democritus, that mirroring is due to the reflection, or bending, of something, *On Sense Perception* 2, 438a8. At *On the Soul* 3.12, 435a5–10, he thinks of it as due to the bending of the influence of colour.

Aristotle also discusses how many colour patches in an area, or how many variations of shade or pitch in a range, are 'separately' perceptible, as opposed to being perceptible in some weaker sense, such as contributing to the perceptibility of a larger whole. He decides the number will be finite, so that there are minimal 'separately' perceptible patches and variations. This introduces an element of discontinuity into his system. But he introduces refinements: a singer's discontinuous change of separately perceptible pitch may be due to a *continuous* change of vocal tension, and similarly with the *continuous* motion of a stopper along a musical string. This permits us to identify the target of certain objections raised by Aristotle's friend and successor, Theophrastus.

Unexpectedly, however, Aristotle goes on a little later to say that, although a perceptible magnitude can *appear* the smallest possible, it cannot in fact be indivisible. I now think that he means to allow what he previously allowed, that it is still the smallest 'separately' perceptible and is only denying that it is indivisible as an area in its own right. He uses an argument that will be the subject of the next chapter concerning the instant of change. But he uses the argument unsatisfactorily in a way that would prove too much by ruling out larger perceptible patches. If there were an indivisible perceptible patch, he says, imagine it approaching an observer until it becomes perceptible. What would be the last distance of imperceptibility and what the first distance of perceptibility? Every answer appears paradoxical. In the next chapter, we shall see Aristotle offering clever answers for some contexts.

Whatever his view of minimal perceptible patches, Aristotle does not welcome a minimal limit for perceptible *times*, with shorter times being imperceptible, an idea which seem to have been required by certain theories that he addresses. Certainly, modern psychology has established that our perception depends on a number of illusions about the relative timing of things perceived, because of the imperceptibility of small time differences. One of the pointilliste theories that Aristotle rejects, of intermediate colours being produced by juxtaposed black and white dots, probably postulated that the effects of the black and white reach the observer at different speeds, and imperceptibly different times. This would protect the observer from having to perceive opposite qualities at the very same time. Another type of theory, including probably Plato's in his *Timaeus*, explains the two notes in a consonant pair as travelling towards us at different speeds, the higher one arriving imperceptibly sooner, and a theory in the pseudo-Aristotelian *On Audibles* postulates undetectably small differences of string vibration. The last description may have been written after Aristotle, but either it or some predecessor may have added further objectionable features, since that would explain why Aristotle adds several extra objections that would not apply to the other theories. Once again, Aristotle's successor Theophrastus is said to have replied that there can be a first instant of having changed, in cases where change takes no time, and he was thought to have been referring to Aristotle's 'leap' of light or freezing.

Chapter IX, the instant of change

The problem of the instant of change is a general problem of physics. But it is applied to the change of becoming perceptible, as we have just seen, and to a change of coming to be wholly of a new colour. If the train leaves at the sizeless instant of noon, what is the first instant of motion and the last of rest? If the first instant of motion coincides with, or precedes, the last instant of rest, we seem to have both motion and rest at the same time, which sounds like a contradiction. If the first instant of motion follows the last instant of rest, we will have neither state during the intervening period, and how can this be? Finally, to say that there is a last instant of rest but not a first instant of motion, or vice versa, appears arbitrary.

I have suggested that different solutions should be found for different contexts. But if, like Aristotle and modern physics, we treat motion as continuous, not jerky like motion on a cinema screen, in that context there would be a way of avoiding arbitrariness. Since in continuous motion, there is no first distance or instant away from the starting point, and no first instant of exceeding zero velocity, it would not be arbitrary (although it would not be mandatory) to prefer a last instant of rest to a first instant of motion, since there are *independent* reasons for denying a first instant of motion.

Are other changes continuous in this way? If shades of colour do not form a continuous series, according to Aristotle *On Sense Perception* Chapter 6, it might seem that a leaf could change discontinuously to a new colour at an instant. But Aristotle points out that the new colour may spread continuously over its surface. Even if the whole leaf changed colour instantly, this might be due to a continuous underlying change, in which case it might be thought of as changing to the new colour continuously, but imperceptibly, according to one suggestion in Aristotle's discussion. In all the cases so far, it would be non-arbitrary to say that there was no first instant of changing, though, as Aristotle is aware, there would be a first instant of having wholly acquired and of having the new colour.

Aristotle offers two solutions for the case of continuous changes. Sometimes he falls foul of modern dynamics by denying that there is any rest or motion at a sizeless instant, since rest or motion must include a 'then' and a 'now', which a sizeless instant cannot do. But modern dynamics is able to make very useful calculations by thinking in terms of velocity at an instant, through a process of thinking of velocity at an instant as the limit of velocities in a surrounding period. Moreover, Aristotle is himself aware that there are many properties which he has to recognise as holding at an instant. A moving thing can have reached a point at an instant, a body can be of a new colour at an instant, and in general a change can have been completed and a new state of affairs have come into being at an instant.

Accordingly, he often suggests a solution like the one I have advocated and even at one point allows that after all there can be a last instant at which something is *resting*. Moreover, he holds that there is a first instant of being in the *terminal* state of a change, but on the other hand, what is changing must already have accomplished some change, and what has accomplished some change, must already have been changing, so that there is *no* first in the series of changes. This last point, no first in the series of changes, is reasonable because of the *continuity* of the changes he is considering, and on which he insists, and I presume he is influenced by the continuity even though he does not actually articulate it as his rationale.

Niko Strobach has written a thorough and interesting book on the instant of change, recording solutions throughout Western history and offering his own. He treats my proposals very fairly, but prefers a different one, because he would like a proposal that fits all cases and even imaginary cases that physics may or may not recognise in the world, such as a discontinuous acceleration in a continuous motion, although I did in passing consider such a case.[20]

Chapters X–XI, Self-awareness in perception and higher order perception and thought

Chapters X–XI discuss self-awareness. But Chapter 10 has a more general theme, the tendency of Platonism to permeate what Aristotle saw as perceptual functions with rational ones. I consider not only self-awareness, but concept formation and perception itself.

As regards concept formation, I argue for the view that Aristotle, in contrast to Plato's recollection of concepts acquired from previous lives, recognised a level of *empirical* concepts, available even to some animals, that amounted to

---

[20] Niko Strobach, *The Moment of Change*, Kluwer, Dordrecht, 1998.

no more than many memories based on *perception*. But scientific concepts, although starting in this empirical way, required more. The concept of lunar eclipse as the moon's loss of light caused by the earth's shadow required *nous*, a kind of intellectual 'spotting' of the cause. Platonist commentators took the opportunity to build up the *nous* required into three kinds of intellect. Aristotle himself also went beyond his usual statement that one perceives something particular, by saying that perception is of the *universal*, e.g. *human*, not just of the human Callias. Once again, he was seeking to give a basic role in concept formation to perception, but he added that we move by induction from the most specific species, such as human, to the universal, such as animal. Into this induction the Platonist commentators inserted many steps. Perception transmits information about *human* first to imagination, which itself is sometimes equated with the lowest form of intellect, and onward in turn to reason. Some Platonists supposed that Aristotle accepted Plato's concepts recollected from previous lives alongside his own gained originally from perception.

The difference between Plato and his pupil Aristotle is starkest in their accounts of *perception*. Plato's *Theaetetus* reduces the role of sense perception, as noticed in Chapter III, to perceiving white and sweet. But for grasping *being* (*ousia*), which perhaps includes the idea that something *is* white, one needs reasoning and opinion (*doxa*). Aristotle, as classificatory biologist, distinguished opinion as a *rational* capacity, along with most forms of knowledge and thought, and hence as unavailable to non-human animals. But he allows the lion to *perceive* that the ox *is* near. More generally, animals can have the perceptual *appearance* (*phantasia*) that things are thus and so, and he strongly insists that they have memory, which is a *perceptual* capacity even when we apply it to remembering intelligibles. This is a total reconstruction of Plato's *Theaetetus*. Plato cuts across two of Aristotle's perceptual faculties and two of his rational, when he says that *opinion* is a function of memory with perception or thought, and he further allows opinion to non-human animals. Again, Plato describes perception and memory as both giving us knowledge, using three different words for knowledge, including one, *epistasthai*, that Aristotle uses for scientific understanding, which requires far more than his perceptual capacities of perception and memory.

If Aristotle reconstructed Plato's mappings, the Platonists cut across his with a vengeance. One talked of *scientific* perception (*epistêmonikos*). Another distinguished two types of reason, scientific and opiniative (*doxastikos logos*), but the latter was based on *perception* and was later said to give knowledge of *bodies*. Perceptibles came to be made objects of *opinion*, and perception got seated in the *opiniative* part of the soul. In perception, we had to project concepts (*logoi*) or forms (*eidê*) of a Platonist kind stored in our reason, in order to correct the inaccurate deliverances of sense perception.

Aristotle sometimes refers to sense perception in general, as opposed to the five specific senses, as having functions of its own that might concern any of the five, and sometimes (not always) calls it then the *common* sense. Awareness of our own perceiving is sometimes attributed to the common sense, and one needs something unitary, as Plato pointed out, for the function of comparing or distinguishing sweet and white. If these qualities were not presented to something unitary, it would be as if *I* perceived sweet and *you* white. Plato assigns the task to reason, Aristotle to the common sense. So far the role of perception in self-awareness was confined by Aristotle to awareness of one's *sensory* activities, except in one passage, cited in Chapter 1 above, but wrongly omitted here, where Aristotle talks of perceiving that one is *thinking*, *Nicomachean Ethics* (*EN*) 10.9, 1170a 31–2. More commonly, however, Aristotle has a different account in which thinking is aware of *itself*, because the intelligibles of which it is aware are in a sense identical with itself.

With Neoplatonism things changed, because it was repeatedly noticed that we are aware not only of our own perceiving, but also of many other kinds of cognition and of many kinds of desiring. Plotinus assigned awareness of perceptions and thoughts to 'inner sense', or more often to the mirror of imagination (*phantasia*), but imagination could be aware of more activities because, unlike Aristotle, he recognised one kind of imagination concerned with intelligibles, which he equated with opinion, and one with sensibles. But others sought something more unitary to provide consciousness (*parakolouthein*) of all our psychological activities. Proclus suggested *reason*, and by using the Stoic term *parakolouthein*, he recognised the idea of a reflective consciousness more general than anything found in Aristotle, whose perception and reason had split up the field of consciousness, leaving him, as Charles Kahn has pointed out, with no general term.[21] More interesting than reason as the unitary faculty was a suggestion ascribed to 'newer interpreters' that we have a faculty of *attending* (the *prosektikon*), to borrow again a Stoic term, *prosokhê*, used in their case particularly for moral self-interrogation. Damascius was certainly' one of the newer interpreters. Greek philosophy was very alive to the importance of attention, and would never have accepted the idea of one's actions being controlled by desires and beliefs only. They were well aware that it matters which beliefs you *attend* to, and in what way. The unitary part was called 'attentive' insofar as it surveyed one's cognitions, but 'conscience' (*suneidêsis*), insofar as it surveyed one's desires.[22] By this time

---

[21] Charles Kahn, 'Sensation and consciousness in Aristotle's psychology', *Archiv für Geschichte der Philosophie*, 48, 1966, pp. 43–81.

[22] Philoponus, *On Aristotle On the Soul* 465,7–17 says vital faculties, but in the same context Damascius and Olympiodorus specify desiring faculties: Damascius, *Lectures on Plato's Phaedo*

the noun or noun phrase (*to suneidos*) had largely shed its ambiguity and was used for moral conscience. Certainly when another sixth century Neoplatonist, Olympiodorus, explained that the *suneidos* was aware of the desiderative faculties, he equated it with Socrates' admonitory guardian spirit, which earlier Platonists had also treated as equivalent to moral conscience.[23]

There was a final twist relevant to permeation, if some Platonists thought that the unitary faculty could still be called by Aristotle's name, 'the common sense' for reasons that Aristotle himself would have repudiated. These Platonists held that self-awareness took not Plotinus' form of mirroring, but the form of turning back in on oneself, a self-penetration which for bodies is impossible. But the common sense is said to be more independent of body than the five senses. Even though it is lower than reason or intellect, it may possibly have been considered a form of opinion.

Recent controversy has debated whether self-awareness of our own psychological activities is due to higher-order perception or thought. But Greek philosophy turns out to have more options than that. Many forms of self-awareness were discussed that did not involve a higher order of awareness. Aristotle's idea of self-thinking is only one such idea. Another is the idea of being present to oneself, which Augustine is likely to have taken from the Platonist Porphyry. But even among those who postulated a higher-order awareness there were other options, such as inner sense, imagination, and the attentive faculty.

In fact, as more fully explained in Chapter XI, I believe that there is something wrong about seeking unity in a single faculty that is aware of all. A variety of faculties is needed. What gives unity to self-awareness, in my view, is that it is one and the same *person*, that is one and the same owner, who *has* all the psychological states that are being surveyed, and who *has* the activity of surveying them.

In Chapter XI, I focus exclusively on self-awareness. Plato questioned its possibility, arguing that it was in danger of being an awareness with no content. Aristotle discussed a different threat, again influenced by Plato, that it might lead to an infinite regress of higher-order awarenesses. My account of Aristotle here replaces what was said in Chapter I, but there is a more detailed account of these threats in Chapter 11 of my book, *Self*.

Several thinkers considered, and so does modern infant psychology, that self-awareness is facilitated by awareness of others. The idea is found in

I, para 271, Westerink, pp. 162–3; Olympiodorus, *Commentary of Plato's First Alcibiades*, 22,14–23,18, Westerink.

[23] Olympiodorus, *On Plato's First Alcibiades*, p. 23, lines 2–7, (p. 17 Westerink); Plutarch, *On the Daemon of Socrates* 592B; Apuleius, *On Socrates' Daemon*, 16.

different forms in Plato, Aristotle, the Stoic Hierocles and the Neoplatonist Plotinus.

This reverses the tradition found in Augustine and Descartes that self-knowledge is indubitable with their different versions of the *Cogito* argument. Augustine may have been influenced by another passage in Plotinus, as well as by Porphyry's idea that the self is present to the self. Descartes combines indubitable self-knowledge with the idea that knowledge of other people is based on inference.

Returning to the theme of the *unity* of self-awareness, and the suggestion that it is due to higher-order perception or thought, I repeat that different faculties are required in different cases, although I may not have chosen the right examples. But an interesting further observation emerges from Aristotle's *On Sense Perception*, that the whole idea of a world of bodies possessing more than one quality, may depend on awareness of such qualities as being presented to oneself as the self-same person at the same time.

Chapter XII, Moral conscience

My chapter on moral conscience is one of two papers that arose out of work on self-awareness in Chapters X–XI, because moral conscience was originally thought of in the fifth century BCE as a *self-awareness* of a defect, usually moral.[24] The original idea was very surprising. The full Greek expression *suneidenai heautôi* literally meant to share knowledge with oneself, and when the 'with oneself' was explicitly included, the knowledge seems always to have been of a defect. The grammar was explained by C.A Pierce in 1955, but not the meaning.[25] Latin did not offer a paraphrase with all its Roman connotations, but helpfully translated the Greek quite literally as *conscientia*, sharing knowledge, and added its own terms for oneself. It has often been thought that the original meaning must have been sharing knowledge with *another*. But in fact the original metaphor was of yourself sharing knowledge with yourself, as if you were split into two. From your own perspective, this may create the fear that another shares the knowledge that you share with yourself. But it is only later, especially with lawyers, that we find stress on *another* sharing the knowledge, especially in talk of witnesses, accomplices and confidants, and then the reference to self-knowledge often ceases to be

---

[24] The other paper, 'Graeco-Roman origins of the idea of moral conscience', *Studia Patristica* vol. 44, 2010, pp. 361–83, went into more detail, but had for reasons of space to exclude some of the later Greek developments.

[25] C.A.Pierce, *Conscience in the New Testament*, SCM Press, London 1955.

made explicit by the reflexive 'with oneself'. In the absence of the reflexive, the knowledge is not always of a defect.

Since I first wrote, it has come to my attention that the meaning has been recognised by two people, but not as the original meaning: Thomas Hobbes and C.S. Lewis. Both put it well in terms of one self knowing a guilty secret and the other self sharing the guilty secret.[26] Hobbes, I think, was trying to show a decline from conscience as belief shared between genuinely different people, to this private belief about past or present fault, to misguided private belief about the wrongness of complying with the State. The notion that one *does share* one's own guilty secret fits the Greek usage better, I think, than the related, but different, suggestion I made in the original text that one *ignores* one's own guilty secret, when one *ought* to share it.

So far the notion of the guilty secret is backward-looking. But conscience acquired forward-looking roles as well. Already Euripides' Phaedra, without speaking of self-shared knowledge, distinguishes good shame which *averts* future wrongdoing, from bad shame which torments one about the past.[27] Another forward-looking function of conscience is *reform*, and the Stoic Seneca credits Epicurus with interest in that, when he praises him for saying that recognition of sin (*notitia peccati*) is the beginning of salvation.[28] Seneca agrees and also treats conscience as averting wrong conduct.[29] When the Christian Lactantius, writing in the third century CE, criticises Cicero as not thinking repentance (*paenitere*) an effective route to reform (*corrigere errorem*), he adds a further future-looking role for the resulting reform, that it can lead to God's *forgiveness* or *remission* of sin.[30]

The late Neoplatonist view recorded by 'Philoponus' in the 6th century is that moral conscience, *to suneidos*, is one species of a faculty of self-awareness or *attention, to prosektikon*. It is directed to the *vital* (*zôtikai*) faculties, and the other species to the *cognitive* faculties. The term *suneidos* is used in the same century by the Neoplatonists Damascius and Olympiodorus in the very same context to say that one and the same faculty is aware of the cognitive faculties and, as conscience (*suneidos*), of the *desiring* faculties (*orektikai*),

[26] Thomas Hobbes, *Leviathan*, I. Ch 7, previously mentioned by me only for one of the other senses, but all three are set out in Mark Hanin, 'Thomas Hobbes' theory of conscience', *History of Political Thought* 33, 2012, pp. 55–85; and a larger number by C.S Lewis, *Studies in Words*, Cambridge University Press, 2nd edition 1967, Ch. 8, 'Conscience and conscious'.

[27] Euripides, *Hippolytus*, 380–7, as analysed by B. Williams, *Shame and Necessity*, University of California, Berkeley, 1993, p. 95.

[28] Seneca, *Letters* 28, 9–10.

[29] Seneca, *Letters* 105,7–8; 117,1; *frag.* 14 Haase (=81 Vottero) from Lactantius, *Divine Institutes*, VI.24.16–17 (a guardian: *custos*).

[30] Lactantius, *Divine Institutes* VI. 24, 1–10.

with the difference that Olympiodorus uses the term *suneidos* additionally
as the generic term for both forms of self-awareness.[31] That *suneidos* refers
to *moral conscience* is clear from the fact that in Olympiodorus this same
suneidos is identified with Socrates' guardian spirit, which had been treated
like conscience or said to take the place of conscience by the earlier Platonists,
Plutarch and Apuleius.[32]

I shall not say much more here, because it will be the subject of my next
book, *Moral Conscience through the Ages*. But I think that the original meaning
continued to have an influence up to the present. Moral conscience continued
to require one's own self-awareness, however much external authorities sought
to impose rules from the outside. There also recurred at intervals the idea of
conscience splitting one into two. The concept started off secular, and has found
no difficulty playing a role in modern secular as well as religious societies. The
17th century was the period in which the concept underwent revolutionary
examination, in some cases critical, but the 18th century, I believe, saw a
number of attempts to rehabilitate the idea of moral conscience. One of these
rehabilitations, Adam Smith's drew heavily on the Stoics. A towering figure
of the 20th century, Gandhi, was influenced in his account of conscience by
Plato's account of Socrates.

I have suggested in my other treatments that the idea of conscience
eventually developed into that of a fallible *belief*, a believing or thing believed,
which may or may not amount to knowledge. The belief concerned both the
backward and the forward-looking roles of conscience. It came to be a belief
about what it *was*, or *would be*, wrong or not wrong for one to do or not to do.
Alternatively, it can be a capacity for such beliefs. Because the belief is about
one's being in the *wrong*, the belief is motivating and causes feelings, facts
which are thereby accommodated without further complications.

Chapter XIII, Will

The topic of will complements the topic of moral conscience. In the chapter on
will I have been influenced by Charles Kahn's point that there are a number of

---

[31] Damascius *Lectures on Plato's Phaedo* I, para 271, Westerink, pp. 162–3; Olympiodorus, *Commentary on Plato's First Alcibiades*, 22,14–23,18, Westerink. The nomenclature is clarified by J.W Atkins, 'Euripides' *Orestes* and the concept of conscience in Greek Philosophy', *Journal of the History of Ideas*, forthcoming.

[32] Plutarch, *On the daemon of Socrates* 591E–592B; Apuleius, *On Socrates' Daemon*, 16. Atkins further confirms by pointing to Olympiodorus' reference in the passage cited to Orestes' conscience at having killed his mother in Euripides' play.

different strands in the idea of the will.[33] Among the strands, as the idea came
to be developed, are the following four.

(i) A desire like will can be *rational* in more than one sense. Aristotle moves
to the idea, at least by the time of *On the Soul* 3.9, 432a18–b7, I believe,
but not everyone agrees,[34] that *boulêsis* as a desire is conceptually distinct
from reason, but, 3.10, 433b 13–16, is in accordance with it (*kata*). This
is not necessarily correct reason; it may be incorrect reason, as implied by
Aristotle's further claim that *boulêsis* is desire only for the apparent good,
except in good people (*spoudaioi*).[35] A different way in which desire can
be rational had earlier been based by Aristotle on Plato. He had said that it
was the rational form of soul that exhorted (*parakalein*) people aright and
to the best, not something conceptually distinct from rationality. But this
rational form of soul might be opposed by an irrational form of soul, which,
however, could listen to reason and was capable of obeying it and was to
that extent rational.[36] Plato had already thought of reason as having its own
desires. It probably had desires for learning,[37] and there was a rational form
of soul,[38] which can draw the soul back and prevent it from doing something
suggested by the appetitive form of soul.[39] It is this second conception of
rational desire, I now think, that is taken up by Augustine when he makes
the will belong to the rational soul.[40] He also sometimes suggests, like
Lucretius, that what wills is the mind (*animus*), Lucretius' central (but
for him not necessarily rational) part of the soul,[41] and Augustine holds
that there is a carnal will that opposes the spiritual will.[42] The carnal will
is presumably not rational except in Aristotle's sense, probably unknown
to Augustine, of being able to listen to reason (*katêkoon*).[43] So there are

---

[33] Charles Kahn, 'Discovering the will: from Aristotle to Augustine', in J. Dillon, A.A.Long,
eds, *The Question of Eclecticism*, Berkeley 1988, pp. 234–59.

[34] I should acknowledge that Terry Irwin, *Aristotle's First Principles*, Oxford 1988, p. 595,
note 2, has argued, that *On the Soul* 3.9, 432a18–b7 rejects only a *spatial* division of soul parts.
But I think the question raised concerns both spatial and conceptual (*logôi*) divisions, a 20, and
once explicitly, b3, and other times implicitly, speaks of an excess or wrong choice of *conceptual*
(*logôi*) divisions arising from the division of the soul into two or three parts.

[35] Aristotle, *Nicomachean Ethics* 3.4, 1113a22–6.

[36] Aristotle, *Nicomachean Ethics* 1.13, 1102b13–1103a3.

[37] Plato, *Phaedo* 114E.

[38] Plato, *Republic* 439E; 440E.

[39] Plato, *Republic* 439B–C.

[40] Augustine, *City of God* 5.11.

[41] Augustine, *Confessions* 8.9; Lucretius 2.270; 4.886.

[42] Augustine, *Confessions* 8.5; 8.9–10.

[43] Aristotle, *Nicomachean Ethics*. 1.13, 1102b31; Plato, *Republic* 440D

exceptions which recognise non-rational will, and similarly there were debates in the twelfth century about will being superior to reason and overriding it.[44] But the idea that will is in some sense *rational* is a highly typical strand in the idea of the will, as it came to be developed.

(ii) Various forms of desire falling under the names *voluntas* or *prohairesis* can be called '*free*'. But these names have various meanings, so we need to consider which can be translated as 'will', just as 'free' has very different senses as well, which I shall discuss more fully elsewhere.[45]

(iii) Very important is the idea of *will power*. At least three people, Kerferd, Dirlmeier, Sedley, have seen this in the *thumos* of Plato's *Republic* Book 4, 440B–D. A key factor is that this is distinct from reason, but normally (except in Book 9, 586C7–D2) *allied* with reason in enforcing reason's judgements and wishes, just as will is often thought of as not reason, but an ally of reason.[46] Again, Mansfeld has argued will power is in Posidonius, the Stoic who (on Galen's evidence which I have supported) went back to Plato's tripartite soul.[47] Posidonius explains (ap. Galen *PHP*, 4.7.36–9) why we sometimes shed tears or cease to, contrary to our *boulesthai*. This is because the emotional movements (*pathêtikai kinêseis*), probably those in the soul which the Stoics regarded as a physical pneumatic gas, press so hard (*sphodra enkeisthai*) that they are not overcome (*krateisthai)* by *boulêsis*, or have so completely ceased that they are no longer aroused by it. I would add that the *voluntas*, willing, of Lucretius exercises power. In the very same passage where he calls it free, 2, 261–93, the *voluntas* of each person's mind (*animus*) gives a start to his movement, and from it the movements flood through the limbs. But when the starting gates are opened in a horse race, the eager might of the horses cannot burst out as suddenly as their minds desire. For it takes time for *voluntas* to rouse the whole mass of matter throughout the limbs, starting from the heart. Conversely, when we are pushed forward by a blow, all the matter of our body is moved against our wishes (*inviti*) and it takes time for *voluntas* to rein it back by use of what is in our breast. There is a further passage, 4. 883–91, in which Lucretius refers again to *voluntas* causing us to start moving, and says that

---

[44] Bonnie Kent, *Virtues of the Will*, Washington 1995, Ch. 3 'Voluntarism'.

[45] Senses of 'free' are discussed not in Ch. XIII, but in a paper in preparation, 'Freedom and will: Graeco-Roman origins'.

[46] Conversation with George Kerferd; Franz Dirlmeier in Aristoteles, *Nikomachische Ethik*, 3rd edition, Berlin 1964, pp. 327f, n.3, cited by Jaap Mansfeld, 'The idea of the will in Chrysippus, Posidonus and Galen', *The Boston Area Colloquium in Ancient Philosophy*, vol. 7, 1991, p. 107, n. 1; David Sedley, in commentary on Mansfeld, op. cit.

[47] Jaap Mansfeld, op. cit.

the mind (*animus*), which he conceives as physical, is what wills (*velit*),[48] and when it does so, it strikes (*ferit*) the force (*vis*) of the soul (*anima*), and the soul in turn strikes the body, until the whole mass is moved. Mind is here the central part of the soul seated in the control centre in the heart, and since it does the willing, *voluntas* is a capacity or act of *animus*, rather than a distinct agent in its own right. I hesitate to translate *voluntas* here as 'will', not for this reason, but because it is not a rational enough desire, since it is found in horses.

(iv) A fourth influential idea is that of Plotinus, that the lower orders of reality were created through intellects and souls breaking away by distancing themselves (*apostasis*) from the Supreme Father, the One, through an act of pride (*tolma*), willing (*boulesthai*) to belong to themselves alone, and enjoying things being under their own control (*autexousion*), 5.1.1 (1–22); 3.8.8 (32–6); 3.7.11 (15–16). This influenced Augustine's idea of a will perverted by pride.

All four of these ideas about will can be found assembled in Augustine, but each originated in different earlier thinkers. The will is *free* when the whole will wills something,[49] but it lost its freedom when lust stopped obeying it in order to punish our ancestor Adam for committing the first sin, and Augustine prefers to speak of it as having free choice (*arbitrium*), rather than as being free, as in the title of his book, *On free choice of the will*. Now it must try to regain control by exercising will *power*.[50] Adam's sin was due to a will perverted by *pride*.[51] Because each of these strands in the idea of will had been arrived at before Augustine, my conclusion is that it may be better not to ask who discovered the will, but rather to trace the different contexts in which the various components were thought up, and when they were first (in Augustine) all assembled.

More than one writer has taken a different view from mine, and I may well be wrong about Maximus.[52] But some other unresolved puzzles about Maximus have been bought to my attention. He collected ancient definitions,[53]

---

[48] Lucretius, *On the nature of things*, Book 4, 886, cf. 2, 270.

[49] Augustine, *On the spirit and the letter*, 31.53.

[50] The will's loss of freedom is discussed by Augustine in passages assembled in my *Emotion and Peace of Mind*, Ch. 26, and its need to use will power in those passages and in the passages cited below about the conflict between carnal and spiritual will.

[51] Augustine, *City of God* 14.13.

[52] I have not had an opportunity to reconsider my remarks in Chapter XIII about Maximus, and I suspect that David Bradshaw may well be right in the draft of his paper 'Maximus the Confessor on the Will', destined for *Studia Patristica*, that I have misunderstood him.

[53] PG 91, cols 149ff; 213ff.

and also had some collections of definitions wrongly ascribed to him, one a collection of definitions of the will (*thelêsis*) allegedly offered by earlier authors.[54] The ascriptions have either proved unverifiable, or turned out to be definitions of something different, *prohairesis* in two cases, although when that is taken in the relevant sense, which is that of Epictetus not of Aristotle, the meaning is not so distant from *thelêsis*. The other rogue definition was originally a definition of *autexousiotês*, which is closer to freedom than to will. If the rogue lists represent inaccurate compilations collected for Maximus and posthumously added to his work, that raises the question whether he was drawing on inaccurate material also in his own definition. I may well be wrong, but he is surely mistaken in another way when he takes it that the problem is to distinguish *thelêsis* from Aristotle's, not from Epictetus', *prohairesis*.

The most comprehensively different view, however, has appeared since I chose to include this chapter, in an important book, which I ought to address at least briefly,[55] Michael Frede's posthumous *A Free Will: Origins of the Notion in Ancient Thought*, sadly unrevised, but beautifully edited by A.A.Long in 2011.Though often speaking only of *free* will, Frede also argues that Epictetus already had, and was the first to have, the idea of the *will*. His introduction and final chapter oppose the thesis of Albrecht Dihle that Augustine originated the concept of will by arguing that Epictetus' treatment of will had largely anticipated him. I myself, in the paper included here as Ch. XIII, described Epictetus' *prohairesis* as *will*, but twice, in 2000 and 2012, I apologised for using that translation because I thought it imprecise,[56] and I will need to say why. But first, I should indicate Frede's reasons for his view.

One good point he urges is that Epictetus already anticipates Augustine by making ubiquitous *prohairesis* in all action. Ch. XIII had indeed pointed out that Epictetus anticipated, at least verbally, even the Aristotelian Alexander in making ubiquitous *prohairesis* in his very different sense of the term.[57]

---

[54] Two are discussed by Mossman Roueché, 'Byzantine philosophical texts of the seventh century' and 'A Middle Byzantine handbook of logic terminology', in *Jahrbuch der Österreichischen Byzantistik*, vol. 23, 1974, 61–76 and vol. 29, 1980, 71–98. The collection of definitions of will at PG 91, cols 275–280 is discussed in a paper by John D Madden, brought to my attention by Roueché: 'the authenticity of early definitions of will (*thelêsis*)', in Felix Heinzer, Christoph von Schonborn, eds, *Maximus Confessor: Actes du symposium sur Maxime le Confesseur*, Fribourg 1982, pp. 61-79.

[55] It is more fully discussed in 'Freedom and will: Graeco-Roman origins', in preparation, on which I shall draw to the extent needed. I there welcome Frede's appeal to Epictetus' use of *prohairesis* to explain the same *terminology* appearing in Christians (exemplified by Gregory of Nyssa in note 41 of Ch. XIII, but not by Plotinus 6. 8. 17 (3 and 8) in note 40).

[56] Richard Sorabji, *Emotion and Peace of Mind*, Oxford and Chicago University Presses, 2000, Ch. 21, 'The concept of will'; *Gandhi and the Stoics: Modern Experiments on Ancient Values*, Oxford and Chicago University Presses, 2012, Ch. 3, 'Individual freedom'.

[57] Michael Frede, *A Free Will*, p. 46; Ch. XIII below, p. 12.

Both anticipate Augustine who makes will ubiquitous because, even when his carnal will overcomes his spiritual will, he says he has control (*potestas*) over his action thanks to the effect still following his (incomplete) will.[58] But I am less convinced by a second claim, that Epictetus also anticipated Augustine in making will ubiquitous in all *cognition*,[59] because what Epictetus makes ubiquitous in cognition is the *assent of reason* to such appearances as, for example the appearance that a stick is straight or bent. But this assent is not on the face of it the same as *prohairesis*, which is what Frede identifies as will. *Prohairesis*, at any rate, and desire in general, is regarded by the Stoics as merely *one* kind of assent, assent (or a disposition to assent) to an '*impulsive*' (*hormêtikê*) appearance, that is to a *motivating* appearance that directly leads you to *act* by setting a value on something.[60] Frede briefly suggests that Epictetus' will can have a wider sense and can include the ability to give assent to *non-impulsive* impressions as well, although without supplying details on what he has in mind.[61] But be that as it may, Epictetus' view does not seem to me the same as Augustine's.

It is true that Augustine's treatment of cognition uses the idea of *will*. But in *On the Trinity*, Augustine's will (*voluntas*) performs the function not so much of *assent*, or *consent* as it is usually translated in Augustine, but often of directing attention. It unites perception with the perceptible, memory with internal vision and intellect with objects taken from memory.[62] In imagination the will also draws on memory, and unites or separates what it finds there to bring before imagination's gaze a black swan or four-footed bird.[63] Emotions are also acts of will (*voluntates*) and are perverted if the will is perverted.[64] So far Augustine's analysis of cognition in terms of will does not seem to be drawing on the Stoic idea of *assent*. But assent or consent of the will do come in when Augustine talks of *faith* (*credere*) and says that one has faith if one wills (*volere*) and having faith is consenting (*consentire*) that what is said is true. He speaks of the will (*voluntas*) by which we have faith, and says that consenting and dissenting (consentire, *dissentire*) are a matter of one's own

---

[58] Augustine, *On the spirit and the letter* 31.53.

[59] Michael Frede, *A Free Will*, pp. 156–9.

[60] Stobaeus, *Eclogae* Book 2, p. 86, lines 17–18, Wachsmuth.

[61] Frede argues that the Stoic notion of will is complex and includes the ability to give assent to *non-impulsive* impressions as part of the activity of thinking, *A Free Will*, pp. 47–8; 108; 157. He does not, however, say what terminology the Stoics used to indicate that they thought this assent too to be an exercise of will. Brad Inwood has argued against the view that assent to cognitive appearances was regarded by the Stoics as an impulse (*hormê*), or desire, *Ethics and Human Action in Early Stoicism*, Oxford 1985, pp. 60; 101 with note 27.

[62] Augustine, *On the Trinity* 11. 2. 2 ff; 11. 2. 5; 11. 3. 1.

[63] Augustine, *On the Trinity* 11. 10. 17.

[64] Augustine, *City of God* 14.6.

will (*voluntas*). It is only by consenting that the soul can accept (*accipere*) God's gift of will, but the acceptance is our own.[65] Unless one has faith in God, and persists in willing to accept (*in accipiendi voluntate*), he does not accept God's gift of the Holy Spirit by which good works can be done.[66] If you have some faith, you have accepted, though it is only God who makes faith grow.[67] Faith, then, for Augustine does involve the consent or assent of the will.

The idea of assent certainly is a Stoic legacy, not particularly from Epictetus, but from the early Stoics before him. But Augustine's assent here is assent of the *will*, not of reason, but of a desire in the rational part of the soul, and sometimes an assent of the mind (*animus*). Augustine does not, as we shall see below, share the Stoic identification of an act of will or other desire with a *judgement* of reason. He does not even necessarily think that all acts of will are *in accordance* with reason, to use Aristotle's term, because of the complication already mentioned, that he believes there is a carnal as well as a spiritual will. Thus, although Augustine owes to the Stoics the important idea of assent, he does not use this idea in most of the cases where he makes cognition depend on will, and in the one case of *faith* where he does use the idea of assent, that assent is not, like the Stoic one, an assent of *reason*, but at most of one of reason's *desires*.

Frede, however, has a third argument, which seems to be that Epictetus had and was the first to have a concept of will, because his *prohairesis* adjudicates between possible desires or assents.[68] Adjudication, as Frede says, is a function given by Plato, and I would add Epicurus, to reason, not to will, while in Aristotle, Frede urges, we do not see adjudication so much as one desire defeating another. I have three doubts here. Talking of acts of *prohairesis*, Epictetus says that even if you act under the threat of death, nothing compelled that in you which is capable of *prohairesis*. Rather, what happened was that one desire (*hormê, orexis*) defeated another desire, and specifically, one *prohairesis* was subjected to necessity by another *prohairesis*, 1.17. 23–6. There is not much adjudication in this context. Your reason just assented to one motivating appearance, that it was appropriate to comply, rather than to another, that it was appropriate to die. It might be only the Stoic sage from whom we could expect adjudication always to replace mere defeat of one motive by another. Moreover, secondly, this much, I think, we would find in Aristotle's wise person (*phronimos*) too. His *phronimos* is always adjudicating the right thing to desire or do in particular situations, admittedly by an intellectual kind

---

[65] Augustine, *On the Spirit and the Letter* 31.54; 34.60

[66] Augustine, *Exposition of certain propositions from the Letter to the Romans*, Ch. 60.

[67] Augustine, *Sermon* 43.4

[68] Michael Frede, *A Free Will*, pp. 24–6, 46.

of perceptivity, *nous*, *Nicomachean Ethics* (*EN*) 6.11, 1143a35–b5. But in Aristotle's wise person, that *nous* is in its turn guided in its adjudications by a *boulêsis* (sometimes mere *wish*, but in this context closer to *will*) whose aim is based on a correct view of the goals that matter in life, *EN* 3.4. And the correct view appears only to someone who is good, *EN* 6.12, 1144a28–b1.

I would add a third doubt, whether adjudication is a regular mark of the will in Augustine. When his carnal will conflicts with his spiritual will, it does not sound as if his will *adjudicates*. The law in his limbs may rather lead him captive (*captivum ducere*), the wrong course ties him in knots (*vincire*).

I should finish by saying why I have not thought Epictetus an easy candidate for having a concept of will, and definitely not for being the first to have such a concept.

(i) The consideration that originally deterred me was that Epictetus makes the connexion of *prohairesis* with reason almost too close. The problem arises not from an act of *prohairesis* being a desire that has the assent of reason, and dispositional *prohairesis* being a disposition to choose such desires. This fits well enough with the idea that will is a kind of desire that conforms with reason, although I believe that Aristotle framed that conception before Epictetus. Rather, the question is whether it is conceptually distinct enough from reason for comfortable comparison with other concepts of will. To take the case where one *act* of *prohairesis* subjects another to necessity, not only is the constraining *prohairesis* equated with a desire (*hormê*) to comply rather than to die, but – and this is an intellectualist conception – the desire is equated with an *opinion* (*dogma*, *dokein*) that it is better to comply than to die.[69] This fits with the treatment of desire which I believe had been the main Stoic view since Chrysippus in the third century BCE, that desire is a *judgement* of reason. This goes further than Plato's view that makes reason partly desiderative by giving it desires of its own, as Augustine agrees when he assigns will to the rational part of the soul. For making reason desiderative is different from making desire a ratiocination. It is made a ratiocination in the sense of being made into an evaluative *judgement* or a disposition for evaluative judgement by reason. I say this not to criticise – I have elsewhere treated it sympathetically – but to say that this intellectualism was not a precedent for later treatments of will, but was instead offering retrospective support for Socrates' intellectualism.

(ii) A second hesitation was that Epictetus does not mention the will *power* that is so important to Augustine. This was no accident, for Stoics do not

---

[69] Epictetus *Discourses* 1.17. 23–6. I have discussed the mainstream Stoic account of various desires from Chrysippus onwards in *Emotion and Peace of Mind*, especially in Chapter 2.

have to grit their teeth in order to endure and stay calm. Their resistance is entirely due to a change of intellectual attitude. They re-consider whether circumstances are really as good or bad or responses as appropriate as appearances might suggest. It would not be Stoic to think circumstances bad but resist them by will power. This is not to deny that great intellectual effort is called for, but not the kind of effort that we associate with will power. By contrast we have found some idea of will power in Epictetus' predecessors, Plato and Posidonius, and of the power of *voluntas* in Lucretius.

(iii) It is true that Epictetus does have the idea of *prohairesis* being free, but this important freedom which would make you immune from both inner and outer tyrants is one so rarely achieved that Epictetus can find only two examples: Diogenes the Cynic and Socrates.[70] It is also compatible with things having all along been inevitable and with every attempt at duress. Although I discuss this only elsewhere,[71] it is, as Frede would be the first to agree, very different from the freedom of the will found in his Christian successors, or with the freedom of *voluntas* invoked before him by Lucretius and Cicero. Frede himself points out that the early Christians wanted *everyone* to be free in some sense to do otherwise than they did, for the totally different reason that this would give us the moral responsibility for action that would justify God's reward and punishment after death, a concept in which the Stoics did not believe.

(iv) Fourthly, we should not expect Epictetus to have the idea of a will perverted by pride, which was an important strand in Augustine's idea, but which emerged only after Epictetus in Plotinus.

The four strands carry different weights. The idea of will as a desire that accords with reason comes close to being a definition of some conceptions of will, except for complications I have mentioned such as Augustine's having a carnal will as well as a spiritual will, and there being debates in the twelfth century about will being superior to reason and overriding it.[72] Other strands are ones which are so prominent in the Christian tradition at least from Augustine onwards that one might hope to find some of the cluster if one was seeking an earlier discoverer of the will. It is agreed that Epictetus did not have the later Christian concept of *freedom*. What I have been arguing is that equally his concept of *will* was not one that Christianity has made familiar to us.

RICHARD SORABJI

[70] Epictetus *Discourses* 4.1; cf. 1.1.23; 4.4.1–2.

[71] See 'Freedom and will: Graeco-Roman origins', in preparation.

[72] Bonnie Kent, *Virtues of the Will*, Washington 1995, Ch. 3 'Voluntarism'.

ACKNOWLEDGEMENTS

Grateful acknowledgement is made to the following persons, institutions, journals and publishers for their kind permission to reproduce the papers included in this volume: Anthony O'Hear, editor of *Philosophy*, Royal Institute of Philosophy (for Chapter I); University of Notre Dame Press, Notre Dame, IN (II); Koninklijke Brill NV, Leiden (V); Duke University Press, Durham, NC (VI); *Classical Quarterly* (VII); the Institute of Classical Studies, London (VIII); the Aristotelian Society, London (IX); Leuven University Press (X); Ontos Verlag, Frankfurt (XI); Parmenides Publishing, Las Vegas, NV (XII); and Thomas Pink, co-editor of *The Will and Human Action from Antiquity to the Present Day* (XIII).

Every effort has been made to trace all the copyright holders, but if any have been inadvertently overlooked the publishers will be pleased to make the necessary arrangement at the first opportunity.

PUBLISHER'S NOTE

The articles in this volume, as in all others in the Variorum Collected Studies Series, have not been given a new, continuous pagination. In order to avoid confusion, and to facilitate their use where these same studies have been referred to elsewhere, the original pagination has been maintained wherever possible. Article V has necessarily been reset, with the original pagination given in square brackets within the text.

Each article has been given a Roman number in order of appearance, as listed in the Contents. This number is repeated on each page and is quoted in the index entries.

I

Body and Soul in Aristotle

1: Aristotle's view

(i) Interpretations of Aristotle's account of the relation between body and soul have been widely divergent.[1] At one extreme, Thomas Slakey has said that in the *De Anima* 'Aristotle tries to explain perception simply as an event in the sense-organs'. Wallace Matson has generalised the point. Of the Greeks in general he says, 'Mind-body identity was taken for granted ... Indeed, in the whole classical corpus there exists no denial of the view that sensing is a bodily process throughout'. At the opposite extreme, Friedrich Solmsen has said of Aristotle's theory, 'it is doubtful whether the movement or the actualization occurring when the eye sees or the ear hears has any physical or physiological aspect.' Similarly, R.D. Hicks thinks that Aristotle makes the faculty of desire wholly psychical as opposed to corporeal, and Jonathan Barnes has described Aristotle as leaning hesitantly towards the view that desire and thought are wholly non-physical. But on the emotions and sense perception, Barnes takes an intermediate position. Aristotle treats these, he says, as including physical and non-physical components. Other writers too have sought a position somewhere in the middle. Thus G.R.T. Ross concedes that we find in Aristotle 'what looks like the crudest materialism'. It appears that objects produce changes in an organism, 'and the reception of these changes in the sense organ *is* perception'. But, he maintains, this gives us only half the picture. The complete theory 'may in a way be designated as a doctrine of psychophysical parallelism'. W.D. Ross also seeks a middle position. He thinks that Aristotle sometimes brings out 'the distinctively mental, non-corporeal nature of the act [of sensation]. ... But Aristotle cannot be said to hold successfully to the notion of sensation as a purely mental activity having nothing in common with anything physical. He is still under the influence of earlier materialism'.

The most popular alternatives have been to regard Aristotle as some kind of materialist, or as some kind of Cartesian. But, as we shall see, there have

63

64

---

1. Thomas Slakey [68], p.470. Wallace I. Matson, 'Why isn't the mind-body problem ancient?', in *Mind, Matter and Method*, ed. Feyerabend and Maxwell (University of Minnesota, 1966), p.93. Friedrich Solmsen [103], p.170, who claims, 'Nor does the "common sense" which receives, collects and synthesizes depend for its functioning on any physiological process'. He does, however, find (and write illuminatingly about) a physiological process that occurs at a different stage in perception. R.D. Hicks [43], p.563. Jonathan Barnes, reprinted as Chapter 2 above. G.R.T. Ross [49], Introduction, pp. 5-7. W.D. Ross [16], p.136.

been other assimilations. I believe that all these interpretations are mistaken, and that Aristotle's view is something *sui generis*. It is not to be identified with the positions of more recent philosophers. Moreover, when we see what his view is, we shall find that it has interesting implications of its own. But first, by way of background information, I must make two preliminary points about Aristotle's concept of the soul.

(ii) *Preliminaries: the soul as capacities.* Aristotle sometimes thinks of the soul as a set of capacities, such as the capacity for nutrition, the capacity of sense perception and the capacity for thought. These capacities are not a mere conglomeration, but are related to each other in intimate ways, so as to form a unity. The lowest capacity (nutrition) can exist without the higher ones, but not *vice versa*.

According to Aristotle's best-known definition, the soul is the form, or first actuality, of a natural body with organs (*De An.* II 1, 412a19, b5). But it is not always noticed that he regards this definition as insufficiently informative. He calls it an 'impression' or 'sketch', and a 'very general statement'. But it would be ridiculous, he says, to give a general definition of the soul, to the neglect of definitions that pick out the particular kinds of soul, the soul of a plant, a beast, or a man (*De An.* II 1-3, 412a7, b4, b10, 413a9-10, 414b25-8, b32-3). An account that does pick out the various capacities by which living things differ from each other will in fact be the most appropriate account of the soul (*De An.* II 3, 415a12-13). And with this statement at the end of *De An.* II 3, he provides the plan of the rest of the *De Anima*. For the rest of the work considers in turn the capacity for nutrition, the capacity of sense perception, the related capacity of imagination, the capacity for thought, and the capacity for voluntary movement.

Aristotle's statement, that the most appropriate account of the soul is the one which picks out these capacities, already suggests the thought that perhaps the soul just *is* these capacities. This thought is confirmed when we notice that Aristotle speaks of the capacities as *parts* of the soul (e.g. *De An.* 413b7, b27-32, 429a10-13, 432a19; *Mem.* 449b5, 450a17). It is confirmed again when, using one of his technical terms, Aristotle calls the soul a first actuality (*De An.* 412a22-8). For a first actuality is also describable as a **65** second potentiality (*De An.* 417a21-b2), in other works as a capacity. The interpretation is also confirmed by Aristotle's claim that the relation of soul to body is parallel to that of sight to the eye.[2]

I shall follow Aristotle below, by thinking of the soul as a set of capacities. The conception does, incidentally, have one great advantage, namely that we undeniably have a soul of the kind Aristotle describes. At least, we have

---

2. *De An.* 412b17-413a3. Willie Charlton and Professor Wiggins have pointed out that Aristotle sometimes thinks of the soul as that which *has* capacities, i.e. the person (Charlton, *Aristotle's Physics Books I and II* (Oxford, 1970), pp. 70-3; Wiggins, *Identity and Spatio-Temporal Continuity* (Oxford, 1967), part 4, sec. 2). This observation is illuminating, especially for the study of *Metaphysics*, Book VII. But it must be insisted that sometimes, and in the *De Anima* often, Aristotle thinks of the soul as being the capacities themselves. He is not thinking of the soul as that which *has* capacities, when he says that a person is angry with his soul (408b1-15), or that the soul is the cause of living, and the efficient cause of perception and growth, and that only what partakes of soul perceives (415b8-28).

a soul, if this means that we have the capacity to grow, perceive and think. But it must be admitted that Aristotle sometimes adds the difficult idea that we have a capacity to perceive and grow which *explains* our perceiving and growing.[3]

(iii) *Preliminaries: the biological conception of the soul.* The word 'soul' may sound archaic to some modern ears, and people may be tempted to substitute the word 'mind'. But then they are likely to confine the functions of the soul to what we call mental acts, and this will take them away from Aristotle's conception of the soul. In all this, people have been influenced by Descartes. He explains that previously the word 'soul' (*anima*) had been applied to the principle of nutrition as well as to the principle of consciousness (*cogitatio*). But he will use the word only for the latter, and, to avoid confusion, will, whenever possible, substitute the word 'mind' (*mens*).[4]

Aristotle's conception of the soul is much broader than this. He takes the view which Descartes castigates, that the nutritive processes are a function of the soul. Plato and others had attributed a soul to plants.[5] Plato had coupled this view with another current view, that plants had sensations and **66** desires.[6] Aristotle retains the first idea, that plants have souls, but sensibly rejects the second, that they have sensations and desires. Instead, he makes sensation the distinguishing mark of animals. But how, then, does he justify continuing to attribute a soul to plants? By extending the concept of soul, so that the non-conscious processes of nutrition and growth will now count as an activity of the soul. This extension may sound strange to us. But appeal to a (non-conscious) soul is needed, Aristotle thinks, to do justice to such facts as that a plant does not expand haphazardly, but preserves, or develops, a certain distinctive organisation.[7] The resulting conception of the

3. It is easy to understand Aristotle's idea that our capacity for desire explains our moving from place to place (*De An.* III 9-10). But it is harder to see how the capacity to perceive can *explain* our perceiving, or how the capacity to retain a certain distinctive organisation while we grow can *explain* our retaining this organisation while we grow (*De An.* 415b23-8, 416a8-9, b21-2).

That the soul is a cause (415b8-28) helps to explain why Aristotle could not accept the view, which is often said to be like his, that the soul is related to the body as its harmony to a lyre (407b27-408a30). A harmony is not a causal agent in the right way.

4. Reply to objections brought against the 2nd *Meditation*, §4, in the 5th *Objections*, translated Haldane and Ross, Vol 2, p.210.

5. Plato *Timaeus* 77A-B. Empedocles believed he had in a previous incarnation been a bush (fragment 117 in Diels, *Die Fragmente Der Vorsokratiker*). It may have been because of his belief that souls could be reincarnated in plants that Empedocles forbade the eating of beans (fr. 141). But members of the Orphic sect allowed that some or all vegetable food lacked a soul (Euripides, *Hippolytus* 952).

6. Plato, *Timaeus* 77A-B. Put into the mouth of Protagoras by Plato, *Theaetetus* 167B. Asserted, if we can believe our late sources, by Empedocles, Democritus and Anaxagoras (see pseudo-Aristotle, *De Plantis* 815a16, b16; Sextus Empiricus, *Adv. Math.* VIII. 286, using as evidence Empedocles, fr. 110; cf. fr. 103).

7. See, e.g., *De An.* 416a6-9. A plant also produces seed for the next generation. And this must be done by converting the nutriment it draws from the soil (see *GC* I 5; *De An.* II 4). An excellent account of Aristotle's biological extension of the concept of soul is given by Solmsen in [53].

soul makes it coextensive with life, that is, with all life. The conception of soul is a biological one, and it encourages Aristotle to stress the continuity, rather than the differences, between processes in plants and processes in humans. Descartes was wrong, in the passage referred to at the beginning of this paragraph, when he ascribed the connection between the soul and nutritive processes to the earliest men. The connection is in fact an innovation of Aristotle's, though it may well be true that Aristotle's predecessors, other than Plato, already ascribed to the soul functions which were not mental ones.[8]

Though Aristotle makes plant growth a function of the soul, he does not take the next step. He does not attribute the movements of earth, air, fire
67 and water to a soul within them, presumably because the four elements are lifeless things. But although the four elements do not have souls to move them, there are analogies between the movement of elements, the growth of plants, and the movement of animals. All three are processes directed towards an end, and all three are due to nature, which in *Physics* II 1 is defined as an internal cause of change (192b20). There is the difference that the nature, or internal cause, is not a soul or a desire, in the case of the four elements. But this only raises the question how the nature that resides in the elements differs from a plant soul or from the desire of animals, a difficult question which we shall encounter again (below, p.59). The *Physics* offer no satisfactory answer, but an answer can be pieced together from Aristotle's later works.[9]

(iv) *The contrast with Descartes*. We can now return to the rival interpretations of the body-soul relation in Aristotle. Some of the
68 interpretations attribute to Aristotle a Cartesian stand. Solmsen and Barnes attach importance to the fact that Aristotle makes perception an act

8. A major function of the soul, among early Greek philosophers, was to cause motion (*De An.* 403b26, 405b11, 409b19). Did the soul always cause motion by means of some mental activity? Aristotle implies not in the case of Democritus (*De An.* 406b24-5), though in this particular instance Aristotle's testimony is suspect. According to another conception, the function of the soul was not connected with consciousness in this life, but was simply to survive, perhaps with a very low level of consciousness, when a man died (see R.B. Onians [57] for such a conception in Homer). For Plato, one function of the soul was to cause motion, but it caused motion by means of some mental activity (*Laws* 896E-897A). I do not believe that *Timaeus* 36E says otherwise.

9. The *Physics* hints at analogies (192a22, 250b14). But it fails completely when it tries to spell out the disanalogies (255a5-20, b29-31). A good account of this failure is again given by Solmsen in [54]. According to later writings, desire in animals differs from the nature of a stone, in that it involves a physiological process in virtue of which desire is a cause of motion (*De An.* I 1; *MA* 6-10). It also differs in being intimately linked with other soul capacities, with nutrition, which maintains the organs in the right state, and with perceiving, imagining, conceiving and judging. For (*MA* 6-8, 11; *De An.* III 9-11) an animal must perceive, imagine, or conceive the end desired, and, in some cases, the means to its realisation. A human being may also make a judgment that the end or means conceived is to be pursued, or not. Desire differs again, in that desires have varying ends (*Meta.* IX 5; *Cael.* II 12), some of them conflicting (*EN* VII 3, Bekker's numbering), some changeable by training (*EN* II 1), some being only apparent goods, not real goods (*EN* III 4).

of the soul. But given Aristotle's biological conception of the soul (which Solmsen has done so much to bring out), this tells us that perception manifests life, not that it manifests consciousness. G.R.T. Ross finds significance in Aristotle's calling perception an *energeia* and *entelecheia*. But when Aristotle insists that perception is an *energeia* and an *entelecheia*, rather than a *pathos* (cf. Barnes, above, p.38), he has in mind that it is an actualisation of a disposition and that the subject of this actualisation is not destroyed but preserved and fulfilled (*De An.* 417a14-16, b2-12). When Aristotle says that perceiving is an *energeia*, rather than a *kinêsis* (*Meta.* 1048b18-36; *EN* 1174a14-b9; *Sens.* 446b2-3), he means that processes are incomplete until they reach their end, but with activities like perceiving one can say 'I have perceived' right from the very beginning. These points do not imply that perceiving is 'something mental' (G.R.T. Ross [49], p.5) or 'an act of mind' (p.6). Living can be called an *energeia*, even when we are talking of the non-mental life of a plant. W.D. Ross and Barnes attach importance to the passage we shall discuss below where Aristotle says that smelling is something else besides (*para*) a physical change (*De An.* 424a32-b18). But they assume without warrant that if there is 'something else', it can only be conceived of as distinctively mental or non-physical. Ross' second piece of evidence is that Aristotle sometimes speaks of perception as involving discrimination. But here too he assumes without warrant that discrimination can only be conceived of as something distinctively mental. Barnes and Hicks think that the faculty of desire is made wholly non-physical at 433b19, where Aristotle contrasts it with the organ which is physical (*sômatikon*), and which is therefore to be discussed in another work that deals with the body as well as the soul. But I believe Aristotle means no more than that the organ differs from the faculty in being a *part* of the body, and that the *De Anima*, though concerned with states that belong to the body and soul alike, is not interested in *parts* of the body as such. Again, crude though the discussion of the soul is in Aristotle's early work, *Physics* VII, I do not see with Barnes any claim at 244b7-15 that the kind of qualitative change represented by sense perception is non-physical.

Turning to the case on the other side for a while, we should notice that Aristotle has no word corresponding to 'mental act', or to Descartes' *cogitatio* (consciousness). Charles Kahn has suggested that the nearest word is *aisthanesthai* (perceiving), for this covers a very wide range of mental acts.[10] None the less, as Kahn carefully points out, the word does not correspond to Descartes' *cogitatio*, for Aristotle draws a sharp distinction between thinking and perceiving. He never suggests that thinking is a kind of *aisthanesthai*. Nor, as we shall see, does he say of *aisthanesthai* the sort of things that Descartes says of *cogitatio*.

In a very un-Cartesian way, Aristotle insists that in some sense of 'is' every mental act is a physiological process. Thus anger is a boiling of the blood or warm stuff around the heart, in a sense of 'is' analogous to that in

10. In Aristotle, pleasure and pain (*PA* 666a12); awareness of memory-images (*Mem.* 450b14, 16, 18, 28); awareness of one's own acts of sense perception (*Som.* 455a17; *De An.* 425b12; *EN* 1170a29-b1); awareness of being asleep (*Insom.* 462a3). In other authors, desire, fear, and intellectual discernment. Kahn's article, reprinted as our Chapter 1, is basic reading for this subject.

69 which a house is bricks (*De An.* 403a25-b9).[11] The point is made about all *pathê* of the soul, the examples in this chapter being anger and calmness, confidence and fear, loving and hating, appetite, pity, joy, perception and thought,[12] though he sometimes prefers to call the last two actions (*poiein*, 403a7), or functions (*erga*, a10) of the soul, rather than *pathê* (a3). About thinking he is at first hesitant, but, as we shall see, human thinking does not seem in the end to differ in a way that seriously affects his point. The point is not made about long-term states (*hexeis*), or capacities (*dunameis*) of the soul.[13] And at one place Aristotle says it is thought to be a mark of the *pathê* rather than of the *hexeis* that they are corporeal (*EN* 1128b14-15). None the less, he does often speak as if *hexeis* and *dunameis* too had some kind of physiological basis.[14]

The statement that anger is a physiological process does not initially sound very Cartesian. But Cartesian interpreters of Aristotle may take courage (cf. Barnes, above, p.37) from Aristotle's insistence that the physiological process is only the matter, or material cause, of anger. There is also a form, or formal cause, namely the desire to retaliate. And anger can be said to *be*[15] this formal cause, or desire, just as a house can be said to *be* a

70 shelter. This statement in 403a25-b9 is reinforced at 424b3-18, where Aristotle says that exercising smell is something else besides (*para*, 424b17-19) merely being affected by something. It is also a matter of *aisthanesthai*. In view of the wide use of *aisthanesthai*, we may take the word as meaning *awareness*. And we may take the point to be that smelling is not simply a matter of being affected by odour, but is also an awareness of odour. The

---

11. Aristotle does not list this as a distinct sense of 'is', when he talks about the different senses of the verb *to be*. But he still treats this use of 'is' in a distinctive way. He notes that ordinary speakers prefer to say that a thing *is composed of wood* (*Meta.* 1033a16-19), or better (1033a19-22) *is wooden*, rather than that it *is wood*. And he has reasons of his own, to be discussed on p.55, for doing likewise, and refusing to say that a thing *is* its matter (*Meta.* 1035a7-10, 1041b12-16).

12. Other examples of *pathê* of the soul are envy, emulation, longing, shame and shamelessness, kindness and unkindness, and indignation at unmerited prosperity (*EN* 1105b19-28, 1128b9-15; *Rhet.* II 2-11; *EE* 1220b10-20). The semi-physiological analysis is mentioned also at *Sens.* 436a6-10, b1-8; *Mem.* 450a27-30; *Som.* 454a7-11, and is connected with yet other mental states, desire in general, pleasure and pain, memory and memory images. For the claim that anger *is* a bodily process, see *De An.* 403a26. In making all *pathê* of the soul physiological, Aristotle is rejecting the claims of Plato, *Philebus* 34B, 35C, 47E.

13. For the distinction see *EN* 1105b19-28, 1106a3, a5, 1157b28-31; *EE* 1220b13-14; *Rhet.* 1378a20; *Cat.* 8b26-9a13, 9b33-10a10. *Pathê* of the soul (e.g. anger) are accompanied by pleasure or pain, and affect one's judgment. We are said to undergo change (*kineisthai*) when we have them. They are not the result of deliberate choice. They are comparatively short-lived and easily removed. A *hexis* of the soul (e.g. good temper) is something in accordance with which we are well or ill disposed in relation to *pathê*. A *dunamis* of the soul (e.g. the ability to be angry) is that in accordance with which we are capable of suffering *pathê*.

14. For examples, see Theodore Tracy [95], *passim*; Sorabji [50], notes on 449b6 and 453a19.

15. A *pathos* of the soul *is* an enmattered form (403a25), just as a house *is* a form (403b6). Again, anger *is* a movement of a faculty (desire?), as well as *being* a physiological movement (403a26-7).

Cartesian interpreter might now read into these two passages the idea that anger or smelling has two 'components'. The physiological process is one component; the other is a purely mental act of desire or awareness.

This interpretation is impossible for two reasons. First, the form of a thing is not a component in it. A shelter is not a component in a house. Aristotle explains this carefully in the *Metaphysics*. His examples are a syllable, a house, and flesh. These are composed respectively of letters, of bricks, and of the four elements. But the form is not a further component. The arrangement of the letters B and A, for example, is not a component in the syllable BA (*Meta.* 1041b19-33, 1043b4-6). On the contrary, it is matter, not form, which constitutes the components. This is how matter is defined (*Phys.* 195a19; *Meta.* 1032a17). There is a second objection to the Cartesian interpretation. Even if there had been a component in anger other than the physiological process, that component could not have been a purely mental act. For Aristotle, no acts are *purely* mental, since *every pathos* of the soul is, among other things, a physiological process.

The Cartesian interpreter must not look, then, for a purely mental component in anger. His only hope lies in finding Aristotle treating anger as a whole as a distinctively mental act, in spite of its also being a physiological process. But it is no longer very clear what it means to call something distinctively mental, if one is at the same time calling it physiological. It is true that many recent materialists, in talking of the identity of mental states and brain states, have spoken as if this were possible. But Richard Rorty is right in taking them to task.[16] The materialist view, as he points out, should be expressed by saying, 'what we thought to be mental acts may after all be physiological processes instead'. If one calls anger a physiological process, one cannot continue to call it distinctively mental. Or if one does, one is departing from a Cartesian concept of mental acts, and will then have to explain what one means by 'mental'. For Descartes, mental activities have 71 no affinity (*affinitas*) with bodily activities.[17] And the mind itself has properties which are actually incompatible with those of the body, for the body is extended and divisible, the mind neither extended nor divisible.[18]

Aristotle is unlike Descartes in several fundamental ways. For one thing, the topic of self-awareness does not play the same role in his account of the soul. Descartes defines the mind as a conscious being (2nd *Meditation*, HR I, p.152), and consciousness (*cogitatio*) as 'all that is in us in such a way that we are immediately aware (*conscii*) of it'.[19] Because of this, the notion of self-awareness is central in Descartes' view of the soul. But Aristotle's remarks on self-awareness are brief, sporadic, and by no means centrally placed. The topic did not have the same interest for him. His most Cartesian remark is perhaps the one in the *Physics*, when he says that a change of quality in the sense organs of a living thing differs from a change of quality

16. Richard Rorty, 'Incorrigibility as the mark of the mental', *Journal of Philosophy* (1970), esp. pp. 399-406.

17. Reply to objection on the 2nd *Meditation*, in the 3rd set of *Objections*, transl. Haldane and Ross, Vol. 2, p.64.

18. 6th *Meditation*, *ibid.*, Vol. 1, pp. 190 and 196, and *Passions of the Soul*, article 30, p.345.

19. Reply to 2nd *Objections*, Definition I, *ibid.*, Vol. 2, p.52.

in a lifeless thing, in that it does not go unnoticed (*Phys.* 244b15-245a2). He also suggests, though sometimes only in an 'if-' clause, that one is inevitably aware of one's own perceiving, thinking, and remembering (*Sens.* 437a27-9, 448a26-8; *De An.* 425b12; *EN* 1170a29-b1; *Mem.* 452b26-8). But in several ways Aristotle's remarks on self-awareness are unlike Descartes'. First, he does not seem to hold consistently to the claims about self-awareness that we have just referred to.[20] Secondly, he is just as ready to entertain the idea that one is inevitably aware of one's own walking (*EN* 1170a30). And there is no attempt to make self-awareness a distinguishing mark of mental acts, by protesting, with Descartes, that awareness of one's own walking is not immediate (see note 19), or by distinguishing between the corporeal act of walking and merely seeming to walk.[21] Thirdly, Aristotle's view of how one is aware of one's own seeing is rather surprising. For *De An.* 425b12-25 equates the question of how we are aware that we are seeing (425b12, b13), or, in other words, how we are aware of our sight (425b13, b16), with the question of how we are aware of the organ that sees (*to horôn*, 425b19, b22).

72   This implies that it is through awareness of the organ that we are aware that we are seeing. He goes on to remind us that the organ is coloured during the perceptual process (425b22-25),[22] and presumably we will be aware of its colouration.[23] This colouration is a physiological process, which could in

20. Processes (*kinêseis*) in the sense organs, and images (*phantasmata*) can after all pass unnoticed, according to *Insom.* 460b28-461a8, 461a19-22, and according to an argument (whose conclusion, however, Aristotle rejects) at *Sens.* 447a12-b6. Moreover, *Mem.* 451a2-5 admits that a man may be remembering, in spite of being in doubt whether he is.

21. 2nd *Meditation*, Haldane and Ross, Vol. 1, p.153; *Principles of Philosophy* I.9, *ibid.*, Vol. 1, p.222; Reply to objections on the 2nd *Meditation*, §§ 1 and 9, in the Replies to the 5th *Objections*, *ibid.*, Vol. 2, pp. 207 and 213.

22. For the view that the organ takes on colour when we see, see *De An.* 424a7-10, 425b22-4, 427a8-9, 435a22-4, 417a20, 418a3, 422a7, 422a34, 423b30, 424a18, 424b2, 429a15, 434a29. The first four passages suggest a literal taking on of colour. The theory has been misunderstood by modern commentators. Professor Hamlyn and Jonathan Barnes think such a theory absurd, and Barnes concludes that Aristotle cannot have held it (Hamlyn [78], pp. 9 and 11; [44], pp. 104 and 113; Barnes, above, p.38). But it is the *korê* which takes on colour (*De An.* 431a17-18; *HA* 491b21; *PA* 653b25), not the eye as a whole, which would indeed be an absurd theory. The theory would still be absurd, if the *korê* were the pupil, as all recent English translators of the psychological works suggest (Beare, Hamlyn, Hammond, Hett, Hicks, G.R.T. Ross, Smith). But the *korê* is in fact the eye-jelly inside the eye (*Sens.* 438a16, 438b5-16, *HA* 491b21, *De An.* 425a4, *GA* 780b23). And it would not have been obvious, with the instruments available to Aristotle, that the eye-jelly did not become coloured during the process of vision, nor yet (to take another example from Hamlyn and Barnes) that the *interior* of the ear did not become noisy. None of the perceptual organs would have been readily open to inspection during the perceptual process; all were internal.

One advantage of assuming a literal taking on of colour is that this explains (*pace* Barnes) how shapes and sizes can be received in the organ: the coloured patches in the eye-jelly have shapes and (small-scale) sizes. For further supporting evidence, see note 28 below.

23. This is part of a two-pronged answer to a puzzle set in Plato's *Charmides* 168D-E. Sight cannot see itself, for only what is coloured can be seen. Aristotle replies (i)

principle, even if not in practice, be seen by other observers, using ordinary sense perception. So what one is aware of on these occasions does not sound like a Cartesian act of mind. The only concession to a Cartesian way of thinking – and it is not a very big concession – comes when Aristotle says that the perceiver does not simply *see* his own organ and act of seeing (*De An.* 425b17-22; *Som.* 455a17), but is aware of it in a different manner.[24]

There is another way in which Aristotle is fundamentally unlike Descartes. He does not divide up the world at the same points. We have already noticed that he does not treat mental acts as a single group, but makes a sharp distinction between perception and thought. Nor does he follow Descartes in trying to separate off from the group nutrition (see note 4), or in distinguishing between corporeal acts of walking or seeing, which do not belong to the group, and seeming to see or seeming to walk, which do **73** belong (note 21). Aristotle groups together thought, perception and walking as activities of which we are conscious, and does not follow Descartes in protesting that we are not *immediately* conscious of corporeal walking (see note 19). Thought, perception and walking are grouped together again, on the grounds that they all belong to humans, none to plants. And they are grouped together with each other and with nutrition, on the grounds that all are due to the soul. Admittedly, walking, weaving and building are not things the soul does, but are merely due to the soul. But *De An.* 408b11-15 explains that this is no less true of thinking and being angry. All are things the man does with his soul, not things the soul does.

If Aristotle comes close to Descartes anywhere, it will be in his account of thinking. Indeed, God's thinking is a wholly incorporeal activity, so that here Descartes and Aristotle meet. But what about human thinking? This will always involve a physiological process, if it is always accompanied by imagery. It might be maintained (cf. Barnes above, p.40) that images are involved only in the *acquisition* of concepts, not in the use of them, not, that is, in thinking proper. But this would be hard to square with the statements of *De An.* 431a16, 431b2, 432a8. Moreover, Aristotle has *theoretical* reasons for wanting all human thinking to involve imagery. One reason (*De An.* 432a3-10) is his desire to refute Plato's view that the objects of dialectical thought are ideal forms, which exist separately from the sensible world. Aristotle thinks that very few things can exist separately from the sensible world; so the objects of thought need a sensible vehicle, and a vehicle is provided by the image in which (cf. also 431b2) the objects of thought reside. Thus Plato is wrong to suppose that dialectical thinking rises above

---

sight is not seen, but only perceived with the aid of sight. (ii) What is perceived on these occasions (the organ) is coloured, so on this score there would have been no barrier to its being seen.

For further references to the idea that, when seeing, one not only receives, but also perceives, processes in one's eye-jelly, see *GA* 780b32, and (in the course of an argument whose conclusion Aristotle rejects) *Sens.* 447a23-7.

24. The *De Anima* suggests that sight plays an indirect role in our awareness of our own seeing, just as it does in our awareness of darkness. We do not *see* darkness, but are aware of it through trying (and failing) to see *other* things. The *De Somno* – supplementing, but not, I think, contradicting the *De Anima* – says that we are aware of our own seeing through the central sense faculty (455a15-25).

the need for images (*Republic* 510B, 511C, 432A). Another reason for requiring images emerges in the *De Memoria*, which is an important source for Aristotle's theory of thinking.[25] If we are thinking of a triangle, we put before our 'eyes' an image of a triangle, but neglect the irrelevant fact that the particular imaged triangle happens to be, say, three inches across, and attend only to the relevant features, such as its having three sides. Similarly, if we are thinking of something non-spatial, we still put before our 'eyes' something extended, but ignore the fact of its being extended (450a1-7; cf. 452b7-15). Obviously such a process requires imagery (and hence a physiological process) at the stage of thinking, and not merely at the stage of concept acquisition. If we are to open a crack for a Cartesian interpretation, we would do better to raise the question whether the physiological process stands to the act of thinking as its matter, or merely as the matter of the imagining which is necessarily involved in human thinking. Similarly, we might ask whether the physiological process stands as matter, or merely in some other relation, to the act of attending to the relevant features of one's image. But a good many more steps would be needed, before we could move from these questions to the conclusion that Aristotle conceived of human thinking, or some aspect of human thinking, in a Cartesian fashion.

(v) *The contrast with Strawson.* This may be enough to make clear that Aristotle cannot be aligned with Descartes. But it should not be thought either than he can be aligned with present-day critics of Descartes. Present-day readers may be reminded of the anti-Cartesian arguments of Strawson,[26] when they see Aristotle refusing to make a sharp break between thinking or desiring on the one hand and walking, weaving, or building on the other. But Aristotle is further away from Descartes than modern critics are. For he equally refuses to make a sharp break between walking on the one hand and nutrition and growth on the other. All are equally due to the soul.

(vi) *The contrast with Brentano.* In 1867, Franz Brentano interpreted several Aristotelian passages as meaning that the object of sense perception or thought is not (or not only) physically present in the observer, but present in a non-physical way as an object of perception or thought (*Die Psychologie des Aristoteles* (Mainz, 1867), pp. 79-81, 86, 120, n. 23). In 1874, he suggested a new criterion of his own for distinguishing mental from physical phenomena. Mental phenomena are directed towards objects, and the objects have 'intentional inexistence'. That is to say, the object of a thought or wish exists in the mind, but does not have to have real existence outside of the mind (*Psychologie vom empirischen Standpunkt*, trans. L.McAlister, London, 1973). Brentano detected in Aristotle this idea of the 'mental inherence' of objects of thought and sense-perception, and he cited some of the same passages as before. The first publication merely spoke of colours and temperatures being in the perceiver as objects (*objectiv*). The later publication filled this out, finding in Aristotle objects of the kind which Brentano believed characteristic of mental acts. In connexion with sense

25. Sorabji [50], pp. 6-8.
26. Strawson, *Individuals* (London, 1959), Ch. 3, esp. §§ 5-6.

perception, Brentano cited as evidence for his interpretation Aristotle's **74** theory that the sense organs 'receive form without matter' (*De An.* 424a18, b2, 425b23, 427a8, 429a15, 434a29, 435a22), the claim that using one's senses is not the ordinary kind of *paschein* (*De An.* 417b2-7), and the claim that the actualised object of sense is within the sense (*De An.* 426a2-4).

Of the three Aristotelian ideas that Brentano cites, the first two are used also by Barnes (p.38 above), but neither idea seems to prove the point. I have already commented on the second (p.46 above). The first concerns receiving form without matter. It is nearly[27] always the sense organ, or the perceiver, not the sense, which is said to receive form without matter. Brentano takes it in his first publication that this reception of form involves the object of perception being present in a non-physical way (pp. 80-1, 86), and Barnes, following him, holds that it introduces a non-physical component into perception. But there is good reason[28] to interpret the reception of form without matter physiologically. It means that e.g. the organ of sight (i.e. the jelly inside the eye, see note 22) takes on the colour of the object seen, without taking on any material particles from the object, such as Empedocles and Democritus had postulated. In that case, in talking of the organ's reception of form without matter, Aristotle is so far talking only of the physiological process.

The third Aristotelian idea that Brentano cites suits his case best. For Aristotle does say that the actualised object of sense inheres in the sense (if we read *têi*, the organ, at 426a4), and he adds that the actualised object of sense lasts only as long as the act of sensing (426a15-26). This fits with Brentano's first, and less explicit, claim that the object of perception for **75** Aristotle is in the perceiver in a non-physical way.[29] But Brentano's later interpretation seems wide of the mark. For Aristotle does not agree that the object of sense need not have real existence outside the mind. On the contrary, the object of sense in its potential state does exist outside the mind (426a15-26). Admittedly, Aristotle acknowledges that there are

27. The exceptions seem to be cases where Aristotle has misleadingly borrowed the terminology of form without matter, to express the quite different doctrine that the act of sensing is identical with the actualised object of sense.

28. Having declined to regard the reception of form without matter as a physiological process, Barnes finds it difficult to attach any very precise meaning to the idea. In fact, the idea is connected with the organ's becoming like the object perceived (*De An.* 429a15-16), and with the taking on of colours or temperatures (see *De An.* 424a7-10, 425b22-4, 427a8-9, 435a22-4). So it seems easier, and it is also appropriate in the historical context, to interpret the reception of form without matter in our way. This physiological interpretation has the added advantage of enabling us to understand what Slakey could not understand, the second of two explanations at 424b1-3 of why plants cannot perceive. Plants cannot receive form without matter, i.e. they can only take on colour and warmth by admitting coloured or warm matter. Barnes' reason for refusing to regard the reception of form as a physiological process of the organ changing colour or temperature is that the resulting theory would have been 'open to devastatingly obvious attack' (above, p.38). Our answer to this is given in note 22 where additional evidence is offered for the physiological interpretation.

29. Perhaps the actualised object of sense is something that *we* would characterise as mental. And this would support Barnes, provided he does not say that Aistotle himself would conceive the actualised object as mental. It does not support Brentano, however, for Brentano believes that only the sense is mental; its object is physical.

53   Body and Soul in Aristotle

mental states whose objects do not really exist. A wish, for example, can be directed towards something impossible, such as immortality. But this is not true of all mental states, nor even of all kinds of desire (*EN* 1111b10-30).

(vii) *The contrast with materialism.* Having failed to align Aristotle with Descartes or Brentano, we should not swing to the opposite extreme and treat him as a materialist. The fullest case for doing so was made by Slakey (note 1 above). But unfortunately Slakey rested his case mainly on an interpretation of *De An.* 423b27-424a10 which I believe to be mistaken. In this passage, Aristotle says that *aisthêsis* is a mean or mid-point (*mesotês*). Slakey takes this to mean that sense (the capacity to perceive) is the capacity of the organ to change to one extreme or the other, to hot or to cold for example. He infers that sensing will simply be the process of the organ's changing to hot or cold. There are several objections to this interpretation.

First, when Aristotle talks here of *aisthêsis*, he seems to be concerned not (or not directly) with sense, as Slakey requires, but with the sense *organ*.[30] For he describes it as changing temperature (424a6-10). Second, even if he had been directly concerned with sense, he would in any case have been assimilating it hereby to the organ, and not, as Slakey suggests, to a capacity of the organ. Aristotle, I believe, is concerned in particular with the organ of touch. He argues that this organ cannot lack temperature (etc.), in the way that the eye-jelly lacks colour. (This is the relevance of 423b27-31). He also argues that its natural temperature is an intermediate one, mid-way between hot and cold. (This is why he calls it a mean or mid-point, 424a4.) That its normal temperature is a mean one is inferred from the supposed fact that we have a blind spot for mean temperatures (*alla tôn huperbolôn*, 424a4). The inability of plants to perceive is explained (424b1, 435a20-b3; cf. 434a27) as due to their lack of an organ of touch, which is in turn due to their being too earthy and cold to have an organ with a mean temperature. We can thus explain three things which Slakey could not account for (for a fourth, see note 28). We see first why Aristotle uses the word *mesotês* which means mid-point, second how he accounts for the insensitivity of plants, and third what relevance he sees in lines 423b27-31.

But even if this particular passage does not support Slakey's materialist interpretation, we ought to take his suggestion seriously. For we could well expect Aristotle to be a materialist, seeing that so many of his predecessors were preoccupied with the physiology of mental acts. Many of their statements, at least if taken in isolation, could suggest that mental occurrences are simply physiological entities. And Aristotle, along with his successor Theophrastus, and later commentators who drew on Theophrastus, often interpreted early writers in this sense.[31] Moreover,

30. Either *aisthêsis* refers to the organ here, or, if it refers to sense, the sense is called a mid-point only derivatively, because the organ is one. The sense does seem to be called a blend (*logos*) later at 424a27, 426a29, b3, b7, but the point being made there is a different one which applies to senses other than touch.

31. See *Meta.* 1009b11 ff.; *De An.* 427a26, on Empedocles and Democritus. Also Parmenides fr. 6, lines 5-6, and fr. 16. Empedocles fr. 105. Anaxagoras, according to Theophrastus, *De Sensibus* §31. Democritus, according to Aëtius, A.30 in Diels. Some of Plato's *Timaeus* also lends itself to this interpretation. On Homer, see R.B. Onians,

many of Aristotle's own remarks, if taken in isolation, seem to suggest a materialist view. Of sense perception he says that it is a matter of being affected by something, that it is a change in the body, that it is a qualitative change, and that a certain change in the eye is seeing.[32]

Even more striking is his treatment of memory-images and dream-images in the *De Memoria* and *De Insomniis*. We are given every reason to think that Aristotle is discussing what we should call a mental image. It is a *phantasma*, is in our soul, and is contemplated by us.[33] None the less, at the same time, he gives this image a very physical interpretation, insisting, for example, that the surfaces within the body must not be too hard to receive it (*Mem.* 450a30-b10), and implying that the image does not depend for its existence on being perceived.[34] At *Insom.* 462a8-12, he says that we can confirm that we observe processes in our sense organs, if we attend to what happens when we are going to sleep or waking up. For sometimes on waking up, we can surprise the images (*eidôla*) that appear to us in sleep, and find that they are processes in our sense organs. **77**

But these statements should not be taken in isolation. They must be read against the background of Aristotle's full theoretical statements in the *De Anima*. The two main theoretical statements are very prominently placed. One comes in the opening chapter of the first book (403a3-b19), the other in the closing chapter of the second book, where it rounds off the discussion of the five senses (424b3-18). We should remember these full explanations when we encounter the more hasty expressions which we have been looking at. Of the two theoretical statements the first is that which says that the physiological process is only the material cause of anger. There is also a formal cause. The second is that which says that smelling is something else besides (*para*) the process of being affected by odour.

The materialist interpreter may take heart when he sees that Aristotle uses the very same kind of analogy as some modern materialists have used. Anger *is* a physiological process in much the same sense as a house *is* a set of

---

op cit. For Aristotle's interpretation of some earlier views on pleasure, see *EN* 1173b7-9.

32. For these four statements, see (i) *De An.* 424a1, 427a9; (ii) *Phys.* 244b11-12; (iii) *Insom.* 459b4-5; *MA* 701b18; (iv) *GA* 780a3.

33. *Mem.* 450a25-451a17; *Insom.* 3. For the word *phantasma*, see *Mem.* 450b10, b24, 451a15, etc.; *Insom.* 461a18, 462a16, a29-31. For '*in* the soul', see *Mem.* 450a28, b10-11, 451a3. (The expression 'a process *of* the soul' would have been less significant, since it could have been applied to plant growth, as well as to a mental entity.) For reference to contemplating and perceiving the image, to taking it as resembling, or as identical with, familiar objects, to its appearing and being noticed, see *Mem.* 450b15-18, 450b24-451a2; *Insom.* 460b10-11, b23-7, 460b31-461a8, 461a19-22, 462a8-12. The significance of the last point, however, the observability of the image, will be reduced, when we recall that Aristotle sometimes speaks of our observing physiological processes within ourselves (see pp.49-50).

34. *Insom.* 460b31-461a8, a19-22. A physical interpretation suggests itself also when Aristotle says that the changes left behind in us by earlier sense-images are located in the blood in our sense organs (461b12, b16-19, 462a9, a12). They can travel down with the blood towards the heart (461a5-7, a28-b1, b12). They may collide with each other (461a10-11), and change their shape (461a10-11, b19-21) like the eddies in rivers, or like figures in clouds (461a8-9, b19-21).

bricks. Some modern materialists have offered the analogy of a bucket of
water *being* a set of H_2O molecules. But Aristotle is more accurate than these

78 materialists. For they want to say that mental states may be *identical* with
physiological processes. Aristotle sees that, at least for some purposes, it is
misleading to say that a house is *identical* with a set of bricks, and in general
that a thing is *identical* with its matter. He denies that the syllable BA *is*, or is
identical (*to auto*) with, the constituent letters, or that flesh *is* its constituent
elements. And he gives the excellent reason that the components can outlast
the compound. Bricks can outlast the house.[35] The same reason has recently
been given by Professor Wiggins for distinguishing between the relation of
identity and the relation of composition.[36] By noticing that, at least for some
purposes, it is wrong to say that a thing is identical with its components,
Aristotle improves on some present-day materialists, and on Descartes.[37]
He often relaxes his ban on saying that a thing *is* its matter. Very
occasionally (in another kind of context, and for another purpose) he even
lets us say that a thing is *one* with its matter (or rather he says that this way
of speaking is 'better' than certain others he has been describing, which
need not mean that it is in every respect all right, *GC* 320b12-14; cf. *Phys.*
190a15-16). But the important point is that he also has strong reasons
against saying that anger is identical with, or one with, a physiological
process. And this differentiates him from the modern materialists we
mentioned.

There are other contrasts too. Aristotle would not agree that perception is
simply a physiological process. For this 'simply' (Slakey's word) would
ignore the formal cause. A house is not *simply* bricks; it is also a shelter. And
this further description is a very important one. Indeed, the formal
description of perception is, if anything, more important than the material
description. For the body exists for the sake of the soul, in the sense that
there would be no point in the existence of bodies and bodily processes, but
for the existence of souls and soul states (*De An.* 415b15-21). Aristotle would
reject the view of some materialists[38] that talk of sensations or houses could
be replaced by talk of physiological processes or bricks, without impairing
our ability to describe and explain. Formal descriptions cannot be replaced
by material descriptions in this way.

79 It should now be clear why Aristotle disapproves of Empedocles and
Democritus for making perception into a mere qualitative change (*Meta.*
1009b13). It also should be clear how we are to interpret the statements
quoted earlier where Aristotle seems to talk as if perception or images were
physiological processes. They are indeed physiological processes in a way,
but only in a sense of 'are' which does not mean 'are identical with', and

35. *Meta.* 1041b12-16; cf. also 1035a7-10, 'the form, or the thing in so far as it has
form, should be said to be the thing, but the material by itself should never be said to
be so'. Presumably, in the case of anger, the physiological process can occur in sleep,
without anger occurring, just as bricks can exist, when a house does not.

36. David Wiggins, *op.cit.* (above, note 2), pp. 10-25.

37. Descartes says in the 2nd *Meditation* that he *is* a mind, and in the 6th that he *has*
a body. But he also says in the 6th *Meditation*, and elsewhere, that he is *composed of*
(*compositus, composé*) mind and body.

38. See Richard Rorty, 'Mind-body identity, privacy, and categories', *The Review
of Metaphysics* (1965).

with the proviso that they are not 'simply' physiological processes.

Aristotle's use of the matter-form distinction in his psychology has been called a strain, a misfit, and an obfuscation.[39] But it has the merit of steering us away from the idea that mental states may be *identical with*, or may be *simply*, physiological processes.

(viii) *What is the formal cause of desire?* A certain question now becomes urgent. We have seen that anger and smelling are not 'simply' physiological processes. But we have also seen that, whatever else they are, the something else cannot be a further component. Nor can it be a Cartesian act of mind. What else, then, can anger and smelling be? The further description should presumably be parallel to the description of a house as a shelter.

Aristotle tells us that anger can be further described as a desire to retaliate, and smelling as an awareness of odour (*De An.* 403a25-b9, 424b17-19). But neither answer is very helpful to people with our interests. For the new terms, 'desire' and 'awareness', are, like the original terms ('anger' and 'smelling'), the names of *pathê* of the soul. They therefore invite the same question all over again, 'What else are desire and awareness, besides physiological processes?' We would like a description that differs in kind, and is not simply the name of a *pathos*. Unfortunately, Aristotle has not addressed himself to this question. In what follows we can do no more than ask whether what he says provides the *materials* for an answer. I propose to take the example of desire.

On the material description of desire we are well informed. According to *MA* 6-10, it is a process of heating or cooling, which results in expansion or contraction of the gaseous stuff called connate spirit, and of the organs, and hence eventually leads to limb movements. The change of temperature involved in the desire to retaliate is not a second physiological process additional to the boiling of the blood around the heart (the material cause of anger). 'Change of temperature' is simply a more general description of the same process.

But what is the formal description of desire? Aristotle places a strong emphasis on the connexion between desire and *action*. One of the most interesting passages is the analysis of abilities in *Metaphysics* IX5. After **80** analysing non-rational abilities, such as the ability of fire to burn, he passes on to rational abilities such as the ability to heal. These latter are connected with desire. Thus one who is able to heal under appropriate conditions necessarily (1048a14) will heal, if (a) he wants to, (b) of the two results, healing or withholding health, this is the one he wants predominantly, (c) he is in the appropriate conditions (e.g. he is in the presence of the patient, the patient is in a suitable state, and there are no external obstacles to action).[40] Although Aristotle's interest is in the notion of ability, his account commits him to a certain view of desire. For it implies that if a man desires to heal, and the desire to heal predominates over any desire to withold health, then necessarily he will heal, provided (i) he has the ability to heal under appropriate conditions, and (ii) he is in those conditions.

A similar view is expressed in Aristotle's account of *akrasia* or weakness of

39. W.F.R. Hardie [61], pp. 64-6; Jonathan Barnes, above, p. 36.
40. For a modern version of this analysis, see Nowell-Smith, *Ethics* (Pelican, 1954).

I

the will (*EN* 1145a15-1152a36). He distinguishes between two kinds of
weak-willed man. One such man has not deliberated at all (*EN* 1150b19-22,
1151a1-3, 1152a19, a27-8). But one has deliberated about the best means to
achieve his ends, for example about how best to keep fit. And having
decided that a diet of chicken is the best means, he has come to want a diet
of chicken.[41] The discussion, then, presupposes a man who desires some
end, such as health, has worked out the best means to it, and desires to
pursue that means. A man with such a desire, we are told, will necessarily
(1147a27, a30) act accordingly and take some chicken, provided that (i) he
has the ability (1147a30), (ii) he is not prevented (1147a30-1), (iii) he is
fully aware of the relevant observational facts (1147a25-6, a29-30, b9-12),
such as 'this is chicken', (iv) he links these facts to the fact that eating
chicken is good for health (1147a26-7). Aristotle has added in (iii) and (iv)
two extra conditions that were not mentioned in the *Metaphysics*. But the
upshot of the two passages is the same, namely that, in certain
81 circumstances, desire necessarily (1048a14, 1147a27, a30)[42] leads to action.

Aristotle links desire and action again, when he says (*EN* 1139a31-2) that
the efficient cause of *praxis* (deliberate action) is *prohaeresis* (a certain kind of
desire). More generally, the efficient cause of animal motion is desire.[43]
Neither these, nor the preceding statements are offered as providing an
analysis of desire. And in some cases the link between desire and action will
be more indirect than that described here. For example, Aristotle
distinguishes between *boulêsis*, desire for an end such as health, and
prohaeresis, desire for something in our power which we have calculated to be
the best means (in our earlier example, desire for a diet of chicken). Desire
for the end, coupled with calculation, is said to be the efficient cause of
desire for the means. And it is only desire for the means which is directly an
efficient cause of action (*EN* 1139a31-3). Desire for the end, Aristotle
explains, may be directed towards things which are not immediately in our

41. Thus he is described as having deliberated, and as having formed a desire
(*prohaeresis*) based on this deliberation, but as not abiding by his deliberation and his
desire (*EN* 1145b11, 1148a9, 1150b19-22, b30-1, 1151a2, a7, a26, a30-5, b26, 1152a17,
a18-19, a26, a28). The chicken example is derived from 1141b16-21. For the meaning
of *prohaeresis* see *EN* 1112a18-1113a14, where it is described as a desire for something
in one's power (and having a chicken diet is presumably in one's power), which one has
calculated to be the best means for achieving one's end. Desire (*boulêsis*) for the end is
attributed to the weak-willed man at 1136b7, 1166b8.

One should not be put off by the statement that the weak-willed man acts without
exercising *prohaeresis* (1111b14, 1148a17). This only means that when he
incontinently seizes beef-steak, he has no *prohaeresis* for *beef-steak*. He still has his
prohaeresis for *chicken*.

42. It would be anachronistic to ask whether the necessity is logical or physical, for
Aristotle does not regard these as distinct kinds of necessity (Sorabji, 'Aristotle and
Oxford philosophy', *American Philosophical Quarterly* 1969). The *De Motu Animalium*
provides physiological grounds for postulating a necessity, while *Metaphysics* IX5
provides conceptual grounds, grounds, however, which relate to the concept of
ability, rather than to the concept of desire.

43. The efficient cause of animal motion is the soul (*De An.* 415b10, b21-2). It
becomes clear that it is in particular one capacity of the soul, the capacity for desire
(*De An.* III 9-10). The *De Motu Animalium* 6-10 explains the physical mechanism by
which desire leads to action.

power, such as health, or towards things which we can't bring about by our own efforts, such as victory for some athlete, or even towards things altogether impossible, such as immortality (*EN* 1111b19-30).

Perhaps we now have the materials for conjecturing what Aristotle might say, if asked for the formal description of desire. Would part of his answer be that desire is, in certain conditions, a necessitating efficient cause of action? By 'action' I mean not merely *praxis*, deliberate action, which is confined to humans, but the various doings of humans and animals. The statement of conditions would include such provisos as that action is in our power, and that we are fully aware of the relevant observational facts. This could not be more than part of Aristotle's answer.[44] Another part would be that every desire has a final cause (*De An.* 433a15). This is the object of desire. And desire, like other activities of the soul, must presumably be defined by reference to its final cause (*De An.* 403a27), and its objects (*De An.* 415a20-2, 418a7-8). Putting this together, we get a fuller, though no doubt still an incomplete, answer to our question, 'what else is desire, besides a process of heating or cooling?' The answer is that desire has an end, and is, in certain conditions, a necessitating efficient cause of our acting towards that end.

If this conjecture is accepted about the formal description of desire, we can draw conclusions for anger, which is a kind of desire. Anger will be not only a physiological process, but also an efficient cause of retaliation. And we can draw conclusions also for certain other *pathê* of the soul. For loving and hating are listed as *pathê* in the *Rhetoric*, and are there treated like anger as being desires (1380b35, 1382a8). They are wishes for good or for harm towards another person. We can expect, then, that they will be efficient causes of corresponding actions.

Our expectation that loving will be connected with action is confirmed in the *Rhetoric* passage. For Aristotle describes loving not only as wishing good to another person, but also as being a doer of good to him, so far as possible (1380b35).[45] But there is something here that we did not quite expect. Aristotle does not say that loving is an efficient cause of doing good to someone. He says that it is being a doer of good to him, i.e. presumably, it is a tendency to do good to him. Modern discussions have suggested that there is a big difference between a mere tendency to do good and an actual cause of doing good. Perhaps Aristotle does not see a distinction here. We shall return to this question shortly.

Though loving is classed as a *pathos* in the *Rhetoric*, friendship is assimilated to a *hexis*, or long-term state, in the *Nicomachean Ethics* (1157b29). For the difference between *pathos* and *hexis*, see note 13. It need

---

44. It is a commonplace to contrast Aristotelian explanations as teleological with Galilean explanations as causal (see e.g. Georg Henrik von Wright, *Explanation and Understanding* (London, 1971), Ch. 1; Charles Taylor, *The Explanation of Behaviour* (London, 1964), Ch. 1). Certainly, Aristotle favoured teleological explanations, but we should not forget (von Wright, p.92; Taylor, pp. 4, 20-5) that he thought teleological explanations compatible with explanations by reference to efficient cause. An action, for example, has some end as its final cause, and some desire as its efficient cause.

45. Similarly, kindness (*Rhet.* 1385a16) is defined by reference to action, as that in accordance with which a person is said to render a kindness.

be no less true of *hexeis* than of *pathê* that some are connected with action. Examples of *hexeis* are the virtues and vices discussed in the *Nicomachean Ethics*. And these are connected not only with *pathê*, but also with action, according to *EN* 1106b23-8. For example, hot-temper is not only a matter of being ill-disposed in relation to the *pathos* of anger. It also manifests itself in **83**   action in various ways. Consequently, a large number[46] of the virtues and vices are analysed by reference to action, and not, or not only, by reference to *pathê*. In many cases, *hexeis* and *dunameis* (capacities) are described not as mere tendencies to act, but as efficient causes of action, and as things 'from which' and 'through which' we act.[47]

If we have not gone too far beyond Aristotle's text, in our speculations, we now have some sort of answer to our question. The answer will only apply to desire and to some *pathê* or *hexeis* of the soul. For Aristotle shows no interest in connecting all *pathê* or *hexeis* with action towards an end. But at least for desire we can suggest a formal description which is not merely the name of another *pathos*.[48] The description is that desire has an end and is (with appropriate qualifications) an efficient cause of action towards that end. If this is the sort of thing that Aristotle would say, we can now understand how he can hold that desire is something else besides a physiological process, without thinking that the something else is a further component, and without thinking that the something else, or the desire itself, is a Cartesian act of mind.[49] Our suggested further description of desire is rather like the description of a house as a shelter, in that it does not name either a component or a Cartesian act of mind.

(ix) *The analogy with plant growth and elemental motion.* We can now return to the point made earlier that Aristotle stresses the continuity between processes in plants and processes in humans. Desire is treated as parallel to the growth of a plant. Neither is called mental. But just as the growth of a plant is not simply a physical process, but also a development towards an

46. Courage,   Liberality,   Magnificence,   Great-Souledness,   Friendliness, Truthfulness, Ready Wit, Justice, and the corresponding vices. Also Self-Indulgence, Hot Temper, Friendship, Technical Skill, Practical Wisdom.

There is a class of virtues (friendliness, truthfulness, ready wit) in connexion with which Aristotle deliberately plays down the rôle of emotion and emphasises the rôle of action. See *EN* 1108a9-31, 1126b11-1128b9 (esp. 1126b22-3), and William Fortenbaugh, 'Aristotle and the questionable mean-dispositions', *Transactions and Proceedings of the American Philological Association* (1968).

47. See e.g. *Phys.* 195a5-11, b23-4; *Meta.* 1019a15-1020a6, *EN* 1129a6-21, 1143b26, *GA* 726b21; *Rhet.* 1366b9, *De An.* 415b10, b21-2.

48. This is not to deny that the notions of having an end, or of acting towards an end, might turn out to involve some indirect reference to *pathê* of the soul. And we have not made a positive suggestion as to how these further *pathê* might be analysed. But we have said enough to show how Aristotle could analyse desire without making it, or its formal cause, into a Cartesian act of mind, and without making its formal cause into a component.

49. D.M. Armstrong (*A Materialist Theory of the Mind* (London, 1968), pp. 11-12) and Barnes (*op. cit.*) ascribe to Aristotle the view that, in so far as man has a soul, he has some non-physical attributes. Is desire, as here defined, a non-physical attribute? Once we observe that it is at any rate not a mental attribute, by Cartesian criteria, the question loses much of its interest.

end, so desire is not simply a physical process, but also an efficient cause of action towards an end. We can also see more clearly the analogy between desire and the *nature* of the lifeless elements. Just as desire is an efficient cause of action towards an end, so the nature of a stone, according to the conception of nature in *Phys.* II 1, is an internal cause of its moving downwards towards an end.

(x) *The contrast with Ryle.* We must ward off a final danger. We have seen **84** that in his divergence from Descartes, Aristotle does not side with the materialists, nor with Strawson. But it may now appear (and it has been suggested in recent literature)[50] that Aristotle takes the same path as Ryle, for Ryle, like Aristotle, stresses the links between mental states and action. This would be a mistake for at least two reasons. First, Aristotle has no general programme for analysing mental states by reference to action. He makes the link only in some cases. Secondly, in *The Concept of Mind*, Ryle analyses many mental states as dispositions or tendencies to act, and he argues that dispositions or tendencies are not causes of action. D.M. Armstrong opposes Ryle in *A Materialist Theory of the Mind* (pp. 85-8). He claims that a disposition necessarily has a 'categorical' basis (cf. Aristotle's boiling of the blood around the heart), with which it can be identified (Aristotle would reject the talk of identification). It is, Armstrong says, in virtue of the categorical basis that the disposition can be a cause of action. While Aristotle would not entirely side with either party in this controversy, some of what he says is closer to Armstrong. For he does speak of desire, and of various *hexeis* and *dunameis*, as efficient causes of action. And he might well agree that desire is an efficient cause of action partly because of its physiological basis.

(xi) It is tempting, when Aristotle says that anger and smelling are something else besides a physiological process, to suppose that the something else can only be a Cartesian act of mind. Conversely, if one notices that he postulates no such act of mind, it is tempting to suppose he must be a materialist. If one notices that these are not the only possibilities, the next temptation is to hunt among other current anti-Cartesian views, and to try and match Aristotle with one of them (with Ryle's or Strawson's perhaps). But so long as commentators hope to fit Aristotle into pigeon-holes of more recent make, they will continue to come out with such widely divergent interpretations as the ones we noted at the beginning.

2: Implications for modern philosophical problems

Aristotle's view of the body-soul relation has implications for various modern problems. Some of these problems arise for Aristotle only in a different form, and some do not arise at all. They do not arise for a number

50. See A.R. White, *The Philosophy of Mind* (New York, 1967), pp. 46-9, '... to possess some knowledge is to have a tendency or an ability to behave in certain ways'.

I

Body and Soul in Aristotle

of reasons, as we shall see, but often because Aristotle's view of the body-soul relation *prevents* them from arising.

85   (i) One problem that has troubled modern philosophers is the problem how a mind can possibly move a body. On Descartes' view, as we have seen, this involves interaction between two things that have no 'affinity' with each other. Aristotle is interested in the method by which the soul moves the body. In Book I of the *De Anima*, he attacks accounts which make the soul into a gas, or other kind of spatial entity, that moves the body by pushing or pulling. Aristotle's biological concept of the soul is not, as we have seen, the same as modern concepts of mind. But he comes fairly close to modern preoccupations in the *Physics*, when he worries about how the soul can move the body conformably with his principles of causation.

One such principle is the time-honoured requirement, first explicitly formulated by Aristotle himself, of no action at a distance.[51] In Aristotle's version, the principle says that what acts and what is acted on must be in contact. This in turn is interpreted as meaning that they must have their extremities or edges together. And 'together' is glossed as 'in one immediate place' (*Phys.* 226b21-227a7). But if a soul is not corporeal (*De An.* 414a20), nor spatially extended (*De An.* 407a2-3), it can have no edges. So how can it act on a body? Instead of concluding, like the Epicureans and Stoics,[52] that since body and soul do interact, the soul must be corporeal, Aristotle appears to be embarrassed into modifying his requirements of contact. At any rate, we find him suddenly switching at *Phys.* 243a3-6, a32-5 to the weaker principle[53] that what acts and what is acted on should be together, which is explained as meaning that there should be nothing in between them. There is no reference to contact or to edges. And when we ask why not, we notice that he is going on to discuss the case of animals who move themselves (243a11-15, a21-3). Now that his requirement is weakened, he is able to say that animals satisfy it. For what acts (and I take it he means the soul) is together with what is acted on (and I take it he means the body),

86   since the former is, in a certain sense, *in*[54] the latter, so that there is nothing in between them. Once again,[55] the *Physics* account of the soul seems to involve hasty improvisation.

By the time he came to write the *De Anima*, Aristotle would have had the means for showing how the stronger contact requirement is satisfied. And he might also have been in a position to answer modern perplexities about

51. *Phys.* III 2, 202a6-9, VII 1, 242b24-7, b59-63, VII 2; *GC* I 6. For the history of this variously interpreted principle, see Mary B. Hesse, *Forces and Fields, The Concept of Action at a Distance in the History of Physics* (London, 1961).
52. See Lucretius *De Rerum Natura* III 161-7. Cleanthes (Nemesius, *De Nat. Hom.*, p.33, in von Arnim's *Stoicorum Veterum Fragmenta* I 518). Iamblichus (quoted in Simplicius' commentary on Aristotle's *Categories*, ed. Kalbfleisch, pp. 302, 28 ff).
53. For a different improvised attempt to weaken the principle, by reference to a special kind of touching, see *Phys.* 258a20, with further explanation at *GC* 323a25-33.
54. In a weak sense of 'in', for the soul does not meet Aristotle's requirements for 'being in a place' (*De An.* 406a12-16). And this is presumably why reference to being in a place is dropped from the modified principle.
55. Cf. the attempt to distinguish animal motion from elemental motion: *Phys.* 255a5-20, b30-1, referred to above, note 9.

the mind moving the body, if he had further exploited his semi-physiological analysis of desire. Desire, as we have seen, is a physiological process of heating or cooling. And it is not philosophically puzzling how heating or cooling, by causing expansion or contraction, can lead to bodily movement. The details of the mechanism are given in *MA* 6-10. At no stage does the process violate Aristotle's requirement of contact, and at no stage do we have the Cartesian problem of interaction between two things that have nothing in common. That desire should cause movement is no more (and no less) puzzling than that heating around the heart should cause expansion. But if desires lead to movement, then there is a sense in which the *capacity* for desire is responsible for movement. For, as we have seen, the soul is a set of capacities, such as the capacity for desire.

Admittedly, in appealing to heating or cooling, we have not given a complete account of how the body is moved. For all non-compulsory animal motion is for an end (*De An.* 432b15). If we want a full explanation of animal motion, we shall have to appeal to this end, which is the object desired. But the end is a final, not an efficient, cause. So it does not raise the Cartesian problem of one thing acting as *efficient* cause upon another with which it has no affinity. Nor does it violate Aristotle's contact requirement, for this requirement too applies only to efficient causation (cf. *GC* 323a25-33).

(ii) We have been talking about how the soul acts on the body. But there is also a problem for modern Cartesians about how the body acts on the soul. How can a physical process in the eye lead to seeing? W.D. Ross (see above, n1), speaking of the physical process in the eye, says, 'it does nothing to explain the essential fact about perception, that on this physical change supervenes something quite different, the apprehension by the mind of some quality of an object'. Earlier on the same page, he speaks of 'the distinctively mental, non-corporeal nature of the act', and of 'a purely mental activity having nothing in common with anything physical'. For Aristotle, however, there is no question of how an act in the body can lead to a purely mental activity. For one thing, 'lead to' is not the right description, **87** he would say, of the relation between the physical process and the apprehension of colour. Bricks do not 'lead to' a shelter, though they are necessary (*De An.* 403b3; *Phys.* II 9), if a shelter is to be realised.[56] For another thing, it is not a purely mental activity for which the physical process is necessary, either in the case of seeing, or in the case of desire. The physical process is necessary for the realisation of the formal cause. In the case of desire, we suggested, the formal cause is not a purely mental activity, but is having an end and being an efficient cause of action towards that end.[57]

56. Similarly, heating and cooling (even if they lead to action) do not lead to an efficient cause of action, but are merely necessary for the realisation of that cause.

57. The formal cause of seeing will be awareness of colour, if seeing is to be treated in the same way as smelling (see p.47). But the awareness is again not a Cartesian act of mind.

(iii) Aristotle's comparison of anger with a house has implications also for present-day questions about the predictability of states of mind. If I can predict what bricks there will be in the world, it does not follow that I can predict whether there will be houses. For that, I should need to know at least how the bricks were arranged, and perhaps also that the arrangements had at some time been used, or intended for use, as shelters. Equally, if I predict what physiological processes will be going on, it does not follow that I can predict whether people will be angry.

(iv) Throughout the discussion so far, we have been guilty of an over-simplification. For we have spoken as if Aristotle were giving a purely physiological description, with no implications for the mind, in his talk of the boiling of the blood around the heart. But in fact he is so impressed by the importance of a thing's function, that he believes a non-functioning heart, or non-functioning blood, is not a heart, or blood, in the proper sense of the word. This theory is applied to the body as a whole, and to many of its components.[58] Aristotle thus gives to the heart or eye a treatment that would be more appropriate for a scrap of paper used as a bookmarker. The scrap becomes a bookmarker, when so used, and ceases to be a bookmarker, when discarded. When it lies in the wastepaper basket, there is nothing distinctive to connect it, rather than thousands of other objects, with bookmarking; its use alone made it a bookmarker. Contrast the severed hand or eye. This still has a distinctive structure to connect it with its former activities, and so it should still (pace Aristotle) qualify as a hand or eye in the primary sense.[59] This is not to deny the important of function. Structure alone, unconnected with function, cannot make something an eye in the primary sense: the eye of a peacock's tail is not. But by making the link between the flesh and its function so tight, Aristotle runs into Ackrill's objection (ch. 4 below), that he is unable to pick out the matter in which soul resides in such a way that that matter could be conceived as existing without soul. If he had made the link looser, in the way recommended, he might have been able to avoid this objection.

88   For our purposes, the interesting thing is the implications of Aristotle's theory for the problem of knowledge of other minds. If true, the theory would mean that the sceptic who doubts his knowledge of other minds cannot express his doubts by saying, 'I see many eyes around me, but I do not know whether they see. I see many bodies, but I cannot tell whether they feel'. According to Aristotle, in admitting the existence of eyes and bodies, he is admitting the existence of sight, which is the function of eyes, and of touch, the distinctive power of animal bodies.

It is interesting to find a similar argument put forward in recent articles by Douglas Long and John Cook.[60] Long points out that the sceptical doubt

58. See *GA* 726b22-4, 734b25-7, 735a8; *Meta.* 1035b16-17, b24-5, 1036b30-2, *De An.* 412b20-5, *PA* 640b34-641a7, *Meteor.* 389b31-390b2, *Pol.* 1253a20-2.
59. It does not need to be transplantable or reversable in order to qualify, as the modified Aristotelian view discussed by Ackrill would suggest (p.71 below).
60. Long, 'The philosophical concept of a human body', *Philosophical Review* (1964). Cook, 'Human beings', in *Studies in the Philosophy of Wittgenstein*, ed. Winch (London, 1969).

I

is often expressed as a question as to whether certain bodies are associated
with minds. He claims that such philosophers as Price, Broad and Strawson
have assumed the existence of other bodies in their discussion of the
problem. And this assumption, according to Long, already implies the
existence of other minds. So much is reminiscent of Aristotle. Long and
Cook go further, and suggest that the sceptic cannot even reformulate his
position.

It never occurs to Aristotle to raise doubts about other minds. Such
doubts would fit very badly with his teleological attitude. If there were
many 'eyes' around, but they had no sight, and many 'bodies', but they had
no sense perception, then nature would have acted in vain. For as he says,
the body exists for the sake of the soul (*De An.* 415b15-21). There would be
no point in the existence of bodies, if there were not souls. Doubts about
other minds would also fit badly with his dialectical method, the method of
starting from opinions that have been accepted by *others*, and salvaging as
much as can be freed from objections (*EN* 1145b2-7, 1146b6-8).

For Aristotle, seeing is, among other things, a physiological process, the
colouration of the eye-jelly. And this process can in principle, even if not in
practice, be observed by others. So there is an answer to the question how
one can possibly know that another person is seeing. One can in theory
observe the fact. Perhaps it will be objected that to observe the colouration
of another man's eye-jelly is to observe only the material cause of his seeing,
not the seeing itself. But this objection fails to do justice to Aristotle's
position in two ways. First, in Aristotle's view, it is by this means that one is
aware of one's own seeing (pp. 49-50 above). One perceives its material
cause, the colouration of the eye-jelly. Secondly, it should not be supposed
that after one has observed the physiological process, there is some purely
mental act still waiting to be detected. The formal cause of seeing will not be,
and will not involve reference to, a purely mental act, one having no 'affinity'
with bodily acts. There are no such acts. If there had been, the sceptical doubt
would have been easier to raise. As it is, we have not discussed the formal
cause of seeing, but we have suggested that the formal cause of desire is
having an end and being an efficient cause of action towards that end. And **89**
this is something with regard to which it is (not indeed impossible, but)
certainly much harder, to raise a plausible doubt.

Aristotle is so far from entertaining doubts about other minds that, in his
discussion of friendship, he almost reverses the sceptical position. Some of
the benefits of friendship arise from the fact that it is easier to contemplate
others than to contemplate ourselves (*EN* 1169b33-5).[61]

61. I acknowledge gratefully the helpful comments of William Charlton, David
Hamlyn, Charles Kahn, A.C. Lloyd, A.A. Long, Norman Malcolm, Malcolm
Schofield, and of my students, Bill Hartley and Philippa Mance. The writings which
I have found most valuable are: Charles Kahn (ch. 1 above); Friedrich Solmsen [53];
Solmsen, 'Nature and soul' [54], pp. 95-102. I am especially indebted to Solmsen's
article in my section I (iii), and to Kahn's for the contrast with Descartes. I have
taken the opportunity of making some revisions in this version, and I have slightly
curtailed the footnotes.

I

BIBLIOGRAPHY for I

Some articles are referred to in the notes by the surname and a number in brackets, relating to the listing in the original publication. These numbers have been given at the end of the reference, where relevant.

Ackrill, J.L. (1972–3), 'Aristotle's Definitions of *psuchê*', *Proceedings of the Aristotelian Society* 73, 119–33, repr. in Barnes, J., Schofield, M., and Sorabji, R. (eds) (1979), *Articles on Aristotle, vol. 4*, 65–75.

Armstrong, D.M. (1968), *A Materialist Theory of Mind*, London: Routledge and K. Paul.

Barnes, J. (1971–2), 'Aristotle's concept of mind', *Proceedings of the Aristotelian Society* 72, 101–10, repr. in Barnes, J., Schofield, M., and Sorabji, R. (eds) (1979), *Articles on Aristotle, vol. 4*, 32–41.

Brentano, F. (1867), *Die Psychologie des Aristoteles, inbesondere seine Lehre von NOUS POIÉTIKOS*, Mainz: Franz Kirkheim.

— (1874, tr. 1973), *Psychologie vom empirischen Standpunkt*, Leipzig: Duncker and Humblot; (2nd. ed.), Kraus, O. (ed.) (1924, 1959), Leipzig: F. Meiner; tr. Rancurello, C., Terrell, D.B., McAlister, L. (1973), London: Routledge.

Chisholm, R. (ed.) (1960), *Realism and the Background of Phenomenology*, Glencoe, Illinois: The Free Press.

Cook, J.W. (1969), 'Human Beings', in Winch, P. (ed.), *Studies in the Philosophy of Wittgenstein*, London: Routledge and K. Paul, 117–51.

Fortenbaugh, W. (1968), 'Aristotle and the Questionable Mean-Dispositions', *Transactions of the American Philological Association* 99, 203–31.

Hamlyn, D.W. (1959), 'Aristotle's Account of Aisthêsis in the *De Anima*', *Classical Quarterly* ns 9, 6–16. **[78]**

Hamlyn, D.W. (1968), *Aristotle's De Anima Books II and III*, Oxford: Clarendon Press. **[44]**

Hardie, W.F.R. (1964), 'Aristotle's Treatment of the Relation Between the Soul and the Body', *Philosophical Quarterly* 14, 53–72. **[61]**

Hesse, M.B. (1961), *Forces and Fields*, London, New York: T. Nelson.

Hicks, R.D. (1907), *Aristotle: De Anima*, Cambridge: Cambridge University Press. **[43]**

Kahn, C. (1966), 'Sensation and Consciousness in Aristotle's Psychology', *Archiv für Geschichte der Philosophie* 48, 43–81, repr. in Barnes, J., Schofield, M., and Sorabji, R. (eds) (1979), *Articles on Aristotle, vol. 4*, 1–31.

I

BIBLIOGRAPHY 2

Long, D.C. (1964), 'The Philosophical Concept of a Human Body', *Philosophical Review* 73, 321–37.

Matson, W.I. (1986), 'Why isn't the Mind-Body Problem Ancient?', in Feyerabend, P.K. and Maxwell, G. (eds), *Mind, Matter, and Method: Essays in Philosophy and Science in Honour of Herbert Feigl*, Minneapolis: University of Minnesota Press, 92–102.

Nowell-Smith, P.H. (1954), *Ethics*, London: Pelican Books.

Onians, R.B. (1951), *The Origins of European Thought: About the Body, the Mind, the Soul, the World, Time and Fate*, Cambridge: Cambridge University Press.

Rorty, R. (1965), 'Mind-Body Identity, Privacy and Categories', *Review of Metaphysics* 19, 24–54.

— (1970), 'Incorrigibility as the Mark of the Mental', *Journal of Philosophy* 67, 399–424.

Ross, G.R.T. (1906), *De Sensu et De Memoria*, Cambridge: Cambridge University Press. **[49]**

Ross, W.D. (1923), *Aristotle: A Complete Exposition of His Works and Thought*, London: Methuen; (1959), New York: Meridian. **[16]**

Slakey, T. (1961), 'Aristotle on Sense Perception', *Philosophical Review* 70, 470–84. **[68]**

Solmsen, F. (1955), 'Antecedents of Aristotle's Psychology and Scale of Beings', *American Journal of Philology* 76, 148–64. **[53]**

— (1960), 'Nature and Soul', in his *Aristotle's System of the Physical World: A Comparison with His Predecessors*, Ithaca, NY: Cornell University Press. **[54]**

— (1961), 'Greek Philosophy and the Discovery of the Nerves', *Museum Helveticum* 18, 150–97. **[103]**

Sorabji, R. (1972), 'Aristotle and Oxford Philosophy', *American Philosophical Quarterly* 6, 127–35.

— (1972), *Aristotle On Memory*, London and Providence, RI: Duckworth and Brown University Press, (2nd. ed.) Chicago University Press 2006, Bloomsbury 2013. **[50]**

Strawson, P.F. (1959), *Individuals*, London: Methuen.

Taylor, C. (1964), *The Explanation of Behavior*, London: Routledge and K. Paul.

Tracy, T.J. (1969), *Physiological Theory and the Doctrine of the Mean in Plato and Aristotle*, The Hague: Mouton. **[95]**

von Wright, G.H. (1971), *Explanation and Understanding*, London: Routledge and K. Paul.

White, A.R. (1967), *The Philosophy of Mind*, New York: Random House.

Wiggins, D. (1967), *Identity and Spatio–Temporal Continuity*, Oxford: Blackwell.

II

THE MIND-BODY
RELATION IN THE WAKE
OF PLATO'S *TIMAEUS*

INFLUENCE OF THE BODY ON THE MIND

Plato in the *Timaeus* allows a very strong influence of the body upon the soul.
The movements of the body affect the movements of the soul, and the soul's
movements, as I shall explain, are thought of as spatial movements. Plato explains these effects of the body in two passages at great length: 43A6 – 44C2
(on which I shall concentrate) and 86B2 – 87B8.

> 43A6 These [revolutions of the soul], confined in the strong river [of the
> body], neither conquered (κρατεῖν) nor were conquered, but carried and
> were carried by force, so that the whole creature was moved, in a disor-
> derly and irrational way wherever it chanced to advance with any of the
> six movements. For the movements were wandering forward and back-
> ward and again to right and left, down and up, in every one of the six
> directions. 43B Though the waves which flooded in and flowed out as they
> provided nourishment were large, greater still was the turmoil for each
> person created by the qualities of those objects which they came into con-
> tact with, when someone's body came upon and collided with alien exter-
> nal fire, or solid rock made from earth, or moist and slippery waters, or
> was caught by a windstorm borne by the air, and the motions produced
> by all this were carried 43C through the body and came into contact with
> the soul. These motions taken all together were on account of this there-
> after called and still are now called sensations. Moreover at that time they
> caused for a while a lot of very great motion, and in conjunction with the
> 43D continuously flowing stream stirred and vigorously shook the revolu-

tions of the soul. The revolution of the same they altogether impeded by flowing in the opposite direction to it, and prevented it from ruling and going on its way; while the revolution of the different they shook so hard that the three intervals of the double and of the triple, as well as the mean terms consisting of the ratios of 3 : 2 and 4 : 3 and 9 : 8 that are the connecting links, were [43E] nonetheless twisted round in every direction, and suffered every possible kind of fragmentation and deviation of their cycles. Thus they barely held together with one another and were carried along, but irrationally so, sometimes in reverse, sometimes obliquely, sometimes upside down. It was just like when someone stands upside down, pressing his head on the ground and throwing his feet up against something. In this situation, for the one undergoing it and for the onlookers, the right-hand parts of each appear left to the other, and vice versa. The revolutions of the soul undergo the same and [44A] similar sorts of intense experience, and when they come upon some external object belonging to the genus of the same or the different, they announce that it is the same as something or different from something when the opposite is true, and so are proven false and foolish. At that time there is no revolution among them which rules or is leader. And when certain sensations carried in from the outside come into contact with the revolutions and drag the whole vessel of the soul along with them, then these revolutions, though they appear to conquer (κρατεῖν), are in fact conquered. Indeed it is because of all these experiences that the soul [44B] today starts out foolish, when it is first bound into a mortal body. But then the flow of growth and nutrition diminishes, and the revolutions regain some calm and go along their own path and become more established as time passes; the rotations are straightened out as each of their cycles takes on its natural form; and they announce both the same and the different correctly, thus making the person who possesses them become intelligent. [44C] So then if some right nurture of education (τροφὴ παιδεύσεως) is recruited, the person becomes whole and entirely healthy, having escaped the worst sickness. (Plato, *Timaeus* 43A6 – 44C2)

It is worth noticing also that at 24C5 – 7 Plato speaks as if climate improves intelligence. In both of our two main passages he allows that education may counteract the effect of the body (44B7; 87A–B).

Galen cites all three of these *Timaeus* passages in his work *Quod Animi Mores*. The full title is "That the Capacities of the Soul follow the Blends of the Body." Galen cites the three *Timaeus* passages in support of his view that mental states *follow* (ἕπεσθαι) the blend (κρᾶσις) of hot, cold, fluid, and dry in our bodies. Galen goes even further in this treatise and makes the human soul, or at least the mortal part of it, actually to *be* the blend of hot, cold, fluid, and dry in the body. The Neoplatonists were horrified by this position and sought to reinterpret Plato's *Timaeus* at all costs, in order to reduce the degree of influence the body could have on the mind.

The story starts in Plato's *Phaedo* 86B7–C2, where Plato considers the suggestion that although the soul is not a body, it is entirely dependent on the body as the attunement of the lyre is dependent on the physical strings and as a blend (*krasis*) of hot, cold, fluid, and dry is dependent on the physical ingredients. Plato's Socrates rejects this suggestion at 92E4–93A7 and 94C3–7, by arguing that an attunement (and the same could be said of a blend) merely *follows* (*hepesthai*) the bodily components, whereas a soul leads them. When the Neoplatonists Plotinus and Porphyry return to the idea that the soul is like an attunement, they say it is like an attunement that, however, moves the strings of the lyre (Plotinus 1.1.4.14–16; 4.3.22.1–9; Porphyry, *Sententiae* 18, p. 9.4–6 Lamberz).

I agree with those who think that Plato views the movements of the soul as spatial movements, even though the soul itself is neither a body nor perceptible to the senses.[1] It is already very hard in our two main *Timaeus* passages not to understand the movements of the soul as spatial movements (43A6–C2; 87A1). It becomes impossible when we see how Plato says the same thing in many other passages. In 67A–B the account of sound and hearing treats hearing as a spatial movement. In 91E–92A Plato makes what is sometimes treated as a joke, but I think he means it to be taken literally. His idea is that if you do not use your reason properly in this life, the circuits of the rational soul in your head will get out of true shape and so you will be reincarnated as an animal with a long snout to house the distorted circuits of the soul. In 36Eff. Plato gives the same treatment to the World Soul that drives the stars around us. It is the spatial circuit of the World Soul that moves the visible stars in circles. Exactly the same happens in a later work, Plato's *Laws* 790D–791B. Plato there explains why when you want a baby to go quietly to sleep, you do not keep it still, but rather rock it. This rocking, just like frenzied Corybantic dancing, can influence the spatial movements of the soul so as to produce quiet and calm.

Many philosophers after Plato like to some extent what he had said. Aristotle also recognizes the influence of the body on states of mind. In *De Anima* 1.1.403a16–27 he explains the strong effect that the body has in encouraging or discouraging emotion. In *De Partibus Animalium* 2.2 and 2.4, he explains how the fibrous character of the blood can encourage the emotion of anger in animals. The Epicurean Lucretius agrees (3.307–15) that character *follows* one's physical nature. Like Plato he allows that education (*doctrina*) can counteract nature, but traces of one's physical nature will still remain. The Stoic philosopher Posidonius agrees (*apud* Galen, *De Placitis Hippocratis et Platonis* 5.5.22–24) that the movements of the soul *follow* the blend of the body. Hence, he says, physiognomy and climate affect character. But Posidonius too thinks that the right education can counteract the body's influence.

Galen announces his main theme in *Quod Animi Mores* 32.1–13, that capacities of the soul *follow* the blends in the body (*Scripta Minora* 2 Mueller), and he there adds that we produce a good blend through food, drink, and daily activities. His most ringing statement comes at 67.2–16, where he asks all those who want their mental state improved to come to him as a medical doctor and start on the right diet. Climate too will have an effect. Moreover, he claims that diet will affect even ethical philosophy, memory, and intelligence. Posidonius, the Stoic, had confined the effect of the body to the irrational capacities of the soul. In a further development, Galen extends it to the rational faculties. Galen wrote another work on the control of emotions, *On the Diagnosis and Therapy of the Distinctive Passions of the Individual's Soul,* and there he gives conventional advice on how to control emotions by rational techniques of altering one's attitude and viewpoint. But here Galen treats diet as a necessary preliminary to the control of the emotions:

> So now at least let those come to their senses who do not like the idea that food can make (*ergazesthai*) people more sensible or more licentious, more in command or less in command of themselves, bold or cowardly, mild and gentle or contentious and competitive. Let them come to me to learn what they should eat and what drink. For they will be greatly helped toward ethical philosophy, and in addition they will progress toward excellence in the capacities of the rational part, by improving their intelligence and memory. Besides food and drink I shall also teach about winds and their blends (*kraseis*) in the environment, and about what locations one should choose and avoid. (Galen, *Quod Animi Mores* in *Scripta Minora* 2.67.2–16 Mueller)[2]

Galen allows (79.4–7) that there can be feedback. Not only does the blend encourage quick temper, but also hot temper can inflame the innate heat in the body. And at 71.11–73.12 Galen has a long discussion of our second *Timaeus* passage, *Timaeus* 87B. When Plato says that the potentially disastrous effect of an unhealthy body on the mind can be counteracted by nurture (τροφή), practices (ἐπιτηδεύματα), and studies (μαθήματα), Galen interprets this as meaning diet (this is special pleading), then gymnastics and music, then geometry and arithmetic. Galen further denies a view which he attributes to earlier Platonists, and which we shall find recurring in Platonism, that the body may be able to hinder the soul but cannot help it (64.19–65.1; 70.11–13).

Finally, moving from states of mind to the soul itself, Galen insists that the soul actually *is* the blend in the body. He congratulates an earlier philosopher, the Aristotelian Andronicus of Rhodes (the name is supplied by the Arabic version of the Greek), for taking a very similar view. But he is afraid that Andronicus may have meant only that the soul is a capacity *following* the blend in the body, and this for Galen is not a strong enough view.

II

Qualms about This Influence

So far the philosophers mentioned have been happy to allow the body a considerable influence on states of mind, but the Aristotelian philosopher Alexander, Galen's contemporary and rival, enters a *caveat*. In *De Anima* 25.4 – 9 and 26.20, he says that the soul is not to be identified with the blend of the body but is rather a capacity or form that *supervenes* (ἐπιγίνεσθαι) on the blend of the body. *Supervening* is here introduced as an alternative to the notion of *following*, which had its origins in Plato's *Phaedo*. Nonetheless, when Alexander turns from the soul to states of mind, like emotions (e.g., 12.24 – 13.8), he endorses Aristotle's view that the state of the body has a very strong influence on these. Moreover, *Mantissa* 104.28 – 34, which may or may not be by Alexander, reverts to saying that differences of soul *follow* (*hep-esthai*) the blends and adds that the blend is the cause (αἰτία) of soul coming into being. Similarly a later commentator on Aristotle, Themistius, *In De Anima* 7.8 – 23, is happy to say that the emotions *follow* the blend of the body.

A more determined opposition to Galen's view is found in Neoplatonism. Plotinus concedes, 4.4.28.28 – 35, that animals' anger *follows* the blends in their bodies, but at 4.4.31.39 – 43 he warns, "Even if you attributed differences of character to them due to bodily blends, which are accounted for by the predominance of cold or heat, how could you relate ill-will, jealousy and immorality to them?"[3]

In other words, not all states of mind can be due to blends. It has been said that Plotinus tries out three views in succession on the extent to which the body can affect the soul. Plotinus' work as we have it is divided into fifty-four treatises. In 1.2.5.1 – 26, which is chronologically the nineteenth treatise and is paraphrased by Porphyry (*Sententiae* 32, lines 33.3 – 34.10 Lamberz), he allows that through purification the soul may acquire partial immunity from being affected by the body. In the twenty-sixth treatise (3.6.4.8 – 41), he canvasses Aristotle's view that the soul is a form that cannot be affected at all. Plotinus suggests that it produces only effects in the body. He is worried that if a soul cannot be affected, purification would not be necessary at all, but he replies that purifying takes the form of redirecting the soul's attention (3.6.5.13 – 25). In some of his last treatises, for example, in the fifty-second (2.3.9.6 – 18), Plotinus decides that it is our lower soul that is affected, but not the higher soul, and it is the higher soul that is the real "us." Plotinus' pupil and editor, Porphyry, agrees that the effect of the body on our reason is merely to make it less accessible (πρόχειρον), not to change it (*De Abstinentia* 3.8.6).

At the beginning of the fifth century, Saint Augustine, who had read some of Plotinus and Porphyry, uses his famous *cogito* argument, the argument later borrowed by Descartes, to argue against the view that the soul is a body or even an arrangement (*compago*) or blend (*temperatio*) of the body (*De Trinitate* 10.10).

Before and after Augustine, we have two important commentaries on Plato's *Timaeus*. One in Latin is by the fourth-century Christian Calcidius. Speaking of *Timaeus* 43 – 44, Calcidius allows the body some influence. He understands Plato to mean that the child's soul is very mobile, partly because the child is not yet rational, but partly also because of the physical influence of fluidity and heat. There is, in contrast, no such concession to the body in the commentary by the pagan Neoplatonist Proclus in the fifth century. In one passage (3.349.21 – 350.8 Diehl), Proclus criticizes Galen directly. He says that the body may hinder the soul but cannot help it, which is exactly the view which Galen had already reported and rejected. The body, Proclus says, only hinders the soul in the way that one might be hindered by a chattering neighbor. What is needed for positively helping the soul is, as Plato said, education (παιδεία). The word echoes Plato's term *paideusis* at *Timaeus* 44B8. In a neighboring passage, slightly earlier, Proclus goes further: it is an illusion that the soul of children is affected by the state of their bodies. It is rather as if someone saw his reflection in a moving river that made his body appear to move sideways and in every other direction. The word *sideways* (πλάγιον) is taken from *Timaeus* 43E. When Proclus takes up Plato's description of the soul's sideways movements (at 341.4 – 342.2), he interprets its movements, unlike Plato, as being nonspatial. Proclus' final view is that only the powers or activities of the soul can be subjected to change, not the soul's essence (3.335.24 – 336.2).

Moving on to the next century, the sixth, we find Proclus' Christian Neoplatonist opponent, Philoponus, elaborating the subject. In his commentary on Aristotle's *De Anima* (51.13 – 52.1) Philoponus speaks against the "doctors" who say that capacities of the soul *follow* the blends in the body. Philoponus replies that by philosophizing and through the philosophical way of life (διαγωγή) one can counteract the blends in the body and acquire a different emotional disposition. One cannot, by contrast, stop being pale, or sallow, or dark even by philosophizing ten thousand times. Philoponus likes his little joke: in his commentary on Aristotle's *Physics,* he denies that even with ten thousand pairs of bellows an army could fire arrows in the way that Aristotle supposes arrows need to be propelled. Philoponus makes his argument about philosophizing to show that emotional characteristics do not *follow,* nor *necessarily follow,* the blends of the body.

In appealing to the counteractive power of philosophy, Philoponus is implicitly appealing to a tradition about Socrates and the physiognomist Zopyrus, as reported by Cicero in the *Tusculanae Disputationes* (4.37.80) and *De Fato* (10) and by Alexander in *De Fato* (171.11–16). Zopyrus said he could tell from Socrates' physiognomy that he had a very bad character. When Socrates' friends laughed, Socrates stopped them and said that the comment was entirely on the mark. By physical disposition he did have very bad tendencies, and he had overcome them only through philosophy. In Cicero's version

158

(*De Fato* 10), it is said that Alcibiades burst out laughing when Socrates was described as a womanizer.

Elsewhere Philoponus (*In De Anima* 439.33 – 440.3; *In Aristotelis Physicorum* 191.11–16) borrows Alexander's word and says that the soul and the faculty of perception *supervene* (*epiginesthai*) on the blend in the body. In his commentary on Aristotle's *De Generatione et Corruptione* (169.4 – 27), Philoponus adds that even colors merely supervene on the state of the body. He does allow that colors follow the state of the body (169.17; 170.28), but for more than one reason he does not allow that colors are results explained (ἀποτέλεσμα) by the blend of the body. One reason is that, as he mentions in two of these passages, forms such as colors are made by God the Creator to supervene on matter, and hence are not explained by the matter itself.

Philoponus' most interesting comment occurs in his commentary on Aristotle's *Physics*, book 7, in the surviving Arabic version translated by Paul Lettinck (771.21–772.3). Philoponus says that lectures can reduce the students' irascibility, but it turns out that they do so by physiological means, that is, by making their bodies lean and dry. Moreover, physiology plays a role in giving us knowledge of other minds. It is thanks to physiology that the lecturer in the classroom is able to see whether he has been successful at communication. The face shows expressions of understanding or not understanding. This is both a contribution to the question of our knowledge of other minds and an indication of Philoponus' commitment to communication in the classroom. "Furthermore, those who frequently attend lectures on the disciplines of knowledge get lean and dry bodies, which results in their <not> easily becoming annoyed. Also, if there were not those alterations and affections connected with the body, we would not be able to explain the expressions in the face of someone showing that he has understood what we say and the other expressions showing that he has not understood us" (Philoponus, *In Aristotelis Physicorum* 7; trans. Lettinck 771.21–772.3).

NONSPATIAL RELATION OF SOUL TO BODY

The last subject I want to discuss relates to a remark in Plato's *Timaeus* at 43A6–7. Speaking of the circular movements described by the soul of the newborn, Plato says, "These [revolutions of the soul], confined in the strong river [of the body], neither conquered (*kratein*) nor were conquered, but carried and were carried by force."[4]

Plato repeats at 44B that the circular movements of the soul sometimes are conquered by sensations even though they appear to conquer. Plato uses the notion of conquering again in the passage earlier cited from the *Laws*, in which he discusses rocking babies to sleep. The rocking motion conquers the unsatisfactory soul movements in the babies. This talk of conquering or not conquering movements of the soul is reinterpreted by the Neoplatonists in a nonspatial sense.

The most interesting passage on the nonspatial relation of soul to body comes from what is believed to be a fragment of the *Summikta Zētēmata* by Plotinus' pupil Porphyry. It is preserved by the Christian bishop Nemesius (*De Natura Hominis* 3.38.20 – 43.16 Morani), and it draws on ideas of Plotinus and of Plotinus' teacher, the shadowy Ammonius Saccas. According to Porphyry's *Vita Plotini* §§3, 13, Plotinus and the other pupils had sworn not to reveal the doctrines of Ammonius. So this is one of the few cases in which we can learn about his thought.

The passage starts by saying that the relation between body and soul cannot be any kind of mixture. It cannot be that bits of body are juxtaposed with bits of soul, or we would have dead bits of body not animated by soul. But neither can there be a genuine chemical mixture or blend between body and soul because, on the view given here, in a genuine blend the ingredients destroy each other. Of course there may be nongenuine blends in which the ingredients are not destroyed. This text provides one of the references to the fact that wine and water when mixed can be reseparated from each other by an oil-drenched sponge. I have myself seen this confirmed in an experiment by Constance Meinwald and Wolfgang Mann. The alternative solution (and this is explicitly said to come from Ammonius) is that intelligible entities can be unified without undergoing the fusion (ἀσυγχύτως) experienced by sensible ingredients like wine and water. An intelligible entity brought into union with a physical entity cannot be destroyed, and the passage appeals to Plato's discussion in the *Phaedo* 103D–106E of how soul cannot be destroyed. A better analogy than the mixture of wine and water is that of light and air, except that soul, unlike sun or fire, is not circumscribed in place. The text here appeals to our passage in *Timaeus* 43A6–7. Soul is present everywhere as a whole because it is not conquered (*kratein*) by the body. Indeed it is not in the body, rather the body is in it. It has a certain relationship (σχέσις) to the body, but it is not in the body as in a place. It is bound to the body in the way that a lover is bound by the beloved. Porphyry, we are told, is in his *Summikta Zētēmata* a witness that soul can be unified with body and yet retain its own nature and individuality. The bishop Nemesius takes courage from Porphyry to say that, along the same lines, the relation of divine to human in Christ can, despite Porphyry's opposition to Christianity, be understood on Porphyry's own model.

Some of these ideas Porphyry draws from Plotinus. In 1.1.4.14–16, Plotinus says that the soul can pass right through the body without being affected, just as the weft that is interwoven need not be affected and just as light need not be affected. The talk of soul being interwoven is found at Plato, *Timaeus* 36E, and this passage is also used by Plotinus at 4.3.22.1–9. Plotinus there says that perhaps soul is present to the body in the way that fire is present in air, for fire too is present without being present. It is not mixed in any kind of mixture with anything. Rather the air flows past, and when the air comes to be outside the region in which the light is, it ceases to be illuminated. So we should say too that the air is in the light rather that the light in the air, and then Plotinus says that is why Plato himself rightly does not put soul in body, in the case of the World Soul, but body in soul. The reference is to *Timaeus* 36D9–E3, which puts the World's Soul outside its body, speaking as follows: "After this [the Creator] began to fashion all that was bodily within (*entos*) the soul, and bringing them together, fitted them centre to centre. The soul was interwoven (*diaplakeisa*) everywhere from the centre to the outermost heaven and covered (*perikaluptein*) the heaven in a circle from the outside (*exōthen*)."[5]

J. Pépin has argued that Porphyry's *Summikta Zētēmata* influenced Augustine.[6] Like Nemesius, Augustine uses the soul-body analogy as a model for the combination of God and Man in Christ (*Letter* 137.11). Moreover, Porphyry's conception of a nonspatial relationship is applied to the Trinity by Augustine in *De Trinitate* (book 9) and by Claudianus Mamertus, who uses Porphyry's term "without fusion" (*inconfusibiliter* in *De Statu Animae* 1.15, p. 59.20–60.1; see also Porphyry's ἀσυγχύτως in Nemesius 40.12 Morani). Augustine, Pépin argues, may be applying the ideas of Porphyry's fragmentary treatise directly to the soul-body relation in *De Immortalitate Animae, De Quantitate Animae, De Genesi ad Litteram,* and *Letter* 166 to Jerome (Corpus Scriptorum Ecclesiasticorum Latinorum 44.551.7–12), including the question whether the body is like a wineskin (*uter* in *De Quantitate Animae* 5.7 and *De Genesi ad Litteram* 8.21; cf. Porphyry's ἀσκός at Nemesius 41.9). In the letter to Jerome the soul is said to be extended through the body not by a spatial diffusion (*localis;* cf. Porphyry's τοπικός in Nemesius 41.19–20), but by a certain inclination (*intentio;* cf. Porphyry's ῥοπή in Nemesius 41.17), and to be present as a whole in every part (cf. 41.6–8). This would in turn add to Augustine's reasons for the attack in *De Trinitate* 10.10, noted above, on the suggestion that the soul is an arrangement (*compago;* cf. ἁρμονία in Plato's *Phaedo*) or blend (*temperatio*) of the body. This is the context in which Augustine uses the famous *cogito* argument, to show that the soul is not bodily, but this, presumably, is not borrowed from Porphyry's now fragmentary treatise.

The idea of a nonspatial relation is repeated by Porphyry in *Sententiae* 3; 27 (Lamberz, p. 16.5–6, 11–13); 31 (Lamberz, p. 21.2). According to Porphyry, the soul is not present to the body spatially but by a relationship (σχέσει). It is everywhere in the body and nowhere. This same idea that the soul has a nonspatial relationship to the body was maintained in Porphyry's treatise *De Regressu Animae,* if Courcelle is right that Porphyry's text is preserved in Claudianus Mamertus' *De Statu Animae.*

Proclus comments on our main passage from *Timaeus* 43–44 (*In Timaeum* 3.326.9–12), taking up the statement at 43A6–7 that the circuits of the soul neither conquered nor were conquered. Proclus refers to the point we found in Porphyry, that the concourse of soul and body is not like the case of things blended so that they destroy each other. Rather, each of the two preserves its own nature when they unite.

Simplicius in turn goes beyond Porphyry. He is inclined (at *In Aristotelis Physicorum* 286.36 – 287.6) to extend the nonspatial relationship even to irrational and vegetative souls. The story I have told is that Plato in the *Timaeus* allows the body a major role in affecting even the rational part of the soul, partly because the soul's movements are spatial. Aristotle and some Hellenistic philosophers also accepted a strong physical influence on the soul, but Galen went too far with his view that mental states simply *follow* the blends in the body, and this provoked reaction, first from Galen's influential rival, the Aristotelian Alexander, who substituted talk of "supervening" (*epiginesthai*). The reaction was strongest in the Neoplatonists, who did not want to concede Aristotle's idea of "following," nor yet the spatiality of Plato's soul-movements. In reducing the role of the body, they came up with many new analogies for describing the soul-body relation, although some concessions to the body are made by the free-thinking Christian Neoplatonist Philoponus.

NOTES

Some, but not all, of this material overlaps with chap. 17 of my book *Emotion and Peace of Mind: From Stoic Agitation to Christian Temptation* (Oxford: Oxford University Press, 2000).

1. David Sedley, "'Becoming like God' in the *Timaeus* and Aristotle," in *Interpreting the "Timaeus-Critias,"* ed. T. Calvo and L. Brisson, International Plato Studies 9 (Sankt Augustin: Academia Verlag, 1997), 327 – 39; Gabriela Carone, "Mind as the Foundation of Cosmic Order in Plato's Late Dialogues" (Ph. D. diss., University of London, 1996).

2. Ὥστε σωφρονήσαντες [καὶ] νῦν γοῦν οἱ δυσχεραίνοντες, ⟨ὅτι⟩ τροφὴ δύναται τοὺς μὲν ⟨σωφρονεστέρους, τοὺς δ᾽ ἀκολαστοτέρους ἐργάζεσθαι καὶ τοὺς μὲν⟩ ἐγκρατεστέρους, τοὺς δ᾽ ἀκρατεστέρους καὶ θαρσαλέους καὶ δειλοὺς ἡμέρους τε καὶ πράους ἐριστικούς τε καὶ φιλονείκους, ἡκέτωσαν πρός με μαθησόμενοι, τίνα μὲν ἐσθίειν αὐτοὺς χρή, τίνα δὲ πίνειν. εἴς τε γὰρ τὴν ἠθικὴν φιλοσοφίαν ὀνήσονται μέγιστα καὶ πρὸς ταύτῃ κατὰ τὰς τοῦ λογιστικοῦ δυνάμεις ἐπιδώσουσιν εἰς ἀρετὴν συνετώτεροι καὶ μνημονικώτεροι γενόμενοι. πρὸς γὰρ ταῖς τροφαῖς καὶ τοῖς πόμασι καὶ τοὺς ἀνέμους αὐτοὺς διδάξω καὶ τὰς τοῦ περιέχοντος κράσεις ἔτι τε τὰς χώρας, ὁποίας μὲν αἱρεῖσθαι προσήκει, ὁποίας δὲ φεύγειν.

3. Οὐδὲ γὰρ εἴ τις τὰς τῶν ἠθῶν διαφορὰς δοίη αὐτοῖς κατὰ τὰς τῶν σωμάτων κράσεις διὰ ψυχρότητα ἐπικρατοῦσαν ἢ διὰ θερμότητα τοιαύτας — πῶς ἂν φθόνους ἢ ζηλοτυπίας ἢ πανουργίας εἰς ταῦτα ἀνάγοι;

II

162

4. Αἱ δ᾽ εἰς ποταμὸν ἐνδεθεῖσαι πολὺν οὔτ᾽ ἐκράτουν οὔτ᾽ ἐκρατοῦντο, βίᾳ δὲ ἐφέροντο καὶ ἔφερον.

5. Μετὰ τοῦτο πᾶν τὸ σωματοειδὲς ἐντὸς αὐτῆς ἐτεκταίνετο καὶ μέσον μέσῃ συναγαγὼν προσήρμοττεν· ἡ δ᾽ ἐκ μέσου πρὸς τὸν ἔσχατον οὐρανὸν πάντῃ διαπλακεῖσα κύκλῳ τε αὐτὸν ἔξωθεν περικαλύψασα.

6. J. Pépin, "Une nouvelle source de Saint Augustin: Le *zētēma* de Porphyre sur l'union de l'âme et du corps," *Revue des Études Anciennes* 66 (1964): 53–107.

III

INTENTIONALITY AND
PHYSIOLOGICAL PROCESSES:
ARISTOTLE'S THEORY OF
SENSE-PERCEPTION

I

THE most valuable aspect of Aristotle's theory of sense-perception is, I believe, one which has been relatively neglected. It lies in his redrawing the map in which perception is located in a debate which is still being conducted in contemporary controversy on perceptual content. I shall discuss this in Section I of this chapter. It has to do with the formal cause of perception. What has been most discussed recently is what I believe to be the material cause. I shall turn to that in Section II, because the formal cause and material cause together complete the definition of perception, as explained at the opening of the *De Anima*.[1]

Perception for Aristotle is not to be viewed as a rudimentary reaction with little content, as is suggested by Plato. Nor on the other hand is it the work of reason and thought (*dianoia, noein, nous*), as was claimed by Aristotle's rebellious successor Strato.[2] It is a half-way house between the two.

Plato's position has been very well described by others: he argues in the *Theaetetus* that the soul uses the senses as channels to perceive sense qualities like whiteness, but cannot use them for distinguishing and comparing qualities, or for hitting on something's being the case (*ousia*) or the truth (*alētheia*); for that requires reasoning (*sullogismos*) and belief (*doxazein*).[3] Reasoning is described in turn as the silent dialectical debate of the soul with itself, and belief either as the conclusion of this debate, or as a silent affirmation, negation, or answer in the debate.[4] Plato's distinction of reasoning and belief from perception reflects Alcmaeon's earlier distinction of perception from understanding and thought

---

[1] *DA*, 403ᵃ25–39. I shall be returning to the subject of the first section in Sorabji, *Mind and Morals, Man and Beast*, in preparation.

[2] Strato *ap*. Plut. *De Sollertia Animalium* 961 A; *ap*. SE. *M*. 7. 350; *ap*. Porph. *Abst*. 3. 21; *ap*. Epiphan. *Against Heresies* in *Dox.Gr*. p. 592, 16–18.

[3] Plato, *Theaetetus* 184 D–187 B. See the illuminating accounts by Burnyeat (1976) and Frede (1987*b*) and before that Cooper (1970).

[4] Plato, *Theaetetus* 189 E–190 A, *Sophist* 263 E ff., *Philebus* 38 C–E.

(*xunhienai, phronein*).[5] But Plato greatly narrows the role of perception. This narrowing only becomes critical when Aristotle revives the other half of what Alcmaeon says by denying reasoning and belief (*logos, dianoia, nous, logismos, doxa,* in Aristotle) to animals other than man.[6] Aristotle is then obliged enormously to expand the content of perception beyond the rudimentary level to which Plato had reduced it. Typically, an animal that follows a scent does not merely perceive the scent in isolation, but perceives it as lying in a certain direction, and otherwise would not go in the right direction for it. But this already involves *predication*: the scent is *connected* with a direction. We can put this by saying that the animal perceives that the scent comes from that direction, or perceives it as coming from there. If animals lack reason and belief, these predications must be something that their perception can carry out.

Plato did not have to face this problem. For even when he is tempted to deny the reasoning part of the soul to animals (and this is a subject on which he wavers to the end),[7] he is still not obliged to deny them belief (*doxa*), since he is perfectly ready to associate belief with the lower, non-reasoning parts of the soul.[8] I know of only two exceptions. One occurs in the *Theaetetus* and related dialogues, where one (not the only) definition of *doxa* makes it the outcome of *reasoning* (references above).[9] The other occurs also in the *Theaetetus*, where the denial of reasoning to some (not all) animals may in the context imply a denial to those same animals of belief.[10] But the *Laws*, written later, does not take any of this as settled.

Aristotle does three things. First, he tidies up the concept of reason (*logos*) in the direction of the *Theaetetus*, by bringing all of *doxa* (belief) under it (*DA* 428ª19–24, see below). Secondly, he gives to perceptual content one of the most massive expansions in the history of Greek philosophy. Thirdly, despite expanding the role of perception, he maintains Plato's denial that perception involves belief or is a function of reason.

As regards the expansion of perceptual content, not only does he incorporate in perception the one function recognized by Plato, perception of whiteness and other sense-qualities perceptible by only one sense, but he adds perception of the common qualities (*koina*) perceptible by more than one sense: movement, rest, shape, extension, number, unity.[11] These are overlooked by Plato when he says

---

[5] Alcmaeon *ap.* Theophr. *De Sensibus* 25. Alcmaeon also distinguishes belief (*doxa*) from perception, if it is his theory that Plato reports at *Phaedo* 95 B, as the reference to the brain has been taken to suggest.

[6] See *DA* 414ᵇ18–19, 428ª19–24, 434ª5–11, *PA*, 641ᵇ7; *EE* 1224ª27, *Pol.* 1332ᵇ5: Alcmaeon *ap.* Theophrast. loc. cit.

[7] Contrast Plato, *Timaeus* 77 A–C, 91 D–92 C, *Statesman* 263 D, *Republic* 620 A–D, *Phaedo* 81 D–82 B, *Phaedrus* 249 B, *Laws* 961 D with *Republic* 441 A–B, *Symposium* 207 A–C, *Laws* 963 E (cf. *Theaetetus* 186 B–C, discussed below).

[8] e.g. Plato *Republic* 442 B–D, 574 D, 603 A, *Phaedrus* 255 E–256 A, *Timaeus* 69 D, *Laws* 644 C–D, 645 A. In *Timaeus* 77 A–C it is plants, not animals, which are distinguished as lacking *doxa*.

[9] Another account of belief, which fits some but not all of the cases, is that it results not from reasoning, but from fitting a memory imprint to a current perception, *Theaetetus* 193 B–195 E.

[10] Plato *Theaetetus* 186 B–C. I thank Myles Burnyeat for the reference.

[11] *DA* 418ª17–18, 425ª16, *Sens.* 442ᵇ5.

that you cannot perceive through one sense what you perceive through another.[12] Moreover, the common properties (*koina*) which Plato does recognize, such as likeness and difference, and which he (Plato) assigns to the province of reason,[13] are assigned by Aristotle to that of perception.[14] This already involves perceiving a proposition, in other words, *that* something is the case—that the qualities differ. It has been shown by Stanford Cashdollar how much propositional perceiving Aristotle recognizes. One can perceive that the approaching thing is a man and is white, that the white thing is this or something else, whether the white thing is a man or not, what the coloured or sounding thing is, or where, that one is perceiving, walking, thinking, living, existing, that one is sleeping, that something is pleasant, whether this is bread, whether it is baked, 'this is sweet' and 'this is drink'. The lion perceives that the ox is near.[15]

It would be wrong to suppose that this propositional perception really involves an inference of reason[16] merely on the ground that sense-qualities, like colour, are said to be essential (*kath' hauto*) objects of perception, whereas the son of Diares and the son of Cleon, who enter into propositions, are said to be coincidental sense-objects (*kata sumbebēkos*). Coincidental does not mean inferential. I have argued elsewhere that the reason why colour is said to be essential to sight is that sight is *defined* as the perception of light, shade, and colour.[17] By contrast the son of Diares is not essentially related to colours seen, and hence not to sight. It is this that accounts for his being called a coincidental object of perception. There is no suggestion that he is perceived only indirectly by way of inference.

Propositions are also involved in *phantasia*, which in Aristotle's *De Anima* is perceptual and post-perceptual appearance.[18] Examples of post-perceptual appearances would be imagination, dreams, and memory, all due to prior perception. An example of perceptual appearance given by Aristotle is the appearance that the sun is quite small, only a foot across. This appearance too is due to (*hupo*) the perceiving.[19] The word *phantasia* is used in connection with perception, propositional or otherwise, just so long as we want to talk of things appearing. Plato and Aristotle in their discussions explicitly connect *phantasia* with the verb 'to appear' (*phainesthai*).[20] To mark the connection of *phantasia* with appearing, and to bring out the continuity between different texts, I shall use the translation 'appearance', although readers should be aware that some translators will render the same word as 'imagination' or as 'impression'. A perceptual appearance is typically an appearance *that* something is the case, or, as we would sometimes prefer to say, an appearance *as of* something's being the case. I shall

---

[12] Plato, *Theaetetus* 184 E–185 A.   [13] Ibid. 184 D–187 B.

[14] Arist. *DA*, 426ᵇ12–427ᵃ14, 431ᵃ20–4ᵇ1, *Somn. Vig.* 455ᵃ17–18.

[15] Arist. *DA* 418ᵃ16, 428ᵇ21–2, 430ᵇ29–30, *EN* 1113ᵃ1, 1147ᵃ25–30, 1149ᵃ35, *MA* 701ᵃ32–3, cit. Cashdollar (1973). Also *EN* 1118ᵃ20–3, 1170ᵃ29–ᵇ1; *DA* 425ᵇ12, *Insomn.* 1, 458ᵇ14–15, 462ᵃ3. I am not quite convinced by Cashdollar's examples from *DA* 418ᵃ21–3, 425ᵃ25–7.

[16] This view is rejected by Hamlyn in Aristotle (1968) and Cashdollar (1973), who cites J. I. Beare, W. D. Ross, Irving Block, and Charles Kahn.

[17] Sorabji (1971).   [18] *DA* 3. 3.   [19] *DA* 428ᵇ26.

[20] Plato, *Sophist* 264 A–B; Arist. *DA* 3. 3, 428ᵃ13–14.

call both of these appearances propositional, meaning by that no more than that something is a *predicated* of something. There is not merely an appearance of whiteness, but of whiteness as belonging to something or as being located somewhere. Aristotle grants perceptual appearance to animals, even though he seems uncertain whether it belongs to all animals,[21] as the Stoics were to insist.

It cannot detract from the clear example of a propositional appearance that the sun is only one foot across that Aristotle later goes on to contrast appearance with affirming or denying as not being true or false, because it involves no combination of concepts (*sumplokē noēmatōn*, 432ª10–12; cf. 431ª8–16). We are free to assume that Aristotle is talking here of another kind of appearance, that involved in imaging (431ª15). We need not therefore resort to the interesting device suggested by Irwin (1988), who concedes that for Aristotle a dog cannot have an appearance with the structure 'that it's red', but urges that we can still describe its appearance that way, because the unstructured appearance explains the dog's behaviour in the same way as would a structured belief.

The propositional content of perception and appearance answers another problem. It has been thought that Aristotle oscillates wildly on the mental capacities he allows to animals. Having distinguished animals from men as lacking reason in the *De Anima*, he none the less allows the lion to entertain propositions about the ox he is going to eat in the *Nicomachean Ethics*. Moreover, there and in the biological works he allows animals emotions, which are elsewhere treated as involving belief (*doxa*) in past or future harm or benefit.[22] I think it can now be seen that this suggested oscillation is apparent rather than real. Perception was all along treated in the *De Anima* as admitting a propositional content. As for emotions, Aristotle (admittedly not out of any concern for animals) defines anger and fear as involving an *appearance* (*phantasia*) of past or future harm, as often as he mentions belief (*doxa*).[23] And the Aristotelian Aspasius (again for independent reasons) later recommends that this become the preferred definition of emotions.[24] Admittedly, *post*-perceptual appearance, mere *imaging* of terrible things, does not provoke fear, according to Aristotle.[25] But there is no reason why *perceptual* appearance should not. There need, then, be no change in the concept of emotion when this is ascribed to animals who lack belief. Had there really been an oscillation, I do not think that Aristotle could have been protected from the charge of confusion by saying that he used different explanatory frameworks in different places. For he is not an anti-realist, who believes that explanations are helpful devices which need not correspond to the real nature of things.

We can now see how generous a content Aristotle gives to sense-perception

---

[21] Contrast *DA* 415ª11, 428ª10, 22, 24 with 433ᵇ28, 434ª1–5.

[22] Fortenbaugh (1971). He has quite correctly put to me that some of the beliefs involve a *moral* judgement that the harm is unjustified. Even so, that is not true of fear, while pity is not ascribed to animals and anger is defined in terms of a moral belief only in the legal context of the *Rhetoric*, not in the biological context of *DA* 403ª25–ᵇ9, nor yet in that of the *Topics*.

[23] Arist. *Rh.* 1378ª31, 1382ª21–2, *Top.* 156ª32–3.

[24] Aspasius, *in EN* 44. 33–45, 10 (Heylbut). So also, for different reasons again, Posidonius in Galen, *PHP* (De Lacy).

[25] A. *DA* 427ᵇ21–4.

compared with most other Greek philosophers. I have already commented on Plato's parsimony. The Platonist author of the *Didaskalikos* sharpens Plato's point when he says that even sense-qualities like whiteness are discriminated (*krinein*) not without a certain empirically based type of reason associated with belief (*ouk aneu doxastikou logou*).[26] The Cyrenaics hold that one can only be aware of one's own experiences.[27] The Epicureans allow all perceptual appearances to be true, but all true only of the films of atoms impinging on the sense-organs, which may not faithfully represent the external causes.[28] The Pyrrhonian sceptics express perceptual appearances as propositions: 'honey is sweet'. But on one interpretation this is no more than a statement of, on another a mere reaction to, how the perceiver is himself perceptually affected.[29] As for the Stoics, although they allow a generous content to perceptual appearances in humans, I shall have to return to the question how much content they allow to perceptual appearances in animals or infants.

Having expanded perceptual content, Aristotle is faced with his remaining task. He needs to show that this expansion does not after all turn perception into belief, or make it a function of reason. For he agrees with Plato that this would be wrong. One of Aristotle's devices for distinguishing perception from belief (*doxa*) is to call it a kind of discriminating (*krinein, kritikē*). It has been argued by Theo Ebert that *krinein* does not in the Greek of Aristotle's time yet mean judgement.[30] If not, there should be no danger of confusing it with *doxa* (belief). But it can cover a wide range of activities short of belief, from the perception of colour to the perception of propositions. It can cover, for example, the kind of activity in which a bird engages in selecting some feathers for its nest while discarding others.

Aristotle has a further device for making perception fall short of belief, but this one commits him to disagreeing with Plato. Plato had defined perceptual appearance (*phantasia*) as a belief formed through sense perception (*doxa di' aisthēseōs*).[31] Aristotle denies that perceptual appearance is belief, and he produces an excellent argument for his denial: we can have the perceptual appearance that the sun is quite small, only a foot across, but we may believe that it is very large.[32] The argument enables Aristotle to treat perception and perceptual appearance as only a half-way house on the way to *doxa*. His argument has been much repeated in the modern literature against the view that perception is some function of belief.[33] Plato by contrast had classified illusion as a case of *doxa*.[34]

---

[26] Albinus (?), *Didaskalikos* 156. 2–10 Hermann. In requiring this type of reason (which is described as a set of acquired, as opposed to innate conceptions), the author diverges from Plato, but in a way that sharpens Plato's view of how little perception can achieve on its own.

[27] Plut. *Col.* 1120 C; cf. Eusebius, *PE* 14. 19. 2–3.

[28] S. E. *M.* 7. 206–10, Plut. *Col.* 1121 A–B.   [29] S. E. *PH* 1. 13, 1. 19–24.

[30] Ebert (1983): except in the sense of a legal judgment.

[31] Plato, *Sophist* 263 E–264 D.   [32] *DA* 428^{b}3–10.

[33] It is recognized as a difficulty by Armstrong (1968, relevant section reprinted in Dancy 1988), and it is urged as a difficulty against theories such as those of Armstrong and Pitcher (1971) by Jackson (1977), Fodor (1983) and Crane (1988, 1989).

[34] Plato, *Republic* 603 A.

Aristotle has two more arguments, separated by a 'furthermore' (*eti*), to show that what animals possess does not amount to belief (*doxa*).[35] First, belief involves being convinced (*pistis, pisteuein*), which animals cannot be. Conviction is more passive than the assent (*sunkatathesis*) later required by the Stoics, but it plays a similar role in the argument that animals cannot be said to have beliefs. Aristotle's other claim involves something slightly closer to assent: belief involves being open to persuasion (*pepeisthai, peithō*), which in turn implies possessing reason (*logos*). This has been called a 'rhetorical' criterion for belief, on the grounds that persuasion involves dialogue with *others*.[36] But I think that what Aristotle actually has in mind is Plato's definition of belief in the *Theaetetus* and *Sophist* as the outcome of a silent dialectical conversation (*logos*) within the soul.[37] Plato says explicitly that others are not involved, and I assume that correspondingly Aristotle would allow his persuasion to be self-persuasion, while complaining that animals are not capable even of this.

So much for Aristotle's distinction of perception from belief. But a difficulty may be felt about his idea that sense-perception enables animals to make predications, for example, to perceive sweetness as belonging to something. How can they perceive anything so complex, if they do not have concepts? To this Aristotle might find two answers. First, some animals may perhaps have concepts. Secondly, Aristotle might take comfort from certain modern discussions which purport to show that perceptual content can be predicational without the use of concepts being implied.

To take the second point first, a number of discussions have urged that perception requires no conception.[38] A person can perceive a building as eight-sided, for example, and generally be able to recognize eight-sided buildings, without having the concept of eight, or other relevant concepts. He may not even be able to count. It may be a controversial claim that his recognitional capacity would not itself amount to his having a concept of eight-sidedness.[39] But there is a more formal argument for perceptual predication without concepts, which can be expressed in terms of an example of Aristotle's already mentioned. The argument is that if you can rationally wonder with regard to the perceived length of a footrule and the perceived diameter of the sun whether these two lengths are really the same, you must be conceptualizing them differently—even if you are conceptualizing each as 'that length'. For after all no one can rationally wonder whether A is A, where A is one and the same concept, but only whether A is B. None the less, even though you are conceptualizing the two lengths differently, you may be perceiving them in exactly the *same* way and (*inter alia*) as the same length, which implies that your *perceiving* them does not involve conceptualizing.[40]

---

[35] *DA* 428ᵃ19–24.   [36] Labarrière (1984) 31–4.

[37] Plato, *Theaetetus* 189 E–190 A, *Sophist* 263 E ff.

[38] See Evans (1982), Peacocke (1986 and forthcoming), Crane (1988), Millar (1985–6); Irwin (1988).

[39] See Geach (1957) and contrast Peacocke (1989), Irwin (1988).

[40] Example adapted from Peacocke (1986 and forthcoming).

There are other modern arguments too of the same general type.[41] The upshot of these arguments is that, although perceiving the sun as a foot across doubtless involves the use of concepts, perceiving it as matching something else in size, or as small, does not necessarily do so. The argument is like Aristotle's in attempting to locate perception on the map somewhere short of belief.

Aristotle's other recourse might be to argue that some animals do in any case have concepts. He does discuss the issue of whether perception involves concepts, in a passage, *APo.* 2. 19, which may again be in the tradition of Alcmaeon.[42] The passage is sometimes taken as a treatment of our acquisition of universal concepts and sometimes as a treatment of our acquisition of universal truths. In fact there is no conflict: to acquire one is to acquire the other, as a preceding discussion in *APo.* 2. 8–11 shows. To acquire the universal truth that lunar eclipse is some kind of lunar loss of light, or that it is a lunar loss of light due to the earth's screening of the sun, *is* to acquire an (increasingly scientific) concept of lunar eclipse. Aristotle firmly argues that sense-perception must chronologically precede (so that it does not presuppose) the formation of universal concepts. On this both Stoics and Epicureans would agree. Perception for them precedes, and cannot pre-suppose, the formation of conceptions (*ennoiai*) and preconceptions (*prolēpseis*).[43]

Aristotle does not deny, however, that those who do have concepts may bring them to bear in perception. Does this include animals? That depends on how we take his remarks on experience (*empeiria*: compare our 'empirical'). Although he says that animals have little experience,[44] this presumably implies *some*, rather than, as the commentator Alexander followed by Asclepius half suspects, none. And does experience involve having universal concepts? This may seem the easiest way to read Aristotle's words, 'experience or the whole universal stabilized in the soul', since it is difficult (not impossible) to take the second of these two descriptions ('the whole universal') as referring to something *distinct* from the

---

[41] Crane (1988) appeals to the possibility of conflicting appearances within sense-perception. An analogous argument applied to the case of a conflict between sense-perception and belief might say that the same subject (the sun) cannot rationally be simultaneously believed to be large and believed to be not large, so long as it is conceived in terms of the same concepts (conceived as the sun) and largeness is conceived in the same way. When therefore we simultaneously believe that the sun is large and *perceive* it as small, this suggests that perception differs from belief in not *conceptualizing* the sun or largeness at all. The simplest reply, as Crane's retraction (1989) makes clear, is that it is perfectly rational simultaneously to *believe* that my bank balance is small and to *wish* that it were large, employing concepts in both cases. So whatever may be the case about two opposite *beliefs*, it remains to be shown what is irrational about an opposition between belief and such *different* states as wishing or perceiving (Cf. Plato, *Republic* 436 A–439 E, 602 E).

[42] The passage is in the tradition of the developmental psychology which is described by Plato at *Phaedo* 95 B, and often attributed to Alcmaeon on the basis of the reference to the brain.

[43] See for the Stoics e.g. Cic. *Acad.* 2. 30–1, 'Plut.' (Aët.) 4. 11. 1–4 (*Dox. Gr.* 400 = *SVF* 2. 83), and for the Epicureans e.g. Diog. Laert. 10. 31, and Philodemus, *On the Gods*, col. 12, 10 (Diels): animals lack *hupolēpseis*. I doubt Diels's view in his edition (p. 63) that in Polystratus, *On Irrational Contempt*, col. 1, the words 'each of these' refer to concepts possessed by animals.

[44] Arist. *Metaph.* A1, 980b26–7, with Alexander, *In Meta.* 4. 15, (Hayduck); Asclepius, *In Meta.* 7. 24 (Hayduck).

first ('experience').[45] Moreover, when an illustration is offered of experience in humans, the man of experience is described as knowing that eating fowl is good for health, a truth which seems general enough. If he is said to know only the particular (*kath' hekasta*) rather than the universal (*katholou*), this is only because he is ignorant of the more universal and explanatory truth that light meat is easy to digest.[46] On the other hand, there is evidence on the other side. For one thing, Aristotle denies that animals (*thēria*) have any universal concept (*katholou hupolēpsis*)—they have only memory and perceptual appearance (*phantasia*) of particulars.[47] Moreover, in the very passage where he allows animals a little experience, he treats experience in humans rather cautiously. It seems to be a conjunctive apprehension (*hupolēpsis*), or set of thoughts (*polla ennoēmata*) about particular cases (*kath' hekaston*), which guides action in the next case, but which does not yet involve a single universal (*mia katholou*). The man of experience knows that this remedy helped Callias when he had this illness, and similarly for Socrates and each of many others. But he has not marked off these people as belonging to a single kind, so that he can say the remedy helps all phlegmatic, or bilious, or feverish people when they have this illness. There is then some universal concept which he has not got.[48]

We may protest that he has other universal concepts, 'this remedy', 'this illness'; why does Aristotle not draw attention to this? Perhaps the answer is that he is here interested only in the universal concepts of *technology* and *science*. But it would be odd if those who lacked these special qualifications had no universal concepts at all. In fact, we have noticed Aristotle granting to laymen a pre-scientific concept, based on prior observation, of lunar eclipse as *some* kind of lunar loss of light. The present passage, then, is not denying the man of experience some pre-scientific and pre-technological universal concepts. And if universal concepts are in another text denied to animals, this is perhaps because that text overlooks the modest concession offered here, that animals do have a *small* share of experience.

It is not quite excluded, then, that Aristotle might grant some animals universal concepts. What is clear is that he grants them predicational perception and a little experience, and these two concessions represent two ways in which he compensates them for their lack of beliefs (*doxai*). But how, it may be wondered, does he distinguish their experiential information from belief? He tries to do so by defining experience as consisting of many memories,[49] and he is peculiarly insistent that memory belongs to the perceptual part of the soul to which percep-

[45] Aristotle *APo.* 100ᵃ6–8. The expression might instead refer, as Myles Burnyeat has pointed out to me, to technological skill (*technē*). This is uneasy, because the end of the sentence then startles us, saying as it does that what has been referred to is merely that from which comes the origin (*archē*) of technological skill. It would need to be reinterpreted as meaning that experience (*empeiria*) provides the origin of technological skill, and technological skill the origin of scientific understanding (*epistēmē*).

[46] Arist. *EN* 1141ᵇ14–21.   [47] *EN* 1147ᵇ5, stressed by Irwin (1988).

[48] Arist. *Metaph.* 981ᵃ5–30.   [49] Arist. *APo.* 100ᵃ5–6, *Metaph.* 980ᵇ29–30.

tual appearance (*phantasia*) also belongs.[50] More exactly, memory is the having of a mental image (*phantasma*, a cognate word) taken (*hōs*) as a copy of that of which it is an image.[51] We can see how concerned Aristotle is to classify states of mind on one side or other of the perception–belief frontier. And we need not think that he has transferred memory to the wrong side of the frontier when he remarks that it involves *saying* in one's soul that one has encountered the thing before,[52] for such metaphorical references to saying are common enough to be discounted.[53]

The Stoics, some of them, would agree with Aristotle, for they too analyse experience and memory in terms of perceptual appearance (*phantasia*). Experience for them is a multiplicity (*plēthos*) of similar appearances from many memories,[54] while memory is a storing of appearances.[55] Despite that, there are differences. For in humans perceptual appearance is, for the Stoics, tantamount to rational thought.[56] Moreover, some Stoics deny animals learning by experience (*experisci, experimentum, usus*) in contexts where others might have ascribed it,[57] and some of them deny animals memory except in the sense of recognition of what is perceptually present, and treat memory proper as requiring rational reflection (*deliberatio, consideratio*).[58]

In another respect the Stoics are very like Aristotle. For they deny to animals reason and belief (although reason is slightly redefined),[59] and so they ought, like Aristotle, to expand perceptual content, if they are to account for the ability of animals to get around in the world. Yet this time the orthodox interpretation creates a problem, since it drastically narrows the perceptual content of animals. On this interpretation, which has attracted the ablest scholars,[60] perceptual appearance (*phantasia*) has propositional content not in animals, but only in humans. I have therefore attempted elsewhere[61] to raise a doubt about the orthodox interpretation, and to suggest that the Stoics allow animal perception as much content as does Aristotle. Here I will only indicate the main lines of that counter-proposal.

One argument for the orthodox interpretation of the Stoics is that neither

[50] Arist. *Mem.* 450ª16–17, 22–3.
[51] Ibid. 451ª15. My understanding of *phantasma* as a mental image in Aristotle, which I take to be confirmed by the very pictorial account of it throughout the *De Memoria* (see Sorabji in Aristotle 1972, *passim*), has been defended by Huby (1975).
[52] Arist. *Mem.* 449ᵇ22–3.   [53] A list is given by Cashdollar (1973), 162.
[54] 'Plut.' (Aët.) 4. 11. 1–4 (*Dox. Gr.* 400 = *SVF* 2. 83).   [55] S. E. *M.* 7. 372 (*SVF* 2. 56).
[56] 'Plut.' (Aët.) 4. 11. 1–4 (*Dox. Gr.* 400 = *SVF* 2. 83); Diog. Laert. 7. 51, 7. 61; Stobaeus 1, p. 136. 21 Wachsmuth (both in *SVF* 1. 165); pseudo-Galen, *Def. Med.* xix. 381 Kühn (*SVF* 2. 89).
[57] Sen. *Ep.* 121. 19–23; Hierocles 1. 51–3. 52 (von Arnim and Schubart).
[58] Only recognition: Sen. *Ep.* 124. 16, Plut. *De Sollertia Animalium* 961 C; Porph., *Abst.* 3. 22. Rational reflection: Calcidius, *In Tim.* 220. Cf. the Antiochan Lucullus in Cic. *Acad.* 2. 38: memory requires assent.
[59] Reason is a collection of conceptions, Galen, *PHP* 5. 3, p. 421 M (*SVF* 2. 841) and as such can by the Middle Platonists be distinguished from the intellect as being its tool, 'Albinus', *Didaskalikos*, ch. 4.
[60] Frede (1983); Inwood (1985), 73–4; Long–Sedley (1987), 240; Labarrière (forthcoming). I ∗ thank all of them for friendly and helpful discussion.
[61] Sorabji (1990). Further objections are addressed there.

animals nor infants have concepts.[62] The infant's mind, in a passage already cited,[63] is compared to blank paper. But we have now seen that the lack of concepts would not, at least in the opinion of various modern philosophers, rob animal perception of propositional (that is, predicational) content. And we cannot assume that the lack of concepts would weigh with the Stoics either.

I am also not convinced by the argument that a *lekton* (a sayable, or, roughly speaking, a proposition) is defined as corresponding only to a rational appearance,[64] that is,[65] to the appearance enjoyed by a rational being, as opposed to an animal. It would be wrong to infer from this that what appears to an animal cannot have corresponding to it a proposition, or sayable. For propositions are here being defined—and it is quite legitimate to define things this way—by reference to a sufficient, not a necessary, condition. What subsists in accordance with the appearance enjoyed by a rational being will be a star example of a proposition (*lekton*). But there may be other *lekta* too, and indeed we know there are. The ones that would interest us would subsist in accordance with the appearance enjoyed by an animal. But we know that there must be *lekta* which correspond to no appearances at all. For the effects of causes are all *lekta*,[66] whether they have ever been noticed and appeared to anyone, or not.

The interpretation for which I have argued is that in Stoicism the perceptual appearances (*phantasiai*) enjoyed by animals are (at least in many cases) verbalizable and conceptualizable by us, even though not by the animals themselves. What has not, I think, been noticed is that appearances that something is the case are repeatedly described, not as verbalized and conceptualized, but as verbalizable and conceptualizable.[67] The point is that it is not said by whom. Evidence already cited suggests that in humans perceptual appearances are always conceptualized, whereas in animals they never are, which is why the *phantasiai* of humans are distinguished as rational (*logikai*) and as thoughts (*noēseis*). But that does not mean that we cannot verbalize and conceptualize how things appear to animals, and do so in propositional form.

The Stoics themselves seem very ready to do so. Chrysippus describes a hunting dog that comes to a crossroads where its quarry might have gone in any of three directions. The dog sniffs the first two, perceives no scent, and takes the third *without* sniffing. It is said 'virtually' (*dunamei*) to go through a syllogism about its quarry: 'The animal went either this way, or that way, or the other way. But not this way, or that way. So that way.'[68] Chrysippus is not conceding that the dog really reasons, or forms *doxai*, beliefs. It is only doing something analogous (*dunamei*). But how could there be an analogy, if its sense-perception

[62] Frede (1983); Long–Sedley (1987), 240.
[63] 'Plut.' (Aët.) 4. 11. 1–4 (*Dox. Gr.* 400 = *SVF* 2. 83).
[64] S. E. *M.* 8. 70; Diog. Laert. 7. 63.   [65] Diog. Laert. 7. 51.
[66] S. E. *M.* 9. 211. The point is well made by Long–Sedley (1987), 201–2.
[67] Diog. Laert. 7. 49; 'Plut.' (Aët. 4. 12. 1) (*Dox. Gr.* 401 = *SVF* 2. 54); S. E. *M.* 7. 244, 8. 70 (*SVF* 2. 187), 8. 10 (*SVF* 2. 195).
[68] S. E. *PH* 1. 69; Plut. *De Sollertia Animalium* 969 A–B; Philo, *De Animalibus* 45; Porph. *Abst.* 3. 6; Aelian, *Nat. An.* 6. 59.

allows it only to grasp a scent? At the least, it must perceive the *absence* of a scent and perceive it as pertaining to one direction rather than another. And this implies that its perceptual appearance involves predication.

Also important is what the Stoics Chrysippus, Seneca, and Hierocles say about the self-preservation of animals depending on their awareness of their own persons, in relation to the surrounding environment.[69] It would not be enough to secure preservation that an animal's body should appear to it without further characterization. The richest set of examples is supplied by Hierocles. Admittedly, neither he nor the others use the verb 'to appear' (*phainesthai*). But he repeatedly speaks of animals grasping (*antilambanesthai*; *katalambanein*), or being conscious ([*sun*]*aisthanesthai*). The frog, for example, is conscious (*sunaisthanetai*) of how far the distance for a leap should be.[70]

A similar view of animals is put in the mouth of a non-Stoic character, but with the standard Stoic example of a syllogistic premise, by Plutarch:

Wolves, dogs, and birds surely perceive (*aisthanesthai*) that it is day and light. But that if it is day, it is light, nothing other than man understands.[71]

This passage, though not explicitly about the Stoics, gains significance from a closely related one which is. The Stoics hold that inference from signs is peculiar to man. Such inference involves syllogistic premises of an 'if…then' variety, like those discussed in the Plutarch passage. In reserving it for man, the Stoics concede that non-rational animals receive perceptual appearances. What then do they deny? Not, it turns out, that these appearances are propositional, although that would have clinched the case, but only that these animals have appearances arising from inference and combination (*metabatikē, sunthetikē*), appearances which explain (*dioper*) our having the concepts of logical implication (*akolouthia*) and sign.[72]

Further, in their efforts to deny reason to animals, the Stoics redefine the kinds of mental capacity available to them. Animals cannot, for example, remember what is absent, but only recognise what is perceptually present.[73] Their memory therefore is merely the apprehension of a proposition (*katalēpsis axiōmatos*) in the past tense of which the present tense has been apprehended from perception.[74] Here in the very act of downgrading animal capacities, the Stoics evidently concede to them the apprehension of propositions.

Exactly the same happens with one of the other Stoic redefinitions. Seneca denies that animals are capable of anger, because they are not rational,[75] whereas anger involves rational assent to the appearance of injustice (*species iniuriae*).[76]

---

[69] Chrysippus *ap*. Diog. Laert. 7. 85; Sen. *Ep*. 121, 7–10; Hierocles, ed. H. von Arnim, *Berliner Klassikertexte* 4 (Berlin, 1906), 1. 39–5–7.

[70] Hierocles 2. 37–8.

[71] Plut. *On the E at Delphi* 386 F–387 A. I thank Brad Inwood for the reference.

[72] S. E. *M*. 8. 276.   [73] Sen. *Ep*. 124, 16.

[74] Plut. *Sollertia* 961 C; repeated by Porph. *Abst*. 3. 22.

[75] Sen. *De Ira* 1. 3. 3–8, esp. 1. 3. 4.   [76] Ibid. 2. 3–4.

They merely seem to be angry because they have an appearance, albeit a muddled and confused one,[77] and an involuntary reaction (*impetus*), which is not, however, a rational one. Once again, in downgrading their capacities, a Stoic none the less concedes that animals entertain at least a muddled appearance. And that muddled appearance is presumably a propositional one—the appearance that injustice has occurred.

On the orthodox interpretation, the Stoics will have been inconsistent in allowing such consciousness to animals. Their official view should have led them to reject Aristotle's expansion of perceptual content. On the interpretation I have offered, they will have endorsed it. Equally, I would give an opposite answer to the interesting question that has been raised by C. Gill (1991), whether we should compare the Stoics with Donald Davidson or Daniel Dennett. Davidson (1982) would be the orthodox choice, because he denies propositional attitudes to animals. But I would prefer Dennett (1976), if a selection is to be made, because he allows the ascription of propositional attitudes to animals, provided their behaviour can be analysed *by us* in intentional terms.

Before returning to Aristotle, I should like just to consider whether the Epicurean school had any alternative strategy to enable animals to get around in the world. The Epicureans fall into two camps. Some, notably Lucretius, allow animals to have a mind or thought, whereas others deny them reason, reasoning, thinking, and belief.[78] Illustrating the first tendency, Lucretius goes to some length to say that animals dream,[79] while arguing that in dreams the mind (*mens, animus, mens animi*), the equivalent of Epicurus' thought (*dianoia*), is at work, selecting for close attention some of the many configurations of atoms that reach the dreamer.[80] In fact he explicitly ascribes a mind (*mens, animus*) to horse, lion, and deer.[81] So he need have no problem about how animals cope.

Other Epicureans deny to animals reason and reasoning (*logos, logismos, epilogismos*).[82] One denies them not only reason, but also thinking (*noēsis*—the terms are not sharply distinguished) and belief, including false belief (*doxa, pseudodoxia*).[83] His method of compensating them for the loss of belief and thought is to say that they have *analogues* of belief.[84]

Another strategy for the Epicureans might be extrapolated from the sugges-

[77] Ibid. 1. 3. 7.

[78] For the contrasting views see H. Diels (ed.) Philodemus *Über die Götter* 1, p. 63; Annas, (forthcoming) in J. Brunschwig and M. Nussbaum (eds.), *Passions and Perceptions*.

[79] Lucr. 4. 984–1010.

[80] Epicurus, *Letter to Herodotus*, ap. Diog. Laert. 10. 51; Lucr. 4. 728–31, 747–8, 750–61, 767, 803–15, 975–7.

[81] Lucr. 2. 265, 268, 270, 3. 299.

[82] Hermarchus ap. Porph. *Abst.* 1. 12 (*logos*); Polystratus, *On Irrational Contempt* col. 6 (*logismos*), col. 7 (*logismos*, at least such as ours) Indelli; Philodemus, *On the Gods*, col. 13, line 2 (*epilogismos*), 15. 28 (*logismos*) Diels.

[83] Philodemus 12. 17, 13. 39 (*noēsis*), 13. 6–7 (*doxa*), 14. 34 (*pseudodoxia*).

[84] Philodemus 13. 17–18 (analogue of *prosdokia*: belief about the future). 14. 6–8 may even go further and contemplate their having analogous beliefs, rather than analogues of belief.

tion[85] that they belong to the same tradition as those empiricist doctors who were called memorists. On the memorists' view, even human beings do not need reason. Thinking is a function of memory, and neither memory nor thinking is a function of reason. Reason is very narrowly conceived as performing certain deductive operations postulated by logicians. Interesting as this view is, I doubt if any of it attracted the Epicureans. For to humans they allow reason,[86] while to animals one, we have seen, denies not only reason, but also thinking and belief. In another author, memory is subordinated to thought (*dianoia*), because in memory thought receives likenesses of what was formerly perceived.[87] Similarly, in yet another, memory is said to be in abeyance during dreams,[88] even while, as we have seen, thought (*dianoia*), or equivalently the mind (*mens, animus, mens animi*) is at work. I believe we find a larger role assigned to memory in such Platonist treatises as the *Didaskalikos* than we do in the empiricist treatises of the Epicureans.

If there is another strategy open to the Epicureans for compensating animals, it would lie in expanding perceptual content, like Aristotle and, I believe, the Stoics. In this some help might be provided by Epicurus. He speaks of perceptual appearances as being true,[89] and he gives a causal analysis of truth not unlike the subsequent Stoic analysis of what it is for a perceptual appearance to be 'cognitive' or warranted,[90] and not unlike certain modern accounts of what it is for primitive perceptual states to have an informational content.[91] Unfortunately there are complications, for Epicurus holds that perceptual appearances are all true, but true only of the films of atoms that impinge on the sense-organs. As regards the physical objects which transmit those films, there is something that can be true or false of these, but that is *opinions* based on the appearances, not the appearances themselves.[92] Nonetheless, he does not seem to deny that perceptual appearances are about the transmitting physical objects, even if they are not true or false of them. Vision sees a tower as small and round or as large and square.[93] It sees not only colour, but the *distance* to the coloured thing, not only light and shade, but *where* they are.[94] There is therefore predication, and the content of vision is propositional in the sense I have been using. It looks as if a perceptual appearance which is true of the impinging film is also true of how the physical

---

[85] Frede (1989). I thank Stephen Everson for drawing my attention to his fascinating account of the memorists.

[86] *Logos* in Hermarchus *ap.* Porph. *Abst.* 1. 12; animals are given the conventional description contrasting them with man as irrational, *aloga*.

[87] Diogenes of Oenoanda, new frag. 5. 3. 3–14, Smith. Admittedly, some memory at least is treated by Hermarchus as irrational (*alogos*) and contrasted with reasoning (*epilogismos*) *ap.* Porph. *Abst.* 1. 10.

[88] Lucr. 4. 765.   [89] S. E. *M.* 7. 205, 8. 63.

[90] Diog. Laert. 7. 46; Cic. *Acad.* 2. 77; S. E. *M.* 7. 248–51; 11. 183.

[91] Dretske (1981); Burge (1986). The debate on the viability of such analyses continues.

[92] S. E. *M.* 7. 208, 8. 63; Epicurus, *Letter to Herodotus*, in Diog. Laert., *Lives* 10. 50–1.

[93] S. E. *M.* 7. 208–9; Lucr. 4. 353–63.

[94] Lucr. 4. 379–86; anonymous Epicurean treatise on the senses Herc. Pap. 19/698, col. 25, fr. 21 Scott, translated Long–Sedley (1987), 80.

object appears, though neither true nor false of how it really is. Given that the appearances are propositional, that appearance is not always a bad guide to future experience, and that memory should enable an animal to act on those appearances which are good guides, our Epicureans may be able to give animals enough perceptual content to manage in the world.

I have presented Aristotle as a catalyst in the debate on how perception relates to other capacities of mind, particularly belief and reason, a debate which was made urgent by his denial of these last capacities to animals. This denial necessitated an expansion of the content of perception and its differentiation from belief—a discussion which is still continuing today.

I can now draw a general conclusion about Aristotle's Philosophy of Mind. He does not try to reduce perception to things at a *different* level, such as physiological states, or behaviour, or the performance of functions. Rather he relates it to capacities at the *same* level, such as belief, reason, appearance, memory, experience, and concept formation. Yet many commentators have seen Aristotle as a reductionist, that is a materialist,[95] at a time when materialistic theories were dominant, and as a functionalist,[96] when theories of that kind prevailed. Some of my own earlier ideas were careless enough to suggest that I too favoured, or at least gave comfort to, a functionalist interpretation.[97] But if I were now to compare Aristotle with any contemporary philosophers, I would compare him with those who are distinguishing the content of perception and thought, thus relating capacities at the same level, rather than reducing them to physiology, behaviour, or function.

I would add more: I think Aristotle's relation of sense-perception to other capacities would be seen by him as throwing light on the *formal* cause of perception, not the *material* cause. The same happens with anger, whose material cause is specified as a physiological process, but whose formal cause relates it to another capacity: desire. For the formal cause of anger is the desire to retaliate.[98] Thus I do not agree with the view that Aristotle's account of perception and anger as each composed of a material and formal aspect really boils down to a polite form of materialism, in which there is nothing more than a physiological process.[99] Rather, the specification of the formal cause by reference to other capacities is meant to tell us something about what we should call the intentional aspect of anger and perception, even if he does not himself characterize it as intentional.

This brings me to the second part of the chapter. For many commentators have picked out a group of phrases (becoming like, being potentially such, receiving form without matter) which I believe describe the physiological process in sense-perception, in other words its material cause. But others have construed

---

[95] Slakey (1961), 470; Matson (1966).

[96] Hartman (1977); Wilkes (1978), ch. 7; Nussbaum (1978), 61–74, drawing on Putnam (1975); Nussbaum–Putnam, 'Changing Aristotle's Mind', pre-publication version of ch. 3 above.

[97] Wilkes (1978); Burnyeat pre-publication version of ch. 2 (hereafter 'Burnyeat'). I argued that Aristotle supplied the materials for defining anger by reference to behaviour. But he did not do this as part of a general programme, and I think it no accident that I found no further similar examples.

[98] *DA* 403^{a}3–^{b}19.   [99] Williams (1986).

them as referring to some cognitive representation. One recent writer, finding this implausible, has suggested that Aristotle had not yet distinguished physiological process from cognitive representation, since he lacked understanding of the intentional character of representation.[100] But I believe that these commentators have been looking in the wrong place. What we should call the intentional aspect of perception is handled in the passages we have already looked at. The passages to which I shall now turn are concerned with its physiological aspect. But the conviction has been so strong that they are concerned with something else that it will take me a little time to put the case.

II

Controversy has centred on an interconnected group of phrases. Aristotle says that in perception the sense-organ becomes like the thing perceived, is potentially such as the thing perceived is already, and receives the form of the thing perceived without matter. Some (myself included) have taken these phrases, despite the mention of form, to refer to the material cause of perception, its physiological process. Others have taken them or at least the last phrase, to refer to the formal cause. There are two corresponding ways of construing the last phrase grammatically. I have followed the oldest interpretation according to which it means that the organ receives form without *receiving* matter. On Philoponus' rival interpretation, the reference is to receiving form without *standing to it as* matter.

My present conviction is that at least two of the phrases, and probably all three, refer to the physiological process, although the case of the 'reception of form' is slightly less certain. Moreover, I still take the physiological process to occur as follows. In vision, for example, the eye-jelly (*korē*) does not receive particles or other bits of *matter* from the scene observed. It simply takes on colour patches (perceptible *forms*) to match it.[101] One advantage of understanding a literal taking on of colour is that this explains how shapes and sizes can be received: the coloured patches in the eye-jelly have shapes and (small-scale) sizes corresponding to those of the scene. The reception of shape and size had previously been thought to constitute a difficulty for any such literal interpretation, and it had also been thought that the literal interpretation would be 'open to devastatingly obvious attack', since we don't find people's eyes going coloured, or their ears noisy.[102] But the relevant organ is deep within, as I argued. For it is the *korē* which takes on colour patches,[103] and the *korē* is not the pupil, as all recent

---

[100] Glidden (1984), 128–9.   [101] Sorabji (1974/1979).

[102] For both points see Barnes (1971–2) 109, repr. (1979*b*) 38 and for the second, Hamlyn in Aristotle (1968), 104 and 113; and (1959), 9 and 11. A related objection concerning size and shape is found in Galen, *On the doctrines of Hippocrates and Plato* VII 7. 4–15, translated by Philip De Lacy in *Corpus Medicorum Graecorum*, V 4. 1–2.

[103] *DA* 431ª17–18, *HA* 491ᵇ21, *PA* 653ᵇ25.

English translators of the psychological works suggest,[104] but the eye-jelly within the eye.[105] It would not have been obvious, with the instruments then available, that the eye-jelly did not go coloured, or the inside of the ear noisy.

Reactions to this literal physiological interpretation have been varied. It has been sometimes accepted and sometimes rejected,[106] the latter in one case on the ground that it would give essential support to the functionalist interpretation,[107] which I have sometimes been taken as upholding.[108] Among those who disagree, one interpretation of the reception of form without matter is that the organ receives a coded message, a vibration for example, not literal coloration.[109] This view still takes the reception of form to be physiological. Others dissent, saying, for example, that to receive form without matter is simply to *become aware of colour*.[110] Brentano adds that it is to become aware of an intentional object.[111] Another writer finds it difficult to attach any very precise meaning to the reception of form,[112] while another offers a non-physiological gloss, but agrees that a literal coloration process *underlies* the reception of form.[113] A final variant is that the reception of form is *both* an awareness *and* a change in the organ which is not, however, a literal coloration process.[114] Evidently disagreement is widespread.

I shall try to show that all these interpretations are mistaken, but one in particular deserves attention, Myles Burnyeat's, because it is the most daring and the most fully argued. It is also the most discussed, even though it has a status like that assigned by Averroës to some of Aristotle's received forms: it is between corporeal and spiritual, because it has never appeared in print, and yet it has been the subject of at least four discussions.[115] Many of the authors concerned with this particular interpretation state their latest views in the present book. My knowledge is necessarily based on a pre-publication version, and I must beg forgiveness for not being able to take account of any changes that may have been made.

In his earlier version, Burnyeat endorsed an interpretation of Aristotle which he called the Christian interpretation, because he found it in three Christians, Philoponus, Thomas Aquinas, and Brentano. This is the interpretation according

---

[104] Beare, Hamlyn, Hammond, Hett, Hicks, G. R. T. Ross, Smith. Philoponus also explains that 'pupil' is only the everyday, not the technical, meaning *In DA* 366, ll. 11–14, 368, 1–3, Hayduck. His own technical meaning differs from Aristotle's.

[105] Arist. *Sens.* 438ª16, 438ᵇ5–16, *HA* 491ᵇ21, *DA* 425ª4, *GA* 780ᵇ23.

[106] Agreement is expressed by M. Cohen (1987) and Charlton (1980). Nussbaum agreed on the need for a physiological process (1978), 147–8, but later pointed out that it would suit the functionalist interpretation if the process was variable (Nussbaum–Putnam pre-publication version of ch. 3). Robinson initially disagreed (1978), but appears not to in (1983). Disagreement is manifested by Hamlyn (1968), 104 and 113; and (1959), 9 and 11; Burnyeat; Glidden (1984); Bernard (1988); Lear (1988).

[107] Burnyeat.   [108] M. Cohen (1987) and perhaps Wilkes (1978).

[109] Glidden (1984), 20–1. This is also one half of Lear's interpretation, I think (1988), 116.

[110] Burnyeat (1992); Robinson (1978); Lear (1988).   [111] Brentano (1874/1959), translated (1973).

[112] Barnes (1971–2).

[113] Bernard has described his interpretation as being that the sense receives the definiteness of the thing perceived.

[114] Lear (1988), 116.

[115] Burnyeat; M. Cohen (1987); Nussbaum–Putnam (1992); Charles (1988), 36–7; Lear (1988), 110–16.

to which to receive form without matter is simply to become aware, but Burnyeat added something of his own which was not in any of these authors. For Aristotle, he held, no physiological process at all is needed for the eye to see, and *a fortiori* not the coloration of the eye-jelly. It is just a basic fact, not requiring further explanation, that animal matter is capable of awareness. And this is why Aristotle's philosophy of mind is no longer credible. For it turns the matter of animal bodies into something pregnant with consciousness, whereas we are wedded to Descartes's conception of matter, which makes it something quite distinct from awareness, so that awareness is something whose occurrence calls for explanation.

I have three initial disagreements with this particular interpretation, the first of merely historical interest—the interpretation advocated is not particularly Christian, as we shall see. Secondly, I do not think that Aristotle can be making a physiological process unnecessary to sense-perception. For the theory of the opening chapter of the *De Anima*, a theory already referred to, is that *every* mental process, with the possible exception of intellectual thought, requires a physiological process. We have already encountered the illustrative example that anger requires the boiling of the blood around the heart. And perception is explicitly included in the theory.[116] Thirdly, on my interpretation, Aristotle's theory comes out prosaic and commonsensical. There is nothing bizarre about the coloration of the eye-jelly. If we want a bizarre theory of matter, we should rather look to Descartes, not, admittedly, to his distinction between matter and awareness, but to his claim that matter is merely three-dimensional extension. We need to go to the further shores of physics, not to common sense, to find anything comparable with this.[117]

To explain my disagreement with the whole range of interpretations, I shall need to go into some exegetical detail,[118] and some readers may prefer to skip to the final section, where I say what I take the significance of my interpretation to be. Roughly speaking, I think it necessary to establish that Aristotle's original doctrine involved literal coloration, if we are to understand the process through which Brentano came to take the opposite interpretation, and to read into the doctrine his own idea of an intentional object.

As a preliminary, we need to note the phrases with which Aristotle expresses his theory of the perceptual process and how they are connected. He says that the organ receives form,[119] receives perceptible form,[120] receives or is affected by forms of perceptibles;[121] and he adds that it does so without matter.[112] In several places, instead of talking of reception (*dechesthai, dektikon*), Aristotle talks of being affected (*paschein*) by form, as if that were a more general description of the same thing.[123] He also says that the sense-organ is potentially such as the

---

[116] Aristotle *DA* I. I, 403ᵃ3–ᵇ19. Sense-perception is included, 403ᵃ7.
[117] Sorabji (1988), chs. 1–3.
[118] I previously confined the case to two footnotes: Sorabji (1974), 22 and 28 of the 1979 version.
[119] *DA* 429ᵃ15–16, 434ᵃ29–30.   [120] *DA* 424ᵃ18.   [121] *DA* 424ᵇ2, 427ᵃ8–9.
[122] *DA* 424ᵃ18–19, 424ᵇ2–3, 434ᵃ30.   [123] *DA* 427ᵃ8–9, 424ᵃ23, cf. 424ᵃ34, ᵇ3.

sense-object is actually.[124] He says further that it starts off unlike the sense-object, but becomes like it.[125]

These phrases are all linked together. For two are combined with an 'and' at 429^{a}15–16, where it is said that if thinking is like perceiving, the thinking part of the soul must be able to receive form and be potentially such as its object. The rest are connected at 418^{a}3–5, where the sentence, 'the organ is potentially such as the sense-object is already, *as has been said*', refers back to the other form of words at 417^{a}20: 'it is while unlike that it is acted on, but once acted on, it is like.'

So far it is still a little unclear what kind of likeness is involved. But there is a significant variant at 425^{b}23, when Aristotle says that what the organ receives is *perceptibles*. These perceptibles are specified elsewhere. For when he says at 423^{b}30–1 that the sense organ is potentially such, the 'such' refers to the 'hot, cold, dry, and fluid' at 423^{b}28–9. A little lower at 424^{a}7–10, he says that the organ is potentially, but not actually, white, black, hot, or cold. And this informative description is intertwined with some of the others, because it immediately follows the explanation that the organ is potentially such (i.e. hot, cold, dry, or fluid, 423^{b}31), and that being potentially such, it is then made such as the object is in actuality (424^{a}1–2). There may be a claim of the same kind at 3. 13, 435^{a}23, where it is said that the organ receives hot, cold, and all the other objects of touch, but the text there is ambiguous, as we shall see.

Except perhaps for the last, all the foregoing expressions are most easily taken as referring to the same process, and they are connected with becoming black, white, hot, cold, dry, or fluid. There are two further references to a process of coloration, both of them linked to the idea of receiving form. The exact meaning is admittedly more disputable this time, but the references are most naturally understood in the same way as the others. At 425^{b}22–4, Aristotle says that what sees is coloured in a way, and he explains this by saying that the organ receives perceptibles without matter. As I understand it, he says 'in a way', because the transparent fluid in the eye is colourless in itself,[126] but receives *borrowed* colour during the sensory process. At 427^{a}8, he says that something indivisible cannot at the same time be white and black, and so cannot receive the forms of these qualities either. I take it that 'and so not either' (*hōste oude*) is not introducing a second process for which becoming white or black is prerequisite (although that would already give a significant enough role to coloration), but is rather supplying a more relevant description of the same process.

I have said that it is the sense-organ that undergoes the process described. This is explicit in five passages where Aristotle refers to the organ with the word *aisthētērion*.[127] In three other passages, he uses an ambiguous expression, which can, however, refer to the organ: 'that which sees' (*to horōn*, immediately glossed by reference to the organ),[128] 'what is going to perceive' (*to mellon aisthēsesthai*),[129]

---

[124] *DA* 418^{a}3, 422^{a}7, 423^{b}31–424^{a}2, 429^{a}16.
[125] *DA* 417^{a}20.　　[126] *DA* 418^{b}26–30, 429^{a}15–26.
[127] *DA* 422^{a}7, 422^{b}1, 423^{b}30, 425^{b}23, and the ambiguous 435^{a}22.
[128] *DA* 425^{b}22.　　[129] *DA* 424^{a}7–8.

'what can perceive' (*to aisthētikon*).[130] In a final passage, he starts off by saying that the *sense* receives the forms of perceptibles without matter,[131] but he qualifies this by saying the organ *aisthētērion* is the primary thing in which a power of that kind resides.[132]

It is necessary to distinguish a different doctrine, which does apply to the sense, not the organ, and which concerns not mere becoming like, but actual identity. This turns on Aristotle's general theory of causation, explained in *Ph.* 3. 3. It is there illustrated by saying that when somebody teaches a pupil, there are not two activities going on, one of teaching and one of learning, but a single activity, which is equally one of teaching and one of learning, and which is located in the learner. The application to sense-perception of this causal theory is that the activity of a sound in working on one's hearing and the activity of hearing it are not two activities, but one and the same activity,[133] and located not in the organ but in the sense (*en tēi kata dunamin*).[134] This doctrine about the activity of the *sense* tells us nothing about whether the *organ* takes on sounds.

A further preliminary point to notice is that Aristotle normally postulates only that we *receive* forms in our sense-organs, not that we *perceive* them there. The only exceptions come in the course of a dialectical argument at *DA* 425ᵇ22–5, in an argument whose conclusion is rejected at *Sens.* 447ᵃ23–7, and in a non-psychological work at *GA* 780ᵇ32.

The foregoing provides the preliminary evidence that for Aristotle sense-per-ception involves the sense-organ's becoming white, black, hot, cold, wet, or dry. It is not essential to my case whether 'receiving form without matter' refers, like the other phrases, to this physiological process, or, as one interpretation holds,[135] to some further process dependent on it. But as a matter of fact, I think the fol-lowing is what actually happens: initially, the reception of form is something in which the sense-*organ* (*aisthētērion*) engages[136] and is connected with being 'potentially such'.[137] In other words, it involves the literal coloration of the organ of sight. But when Aristotle compares perception with *thought*, he realizes that the desired analogy is only partial. Certainly, when a person thinks of a stone, matter is left behind, because the stone is not in his or her soul, only its form.[138] But Aristotle refrains, when he gets beyond the first tentative comparison in *DA* 3. 4, from repeating the standard expressions. The stone is not described as 'mat-ter', and its form is not spoken of as being 'received', probably because these words had expressed a doctrine about the sense-*organ*, and thinking does not in the same way involve an organ, in his view. Instead, the comparison is with the doctrine which concerns not the organ but the sense, that the activity of sound is in the sense and is not merely such as, but identical with, the activity of hearing.

---

[130] *DA* 418ᵃ3.   [131] *DA* 424ᵃ18–19.   [132] *DA* 424ᵃ24–5.

[133] *DA* 425ᵇ26–426ᵃ26.   [134] *DA* 426ᵃ4.

[135] Bernard (1988). The best candidate for this further process might be not Bernard's, but Lear's action of sound on the sense (425ᵇ26–426ᵃ26), which, however, I would construe somewhat differently from Lear (1988).

[136] *DA* 425ᵇ23.   [137] *DA* 429ᵃ15–16.   [138] *DA* 431ᵇ28–432ᵃ1.

In this roundabout way, the idea of form, though not in so many words the idea of reception of form, gets connected with a second, non-physiological, doctrine, but only in the case of thought, not in the case of perception. It is this second, non-physiological application of the word 'form', confined to the case of thought, which has in at least one case absorbed attention and led (mistakenly, I think) to a rejection of the physiological interpretation of the reception of form for the case of perception.[139]

So much for preliminaries. That a literal coloration process is involved in (visual) perception can be made undeniable, I believe, by examining a virtually continuous passage, *DA* 423^{b}27–424^{b}18. Here Aristotle finds that there is a problem affecting the organ of touch, but no other sense. For the eye-jelly is colourless and the interior of the ear soundless. Otherwise they would obtrude their own character and interfere with the reception of form.[140] But the organ of touch cannot equally be free of the qualities of heat, cold, fluidity, and dryness, for these, as explained in *On Generation and Corruption*, are the defining characteristics of the four sublunary elements (423^{b}27–9). This creates a problem: the organ of touch cannot afford to possess already the degree of heat, cold, fluidity, or dryness which it is to perceive, since the perceptual process involves starting off merely potentially such as the sense-object, and being subsequently made such as it. The organ cannot be made to acquire in this way the temperature it already possesses (423^{b}30–424^{a}4). The conclusion must be that we have a blind spot for that particular temperature. And indeed that is why (*diho*, 424^{a}2) we do in fact have a blind spot for what is as hot, cold, hard, or soft as we are (*diho tou homoiōs thermou kai psuchrou ē sklērou kai malakou ouk aisthanometha*, 424^{a}2–3). The empirical fact is that we notice only extremes (*alla tōn huperbolōn*, 424^{a}4). And this shows, by inference to the best explanation, that the sense organ is somewhere in the middle range of temperatures, etc., and that derivatively the sense is as it were a mid-point (*hōs tēs aisthēseōs hoion mesotētos tinos ousēs tēs en tois aisthētois enantiōseōs*, 424^{a}4–5). Just as what is going to perceive white and black must be neither of these in actuality, but both in potentiality, so in the case of touch it must be neither hot nor cold in actuality, though both, presumably, in potentiality (424^{a}7–10).

There are three reasons why I think this first part of the passage cannot be handled by those who deny that Aristotle is referring to a literal taking on of temperatures and other qualities. First, a relevance must be supplied for the sudden reference in the middle of the *De Anima* to *On Generation and Corruption* and its doctrine that hot, cold, fluid, and dry are the defining characteristics of the four elements. Secondly, and most crucially of all, the *diho* ('that is why') at 424^{a}2 appears to become unintelligible on other interpretations. *Diho* offers to explain why there is a *barrier* to our perceiving certain temperatures. No barrier would have been presented to our perceiving medium temperatures, if the organ

---

[139] Lear (1988).

[140] *DA* 418^{b}26–30, 429^{a}15–26. No exception is provided by the fact that the ear produces an echo, for this is said to be a foreign (*allotrios*) sound, not its own (*idios*), 420^{a}17–18.

merely had to receive a coded message, for example a vibration, or if we were merely being told that the organ becomes aware of temperature. The barrier arises because the organ needs to acquire the temperature to be perceived, and is debarred from acquiring the temperature it possesses already. The inability of coded messages, or of references to awareness, to supply a barrier, affects not only the present passage in 2. 11, but also the statement in 3. 4 that what is to receive forms must obtrude no interfering characteristics of its own. My case could very well rest on the single word *diho*. The third question is why Aristotle says that what is going to perceive black and white must be potentially both, and similarly for what is going to perceive hot and cold. This cannot be brushed aside as if it were the merely negative point that the thing must not be actually black or white. It means more to say that it is potentially these.

I would add a fourth point, although it is not decisive, that the meaning of the word *mesotēs* (424ᵃ4) must be respected. Literally, it means something in the middle. Of course, sense is only said to be *as it were* a *sort of* mid-point, but some connection with the literal meaning must be retained. Admittedly, this constraint is probably no harder for others than for me, since I too must explain how senses other than touch are to be viewed as mid-points: the eye-jelly does not have a medium colour.[141] But it is a constraint that is seldom at present observed. Let me now give a translation of the passage:

It is the differentiating characteristics of body *qua* body which are the objects of touch. By differentiating characteristics I mean those which define the elements, namely, hot, cold, dry and fluid, about which we have spoken earlier in the work on the elements. And their organ (*aisthētērion*), which can exercise touch and in which first of all the sense called touch resides, is the part that is potentially such (*dunamei toiouton*). For perceiving is being affected in some way. So what makes a thing such (*hoion*) as it itself is in actuality makes it such (*toiouton*) because it is potentially (*dunamei*) so. And that is why (*diho*) we do not perceive what is similarly hot or cold, hard or soft, but perceive the extremes, which suggests that sense is as it were a sort of mid-point (*mesotēs*) between opposites in perceptibles. And it is for this reason that sense discriminates (*krinei*) perceptibles, for the middle is discriminating (*kritikon*), since it comes to be to each of the two extremes its opposite. And just as what is going to perceive white or black must be neither of them in actuality, but potentially both (*dunamei d' amphō*), and similarly too in the other cases, so also in the case of touch it must be neither hot nor cold.[142]

Shortly afterwards, Aristotle concludes his chapter on touch, 2. 11, and begins his survey of all five senses in 2. 12. Whereas the previous chapter had talked about being 'potentially such', the new chapter brings in another of the interlinked phrases and affirms that with all five senses the organ receives the perceptible forms without matter. It then offers to explain various phenomena on the basis of what precedes. One thing to be explained (424ᵃ32–ᵇ3) is the fact that plants do not perceive, even though they are alive and are affected (*paschein*) by

---

[141] Different evidence for the sense of sight being an intermediate blend (*logos*) is that extremes of dazzle or darkness impair its functioning, 424ᵃ27–32.

[142] *DA* 423ᵇ27–424ᵃ10.

heat and cold, as shown by their being warmed or cooled. The explanation is twofold: plants do not have a mid-point (*mesotēs*), and they cannot receive the forms of perceptibles, but are acted on in company with matter. The first part of this explanation, the lack of a *mesotēs*, has on some interpretations been found unintelligible,[143] but it is elucidated in 435^{a}20–^{b}3. Plants are made predominantly of earth, and the characteristic properties of earth are cold and dryness. But touch needs to be a sort of mid-point (*mesotēs*) among all the tangible qualities, and its organ has to be able to receive (*dektikon*, 435^{a}22) not only the characteristics of earth (cold and dryness), but heat and cold and all the other tangible qualities.

If 'receive' here refers as usual to the perceptual process, there will have been some carelessness, because cold and dryness are precisely what plants, being already cold and dry, could *not* receive. If such carelessness is accepted, there will be further confirmation of my claim that the reception of perceptible form is the literal taking on of heat, cold, fluidity, and dryness, etc. Alternatively, Aristotle may be using the idea of qualities received in a less usual way to refer to the organ's standard qualities, not to those which it temporarily assumes during perception. He will be saying that the organ is standardly characterized by an intermediate blend of hot and cold, of fluid and dry, etc., and cannot just be cold and dry. That too would confirm part of what was said above, but would throw no light on what happens to the organ at the very moment of perception. The conclusion of the argument is that plants could not have the sense of touch, and without touch no other sense is possible.

There is an underlying assumption, rather contrary to the spirit of functionalism, if that is taken at its broadest to be the idea that mental processes can be defined by functions that can be realized in various different types of matter. For Aristotle is here assuming that sense-perception can only be realized in an organism with a mean temperature not too far from our own. Admittedly, Aristotle does elsewhere allow for certain other variations of mechanism. For smelling, fish use their gills, dolphins their blowhole, and insects the middle part of their body,[144] the first two of which contain water, not air.[145] Indeed, it is a major theme of Aristotle's biological groupings that, in different genera, parts can be analogous in function but different in structure, and a case in point is the nostrils, the gills of fish, and the middles of insects. He also entertains what we should call the conceptual possibility that colours, sounds, and odours might have been perceived through direct application of a balloon-like membrane to the thing perceived.[146] Even when he argues that there could be no sixth organ to create a sixth sense, he still recognizes the epistemic possibility that there might be some unknown substance or property not possessed by anything on earth, but capable of constituting a sixth organ.[147] The anti-functionalist restriction to mean temperatures is then perhaps the exception, rather than the rule.

[143] Slakey (1961).
[144] *PA* 659^{b}14–19. For further details, see Sorabji (1971), 57–8, repr. (1979), 77–8.
[145] *DA* 425^{a}5. [146] *DA* 423^{a}2–12. [147] *DA* 425^{a}11–13.

The second explanation in 2. 12 of why plants do not perceive is that they can-not receive (*dechesthai*) the forms of perceptibles, but are affected (*paschein*) in company with (*meta*) matter. The word for being affected here, as elsewhere,[148] stands in as a more general description of receiving. I prefer the oldest interpretation, according to which plants become warm by letting warm air or other warm matter into their systems, instead of leaving the matter behind. It has been objected that this is plainly false,[149] but I do not think so. Nor is there any need that it should be *plainly* true, for it is not an observation, but a hypothesis constructed to help explain the insensitivity of plants, and it would again have been difficult with the instruments available to discover whether it was true or false. The main rival interpretation takes the point to concern the matter of the plants themselves, not the matter they receive. On this view, for the plants to receive form in company with matter is for their matter to take on heat and cold, while for them to receive form without matter would be for them not to stand as matter to, but simply to become aware of, heat and cold.[150] But this reading gives us a tautology, instead of an explanation, because it merely tells us that plants do not become aware of heat, but grow hot instead. This does not *explain* why they don't perceive. Of course, it is part of this interpretation that Aristotle does not think it appropriate to explain such a thing. But in fact he purports to be offering an explanation (*dia ti, dia touto, aition*)[151] in both of the chapters where he discusses the question. The passage in 2. 12 reads:

And [it is clear from the preceding] why (*dia ti*) ever it is that plants do not perceive, although they have some part of the soul and are affected (*paschein*) in some way by the tactile qualities themselves. For they are heated and cooled. The explanation (*aition*) is that they do not have a mid-point (*mesotēs*), nor a principle of a sort to receive (*dechesthai*) the forms of perceptibles. Rather they are affected in company with matter (*paschein meta tēs hulēs*).[152]

It is difficult to see how this can fail to be offering an explanation, or how it could instead be saying that no explanation is needed, because the ability or inability to perceive is a basic fact which needs no explanation.

But there is more to come, and the point that follows has not, I think, received attention. I am not referring merely to the fact that it would be historically appropriate for Aristotle to insist that sensory reception involves leaving matter behind—although it is relevant that that would be appropriate, because so many of his predecessors had made sense-perception depend on receiving matter from the object perceived. But far more important is the little-considered question of the relevance of the rest of the chapter. Aristotle devotes the remainder to a puzzle which he finds so obviously relevant that he does not even think it neces-sary to state what the relevance is, merely saying: 'But someone might be puzzled.' As I see it, the relevance is in fact immediate. I have taken Aristotle's point to be

---

[148] *DA* 424ᵃ23, 427ᵃ8–9.   [149] Burnyeat.   [150] Ibid.
[151] *DA* 424ᵃ32–3, 435ᵇ1.   [152] *DA* 424ᵃ32–424ᵃ32ᵇ3.

that being acted on by heat without receiving air or other matter is a *necessary* prerequisite for perceiving heat, odour, etc. This at once makes relevant the question: is it also *sufficient* for perceiving heat and odour? Or, equivalently, could something that didn't perceive still be acted on by heat or odour—that is, without receiving air or other matter?

It may be thought an obstacle that Aristotle does not explicitly add the words 'without receiving air or other matter'. All he says is:

Rather they are affected in company with matter. But someone might be puzzled whether something incapable of exercising smell would be affected at all (*paschein ti*) by odour, or something incapable of seeing by colour, and similarly for the other cases.[153]

So far my ground is only that the necessary relevance is provided, if we understand Aristotle still to have in mind what he has just been discussing: the possibility of being affected by perceptible qualities *without* receiving matter. But in fact this interpretation is strikingly confirmed. For Aristotle goes on to consider the case of something insentient, timber, being split in a thunderstorm, and he insists that this is not a case of sound acting on a body. Why not? Because it is the air accompanying the thunder that acts. The word for accompaniment is *meta*, the same word that was used when Aristotle complained that plants are affected in company with (*meta*, 424^{b}3) matter. Evidently the subject of his puzzle is whether insentient things can be affected by perceptible qualities, rather than by the *matter* accompanying those qualities. On the alternative interpretation, no particular relevance is apparent either for Aristotle's puzzle, or for his example of air entering the timber:

And it is at the same time clear in the following way too: it is neither light and darkness, nor sound, nor odour that acts (*poiein*) at all on bodies, but rather that in which they reside. It is the air, for example, accompanying (*meta*) thunder that splits the timber.[154]

It is important that the entire discussion down to the end of the chapter should be shown to be relevant, and in particular the question that Aristotle goes on to ask at 424^{b}16–17:

What, then (*oun*), is exercising smell (*osmasthai*) besides (*para*) being affected in some way?

Let us see how the alternative interpretations fare in providing relevance. Aristotle goes backwards and forwards on whether the various perceptible qualities, as opposed to the matter accompanying them, can act on something insentient. He first puts the case on the other side, but finally decides (*alla* = 'but', 424^{b}12) that the tactile qualities, hot, cold, fluid, and dry, and flavours can so act, and that odour and sound can so act on stuff like air, which is free-flowing. Air, for example, can be made smelly (424^{b}12–16), and he means, I am sure, without taking on cheesy matter. This, of course, shows that being affected by odour without receiving matter is *not* sufficient for exercising the sense of smell

---

[153] *DA* 424^{b}2–5.   [154] *DA* 2. 12, 424^{b}9–12.

(*osmasthai*). His question now is not merely relevant: it cries out for an answer (424ᵇ16–17):

What, then, is exercising smell besides (*para*) being affected in some way?

The implication is that exercising smell is partly a matter of being affected by odour, but is also something else besides (*para*).

It is not only relevance that is decisive here, but also the word *para* (besides). This word implies that exercising smell has two aspects. If no physiological process were needed, as maintained by the alternative interpretation, there would be no room for two aspects. So that interpretation must reconstrue the *para* sentence. It might do so by taking the sentence in effect to be asking, 'What is exercising smell as opposed to being acted on in the way the air is?' But *para* does not mean 'as opposed to'; it means 'besides'. Furthermore, the proposed question would rob the second half of the chapter from 424ᵇ3 to 424ᵇ18 of relevance and connection of thought. The question of relevance has come up three times. First, why does Aristotle raise the puzzle whether something insentient can be acted on by perceptible qualities? Secondly, why in discussing the question does he make so much of the air accompanying the thunder as the agent that splits the timber? Thirdly, why after answering the question does he think it relevant ('what, *then* (*oun*),...?') to ask what exercising smell is besides being acted on? I have tried to show how one point flows naturally from another.

Aristotle's answer to the question, 'what is exercising smell besides?' may be to us disappointing. He is only able to say that it is perceiving (*aisthanesthai*), thereby supplying the genus, since the sense of smell is defined by genus and differentia as one kind of perception, the perception of odour. But his silence cannot lend any support to the rival interpretation, because the *para* sentence has told us that exercising smell is partly a matter of being affected by odour and partly something else. It is not in any case surprising if he does not, at the tail end of his discussion of the five special senses, and before his discussion of the generic functions of sense-perception, give us a formula to tell us more about what perceiving is. For though he has a great deal more to say about what it is, that more does not take the shape of a formula. Some of it was said in 2. 6, ch. but much is reserved for book 3 of the *De Anima*, after the discussion of the five special senses is concluded, and I have tried to bring out what it is in Section I above.

Much has been made of the fact that there is no manuscript warrant for reading *kai* (also) into Aristotle's answer, so that it tells us that exercising smell is *also* perceiving. But my interpretation rests not on Torstrik's conjecture of *kai*, but on the word *para*, 'besides'. The passage in its entirety reads as follows:

(424ᵃ32) And [it is clear from the preceding] why (*dia ti*) ever it is that plants do not perceive, although they have some part of the soul and are affected (*paschein*) in some way by the tactile [qualities] themselves. For they are heated and cooled. The explanation (*aition*) is that they do not have a mid-point (*mesotēs*), nor a principle of a sort to receive (*dechesthai*) the forms of perceptibles. Rather they are affected in company with matter (*paschein meta tēs hulēs*).

(424^{b}3) But someone might be puzzled whether something incapable of exercising smell would be affected (*paschein*) at all by odour, or something incapable of seeing by colour, and similarly for the other cases.

(424^{b}5) But if the object of smell is odour, if it produces anything at all, odour produces an exercise of smelling, so that none of the things which cannot exercise smell can be affected (*paschein*) by odour, and the same story goes for the other cases too. Nor can any of the things which can exercise smell be affected by odour except in their capacity as perceivers. And it is at the same time clear in the following way too: it is neither light and darkness, nor sound, nor odour that acts (*poiein*) at all on bodies, but rather that in which they reside. It is the air, for example, accompanying (*meta*) thunder that splits the timber.

(424^{b}12) But (*alla*) the objects of touch and flavours do act (*poiein*). For otherwise by what would inanimate things be affected (*paschein*) and qualitatively changed? So do the other sense-objects also act on things (*empoiein*)? Or rather not every body can be affected (*pathētikon*) by odour and sound, and the ones which are affected (*paschein*) lack definite boundaries and do not stay put, for example, air, for this is smelly as if it had been affected (*paschein*) in some way.

(424^{b}16) What then (*oun*), is exercising smell besides (*para*) being affected (*paschein*) in some way? Rather, exercising smell is perceiving (*aisthanesthai*), whereas the air on being affected (*paschein*) quickly becomes perceptible (*aisthētos*).

I have now surveyed the evidence that Aristotle thinks perception requires a physiological process, that that process is one of the organ's taking on colour, temperature, and other qualities, and that that is what he is referring to by a group of interlinked phrases. I think it highly probable, although it is not essential to my case, that one of those phrases is 'receiving form without matter'. It is now necessary to consider the evidence on the other side for the view that what is being described is only a becoming aware of sense-qualities, and for the further view that no physiological process is needed. I am aware of three pieces of positive evidence.

One piece of evidence, *DA* 2. 5, has, I believe, often been misunderstood. It was used by Brentano to prepare the ground for his view that in Aristotle the sense-objects, colour and temperature for example, are not, or not only, physically present in the observer, but present as objects of perception.[155] It has been used as one of the arguments against the materialist interpretation of Aristotle as holding that perceiving is nothing but a physiological process.[156] It has been used to show that the change involved in perception cannot be anything like becoming red or smelly,[157] and finally to show that no physical change at all is needed in perception.[158]

The relevant passage is not discussing perceiving so much as the *switch to* perceiving after one has not been using one's senses. This should either not be called being affected (*paschein*) and qualitatively changed (*alloiousthai*), or should be recognized as a distinct way of being affected or qualitatively changed. But the

---

[155] Brentano (1867), 79–80, translated (1977), 54.
[156] Barnes (1971–2) 109 = (1979) 38. Barnes also cites *Ph.* 244^{b}7–15. But I think that says only that perceptual alterations are noticed, not that they are non-physical.
[157] Burnyeat; Lear (1988), 111–12.   [158] Burnyeat.

point is not, as supposed, that the switch is not a physical one, nor even that it is not wholly physical. The point is put in terms entirely different from that, by reference to a series of Aristotelian concepts.[159] First, the change should not be called *alloiousthai*, because the literal meaning of *allo-iousthai* is 'becoming other', whereas the being who switches to using his sense or intellect is rather developing more into himself (reading *eis hauto*, 417ᵇ6) and finding fulfilment (*entelecheia*, 417ᵇ7). Again, nothing has been subjected to destruction (*phthora*); rather that which was in a potential state before is preserved (*sōtēria*) by the switch to perception (417ᵇ3). The same is true, in the case of the intellect, with regard to an earlier stage of development. The learner who switches from not knowing to knowing is not switching to a privative phase (*sterētikai diatheseis*), but to a stable possession (*hexeis*), and to his real nature (*phusis*, 417ᵇ15–16). None of this is couched in terms of the switch being wholly or partly non-physical. And indeed it could not be wholly non-physical, because one of the examples given is that of a builder switching to actually building (417ᵇ9). I presume that the point could even be extended to a purely physical switch, such as a rock's switching from its perch on a ledge to falling in the direction of its natural position, just so long as that could be viewed as a switch towards its true nature.

The second piece of positive evidence adduced comes from the opening of *DA* 2. 12, briefly discussed above, where Aristotle first states that the sense-organ receives perceptible forms without matter. In doing so, he uses the analogy of a signet-ring imprinted in wax. Plato had used the model of imprints in a wax block, it is said, to illustrate the wide gap between perception and judgement. In perception there is no awareness, just a causal interaction with sensible qualities in the environment. To judge what these qualities are, or that 'this is Theodorus', one needs to go beyond one's present perception and compare it with the imprints one has retained as if in wax. Only then do awareness and judgement come in. If Aristotle believes instead that wax imprints are an appropriate model for perception itself, he must be denying Plato's view of perception. Two inferences are drawn, the first that the reception of sensible forms must be understood in terms of *becoming aware of* colours, sounds, smells, and other sensible qualities, not as a literal physiological change of quality in the organ. The second inference is that no physiological change is needed at all.[160] I do not believe that these inferences are justifiable. Aristotle uses the signet-ring model in his treatise *On Memory*, where he clearly intends a physiological interpretation, explaining various different forms of memory failure by the surface imprinted being too hard, too fluid like running water, or too worn like the old parts of buildings.[161]

A third reason for holding that there is no *physical* difference which accounts for our perceiving, while plants do not, draws on a difficulty in Aristotle's thought, which is not particularly tied to the theory of perception. Aristotle holds that an eye is *essentially* sighted and flesh *essentially* alive, so that a dead eye and

[159] This is very well explained by Van Riet (1953).   [160] Burnyeat.   [161] *Mem.* 450ª27–ᵇ11.

dead flesh do not even have the same definition. There is then no specifiable physiological difference which accounts for our advantage over plants, because in specifying the difference we should be forced to presuppose the very perception we wanted to explain. This difficulty has been much discussed,[162] and I would agree it is a real one. But I am not convinced that Aristotle's idea of the eye as *essentially* alive is part and parcel of his whole approach to perception, rather than an idea whose relation to the rest of his theory he has insufficiently considered. In any case, it has been pointed out that strictly speaking there is no disharmony with the theory of perception as I have explained it.[163] For Aristotle believes that the concept of an eye can be used in different, though related, senses. An eye that is at one time alive and at another time dead can still be referred to as an eye all right, even though it is not an eye in the fullest sense. It is an eye in this secondary sense to which we need to refer in explaining the perceptual advantage which we have over plants.

I have called these three pieces of evidence positive, because I believe the remaining evidence consists in, or depends on, objections to the alternative account which I have given. Consequently, much of it has been addressed already. But I need to consider two outstanding types of objection. One set of difficulties concerns the implausibility of the view I ascribe to Aristotle. Does my heart go hard as concrete, for example, when I feel concrete?[164] I think Aristotle could answer this by reference to the idea of small-scale models which he uses in his treatise *On Memory*. We think about the relative sizes of two or more objects by having images which serve as small-scale models.[165] Similarly a small-scale hardening within the heart might serve as the basis for feeling the hardness of concrete. I say that Aristotle *could* answer this way, because I do not think he did in fact think much in this context about the tactile qualities other than hot, cold, fluid, and dry. These are the four that define the four elements, and many of the others can, in his view, be reduced to them.[166] What is more difficult is Aristotle's inference (and I have treated it as an inference, not an observation) that the organ in our hearts (perhaps some of the blood in it) has a medium temperature. This would not necessarily be contradicted by observation, since blood heat might be thought of as medium. But it does seem to be in conflict with Aristotle's theory in *Juv.* and *Resp.* that the heart is the centre of vital heat and needs to be cooled by incoming air. I doubt if such a conflict of theories, however, is sufficiently improbable to discredit the interpretation. It has been overlooked by modern critics, and could have been overlooked by Aristotle.

A final objection appears to me to be mistaken. It is complained that form is not the sort of thing that could pass into my organ, or anywhere else, without being carried by a material vehicle.[167] What is true is that sensible forms cannot exist without being embedded in some matter or other at every moment, and also that the transfer or spread of sensible forms is not to be viewed as a genuine case

---

[162] Ackrill (1972–3); Williams (1986); Burnyeat; Cohen (1987).
[163] Cohen (1987), drawing on Williams (1986).
[164] Burnyeat.   [165] *Mem.* 452^{b}8–15.
[166] *GC* 2. 2.   [167] Burnyeat.

of motion (*phora*).[168] That said, however, Aristotle allows all sorts of possibilities to sensible forms. We have noticed him allowing that a thing's odour can float off into the air, however much difficulty that may give the ancient commentators, when they think about the doctrine that particular qualities are inseparable from what they inhere in.[169] In the *De Sensu* he describes the instantaneous spread of heat from one block of material to another.[170] The transmission of effects through an intervening medium to an observer is different from either of these two cases, and different, as the commentators will stress, for each of the three long-distance senses, sight, hearing, and smell. Most obviously in the case of sight the intervening medium does not become coloured. But the same principle applies, that a sensible form, or its effect, located in one piece of matter can cause another instance of the same form to appear in an adjacent piece of matter.

Such are the objections to the literal physiological interpretation. Although not accepting them, I ought to qualify what I said in my original publication.[171] Aristotle sometimes says that physiological explanations play a subordinate role, when there is a purposive explanation available, and tell us only how, not why (*dia ti*) something happens: they tell us only the instrument (*organon*).[172] He is by no means consistent about this, and frequently allows throughout his biological works that physiology is straightforwardly explanatory (*dia, aition, aitia, diho, dihoper, gar, men oun, dihoti, hoti, hōste*), not only where purposive explanations are missing,[173] but also where they are available.[174] However, there is one mood in which he confines them to telling how. Equally, he holds that the powers which constitute the soul, powers of growing, perceiving, and desiring, and indeed the soul itself, can *explain* growing, perceiving, and desiring.[175] One way in which he thinks them explanatory is that he treats it as a *basic* fact about the universe that such powers exist. Appeal to basic facts is explanatory in a way: it can be used to explain the occurrence of the requisite physiological processes. They are only to be expected as necessary for the operation of the powers which are taken as basic. But this is not to treat the powers as basic in the sense that their operation has no explanation in terms of physiological processes. At most, it implies that the physiological processes tell us how, rather than why, the basic powers can operate. And even this perspective is, as I say, not consistently maintained in the biological works. On my interpretation, it is not maintained here in the *De Anima* either, because he cites the physiological process to explain why (*dia ti*) plants do not perceive.[176]

---

[168] *Sens.* 446^{b}28–447^{a}1.

[169] *Cat.* 1^{a}25. I shall discuss the commentators' treatment of this in my (1991).

[170] *Sens.* 446^{b}28–447^{a}6.

[171] The original article was my (1974). The reasons for qualification are explained in my (1980), 166–74.

[172] *GA* 789^{b}3–22.   [173] *PA* 677^{a}18, *GA* 778^{a}35–^{b}1, ^{b}14, ^{b}18, 782^{a}20–783^{b}8, 789^{b}20.

[174] *PA* 658^{b}2–5; 663^{b}14; 677^{b}25–30; 679^{a}28; 694^{b}6; *GA* 738^{a}33–4; 743^{b}7–18; 755^{a}21–4; 766^{a}16–30; 767^{b}10–23; 776^{a}25–^{b}3; 788^{b}33–789^{a}4; 789^{a}12–14.

[175] *DA* 415^{b}8–12; ^{b}21–8; 416^{a}8–9; ^{b}21–2; *GA* 740^{b}25–741^{a}2; cf. 726^{b}18–21; 729^{b}27; 739^{a}17; *PA* 640^{a}23.

[176] *DA* 424^{a}32–3.

III

With the idea of a literal coloration process defended, I can now bring out its historical significance. It was seen in Section I that Aristotle had plenty to say about what *we* should call the intentional objects of perception. But Franz Brentano thought that Aristotle had actually himself framed the concept of an intentional object. This seminal notion was introduced by Brentano into modern philosophy in 1874. His idea was that if I inherit a fortune, the fortune must exist, in order to be the object I inherit. But if I hope for a fortune, the fortune need not exist outside my mind, in order to be the object of my hopes. This feature—not having to exist outside the mind in order to serve as an object—is called by Brentano intentional inexistence. Furthermore, he proposes it as the distinguishing feature of mental, as opposed to physical, phenomena, that they are one and all directed to objects of this kind. Even in sense-perception, the square shapes I may represent some scene as containing need not really exist in the external scene, in order to be the objects my sense-perception represents as being there. Descartes's earlier distinction between the mental and the physical, according to which we have infallible awareness of our own mental states, is hard to accept in the age of Freud, and so the completely different criterion proposed by Brentano has merited attention.

But where did he find the idea of an intentional object expressed in Aristotle? Curiously enough, in the doctrine, which I have interpreted as physiological, of form received without matter. In *Die Psychologie des Aristoteles* (1867), Brentano interpreted that doctrine as meaning that the object of sense-perception (colour or temperature, for example) is not, or not only, physically present in the observer, but present as an object (*objectiv*), that is, as an object of perception.[177] In *Psychologie vom empirischen Standpunkt* (1874), he went further: in his doctrine that the senses receive form without matter, Aristotle was already referring to intentional inexistence. The forms received without matter were intentionally inexistent objects.[178] Throughout, Brentano claimed to be following the medieval scholastics, and his earlier interpretation at least would have been readily suggested by Thomas Aquinas' insistence on the intentional status of what is received.

In fact, however, Brentano's interpretation was only made possible by a long history of distortions, a history which I shall be telling elsewhere,[179] and which here I will only sketch. First, the Greek commentators, Alexander, Themistius, and Philoponus, dephysiologized Aristotle's theory of the reception of form without matter. Their motive was not to give the most straightforward reading of the text, but to rescue Aristotle from certain particular problems in physics and logic. If literal coloration was transmitted to the eye, we might get different colours colliding in the same place. Again, if Socrates' fragrance was transmitted to the

---

[177] Brentano (1867), 79–81, 86, 120 n. 23, translated (1977), 54, 58, 229 n. 23.
[178] Brentano (1874/1959), 125, translated (1973), 88.   [179] Sorabji (1991).

observer's nostrils, we might violate the logical requirement in Aristotle's *Categories*, which was taken to mean that Socrates' particular fragrance cannot exist separately from him. The commentators' interpretations were designed to give Aristotle the most defensible view.

The result was a theory in which, except for the case of the tactile qualities, hot, cold, fluid, and dry, the reception of form was no longer to be understood as a physiological process. By Philoponus it is called a cognitive (*gnōstikos*) reception. The Islamic philosopher Avicenna added in the idea of an intention or meaning (*maᶜnā*, in the Arabic), giving as examples shape, colour, quantity, quality, where (*pou*) and posture. Sense-perception does not abstract from these. In the medieval Latin translations of Avicenna and Averroës available to Albert and his pupil Thomas Aquinas, the Arabic word was translated *intentio*, and *intentio* in perception now appears to be a kind of message which is physically housed. It is the information housed, not the physical housing. It can still in these authors exist in mid-air between perceiver and perceived, and so it is not a message of which anyone is inevitably aware, but Brentano was to change this. For him an intentional object is the object of a mental attitude.

The irony in all at this will now be apparent. Brentano's idea of intentionality was lent the authority of Aristotle, but only through the distortions of successive commentators. We can also see the value of getting clear on the physiological interpretation which I have argued Aristotle originally intended. Only so can the distortions be detected. The purpose of the best commentators is not simply to reflect Aristotle, but to reconstruct him, and that invites originality. The reinterpretation of Aristotle was not perfectly uniform—Philoponus, Aquinas, and Brentano had different versions—much less was it specifically Christian. It was the work of commentators, whether Christian, pagan, or Muslim. It was the commentators who made possible Brentano's interpretation and who lent authority to his important new proposal for the philosophy of mind. Brentano's interpretation should not be taken at face value, but seen for what it is, the culmination of a series of distortions. The moral is that in the history of philosophy the distortions of commentators can be more fruitful than fidelity.[180]

---

[180] I am extremely grateful to Myles Burnyeat for ammunition both for and against my suggestions in Section 1, as well as for pressing the issue in Section 11. Further acknowledgements for my discussion of the Stoics in Section I are given in my (1990) and in n. 60, and for Section II will be given in my (1991), but I should like here to acknowledge John Ellis's work on the inseparability of Socrates' fragrance (1990 and London Ph.D. Diss. 1991).

---

* Labarrière, J.-L.(1993), 'De la "nature phantastique" des animaux chez les Stoïciens', in Brunschwig, J. and Nussbaum, M.C. (eds), *Passions and Perceptions*, Cambridge: Cambridge University Press, 225–49.

BIBLIOGRAPHY for III

Ackrill, J.L. (1972–73), 'Aristotle's Definitions of *psuchê*', *Proceedings of the Aristotelian Society* 73, 119–33, repr. in Barnes, J., Schofield, M., and Sorabji, R. (eds) (1979), *Articles on Aristotle, vol. 4*, 65–75.

Annas, J. (1993), 'Epicurus on Agency', in Brunschwig, J. and Nussbaum, M. (eds), *Passions and Perceptions: Studies in Hellenistic Philosophy of Mind*, Proceedings of the Fifth Symposium Hellenisticum, Cambridge: Cambridge University Press, 53–71.

Armstrong, D.M. (1968), *A Materialist Theory of Mind*, London: Routledge and K. Paul, and section repr. in Dancy (1988).

Barnes, J. (1971–72), 'Aristotle's concept of mind', *Proceedings of the Aristotelian Society* 72, 101–10, repr. in Barnes, J., Schofield, M., and Sorabji, R. (eds), (1979), *Articles on Aristotle, vol. 4*, 32–41.

Bernard, W. (1988), *Rezeptivität und Spontaneität der Wahrnehmung bei Aristoteles*, Baden-Baden: V. Koerner.

Brentano, F. (1867), *Die Psychologie des Aristoteles, inbesondere seine Lehre von NOUS POIÉTIKOS*, Mainz: Franz Kirkheim.

— (1874, tr. 1973), *Psychologie vom empirischen Standpunkt*, Leipzig: Duncker and Humblot; (2nd. ed.), Kraus, O. (ed.) (1924, 1959), Leipzig: F. Meiner; tr. Rancurello, C., Terrell, D.B., McAlister, L. (1973), London: Routledge.

Burge, T. (1986), 'Individualism and Psychology', *Philosophical Review* 95, 3–45.

Burnyeat, M. (1976), 'Plato on the Grammar of Perceiving', *Classical Quarterly* 26, 29–51.

— (1992), 'Is an Aristotelian Philosophy of Mind Still Credible? A Draft', in Nussbaum, M.C. and Rorty, A.O. (eds), *Essays on Aristotle's De Anima*, Oxford: Oxford University Press, 15–26.

Cashdollar, S. (1973), 'Aristotle's Account of Incidental Perception', *Phronesis* 18, 156–75.

Charles, D. (1988), 'Aristotle on Hypothetical Necessity and Irreducibility', *Pacific Philosophical Quarterly* 69, 1–53.

Charlton, W. (1970), *Aristotle's Physics I–II*, Oxford: Oxford Clarendon Press.

Cohen, S.M. (1987), 'The Credibility of Aristotle's Philosophy of Mind', in Matthen, M. (ed.), *Aristotle Today: Essays on Aristotle's Ideal of Science*, Edmonton, Alberta: Academic Printing and Publishing, 103–25.

Cooper, J. (1970), 'Plato on Sense Perception and Knowledge: *Theaetetus* 184–186', *Phronesis* 15, 123–46.

Crane, T. (1988), 'The Waterfall Illusion', *Analysis* 48, 142–7.

— (1989), 'The Content and Causation of Thought', Cambridge: PhD Dissertation.

Dancy, J. (1988), *Perceptual Knowledge*, Oxford: Oxford University Press.

Davidson, D. (1982), 'Rational Animals', *Dialectica* 36, 318–27; repr. in LePore, E. and McLaughlin, B. (eds) (1985), *Actions and Events: Perspectives on the Philosophy of Donald Davidson*, Oxford: Blackwell, 472–80; repr. in Davidson, D. (2001), *Subjective, Intersubjective, Objective*, Oxford: Clarendon, 95–106.

Dennett, D. (1976), 'Conditions of Personhood', in Rorty, A.O. (ed.), *The Identities of Persons*, Berkeley and Los Angeles: University of California Press, 175–97.

Dretske, F. (1991), *Knowledge and the Flow of Information*, Cambridge, Mass.: MIT Press.

Ebert, T. (1983), 'Aristotle on What is Done in Perceiving', *Zeitschrift für philosophische Forschung* 37, 189–98.

Ellis, J. (1990), 'The trouble with Fragrance', *Phronesis* 35, 290–302.

Evans, G. (1982), *The Varieties of Reference*, Oxford: Oxford University Press.

Fodor, J. (1983), *The Modularity of Mind*, Cambridge, Mass.: MIT Press.

Fortenbaugh, W. (1971), 'Aristotle: Animals, Emotion and Moral Virtue', *Arethusa* 4, 137–65.

Frede, M. (1983), 'Stoics and Skeptics on Clear and Distinct Impressions', in Burnyeat, M. (ed.), *The Skeptical Tradition*, Berkeley: University of California Press, 65–93; repr. in Frede (1987a), 151–76.

— (1987a), *Essays in Ancient Philosophy*, Oxford: Oxford University Press.

— (1987b), 'Observations on Perception in Plato's Later Dialogues', in Frede (1987a), 3–8.

— (1989), 'An Empiricist View of Knowledge: Memorism', in Everson, S. (ed.) (1990), *Epistemology: Companions to Ancient Thought* 1, Cambridge: Cambridge University Press, 225–50.

Geach, P. (1957), *Mental Acts: Their Content and Their Objects*, London: Routledge.

Gill, C. (1991), 'Is there a Concept of Person in Greek Philosophy?', in Everson, S. (ed.), *Psychology: Companions to Ancient Thought* 2, Cambridge: Cambridge University Press, 166–93.

Glidden D. (1984), 'Aristotelian Perception and the Hellenistic Problem of Representation', *Ancient Philosophy* 4, 119–31.

Hamlyn, D. (1959), 'Aristotle's Account of Aisthêsis in the *De Anima*', *Classical Quarterly* ns 9, 6–16.

— (1968), 'Koinê Aisthêsis', *The Monist* 52, 195–200.

Hartman, E. (1977), *Substance, Body and Soul: Aristotelian Investigations*, Princeton: Princeton University Press.

Huby, P. (1975), 'Aristotle De Insomniis 462a18', *Classical Quarterly* 25, 151–2.

Inwood, B. (1985), *Ethics and Human Action in Early Stoicism*, Oxford: Oxford University Press.

Irwin, T. (1988), *Aristotle's First Principles*, Oxford: Oxford University Press.

Jackson, F. (1977), *Perception*, Cambridge: Cambridge University Press.

Labarrière, J.-L. (1984), 'Imagination humaine et imagination animal chez Aristote', *Phronesis* 29, 17–49.

— (1993), 'De la "nature phantastique" des animaux chez les Stoïciens', in Brunschwig, J. and Nussbaum, M.C. (eds), *Passions and Perceptions*, Cambridge: Cambridge University Press, 225–49.

Lear, J. (1988), *Aristotle and the Desire to Understand*, Cambridge: Cambridge University Press.

Long, A.A. and Sedley, D.N. (1987), *The Hellenistic Philosophers*, Cambridge: Cambridge University Press.

Matson, W.I. (1986), 'Why isn't the Mind-Body Problem Ancient?', in Feyerabend, P.K. and Maxwell, G. (eds), *Mind, Matter, and Method: Essays in Philosophy and Science in Honour of Herbert Feigl*, Minneapolis: University of Minnesota Press, 92–102.

Millar, A. (1985–86), 'What's in a Book?', *Proceedings of the Aristotelian Society* 86, 83–97.

Nussbaum, M.C. (1978), *Aristotle's De Motu Animalium*, Princeton: Princeton University Press.

— and Putnam, H. (1992), 'Changing Aristotle's Mind', in Nussbaum, M.C. and Rorty, A.O. (eds), *Essays on Aristotle's De Anima*, Oxford: Oxford University Press, 27–56.

Peacocke, C. (1986), 'Analogue Content', *Proceedings of the Aristotelian Society*, supp. Vol. 60, 1–17.

— (1989), 'What are Concepts?', *Midwest Studies in Philosophy* 14, 1–28.

— (1990), 'Perceptual Content', in Almog, J., Perry, J., and Wettstein, H. (eds), *Themes from Kaplan*, New York: Oxford University Press, 297–330.

Pitcher, G. (1971), *A Theory of Perception*, Princeton: Princeton University Press.

Putnam, H. (1975), 'Philosophy and our Mental Life' in *Mind, Language and Reality: Philosophical Papers ii*, Cambridge: Cambridge University Press, 291–303.

Robinson, H. (1978), 'Mind and Body in Aristotle', *Classical Quarterly* 28, 105–24.

— (1983) 'Aristotelian Dualism', *Oxford Studies in Ancient Philosophy* 1, 123–44.

Slakey, T. (1961), 'Aristotle on Sense Perception', *Philosophical Review* 70, 470–84.

Sorabji, R. (1971), 'Aristotle on Demarcating the Five Senses', *Philosophical Review* 80, 55–79; repr. in Barnes, J., Schofield, M., and Sorabji, R. (eds) (1979), *Articles on Aristotle, vol. 4*, 76–92; repr. as article VI of current volume.

— (1972), *Aristotle On Memory*, London and Providence, RI: Duckworth and Brown University Press; (2nd. ed.) Chicago University Press 2006, Bloomsbury 2013.

— (1974), 'Body and Soul in Aristotle', *Philosophy* 49, 63–89; repr. in Barnes, J., Schofield, M., and Sorabji, R. (eds), (1979), *Articles on Aristotle, vol. 4*, 42–64, repr. in ch.1 of current volume.

— (1980), *Necessity, Cause and Blame*, London and Ithaca, NY: Duckworth and Cornell University Press; Chicago University Press 2006; Bloomsbury 2013.

— (1988), *Matter, Space and Motion*, London and Ithaca, NY: Duckworth and Cornell University Press; Chicago University Press 2006.

— (1990), 'Perceptual Content in the Stoics', *Phronesis* 35, 307–14.

— (1991), 'From Aristotle to Brentano: The Development of the Concept of Intentionality', in Blumenthal, H. and Robinson, H. (eds), *Aristotle and the Later Tradition*, *Oxford Studies in Ancient Philosophy*, Suppl., Oxford: Clarendon Press, 227–59, repr. as article IV of current volume.

— (1993), *Animal Minds and Human Morals: The Origins of the Western Debate*, London and Ithaca, NY: Duckworth and Cornell University Press.

Van Riet, G. (1953), 'La théorie thomiste de la sensation externe' *Revue philosophique de Louvain* 51, 374–408.

Wilkes, K.V. (1978), *Physicalism*, Atlantic Highlands, NJ: Humanities Press.

Williams, B. (1986), 'Hylomorphism', *Oxford Studies in Ancient Philosophy* 4, 189–99.

APPENDIX: FURTHER READING

(On coloration of the eye jelly and physiological process in perception).

Compiled by Joachim Aufderheide with additions by Peter Lautner, Roberto Grasso, Kunio Watanabe and Richard Sorabji.

Bowin, John, 'Aristotle on Various Types of Alteration in *De Anima* II 5', *Phronesis* 56, 2011, 138–61.

—, '*De anima* II 5 on the Activation of the Senses', *Ancient Philosophy* 32, 2012, 1–18.

Broackes, Justin, 'Aristotle, Objectivity and Perception', *Oxford Studies in Ancient Philosophy* 17, 1999, 57–113.

Broadie, Sarah, 'Aristotle's Perceptual Realism', in J. Ellis (ed.), *Ancient Minds*, *Southern Journal of Philosophy* 31, suppl. 1993, 137–59.

Burnyeat, Myles, 'Aquinas on "Spiritual Change" in Perception', in D. Perler (ed.), *Ancient and Medieval Theories of Intentionality*, Brill, Leiden 2001, 129–53.

—, 'De anima II 5', *Phronesis*, 47 (2002), 28–90.

—, 'How Much Happens When Aristotle Sees Red and Hears Middle C? Remarks on De anima 2. 7–8', in Nussbaum and Rorty (eds), *Essays on Aristotle's De anima* (1995 edn.), 421–34.

—, 'Introduction: Aristotle on the Foundations of Sublunary Physics', in F. De Haas and J. Mansfeld (eds), *Aristotle: On Generation and Corruption, Book 1*, Oxford University Press, Oxford 2004, 7–24.

—, 'Is an Aristotelian Philosophy of Mind Still Credible? (A Draft)', in M. Nussbaum and A. Rorty (eds), *Essays on Aristotle's De anima*, Oxford University Press, Oxford 1992, 15–26.

Caston, Victor, 'The Spirit and the Letter: Aristotle on Perception', in Salles, R. (ed.), *Metaphysics, Soul, and Ethics in Ancient Thought: Themes from the Work of Richard Sorabji*, Oxford University Press, Oxford 2005, 245–320.

Everson, Stephen, *Aristotle on Perception*, Oxford University Press, Oxford 1997.

Heinaman, Robert, 'Aristotle and the Mind–Body Problem', *Phronesis* 35, 1990, 83–102.

—, 'Actuality, Potentiality and De Anima 2.5', *Phronesis*, 52, 2007, 139–87.

Johansen, Thomas., *Aristotle on the Sense-Organs*, Cambridge University Press, Cambridge 1998.

III

Lautner, Peter, 'Methods in examining sense-perception: John Philoponus and ps-Simplicius', *Laval Théologique et philosophique* 64, 2008, 651–61.

—, '*Gnôstikôs* and/or *hulikôs*: Philoponus' account of the material aspects of sense-perception', in preparation.

Lorenz, Hendrik, 'The assimilation of sense to sense-object in Aristotle', *Oxford Studies in Ancient Philosophy* 33, 2007, 179–220

Magee, J.M, 'Sense Organs and the Activity of Sensation in Aristotle', *Phronesis* 45, 2000, 306–30.

Menn, Stephen, 'Aristotle's Definition of Soul and the Programme of the De anima', *Oxford Studies in Ancient Philosophy* 22, 2002, 83–139.

Miller, Fred D., 'Aristotle's Philosophy of Perception' *Proceedings of the Boston Area Colloquium in Ancient Philosophy* 15, 1999, 177–213.

Modrak, Deborah, *Aristotle: The Power of Perception*, University of Chicago Press, Chicago 1987.

Murphy, D., 'Aristotle on Why Plants Cannot Perceive', *Oxford Studies in Ancient Philosophy* 29, 2005, 295–339

—, 'The Debate of Spiritualists, Structuralists, and Literalists and De anima 423b30–424a10' *Ancient Philosophy* 26, 2006, 305–32.

Price, Anthony, 'Aristotelian Perceptions', *Proceedings of the Boston Area Colloquium in Ancient Philosophy* 12, 1996, 285–309

Polansky, Ronald, *Aristotle's De Anima*, Cambridge University Press, Cambridge 2007.

Rapp, Christof, 'Intentionalität und *phantasia* bei Aristoteles', in D. Perler (ed.), *Ancient and Medieval Theories of Intentionality*, Brill, Leiden 2001, 63–97.

Scaltsas, T, 'Biological matter and perceptual powers in Aristotle's *De anima*', *Topoi* 15, 1996, 25–37.

Shields, Christopher, 'Intentionality and Isomorphism in Aristotle', *Proceedings of the Boston Area Colloquium in Ancient Philosophy* 11, 1995, 307–30.

Silverman, Alan, 'Color and color-perception in Aristotle's *De anima*', *Ancient Philosophy* 9, 1989, 271–92.

Sisko, John, 'Material alteration and cognitive activity in Aristotle's *De anima*', *Phronesis* 41, 1996, 138–57.

—, 'Alteration and Quasi-Alteration: A critical notice of Stephen Everson, *Aristotle on Perception*', *Oxford Studies in Ancient Philosophy* 16, 1998, 331–52.

Sorabji, Richard, 'Body and Soul in Aristotle', *Philosophy* 49, 1974, 63–89.

—, 'Intentionality and Physiological Processes: Aristotle's Theory of Sense-Perception', in M. Nussbaum, A. Rorty (eds), *Essays on Aristotle's De anima*, Oxford University Press, Oxford 1992, 195–225.

—, 'Aristotle on Sensory Processes and Intentionality: A Reply to Myles Burnyeat', in Dominik Perler (ed.), *Ancient and Medieval Theories of Intentionality*, Brill, Leiden 2001, 49–61.

Ward, J, 'Perception and logos in *De anima* II, 12', *Ancient Philosophy* 8, 1998, 217–33.

Woolf, Ralph, 'The Coloration of Aristotelian Eye-Jelly: A Note on *On Dreams* 459b-460a', *Journal of the History of Philosophy* 37, 1999, 385–91.

IV

FROM ARISTOTLE TO BRENTANO: THE DEVELOPMENT OF THE CONCEPT OF INTENTIONALITY

ARISTOTLE's *On the Soul* or *De anima* is probably the most variously interpreted of his works. Modern interpretations have disagreed chiefly on how Aristotle's psychology stands in relation to Descartes.[1] The ancient Neoplatonist commentators, in order to harmonize him with Plato, insisted on his belief in the immortality of the rational soul, and thereby unwittingly made Aristotle safe for Christianity. In this paper I want to take Aristotle's theory of sense-perception and show how there too the ancient commentators started the process of reinterpretation, and handed it on to the Middle Ages. I hope that Tony Lloyd will consider this a suitable theme with which to honour him, since he has led the way in showing that professional philosophers need not and should not leave all the work to others in studying the philosophy of late antiquity.

Among the ancient commentators I shall select three, Alexander of Aphrodisias, Themistius, and Philoponus, and I shall concentrate on two types of revision that they introduced. First, they sought to give Aristotle's account of sensory processes a less material interpretation. Secondly, in doing so they began to emphasize the great diversity of the different senses, some being more and some less material, where Aristotle had stressed uniformity. Their reasons for revision had to do with particular problems of physics and logic quite other than those which have motivated modern interpretations. The Arabic writers

Besides my special debt to John Ellis, I owe thanks to Wolfgang Bernard, Charles Burnett, Jill Kraye, Alan Lacey, Gül Russell, Robert Sharples, and Alan Towey for their valuable comments.

[1] Richard Sorabji, 'Intentionality and Physiological Processes: Aristotle's Theory of Sense Perception', in A. Rorty and M. Nussbaum (eds.), *Aristotle's* De Anima, (Oxford, 1991).

228

contributed to the process of dematerialization the idea of an intention, understood as a non-physical message, or information, and handed it on to Thomas Aquinas and others in the thirteenth century. By Brentano's time this was reinterpreted in terms of an awareness of the message. Moreover, Brentano added his own peculiar idea of an intentional object, thus giving a further twist to the interpretation of Aristotle and lending authority to one of the most important substantive theories in modern philosophy of mind.

That is the outline of my account, but let us start with Aristotle. When I see a coloured scene, my eye-jelly (*korē*) takes on colour-patches whose colours, shapes, and positions match the scene. That, as I have argued elsewhere,[2] is Aristotle's theory of the physiology of the visual process. Similarly, when I hear, smell, taste, or feel anything, the inner organ takes on sounds, odours, flavours, temperatures, and so on. It is to this theory that Aristotle refers when he says that the sense-organ receives form without matter, becomes like the sense-object and is potentially such as it is. What the commentators began to revise was partly this account of what goes on in the sense-organ, and partly, as we shall see, Aristotle's theory of what goes on in the medium that intervenes between the sense-organ and object perceived.

The word *korē*, Latin *pupilla*, in its everyday use means pupil of the eye, but in Aristotle means the eye-jelly.[3] By the time of the commentators, more distinctions had been made among the fluids in the eye, and Philoponus uses the word instead for the channel of the optic nerve.[4] For some later authors I shall leave the word untranslated.

The first of the three Greek commentators to be discussed is Alexander of Aphrodisias, who developed Aristotelianism to its greatest extent around 200 AD. He dematerialized Aristotle's account of sense-perception in more than one way. First, he took up a problem anticipated by Aristotle, but applied by him only to the central sensory faculty which compares and distinguishes the reports of the five individual senses. Those reports must be made, Aristotle argues, to some-

---

[2] Sorabji, 'Intentionality and Physiological Processes'. The most important evidence is contained in Arist. *De anim.* 2. 11, 423^{b}27–424^{a}10. Even Ibn al-Haytham, as A. I. Sabra has pointed out to me, shares this aspect of his theory with Aristotle (*Optics*, 2. 3. 54, ed. Sabra), despite taking the study of vision so much further than Aristotle (see Gül
* Russell, 'The Emergence of Physiological Optics', in preparation).

[3] Richard Sorabji, 'Body and Soul in Aristotle', in J. Barnes, M. Schofield, and R. Sorabji (eds.), *Articles on Aristotle*, (London, 1979), at 49 n. 22 (repr. from *Philosophy*, 49 (1974), 63–89).

[4] Philoponus, *In De anim.* 366. 11–14; 368. 1–3.

thing spatially and numerically indivisible.[5] Otherwise it would be like a case of my perceiving one thing, and you another, which does not yet permit comparisons to be made.[6] But the problem for something spatially and numerically indivisible is that 'it cannot be simultaneously white and black, and hence it cannot be affected by the forms of these [white and black] either, if that is what thinking and perception are like'.[7]

I shall call this the 'contraries' problem. It is applied to the central sense, or to the soul, by the commentators Alexander, Themistius, and Averroes.[8] And it is extended by them, along with Philoponus, Albert the Great, and Thomas Aquinas, to the medium intervening between the observer and the observed. The point where our gazes intersect cannot be coloured both white and black, they say, when I am looking at something white and you at something black (Texts 1, 15, 22).[9] What is interesting about Alexander is that in one of these texts he extends the problem also to the sense-organs (*aisthētēria*), needlessly, it seems, since in the eye-jelly the black and white patches can be adjacent to each other, and need not coincide at the same point. However, Alexander ignores this, and concludes that the sense-organ cannot serve as matter receiving such qualities as white and black. Indeed, we see that sight does not become white or black (Text 2).[10] In other words, Alexander uses the contraries problem to deny the coloration of the organ of sight, a very different reason from any that has inspired modern interpreters. He compares what happens in a mirror,[11] but this can be no more than a comparison. For it would not solve the contraries problem to suggest that what happens in the organ is literally a mirroring, or any other kind of coloration, because the collision of contraries like white and black is no easier to accept in a mirror than it is elsewhere, as Avicenna later points out.[12] In fact, the mirror is invoked simply to illustrate what is

---

[5] Arist. *De anim.* 3. 2, 427ᵃ5.
[6] Ibid. 426ᵇ19–20.   [7] Ibid. 427ᵃ8–9.
[8] Alexander, *De anim.* 61. 30–62. 1 Bruns; Themistius, *In De anim.* 57. 2–12; 86. 29 Heinze; Averroes, *Epitome of* Parva naturalia (medieval Latin versions of Arabic, ed. Blumberg), p. 29 (Text 15); and ap. Albert. Magn. *Summa de creaturis*, pt. 2 (*De homine*), q. 21, a. 5, xxxv. 206ᵇ–207ᵇ Borgnet. ('Text' refers to the passages printed at the end of this paper.)
[9] Alexander, *De anim.* 62. 5–13 (Text 1). Similarly, Alexander (?), *Mantissa*, 147. 16–25 Bruns; Themistius, *In De anim.* 59. 24–6; Philoponus, *In De anim.* 329. 14–30; Averroes, loc. cit. (n. 8) (Text 15); Albert, op. cit. (n. 8), 206ᵃ; Aquinas, *In De anim.* 493 (Text 22).
[10] Alexander, *De anim.* 62. 1–5 (Text 2). I am grateful to Wolfgang Bernard for insisting on the reference to the organs.   [11] Ibid. 62. 13–22.
[12] Avicenna records, but rejects, the view that contrary forms can coexist over the

230

a necessary, but not a sufficient, condition for avoiding coloration, namely, that the organ should not serve as matter to colour. Neither eye nor mirror serves as matter to colour, because each depends for its function on the continuing proximity of the coloured object (these two ideas are more than once connected).[13] In other works Alexander does not apply the contraries problem to the organ, and is consequently free to take a more ambivalent, or even a favourable, attitude towards the view that colours show (*emphainesthai*) in the eye. So the dematerialization evident in this one text is not quite steadily maintained (Texts 3–7).[14]

If we turn to the process of hearing, we find that Alexander dematerializes this too, in probable agreement with his contemporary Galen. His revision of Aristotle consists in saying that what travels through the medium of hearing is not a block of air, but only a *shape*, or as we would say a wave, passed on by one block of air to the next (Text 8).[15] Themistius and (writing in Latin) Boethius actually call it a wave (*kuma, unda*).[16] They along with Simplicius (if he is the author of the *De anima* commentary) and Philoponus all endorse this idea, and the last two credit it to Alexander.[17] Earlier references to a shape in Aristotle

whole of a mirror: *Shifā'* in medieval Latin translation, ed. van Riet, *Avicenna Latinus, Liber de Anima*, i (Louvain and Leiden, 1972), pt. 3, ch. 7, p. 258. 61–7.

[13] Cf. also Alexander, *De anim*. 42. 21–43. 1; 83. 16; 83. 23–84. 6; *Mant*. 147. 21–3.

[14] In *Mant*. 142. 21–143. 2. (Text 3; cf. 147. 23), if he is the author, he affirms that colour *does* show (*emphainesthai*) in the eye. In *In De sensu*, 24. 26–7 and 25. 4–5 Wendland (Texts 4 and 5), thought to be a late work, he correctly reports Arist. *De sensu*, 2. 438[a]5–12 (Text 7), as denying that the showing (*emphasis*) of a mirror image in someone's eye is relevant to that person's vision. (Those MSS which omit the word 'not' at 24. 27 are proved wrong by the sequel at 25. 4–5.) But Alexander is still drawn by the idea that the eye does not merely let colours show *through* it (*diaphainesthai*) like a transparent (*diaphanēs*) medium, but also lets colours show *in* it (*emphainesthai, emphanēs*, 26. 23–6; 36. 2–4). He therefore has to remind himself sternly (26. 25–6) that Aristotle has just ruled out the relevance of an image showing (*emphasis*) in the eye (see Text 6 = 26. 23–6). The only other Greek commentator on Aristotle to allow the relevance of things showing (*emphainesthai*) in the eye is Simplicius, if he is the author of the *De anima* commentary commonly ascribed to him (*In De anim*. 165. 3; 166. 19–31 Hayduck). Aristotle's own argument against the relevance of mirroring is expressed by saying that the *emphasis* resides not in the eye observed, but in the observer of the eye. I take it he means that what is reflected in the eye observed depends on the angle from which the observer views the eye (Text 7).

[15] Alexander, *De anim*. 48. 7–21 (Text 8); similarly 50. 15–16; cf. Galen, *De usu partium*, 8. 6 = iii. 644 Kühn. For Aristotle's moving block of air see *GA* 5. 7, 787[a]30–[b]19, and the strong suggestions at *De anim*. 2. 8, 419[b]25–7, 420[a]8–9.

[16] Themistius, *In De anim*. 65. 31–6; Boethius, *De musica*, 1. 14, 200. 6–21 Friedlein.

[17] Simplicius *In De anim*. 141. 15–38; Philoponus, *In De anim*. 361. 5–362. 8. For the medieval uptake of the idea, whether from Boethius' Latin or from Greek or Arabic

and Theophrastus, or to a wave in Zeno the Stoic, will not be significant, unless they can be divorced from the idea of a moving block of air.[18] But Alexander's concept of the transmission of an impulse through successive blocks of air is to be found in the pseudo-Aristotelian *Problems*, where an interesting Aristotelian parallel is given. For the idea of transmitting an impulse from one block of air to the next is part of Aristotle's account of what keeps a projectile moving after it has lost contact with the thrower.[19] No doubt Alexander would have found it intolerable to allow sounds to be moving blocks of air, since he raises the objection against analogous theories of vision, which make vision depend on the emission of physical rays from the eyes, that the emitted bodies would collide (an objection later used against Naẓẓām's theory of sound as a body).[20] Perhaps he thinks that the problem of collision is obviated, in the case of sounds, so long as sounds are not bodies.

Two other instances of dematerialization in Alexander proved influential, though they are neither of them revisions of Aristotle, but rather support for him. For against the un-Aristotelian idea that vision depends on the travel of bodies, whether emitted or received, he adds the further objection that such bodies would be blown about by winds.[21] And against the second variant, according to which the bodies are received into the eyes, he argues rather like his contemporary Galen that the *korē* is too small to take in more than a little of the available effluence at a time, so that we would not see the object whole.[22]

The second Greek commentator, Themistius (*fl.* late 340s to 384 or 385), begins to bring out the diversity of the five senses in respect of their

sources, see Charles Burnett, 'Sound and its Perception in the Middle Ages', in id. (ed.), *Hearing and Musical Judgment* (London, forthcoming). I owe to him, *inter alia*, the references to Boethius and the pseudo-Aristotelian *Problems*.

[18] Arist. *De sensu*, 6, 446ᵇ6–9; Theophrastus ap. Priscian, *Metaphrasis in Theophrastum*, 14. 10–12 Bywater, and ap. Stob. = fr. 89. 10 Wimmer; Zeno ap. D.L. 7. 158; cf. for the Stoics Aetius, 4. 19. 4 (= *SVF* 2. 425). I regard with caution R. Siegel, *Galen on Sense Perception* (Basle, 1970), 134–5. The most vigorous case for the Stoics already transcending the idea of a moving block of air is made by S. Sambursky, *Physics of the Stoics* (London, 1959), ch. 2, sect. 1.   [19] [Arist.] *Problems*, 11. 6.

[20] Alexander, *In De sensu*, 30. 6–21; 130. 2–6. The objection to Naẓẓām is in Abū Rashīd al-Nishābūrī, *Ziyādat al-Sharḥ fīl Tawḥīd*, ed. Abū Rıḍā, pp. 30–40. I owe the reference to Alnoor Dhanani.

[21] Alexander, *In De sensu*, 28. 27–8; 57. 10; 57. 26–7; Alexander (?), *Mant.* 129. 21–4; 136. 3–5, 21–4. Similarly Philoponus, *In De anim.* 327. 34–8; 400. 20–1.

[22] Alexander, *In De sensu*, 31. 25–7; 57. 23–5. Cf. Alexander's contemporary Galen, *On the Doctrines of Hippocrates and Plato*, 7. 5. 2–4, trans. Philip de Lacy in *Corpus Medicorum Graecorum*, v/4. 1. 2. Plotinus later makes the different claim that the soul could not even receive an impression (*tupos*) from something as large as the sky, 4. 6. 1. 27–8.

IV

corporeality, a subject mentioned, but certainly not emphasized, by
Aristotle.[23] Touch is the most corporeal (*sōmatikōtatē*) of the senses, he
says, because the part of the body in which the faculty resides is
potentially hot, cold, and like the other tactile qualities,[24] whereas the
korē of the eye does not become white or black, nor does the air lodged in
the ear become high- or low-pitched.[25] It is the same with the medium of
touch. Themistius accepts Aristotle's idea that the real organ of touch is
within, in the heart, and that the flesh serves only as a medium. This
medium, as well as the inner organ, is heated and cooled, and serves as
matter to the corresponding qualities, and the same goes for taste,
whereas with the other three senses neither medium nor organ is so
affected.[26]

With the third Greek commentator, Philoponus, in the sixth century,
the revision of Aristotle goes furthest of all. First, he qualifies
Themistius' claim about the corporeality of touch and taste. The organ
of touch is the only one that literally takes on sense-qualities, and it
takes on only the four, hot, cold, fluid, and dry, not heavy and light,
viscous and crumbly, rough and smooth. As for the long-distance sense-
organs, he agrees with Themistius that they do not become coloured or
odorous at all (Text 9).[27] The organs receive the other forms only
cognitively (*gnōstikōs*), just as the sense-faculty receives them (Text 9).[28]
Correspondingly, the *korē* for Philoponus is filled not with liquid, but
with *pneuma* or spirit, an inappropriate vehicle for receiving colour.[29]

Secondly, Philoponus dematerializes Aristotle's account of what
happens to the medium through which vision occurs. Aristotle had been
prepared to say that the medium is affected (*paschei*) by the sense-
object.[30] According to Philoponus, on the contrary, the air is not
affected (*apathēs*); it merely lets through what Aristotle had called the

[23] Arist. *NE* 10. 5, 1175ᵇ36–1176ᵃ1, compares the senses in respect of purity (*kathareiotēs*).
[24] Themistus, *In De anim.* 76. 32–77. 22.
[25] Ibid. 75. 17–19; 79. 29–37.
[26] Ibid. 75. 10–19; 79. 29–37. This is Themistius' interpretation of Aristotle's idea that the medium of touch does not act on the organ of touch, but rather both are acted on together by the sense-object, as a soldier and his shield are both struck together by the enemy's blow, *De anim.* 2. 11, 423ᵇ12–17.
[27] Philoponus, *In De anim.* 432. 33–433. 11; 438. 9. See Text 9 = 432. 32–433. 11; 438. 6–15.
[28] Philoponus, *In De anim.* 303. 4–6; 309. 17–25; 432. 38 (see Text 9): 437. 10–11; 438. 13 (see Text 9); cf. Moerbeke's Latin version of *In De anim.* 3. 4–8 (= *De intellectu*), 9. 11–12; 32. 57–8 Verbeke, and [Philoponus?], *In De anim.* 3, 481. 24–33.
[29] Philoponus, *In De anim.* 366. 11–14.
[30] Arist. *De anim.* 3. 12, 435ᵃ1–8; *De sensu,* 6. 447ᵃ9; cf. *alloiousthai, Phys.* 7. 2. 245ᵃ2–11.

process (*kinēsis*)[31] and what Philoponus calls the activity (*energeia*) of the colour seen. Aristotle himself must believe, according to Philoponus, that these activities are distributed throughout the air, since observers with different vantage-points are equally affected. If, then, the activities so affected the air as to make it show (*emphasis*) the thing seen, we should be able to see an object whatever the direction of our gaze, because we would be confronted by displays of it in every direction. In fact, however, the activities should rather be compared with what happens when a sunbeam shines through stained glass. The beam throws a pool of colour on the wall opposite, *without* colouring the intervening air. This is only a comparison, intended to bring out how the air could avoid being affected. It is explicitly stated that the stained-glass mechanism is not the same as that of vision (Text 10).[32]

But Philoponus does not only dematerialize the sensory processes; he also stresses their diversity in this regard. Touch is the most material (*prosulos*), the most corporeal (*sōmatoeidēs*) and the most physical (*pachumerēs*) of the senses.[33] But in addition smell is more 'corporeal' and more 'physical' than hearing, because the air is affected by odour much of the way, though not quite all the way, to the sense organ.[34] Hearing and smell are both more 'physical' than sight, because the air is affected materially (*hulikōs*) in both of these, becoming fragrant or sonorous, whereas the air does not become coloured.[35] Given this diversity, we should not be surprised if touch is idiosyncratic in yet other ways too (Text 11).[36]

In the case of smell, the diversity is such as even to threaten the dematerialization of sensory processes. The background to this problem has been uncovered in some important work by John Ellis.[37] It started in the unexpected context of logic, where Philoponus' teacher, Ammonius, offered a new solution to an old problem about Aristotle's *Categories* and its criterion for distinguishing individual qualities from other things. Individual qualities are distinguished as being unable to exist '*separately*' from what they are in. But the fragrance of an apple can float off into the surrounding air, it seems, and thus exist *separately* from the apple it is in. In fact, I would construe Aristotle as allowing that at *De*

---

[31] Arist. *De sensu*, 2, 438^b4–5; 6, 446^a21; *GA* 5. 1, 780^a29; 780^b35–781^a12.
[32] Philoponus, *In De anim.* 334. 38–336. 3 (Text 10).
[33] Ibid. 416. 23; 417. 37.   [34] Ibid. 413. 7–12.
[35] Ibid. 413. 6–7; 416. 30–5.
[36] Ibid. 416. 34–5; 421. 35–422. 1. (See Text 11 = 413. 4–12; 416. 30–4.)
[37] John Ellis, Ph.D. diss. (London), in progress, and 'The Trouble with Fragrance', *Phronesis*, 35 (1990), 290–302.

anim. 2. 12, 424^{b}14–16.[38] The question is 'How can he, consistently with the *Categories?'* Ammonius' new solution insists that some of the substance of the apple comes off into the air, so that the fragrance is not at any stage *separated* from the substance of the apple after all.[39] This rescues the *Categories*, and Philoponus is at first happy to repeat the solution in his *Categories* commentary.[40] But in his *De anima* commentary, which refers back to that on the *Categories*,[41] and which is said to be taken 'from the seminars of Ammonius' but 'with some personal reflections' added, he realizes that this will not do. If the *Categories* is to be saved in this way, the *De anima* will be wrecked. For Aristotle there insists that smell never operates by direct contact with the substance perceived (with the apple, for example),[42] whereas taste, despite appearances, operates by direct contact always.[43] Philoponus puts Aristotle's view by saying that odours are conveyed to the sense-organ incorporeally (*asōmatōs*) through the 'diosmic' power of the air, a power which lets through odour as transparency lets through light and colour, without an accompanying substance.[44]

Philoponus' new suggestion is that after all corporeal effluences (*aporrhoiai*) only bring the odour *part* of the way to the organ, an aid that we need because of the weakness of our sense of smell. After that, even if the effluence has got as far as our nostrils, it is still necessary for the activity (*energeia*) of the odorous body to be transmitted by a medium to the inner organ, unaccompanied by any substance (Texts 12 and 13).[45] Whether that would avoid the *Categories* problem he does not say, but perhaps the *activity* of the odorous body is sufficiently distinct (see

---

[38] It is not clear, however, that Ammonius' pupil, Philoponus, construes it that way: *In De anim.* 443. 11–444. 8.　　　　　[39] Ammonius, *In Cat.* 28. 15–18 Busse.

[40] Philoponus, *In Cat.* 35. 24–31 Busse.

[41] Philoponus, *In De anim.* 391. 32.　　　　　[42] Arist. *De anim.* 2. 7, 419^{a}25–35.

[43] Apparent examples of tasting at a distance are explained away at *De anim.* 2. 10, 422^{a}8–16. The olive at the bottom of my Martini is partially dissolved in the drink, and so after all in direct contact with my tongue, if not with my inner organ: Richard Sorabji, 'Aristotle on Demarcating the Five Senses', *Philosophical Review*, 80 (1971), 55–79, at p. 71, repr. in Barnes, Schofield, and Sorabji (eds.), *Articles on Aristotle*, iv. 76–92, at p. 87.

[44] Philoponus, *In De anim.* 391. 38–392. 3. The term 'diosmic' is a contribution of Theophrastus, according to Philoponus, *In De anim.* 354. 12–16.

[45] Philoponus, *In De anim.* 392. 8–11; 392. 19–31; 413. 11–12; 420. 22. (See Text 12 = 413. 9–12 and Text 13 = 392. 3–19.) I do not know if the conflicting testimony on the role of effluence in Theophrastus' much earlier theory of smell may reflect a two-stage theory of the same sort. For the conflicts see Robert Sharples, 'Theophrastus on Tastes and Smells', in W. Fortenbaugh (ed.), *Theophrastus of Eresos: On his Life and Work* (Rutgers Studies in Classical Humanities, 2; New Brunswick, 1985), 183–204, at pp. 193–7, with further comment by David Sedley at pp. 205–7.

Text 13) from the odour itself to avoid counting as a case of odour separated from the substance it started in.

The fact that effluences travel some of the way makes smell very different from sight, where Philoponus argues at length that no physical bodies are transmitted in either direction. For one thing, the *korē* of the eye is too small to emit bodies covering a quarter of the universe.[46]

Ammonius' arguments for odorous effluences reaching *all* the way had included the fact that an apple shrivels as it lets off fragrance, and that the smoke of incense can actually be seen.[47] Philoponus gives us his teacher's arguments, and adds that we can waft odours towards us, unlike colours or sounds, with our hands, and that the 'contraries' argument can be stood on its head, because contrary odours do mask each other, which shows that they are carried by vapours.[48] But he replies that this masking proves nothing, because equally in the case of sound, where there is no effluence, and of brightness, the louder or brighter overpowers the other.[49] Moreover, an effluence could not reach the tens of thousands of distances to the vultures who smell carrion from afar (Text 13).[50] The programme of dematerialization is thus rescued after all.

In discussing Themistius and Philoponus, I have left out a figure earlier than either: Plotinus. Plotinus' view has been interpreted by Eyjólfur Emilsson in a way that makes him sound close to the commentators. In Emilsson's wording, the colours of external things exist in our visual fields in a non-material way.[51] None of this is Plotinus' own wording, but Emilsson does make a good case for saying that Plotinus understands the idea of reception of form, which he borrows from Aristotle, non-physiologically. This would be equally true of Alexander before him, at least in some of Alexander's works. But in addition Plotinus makes use of the idea of intermediacy, which we shall find in Averroes (Text 15), when he (Plotinus) says that the effect (*pathos*) which the perceiver undergoes must have an intermediate status, if it is to mediate between the object of sense on one side and the perceiving soul on the other.[52] I am inclined to leave Plotinus aside, however, not only because of the difficulty of being sure about his intentions and of

[46] Philoponus, *In De anim.* 325. 30–2.
[47] Ammonius, *In Cat.* 28. 15–18; 28. 30–29. 4.
[48] Philoponus, *In De anim.* 391. 11–29.   [49] Ibid. 392. 6–8.
[50] Ibid. 392. 11–19. (See Text 13 = 391. 11–29; 392. 3–19.)
[51] Eyjólfur Emilsson *Plotinus on Sense-Perception: A Philosophical Study* (Cambridge, 1989), 67–93, 142–5.
[52] Plotinus, 4. 4. 23. 22–33, cf. 4. 5. 1. I am grateful to John Ellis for this point.

knowing how the commentators themselves construed him, but because it is even unclear how far they attended to him at all on this subject, rather than to Alexander and Galen, on whom he draws. Certainly, the Islamic commentators are not known to have possessed the most important passage in Plotinus: 4. 4. 23. The passage which they did have in paraphrase, 4. 5. 1, insists only on the intermediate status of the *medium*, not like Averroes·on the intermediate status of the sense-object in the organ and medium.[53]

Of the three Islamic thinkers to be mentioned, Avicenna, Ghazali, and Averroes, the first, Avicenna (*c.*980–1037), rematerializes the account of perception. First, he restores the full effluence theory of smell, citing among other evidence the apple that shrivels as it gives off its fragrance. As for the vultures, winds could blow an effluence as far as them.[54] Meanwhile, for all five senses, the reception of form without matter is interpreted as making the perceiver become like the form of the thing perceived.[55] He hints that the process in vision is less material than that in smell or touch, but even in vision he takes it to mean that the eye receives a replica ('oculus recipit simulacrum', in the medieval Latin translation), just as an illuminated body can tinge something opposite with its own colour 'inficere suo colore').[56] Although the form is received stripped of its original matter, the abstraction from matter in sense-perception is not so complete as in the estimative faculty or in the intellect. For sight cannot abstract the form it receives from such material intentions (*intentiones*) as how much, of what quality, where, and position (Text 14).[57]

Despite the acceptance of something like a literal coloration process, Avicenna here introduces an idea that was eventually to be exploited in favour of a non-literal interpretation. For he brings in the notion rendered in medieval Latin translation as *intentio* (intention), the origin of our idea of an intentional object. His own word

---

[53] *Dicta Sapientis Graeci*, 5, translated into English ad loc. by G. Lewis in the Henry–Schwyzer edition of Plotinus.

[54] Avicenna, *Shifā'* in medieval Latin translation, ed. van Riet, *Avicenna Latinus, Liber de Anima*, vol. i, pt. 2, ch. 4, 148. 43–154. 30, with comments by Verbeke, introduction, 58–9.   [55] Ibid. 2. 2, 120. 42–122. 56; 3. 7, 254. 97–100.

[56] Ibid. 3. 7, 254. 7; 255. 17–19. For smell and touch see 254. 98–100. In insisting (254. 97–8) that the form received in vision is similar, but not identical, to the form in the object seen, he adopts a view exploited by some of the Greek commentators for denying that the fragrance which separates itself from Socrates is identical with his very own fragrance.

[57] Ibid. 2. 2, 116. 84–7 (Text 14), and see for the other faculties pp. 117–120. Cf. Alexander, *De anim.* 83. 20–2.

was *ma'nā*, a meaning. He gives the name 'intention', sometimes 'material intention' (*intentio materialis*), to shape, colour, position, how much, of what quality, and where (Text 14).[58] These passages are more relevant than the better-known one where he suggests that we should speak of form, rather than intention, as being apprehended in sense-perception. According to this better-known account, the context in which to speak of a sheep as apprehending its *intention* of the wolf is when its mind apprehends something about the wolf that is *not* in any way apprehended by the senses, such as why it ought to be afraid of the wolf and run away.[59] But our passages connect intentions with sense-perception.

Averroes (*c.*1126–98) returns to the side of the dematerializers (Text 15).[60] He uses the 'contraries' argument to show that such forms as colours do not have a corporeal, but a spiritual, existence in the sense-organs. Or rather, they have a spiritual existence in the soul, and an existence intermediate between spiritual and corporeal in the organ and medium. An additional argument against corporeal existence is the small size of the *pupilla* (Philoponus' *korē*). The medieval Latin translation of the Arabic uses quite freely the notion of the *intention* of colour (Text 15), although the qualification '*material intention*' is dropped.

Averroes also argues for the *diversity* of the different sense-processes as regards their degree of materiality (Text 16).[61] The being of odour is *less* spiritual than that of colour, because it is blown about by winds. On the other hand, this does not prove that odour must be a body, because sounds too are blown by winds, and sounds are agreed not to be bodies, but rather disturbances (*passiones*) in a body. Equally for odour, then, the point is simply that winds make a difference because odour is a disturbance *in* air. Odour can still be said none the less to have spiritual being in the medium. The liability of bodies to be

---

[58] Ibid. 2. 2, 116. 76; 118. 7 (Text 14). Victor Caston has now made a very interesting ✳
case for tracing Avicenna's use of *ma'nā* back to the Stoic idea of a *lekton* (thing said, proposition) in 'Two Stoics on Concepts and Universals', in preparation.

[59] Ibid. 1. 5, 86. 93–6.

[60] Averroes, *Epitome of Aristotle's* Parva Naturalia, medieval Latin translation, ed. Shields and Blumberg, 29. 15–30. 28 and 31. 45–32. 49 = Text 15 (in Blumberg's translation, *Epitome of* Parva Naturalia, 15–16). The *Long Comm. in De Anima* assigns spiritual being to odour and colour in the medium, but finishes up with much the same intermediate status for odour, by giving it a *less* spiritual being there than colour: medieval Latin translation, ed. Crawford, 2. 97, 277. 28–33 and 278. 69–70.

[61] Averroes, *Long Comm. in De Anima*, medieval Latin translation, ed. Crawford, 2. 97, 278. 68–77 (Text 16).

238

blown by winds we saw introduced into the discussion by Alexander, followed by Philoponus, as a proof that vision does *not* involve the travel of bodies.[62] But a closer parallel is provided by Philoponus (Text 13) when he compares and contrasts odour with sound. On the one hand, he argues that odour is *unlike* sound and colour, in that it can be wafted by the hands.[63] On the other, he contends that it is *like* sound and brightness, in that contraries mask each other, and that consequently the inference from masking to corporeality is no more valid for odours than it would be for sounds.[64]

Averroes, like Ghazali before him (1058–1111), appeals to the vultures to show that odour could not be carried such a distance by vapour,[65] although this may represent a shift of view on his part. For in his epitome of Aristotle's *Parva naturalia* he still says that the objects of smell have a smoky nature and that odours belong to the genus of smoky vapours.[66] It is in his long commentary on the *De anima* that he takes the other view, and there he suggests some awareness of the *Categories* controversy. For he insists against some unnamed opponents that an odour can be *separated* from the odoriferous body that carries it.[67]

All the Arabic texts mentioned were translated into Latin in time to be well known to Christian philosophers of the thirteenth century. Albert the Great (*c.* 1200–80), the teacher of Thomas Aquinas, presents his views in three works, the *De homine* (which is part of the *De creaturis*), and in two inventive paraphrases of Aristotle, named after the Aristotelian originals, the *De sensu et sensato* (part of the *Parva naturalia*) and the *De anima*.[68] My impression is that in the comparatively early *De homine* Albert had thought about the *De sensu* part of Aristotle's *Parva naturalia* and about Averroes' epitome of it, but

[62] Alexander, *In De sensu*, 28. 27–8; 57. 10; 57. 26–7; Alexander (?), *Mant.* 129. 21–4; 136. 3–5; 21–4; Philoponus, *In De anim.* 327. 34–8; 400. 20–1.
[63] Philoponus, *In De anim.* 391. 26–7.
[64] Ibid. 392. 3–8.
[65] Ghazali, *Intentions of the Philosophers*, medieval Latin translation in *Algazel's Metaphysics*, ed. J. T. Muckle (St. Michael's Medieval Studies; Toronto, 1933), 165. 26–31; *Comm. in De anim.* 2. 97, 277. 33–278. 56.
[66] Averroes, *Epitome of Aristotle's* Parva Naturalia, ed. Shields and Blumberg, 24. 14–20 (trans. Blumberg, 13).
[67] Averroes, *Long Comm. in De anim.* 2. 97, 277. 34. The controversy is not, however, mentioned in his commentary on the *Categories*, nor in the earlier middle commentary of Farabi on the *Categories*.
[68] I have learnt particularly from the important account of Albert by Lawrence Dewan, 'St. Albert, the Sensibles and Spiritual Being', in James A. Weisheipl (ed.), *Albertus Magnus and the Sciences: Commemorative Essays* (Toronto, 1980), 291–320.

that careful reflection on Averroes' commentary on Aristotle's *De anima* is manifested only when he comes to write his own *De anima*.

Let me take the first two works first. Already in the *De homine* he suggests the dematerializing view that the eye does not get coloured in the visual process, since he says that the air colours nothing (*nihil colorat*),[69] and he uses the old 'contraries' argument to show that the medium too cannot be coloured.[70]

Albert also tries to uphold the dematerialization of smell. Like Aristotle in the *De sensu*, he castigates Heraclitus both in his *De homine* and in his *De sensu* for allegedly making odour into a smoky vapour.[71] As to whether some other kind of vapour is involved, he cites the conflicting evidence of the shrivelling apples and the distant vultures. Whereas the apples suggest that the odoriferous body gets mixed with the medium to form some kind of vapour, the great distance of the vultures suggests that the medium is merely transformed by the odoriferous body, without any mixture taking place. Albert's solution is that a vapour is often produced by mixture, but that where the vapour stops, it can still transform the air beyond it.[72] So the project of dematerialization is saved.

Albert further argues for the diversity of the senses. As regards the three long-range ones, he accepts the position of Averroes' *Epitome* that the objects of sight, smell, and hearing have an intermediate status in the medium. They have material being in the physical object, spiritual being in the sense, but in the medium what he calls sensible being (*esse sensibile*).[73] The objects of taste and touch are different: they reach the sense-organ (*organum*) still in an actual state (*in actu*), and it is only after that that they acquire spiritual being, and that the 'intention' of heat is drawn off and passed to the brain, which would otherwise get over-heated.[74]

When we turn to Albert's *De anima*, we find him taking still further the theme of the diversity of the different senses, as regards their spirituality. As we noticed in Averroes' *De anima* commentary, winds have a different effect on odours, sounds and colours. As for touch, the sense-objects act on both medium and organ with material being

[69] Albert, *De creaturis*, 2. q. 34, a. 2, xxxv. 300^b Borgnet.
[70] Ibid. 2, q. 21, a. 5, xxxv. 206^a Borgnet.
[71] Albert, *Parva naturalia, Liber de sensu et sensato*, 2. 10, ix. 64^b–65^a Borgnet; *De creaturis*, 2, q. 30, xxxv. 260^{a-b}, 270^{a-b} Borgnet; Arist. *De sensu*, 5, 443^{a}21–^{b}2.
[72] Albert, *De creaturis*, 2, q. 30, xxxv. 269^b–270^a, 270^b–271^b Borgnet.
[73] Ibid. 2, q. 34, a. 2, xxxv. 300^b Borgnet.
[74] Ibid. 301^a.

(Text 17).[75] Later in the same work, however, Albert appears to reduce the amount of diversity by dematerializing the tactual processes after all. For however the outer parts of the body may be affected, the organ within (the heart) receives only the 'species' with intentional being.[76] As announced in the *De homine*, he uses the terms 'species' and 'intention' interchangeably.[77]

Albert's *De anima* reaffirms the immateriality of the visual process, explicitly confirming that the eye does not get coloured (Text 18).[78] He further dematerializes the processes of smell and hearing, but he now gives their objects two alternative statuses, rather than a single intermediate status, in the medium. As regards smell, he refers back to the *Parva naturalia*, but Plato and Avicenna replace Heraclitus as the materialistic proponents of an effluence account of odour.[79] The effluence view uses as evidence the shrivelling apples and meets the problem of the vultures by postulating winds to blow the effluence. In his dematerializing reply, Albert now cites Averroes, relying presumably on the *De anima* commentary, since the epitome of the *Parva naturalia* would have been of little help. Odour is spread through spiritual and intentional being.[80] Admittedly, odour can have more than one status in the medium, intentional being when we smell a distant object (*in remoto*), and some (*de*) material being in the case of a near object (*in propinquo*) (Text 19).[81] Unlike Philoponus, Albert allows that sometimes a vapour reaches right up to the organ of smell, but he still insists that in such cases the odour has intentional being (Text 20).[82] Presumably this is an instance in which it has 'some' material being as well. Such a double status would replace the earlier suggestion of intermediate status.

Albert accords to sound too a double status in the medium: material being in the air, but spiritual being through echo (*reflexio*).[83] The double status is illustrated in Albert's discussion of a version of the contraries problem: how do sounds intersect without interfering with each other? Albert replies that the circular waves break each

---

[75] Albert, *De anim.* 2. 3. 6, v. 242[b] Borgnet (Text 17).
[76] Ibid. 2. 3. 34; 2. 4. 3, v. 290[b]; 297[b] Borgnet.
[77] Albert, *De creaturis*, 2, q. 34, a. 2, xxxv. 298[a] Borgnet.
[78] Albert, *De anim.* 2. 3. 6, v. 241[a] Borgnet (Text 18).
[79] Cf. Plato, *Tim.* 66 E.
[80] Albert, *De anim.* 2. 3. 25, v. 277[a]–278[b] Borgnet.
[81] Ibid. 2. 4. 3, v. 297[b] Borgnet (Text 19).
[82] Ibid. 2. 3. 25, v. 278[b] Borgnet (Text 20).
[83] Ibid. 2. 4. 3, v. 297[b] Borgnet.

other at what is little more than a point. Moreover, this damage is repaired because the intact parts of the circles produce a reflection or echo (*reflexio*) which fills the gaps. It is further suggested that in these places the sound exists in the air only by way of intention (*per intentionem*), and that this makes sound easy to produce (Text 21).[84] The problem of sounds intersecting without interference had already been raised in the *De homine*.[85] But there it was raised as a threat to the idea that sounds have an intermediate status, rather than a purely spiritual or intentional one (the terms are used interchangeably).

A final word is needed about Albert's use of the terms 'intention' and 'spiritual'. In distinguishing intentions from forms, he says that form gives being to the compound of matter and form and is part of it, whereas intention does not bestow being, but provides a sign (*signum, significare, significatio*) of something and a mark (*notitia, notificare*) of the whole thing.[86] This is not far from the original sense of *ma'nā* as meaning or message in Avicenna. We have seen, however, that the intention can exist in the intervening medium (Texts 20 and 21),[87] and the existence of a message there cannot yet imply *awareness* of the message. As regards spirituality, Albert is quite conscious of an ambiguity.[88] To call something spirit or spiritual, he says, can be to imply that it is not a body at all (*non corpus*) and that it is a merely qualitative effect. But it can be to refer to a tenuous body, since the Latin *spiritus* is a translation of the Greek *pneuma*, which started its career by referring to a tenuous, gaseous body—a usage which lingers in a talk of animal spirits, or of alcohol as a spirit. Except where he gives notice otherwise, Albert normally appears to intend the incorporeal meaning, although an exception is provided by the passage mentioned above, where he says that vapour is spiritual (Text 20).[89]

Albert's pupil, Thomas Aquinas, is like Albert and Averroes in giving an intermediate degree of immateriality to what he calls

---

[84] Ibid. 2. 3. 19 (Text 21). The corrupt text in Borgnet v. 268[b] is improved in the Cologne edition, *Opera Omnia*, vii/1, ed. Stroick, 127. 87–128. 1, despite the general strictures on the edition of R.-A. Gauthier, introduction to the Leonine edition of Thomas Aquinas, *In De anima*, in *Opera Omnia*, xlv/1. The greater clarity of an echo as compared with an unreflected sound is already discussed in [Arist.] *Prob.* 11. 23 and 51; see Charles Burnett, 'Sound and its Perception in the Middle Ages'.

[85] Albert, *De creaturis*, 2, q. 24, a. 6, xxxv. 241[a]–242[b] Borgnet.

[86] Albert, *De anim.* 2. 3. 4, v. 238[a] Borgnet.

[87] Ibid. 2. 3. 16; 2. 3. 18; 2. 3. 19 (Text 21); 2. 3. 20; 2. 3. 25 (Text 20), v. 263[a]; 266[b]; 268[b]; 269[b]; 278[b] Borgnet.

[88] Albert, *De creaturis*, 2, q. 21, a. 5, xxxv. 207[a] Borgnet; *De anim.* 2. 3. 25, v. 278[a] Borgnet.   [89] Albert, *De anim.* 2. 3. 25, v. 278[b] Borgnet.

sensible being. But he explains this in a manner reminiscent of Avicenna. In sense-perception, a thing has its being free from matter, but not free of individuating material conditions, because sense-perception is directed to particulars, not universals.[90] Elsewhere he gives as an example of individuating material conditions this flesh and these bones, and implies that sense does not abstract from these.[91]

Thomas takes the theme of the diversity of the senses as regards spirituality still further than Albert. In sections 418 and 493 of his commentary on Aristotle's *De anima*, Thomas repeats that in the case of touch something gets heated or cooled in the perceptual process, as well as undergoing a spiritual change. The next most material sense is smell, because the change induced by odour comes about together with (*fit cum*) a smoky vapour. Moreover, odour is blown about by winds, and, as we found already noticed by Philoponus,[92] the contraries argument yields an opposite result for odour and for colour, since contrary odours do mask each other. As regards sound, the change it induces comes about together with motion, and again sound is blown by winds. Seeing alone involves a purely spiritual change, as is shown by the possibility of two observers seeing contrary colours even when their gaze intersects (Text 22).[93]

Thomas gives a double status to odour. He repeats the argument that a vapour could not be sufficiently attenuated to reach all the way to the vultures (Text 23).[94] But in his *De anima* commentary he uses it to draw a conclusion like that of Philoponus, rather than like that of Albert: the odoriferous body can let off a vapour some of the way, but it never reaches as far as the point where the odour is perceived. Beyond the point where the vapour can reach, the medium is affected only spiritually (Text 24).[95] One should not be deceived by the fact that odours can be blown about, or mask each other, into thinking that the vapour reaches all the way (Text 22).[96]

Once again, one has to be careful about what Thomas means by 'spiritual' and 'intention'. By far the commonest view is that inten-

---

[90] Thomas Aquinas, *In De anim.* 284.
[91] Thomas Aquinas, *Quaestiones de veritate*, 10. 4, ad 6. I owe the reference to Joe Christianson, diss. Ph.D., St Patrick's College, Maynooth.
[92] Philoponus, *In De anim.* 391. 11–21.
[93] Thomas Aquinas, *In De anim.* 418 and 493 (Text 22). Cf. *Summa Theologiae*, 1, q. 78, a. 3 'I answer', for the claim that only touch and taste involve a physical change in the organ and that the pupil does not become coloured.
[94] Thomas Aquinas, *In De anim.* 494 (Text 23).
[95] Ibid. 495 (Text 24).
[96] Ibid. 493, cited above (Text 22).

tional being in Thomas has to do with awareness. Thus, *esse inten-tionale* is standardly translated as 'the existence of being known', and intention is explained as cognitive or causing knowledge.[97] For Thomas, it is said, the eye's taking on colour is just one's becoming aware of some colour, and this view is also ascribed to Philoponus (correctly) and with some plausibility to Brentano.[98] But, as has occasionally been noticed, there is a serious objection against ascribing it to Thomas. For an intention, according to both Thomas and his teacher Albert, can exist *outside* the observer in the medium (Texts 20, 21, 22),[99] so that although an intention involves a message, it cannot imply as a matter of necessity *awareness* of that message.

Accordingly, one recent author has swung to the opposite position, and argued that in Thomas the sensory process is wholly physical, suggesting that it may be some kind of mirroring.[100] Certainly, Thomas is, like Albert, aware that 'spirit' can refer to something tenuous and physical.[101] And certainly he views phantasms (*phantasmata*) as physical. But intentions are different, and I believe the evidence cited shows no more than that intentions can be *housed* in something physical. This leaves it open that an intention may itself be not a physical change, but a non-physical message. That is, a message in the sense of non-physical information, which may be physically housed, not in the sense of the physical housing. This would be in line with the sense of 'intention' we found in Avicenna and Albert. Better evidence would be needed for the particular suggestion that the process is one of mirroring, since the author's ascription of this view to Avicenna and (with misgivings) to Aristotle appears incorrect. I have spoken of Aristotle above (n. 14 and Text 7). Avicenna explicitly

[97] Ibid. 418 (Text 22) in the translation of Kenelm Foster and Sylvester Humphries; Aquinas, *Summa Theologiae*, 1, q. 56, a. 2, ad 3, in the new standard Dominican translation by Kenelm Foster. Cf. Sheila O'F. Brennan, 'Sense and Sensitive Mean in Aristotle', *New Scholasticism*, 47 (1973), 279–310, at pp. 304–5. Other examples of the standard interpretation are given by Sheldon M. Cohen, 'Thomas Aquinas on the Immaterial Reception of Sensible Forms', *Philosophical Review*, 91 (1982), 193–209, at pp. 193–4.

[98] Myles Burnyeat, 'Is an Aristotelian Philosophy of Mind still Credible?', unpublished paper, of which a version will appear in Rorty and Nussbaum (eds.), *Aristotle's De Anima*, (Oxford, 1992).

[99] Thomas Aquinas, *In De anim.* 418 (Text 22); *Summa Theologiae*, 1, q. 56, a. 2, ad 3; 1, q. 67, a. 3. The point is made by Dewan, 'St. Albert, the Sensibles and Spiritual Being', 290–1. For Albert see Texts 20 and 21 and n. 87.   [100] Cohen (see n. 97).

[101] Thomas Aquinas, *In Sent.* 1, 10. 1. 4, sol.; *Summa Theologiae*, 1, q. 36, a. 1, ad 1, cited by George P. Klubertanz, '*De Potentia* 5. 8: Note on the Thomist Theory of Sensation', *Modern Schoolman*, 26 (1949), 323–31.

denies that a mirror undergoes the same effect as an eye. It is not in any way struck (*offensio*).[102] Mirroring provides only a simile: the eye is like a mirror and the transmission of form to the eye is like mirroring.[103] Similarly, we have seen that Thomas's teacher Albert denies any kind of coloration process in the eye, and this presumably excludes mirroring.

There is yet another interpretation, which represents Thomas as inconsistent, on the grounds that he often views the intention as immaterial, yet needs the sensory process to be physical, in order that it may be directed to, i.e. causally related to, particulars.[104] However, according to the interpretation of Joe Christianson, which I have followed above, the sensory process is directed to particulars not in the way suggested, through being a physical process, but through failing to abstract from particular features of the thing perceived, which are incorporated in the message.[105] I am therefore drawn back to the interpretation of Thomas's intention as non-physical information which may be physically housed. It may even depend on a physical coding, as in Albert the intentional sounds restored by echo seem to depend on the restoration of the sound-wave. But I suspect that the more fully intentional it is, the less it depends on a physical coding in order to perform its role as a message. That would account for the decreasing effect of winds on smells, sounds, and colours.

A particularly good account of many of the relevant terms is given by Thomas's older contemporary, Roger Bacon (1214/20–1292). He says that the word *species* is taken from the Latin rendering of Aristotle's doctrine that the senses receive *form* (*eidos*) without matter. And so this word is used when the aim is to emphasize its relation to the *senses*. But the alternative word *intentio* is used, when the interest is in stressing its falling short of being a real thing (*res*). Furthermore, Bacon supplies an example of *species* by describing the stained-glass phenomenon that was first introduced by Philoponus. The colour

---

[102] Avicenna, *Shifā'*, in medieval Latin translation, ed. van Riet, *Avicenna Latinus, Liber de Anima*, vol. i, pt. 3, ch. 7, pp. 259. 89–262. 40.

[103] Avicenna, *Najāt*, translated in part in F. Rahman, *Avicenna's Psychology* (London, 1952), 27; *Dānishnāma*, translated into French by M. Achena and H. Massé, *Le Livre de science* (Les Belles Lettres Unesco; Paris, 1955–8), ii. 60; both passages rendered into English in David C. Lindberg, *Theories of Vision from al-Kindi to Kepler*, (Chicago, 1976), 49.

[104] John J. Haldane, 'Aquinas on Sense-Perception', *Philosophical Review*, 92 (1983), 233–9.

[105] For this reply see Christianson (n. 91 above).

thrown on to an opaque surface by a ray as it passes through stained glass is an example of a *species* (Text 25).[106]

I shall finish the discussion of the Latin writers with William of Ockham (*c.*1285–1349), who takes up the stained-glass phenomenon and the pool of colour thrown on the opposite wall, and denies that it proves the existence of species. 'Multiplicity is not to be postulated unnecessarily,' he says, and therefore we ought not to postulate species as well as colour. What the stained-glass phenomenon proves is that colour itself is in the medium, and we can suppose that it is always there—just too weak to see. But it is postulated only because of the evidence of the stained glass, not because it is needed for seeing (Text 26).[107]

On looking back over the Arabic and Latin writers, I find it impossible to believe that Philoponus' discussion was not among those available to them. Of course, they also had Alexander's *Mantissa*, but the influence of Philoponus seems more pervasive still. We have just noticed the recurrence of the stained-glass analogy in Bacon and Ockham. It is Philoponus most of all who before Averroes stresses the diversity of the five senses and compares them all in respect of their corporeality. The influence of Philoponus' discussion of smell is still more undeniable. The vultures are to be found in Avicenna, as well as in the subsequent writers. Averroes' comparison of colour, sound, and smell in respect of spirituality may well owe something to Philoponus, when he discusses the effect of winds on the three of them. Albert sounds like Philoponus when he gives odour a double status: it sometimes has material being, sometimes intentional being in the medium. But it is Thomas Aquinas who insists, like Philoponus, that the material vapour which sometimes carries odour never reaches all the way to the organ, and who refers to the argument, first recorded by Philoponus, which stands the contraries argument on its head, and

---

[106] Roger Bacon, *Opus maius*, ed. Bridges, ii (Oxford, 1897), 409–10 (Text 25).

[107] William of Ockham, *Reportatio* or *Quaestiones in Sent.*, in Ockham, *Theological Works*, vi (St Bonaventure, NY, 1982), bk. 3, q. 2, Prima experientia, p. 45, line 16, with reply p. 56, line 8; Responsio propria (1), pp. 59–60 (see Text 26); Responsio propria (2), p. 61 (see Text 26); Responsio propria (4), reply concerning second doubt, pp. 92–3; reply concerning third doubt, p. 93; bk. 3, q. 4, Utrum potentiae sensitivae differant, pp. 141–2 (see Text 26). For similar rejections of species by Durandus and Mirecourt and for Mirecourt's explanation of the stained-glass phenomenon as one of displacement by reflection, see Anneliese Maier, 'Das Problem der "species sensibiles in medio" und die neue Naturphilosophie des 14. Jahrhunderts', repr. in her *Ausgehendes Mittelalter*, ii (Rome, 1967), 419–51, from *Freiburger Zeitschrift für Philosophie und Theologie*, 10 (1963), 3–32.

infers the corporeal character of odours from the fact of their masking each other. I would add that it is Philoponus who first records the alternative interpretation of Aristotle's idea that the sense-organs receive form without matter, as meaning that the *organ* does not serve as matter to the qualities received.[108] This new interpretation is taken up with variations instead of, or as well as, the other by Albert and Thomas Aquinas.[109]

The mechanism of transmission for Philoponus' ideas may seem a mystery, because no Arabic translation of his *De anima* commentary is recorded, and the Latin translation made for Thomas Aquinas in 1268 by William of Moerbeke covered only book 3, chapters 4 to 8, which concerns the intellect, not the senses. The answer must lie in the widespread practice of annotating texts or translations of Aristotle in the margins with scholia drawn from the commentators. The practice is actually copied by Avicenna himself, who had probably seen such exemplars. It has been argued that the marginal glosses written by Avicenna into his Arabic version of Aristotle's *De anima* include ideas from at least five different parts of Philoponus' commentary.[110] The Latin authors had not only the Arabic texts in Latin translation to draw on, but also a Latin translation of Aristotle's *De anima* made from the Greek by James of Venice, which was itself equipped with a system of glosses.[111] And it has been independently argued that James had access to scholia drawn from certain other works of Philoponus in Constantinople, perhaps through the good offices of Michael of Ephesus.[112] Michael would have been collecting scholia on psychology, *inter alia*, for his commentary on Aristotle's *Parva naturalia*. Finally, William of Moerbeke translated two scholia from Philoponus' *De anima* commentary which he found written in the margins of

---

[108] Philoponus, *In De anim.* 440. 20–441. 11. See Oivind Andersen, 'Aristotle on Sense-Perception in Plants', *Symbolae Osloenses*, 51 (1976), 81–6. The general idea of not serving as matter is already present in some of the Alexander passages discussed above, as well as in Philoponus (see Texts 2 and 9).

[109] e.g. Albert, *De anim.* 2. 4. 1, v. 294 Borgnet; Aquinas, *In De anim.* 552–3; 557. Cf. later still Sophonias, *Comm. in Arist. Graeca* xxiii/1. 104 Hayduck, who often repeats Philoponus.

[110] Richard M. Frank, 'Fragments of Isḥāq's Translation of the *De Anima*', *Cahiers de Byrsa*, 8 (1958–9), 231–51, at pp. 235–6, cites the following passages: 24. 32 ff.; 25. 22 ff.; 28. 29–32; 46. 10 ff.; 158. 10 ff.; 158. 26 ff.; 271. 33.

[111] R.-A. Gauthier's introduction to the Leonine edition of Thomas Aquinas, *Opera Omnia*, xlv/1. *In De anim.*, pp. 201*–235* and 256*–259*.

[112] So Sten Ebbesen, e.g. in 'Philoponus, "Alexander" and the Origins of Medieval Logic', in Richard Sorabji (ed.), *Aristotle Transformed: The Ancient Commentators and their Influence* (London and Ithaca, NY, 1990), ch. 19.

Themistius' commentary on the *De anima*, a commentary which he translated into Latin in 1267.[113] Moreover, William made a Latin translation of the *De anima* itself for Thomas Aquinas between 1265 and 1268, and would have annotated it,[114] drawing on Greek sources as well as on translations from Arabic.

I come now to the part which, from the point of view of modern philosophy, is the most interesting. In 1874 Franz Brentano introduced into the philosophy of mind the seminal idea of an intentional object. If I inherit a fortune, the fortune must exist, in order to be the object I inherit. But if I hope for a fortune, the fortune need not exist outside my mind, in order to be the object of my hopes. This feature— not having to exist outside the mind in order to serve as an object—is called by Brentano intentional inexistence. Furthermore, he proposes it as the distinguishing feature of mental, as opposed to physical, phenomena that they are one and all directed to objects of this kind. Descartes's earlier distinction between the mental and the physical, according to which we have infallible awareness of our own mental states, is hard to accept in the age of Freud, and so the completely different criterion proposed by Brentano has merited attention. Another feature of Brentano's intentional objects can be illustrated by the fact that if I inherit the family fortune, and the family fortune is the worst thing that could happen to me, I inherit the worst thing that could happen to me. But if I hope for this same fortune, it does not follow that I hope for the worst thing that could happen to me. The non-substitutability of expressions which refer to the same object (in this case, to the family fortune) has been another major locus of discussion. Current debate incorporates yet another question, the difference between the intentional objects of perception and belief, and I have spoken of this elsewhere.[115]

But what has this to do with Aristotle? In *Die Psychologie des Aristoteles* (1867) Brentano interpreted Aristotle's doctrine that the senses receive form without matter as meaning that the object of sense-perception (colour or temperature, for example) is not, or not only, physically present in the observer, but present as an object (*Objektiv*), that is, as an object of perception.[116] In *Psychologie vom empirischen Standpunkt* (1874)

---

[113] G. Verbeke, *Jean Philopon: Commentaire sur le De Anima d'Aristote* (Corpus Latinum Commentariorum in Aristotelem Graecorum, 3; Louvain and Paris, 1966).

[114] See R.-A. Gauthier, loc. cit. (n. 111 above).

[115] Richard Sorabji, 'Intentionality and Physiological Processes' (n. 1 above).

[116] F. Brentano, *Die Psychologie des Aristoteles* (Mainz, 1867), 79–81, 120 n. 23. The classic article on Brentano, with an overview of scholastic uses of *intentio* and *intentionalis*, is

IV

248

he went further: in his doctrine that the senses receive form without matter, Aristotle was already referring to intentional inexistence. The forms received without matter were intentionally inexistent objects.[117] Throughout, Brentano claimed to be following the medieval scholastics, and his earlier interpretation at least would have been readily suggested by Thomas Aquinas's insistence on the intentional status of what is received.

Even so, Brentano's interpretation was not faithful to Thomas, for whom intentional being did not imply awareness, although it may have implied a message. And Thomas in turn was able to make his interpretation of Aristotle only because of the earlier tradition of commentators who had transformed him. They had transformed him in an effort to deal with quite particular problems of physics and (in the case of smell) of logic. The purpose of the best commentators is not simply to reflect Aristotle, but to reconstruct him, and this invites originality. The interpretations of Philoponus, Thomas Aquinas, and Brentano have recently been labelled a Christian view, and taken to be more or less uniform.[118] But we have seen that the reinterpretation of Aristotle was neither uniform nor specifically Christian. It was the work of commentators, whether Christian, pagan, or Muslim. It was the commentators who made possible Brentano's interpretation and who lent authority to his important new proposal for the philosophy of mind. Brentano's interpretation should not be taken at face value, but seen for what it is, the culmination of a series of distortions. The moral is that in the history of philosophy the distortions of commentators can be more fruitful than fidelity.

Herbert Spiegelberg, '"Intention" and "Intentionality" in the Scholastics, Brentano and Hegel', trans. from the German of 1936 in Linda McAlister (ed.), *The Philosophy of Brentano* (London, 1976), ch. 9.

[117] F. Brentano, *Psychologie vom empirischen Standpunkt* (Leipzig, 1874; 2nd edn. by Oskar Kraus and Felix Meiner, Leipzig, 1924, repr. Hamburg, 1959, i. 125); trans. C. Rancurello, D. B. Terrell, and Linda McAlister as *Psychology from an Empirical Standpoint* (London, 1973), 88.

[118] Burnyeat, 'Is an Aristotelian Philosophy of Mind still Credible?', a much-discussed but unpublished paper, of which a published version is about to appear (n. 98 above).

Texts
Text 1. Alexander, *De anima*, p. 62. 5–13 Bruns

But neither does the illuminated air, in spite of serving sight for the grasping of colours, do this through itself being first changed by the colours and itself becoming black or white (*oude dia tou melas autos ē leukos ginesthai*). At least nothing prevents one person apprehending black and another white through the same air, when the white and black lie directly in front of the observers, but each looks at the colour lying not by himself but by the other person. Even if a black and a white person were to see each other, the intervening air is still not prevented from serving both of them simultaneously, because it is not changed by the colours qualitatively (*pathētikōs*), and does not come to act as the matter (*mēde hōs hulē ginomenos*) of the colours.

Text 2. Alexander, *De anima*, p. 62. 1–5 Bruns

But if it is in a different way that sense-perception is changed by perceptibles, and the organs (*aisthētēria*) do not serve as matter receiving the qualities of the perceptibles, it would no longer be such an impasse. For it is evident that sight does not serve as matter receiving the qualities, for we see that sight does not become black or white when it perceives these.

Text 3. Alexander (?), *Mantissa*, pp. 142. 21–143. 2 Bruns

Colour does not evidently show in (*emphainetai*) the air, but in the eye-jelly (*korē*), because some transparent (*diaphanēs*) things are merely transparent (*diaphanēs*), while others, besides being transparent, let things show within (*emphanēs*) because their smoothness and density enable them to protect the process of showing (*emphasis*) and gather it together. Things that are merely transparent do not preserve the thing seen in themselves in such a way that it actually shows (*emphainesthai*) in them. Tenuous transparent bodies like air do not. But transparent things that have some density and solidity do preserve the image (*eikōn*) or shadow (*skia*) of the thing seen and display it (*diadeiknunai*) within themselves. Mirrors, glasses, and transparent stones do this, and so indeed does water, since it has more solidity and thickness than air, and is better able to protect the images and shadows coming from the things seen and to gather them together. The eye-jelly and the channel which extends from it to the primary perceptual centre are both watery, and so receive from what is seen the form and colour and announce it to the perceptual centre, which discriminates the impinging colour thanks to the projection (*prosbolē*) reaching it from these organs.

250

Text 4. Alexander, *In De sensu*, p. 24. 26–7 Wendland

But Democritus is not right to think that seeing is a process of showing (*emphasis*)—that is, he is not right to think that showing (*emphasis*) is the explanation (*aitia*) of seeing.

Text 5. Alexander, *In De sensu*, p. 25. 4–5 Wendland

For what he means is: for seeing does not reside in that, that is, it is not due to (*dia*) showing, nor does it reside in showing but in the observer.

Text 6. Alexander, *In De sensu*, p. 26. 23–6 Wendland

It is enough if that through which we see is transparent (*diaphanēs*), but that with which we see should let things show (*emphanēs*) and be such as can receive and preserve the forms of what is seen. Or as he said, showing (*emphasis*) contributes nothing to seeing, and transparency is sufficient.

Text 7. Aristotle, *De sensu*, 2. 438ª5–12

Democritus is right to say that [the eye] is water, but not right to think that seeing is a process of showing (*emphasis*). For that happens because the eye is smooth, and it resides not in it [the eye] but in the observer, for the phenomenon is reflection (*anaklasis*). But in general nothing was yet clear, it seems, about what shows (*emphainomena*) and reflection. It is also strange that it did not occur to him to be puzzled why only the eye sees and none of the other things in which images (*eidōla*) show (*emphainesthai*).

Text 8. Alexander, *De anima*, p. 48. 7–21 Bruns

We can also say it is not that the first air to be struck travels to the concave body and to the air trapped in it and returns back again from these to the same spot. If that happened, there would be a double circular movement, as the air beyond the struck air, which was itself [reading *auton*] in motion to the concave region, yielded and returned again. Rather, the first air to be struck will remain continuous and undivided because of the speed of the blow and shape the air beyond it with a similar blow, and this air will shape the air beyond it, and so the advance of the sound will be effected by continuous transmission up to the containing cavity. But when the last air beside the cavity is struck and shaped, it will be prevented by the cavity from transmitting the blow further forward, and will be pushed back again by the resistance of the solid, like a ball off something solid. Thus it will strike and shape once again the air on its nearer side, and this air will again shape the air before it.

And so the transmission of the blow and the sound will be brought to the same place from which it started at the beginning, just as people see themselves in the case of mirrors.

Text 9. Philoponus, *In De anima*, pp. 432. 32–433. 11; 438. 6–15 Hayduck

And yet the distinctive character of touch is not destroyed, for the medium itself is acted on and becomes matter for the heat, cold, fluidity, or dryness, and so also does the organ in company with it, which was not the case with the other senses, for they received only the activities (*energeiai*) of the perceptibles. But we must recognize that not even the organ of touch is acted upon by every sense, for when it grasps heavy and light, viscous and crumbly, rough and smooth, the flesh does not become like that, but receives the forms of those qualities only cognitively (*gnōstikōs*). But since, as has often been said, every body is constituted from the mixture of fluid, dry, hot, and cold, because of this, when it is affected by these qualities, as sense it grasps them and recognizes (*ginōskei*) them, but as a natural body it is affected materially (*hulikōs*) by them. It can be concluded that these are the only two contrary pairs from which a natural body is constituted. For only these act on the organs which they affect and come in their essence (*ousiōdōs*) to be in them, whereas weight and lightness, despite accompanying every body (for every created body is heavy or light), do not for all that convert the flesh into their own distinctive likeness (*idiotēs*), as do heat, fluidity, cold, and dryness.

Sense is not affected by the combination of matter and form, but only by the form, as wax is affected by the seal. Nor is it affected *as* a combination, for the organ does not become coloured or odorous, but is affected only in respect of its form, I mean the perceptive capacity itself. The body does suffer the effect of heat, and the sense of touch suffers, but not the same effect. The sense is affected cognitively (*gnōstikōs*), and only by the form of the hot thing, whereas the organ, the flesh, as matter, is affected as a combination, becoming a subject for the heat to inhere in, and being affected as a whole by the heating agent as a whole.

Text 10. Philoponus, *In De anima*, pp. 334. 38–336. 3 Hayduck

The philosopher Aristotle replied to this that the activities (*energeiai*) do not travel to our eyes, but that quite generally the whole air is filled with all the objects of vision. But that is even more problematic and strange. For first, the original problem remains: if all the air alike is filled with showings (*emphaseis*) of the objects of vision, how do we judge distances? For things near and far ought to look alike. Even the most distant things ought not to escape our senses, if the whole of the air is filled with all the showings. Perhaps he could

252

reply that our hypothesis about activities is the same as theirs about the travel of vision: just as they say that vision weakens when it goes out a long way, and that this is why we do not see distant things, so we say that the activities weaken when they go a good distance. But what can he say to the next question? If all the air is filled with showings, what use is it to assume the idea that the activities move in straight lines? We ought rather to see things, including near things and indeed all that we are capable of seeing, wherever we look, once the air is filled with showings. So why do we not see the heavens and all visible things without gazing towards them? Yet we can invoke evident facts in support of Aristotle's view [that seeing depends not on vision travelling out, but on activities].

335. 14 [Attempted solution]. We see that, when a beam of sunlight falls through a glass that is coloured red or some such colour, the air remains unaffected (*apathēs*) and lets through the colour and outline of the glass, until they make contact with a solid body, and colour and outline finally wipe off (*enapomattesthai*) on to that solid. It really is remarkable to see: for if you gaze at the air through which the beam passes, you see it unaffected by the colour and outline of the glass, but colour and outline are seen on the solid body at which the beam finishes up. And you must not explain it by a reflection of the vision as it reaches that point, for this sort of thing happens not only on smooth surfaces, but also on wool, if that is what the beam falls on, or on a cloak, or on sand, or on anything, even when your vision is arbitrarily situated, so that there could be no reflection from that surface to the glass. It is clear from this that the activities of what we see really do go through the air without affecting it (*apathōs*), arrive at the sense-organ, and, since this is a solid body, imprint (*entupoun*) there the colours and shapes of the things seen. Hence the organ is affected (*paschein*) by them, and the discrimination of them passes through to the sense-faculty.

335. 30 [Caveat]. But it can be replied that we do not find the same thing happening in the case of what we see as in the case of our model. For the phenomenon described does not happen unless a beam falls on something after passing through the glass, whereas we see things even when no beam falls on them directly from the sun. And besides in the case of the glass the colour appears in anything on which the beam falls, whereas there is no appearance (*phantasia*) of this kind in the case of things that we see. For they evidently do not act on other bodies, even if a beam passes through them. So what happens in the case of the model is different from the activity of what we see, and in general from our apprehension of it.

Text 11. Philoponus, *In De anima*, pp. 413. 4–12; 416. 30–4 Hayduck

Thus at least it was shown in the *Meteorology* that although the thunder occurs first, we apprehend it after, and although the lightning occurs later, we apprehend it first, both because hearing is more physical (*pachumeresteron*) and because the motion of light is quick (*kinēsis oxeia*). So too with rowing, we see the oar-handle lifted first and then perceive the sound. Similarly smell, being more corporeal (*sōmatoeidestera*) than hearing, needs more time for apprehending, even if the object of smell is quite close, while the air is affected and reaches the nostrils, so that the quality may more speedily reach the organ itself.

Again with the other senses the air itself has to be affected materially, in order that so the sense may be affected. For example, it must become fragrant or sonorous, but with sight it is not so, for the air is not coloured. And take the fact that sight does not operate without light, but the other senses do. There is no need then for the same things to happen with all the senses.

Text 12. Philoponus, *In De anima*, p. 413. 9–12 Hayduck

Similarly smell, being more corporeal (*sōmatoeidestera*) than hearing, needs more time to grasp its object, even if it is quite close. It needs time for the affected (*pathōn*) air to get through to the nostrils (*muktēres*) in order that the quality (*pathos*) may more quickly get through to the sense-organ (*aisthētērion*).

Text 13. Philoponus, *In De anima*, pp. 391. 11–29; 392. 3–19 Hayduck

The following problem might be raised. If smell apprehends through a medium, air or water, why does one odour overpower another? Often a fragrant odour supervenes on a bad one and overpowers it or vice versa, which ought not to happen if the air transmitted odours, and it was not the smellable vapours themselves that came to the organ, just as the air transmits all colours, and never does the activity of, say, white or of any other colour, black for example, overpower another. That is because it is not the colours themselves that are produced in the air, but their activities (*energeiai*). That is what ought to happen with odours too, if the air transmitted only their activities and not actual vapours which are physical bodies. Again the same problem is intensified by the following, I mean the problem that sense does not apprehend the object of smell through a medium, but the object of smell itself comes to the organ: we apprehend incense precisely when it is placed on a fire and dissolved into vapour. The smoke is seen quite evidently rising and coming towards us. And indeed when we want to apprehend the odour more quickly, we waft the smoke to our nose with our hands. So evidently some bodily effluence arises from the fragrant bodies themselves, and the air does not transmit their activities, as with colours and sounds.

We reply that there do indeed occur fine effluences of bodies from fragrant things and especially from burning incense. And for that reason, when they

254

are produced in the air, the greater and that which has the more vigorous odour overcomes the lesser. For even with sounds, where there is no effluence of bodies, the louder sound overpowers the softer, and the very brilliant over-powers the less brilliant. But even if some effluence does occur, it does not itself occur in the organ and bring about apprehension. Rather, a medium, either water or air, is needed, which transmits the activities of the objects of smell. For how do water animals smell what is above the surface of the water? It is not plausible that this effluence goes downwards through the water. It will rather go upwards, if it is vaporous or smoky as Aristotle says next. But as it is, crocodiles smell flesh suspended above the surface of the water. And it is clear from the case of those which hunt by night that they pursue it not by sight, but by smell. Vultures too perceive dead bodies from tens of thousands of distances away, and surely effluences do not travel from the bodies as far as that.

Text 14. Avicenna, *Shifā'*, in *Avicenna Latinus, Liber de Anima*, vol. i, pt. 2, ch. 2, pp. 115. 73–116. 81; 116. 84–7; 118. 6–10

If human nature, by virtue of what it is, had this or that fixed mode of quantity, quality, whereabouts, or posture (*quanti et qualis et ubi et situs*), then by virtue of what human nature is, each man ought to be like every other in these inten-tions (*intentiones*). And if human nature, by virtue of what it is, had some other mode of quantity, quality, whereabouts, or posture, then all men should be alike in that mode. So the human form does not need of its essence to have those accidents (*accidentia*) which are its regular accidents, but is on account of matter possessed in company with those accidents.

Sight needs these accidents when it apprehends form, because it does not abstract form from matter with a true abstraction. Matter must be present if this form is to be apprehended in the matter.

But the estimative faculty scarcely transcends this level of abstraction, since it apprehends material intentions (*intentiones materiales*) which are not in their matter, although accidentally they are in matter, because shape, colour, posture (*figura et color et situs*), and such like are things which can be possessed only by corporeal matter.

Text 15. Averroes, *Epitome of* Parva Naturalia, pp. 29. 15–30. 28; •31. 45–32. 49 Shields and Blumberg

The account of those who say that the forms of sense-objects are impressed in the soul with a corporeal impression is refuted by the fact that the soul receives the forms of contraries simultaneously. And this is found not only in the soul, but in the medium. For it is evident that the observer receives contraries, white and black. And another sign that colours do not exist in the *pupilla* with a corporeal, but rather with a spiritual, existence is the observed fact that the largest bodies are comprehended by sight through the *pupilla*, small though it is, to such an extent that it comprehends the hemisphere of the cosmos. And on that account it is said that those senses do not comprehend the intentions (*intentiones*) of sense-objects except as abstracted from matter. For they do not grasp the intention of colour except as abstracted from matter. And the same goes for the sense of smell and the sense for flavour and the other senses for other sense-objects.

The existence of forms in the medium has a manner intermediate between spiritual and corporeal. For forms outside the soul have a purely corporeal existence, within the soul a purely spiritual one, and in the medium one intermediate between spiritual and corporeal, where by 'medium' I here mean the sense-organs and what is external to sense.

Text 16. Averroes, *Long Comm. in De anima*, 2. 97, p. 278. 68–77 Crawford

But it is evident that the being of colour is more spiritual than the being of odour, for winds are seen to bring up odours. Indeed, this is why it was thought that odour was a body. But in this context the same is true of colour as of sound. For sound is produced by a disturbance in the air, but is also impeded by winds. Yet it does not follow from that that it is a body. It is as if it is necesssary therefore in the case of the two disturbances of sound and odour, when they have come to be in the air, that there should not be movements there in the air in one direction and not another.

Text 17. Albert, *De anima*, 2. 3. 6, v. 242^b Borgnet

Intentional and spiritual being does not have the same intrinsic character in the case of different senses. For one sense-object is much more spiritual than another, since one affects both medium and organ, acting on it with material being, as happens with the objects of touch. And for those objects which have the same medium, as do things visible, audible, and smellable, the medium does not have one and the same nature as a medium, but different natures, as we shall go on to show. And the being which they have in the medium itself is not of one single intrinsic character, because the being of colour is more spiritual than that of sound in the medium, and again that of sound in the medium more spiritual than that of odour. And that is why the wind does not carry colours away or bring them up, but does dull sounds, carrying them partially, but not wholly, away. Odours, however, it both brings up and carries away wholly, as Avicenna [Averroes?] says.

IV

Text 18. Albert, *De anima*, 2. 3. 6, v. 241ᵃ Borgnet

If colour were in the air as in a coloured thing we ought to see the air coloured and the eye coloured by the colour it receives. And we see the opposite of this. So in abstraction it exists with a different being from that which it has in its own proper matter.

Text 19. Albert, *De anima*, 2. 4. 3, v. 297ᵇ Borgnet

The sense-objects are not things, as we have said, but certain intentions of things, and especially in the case of sight. But in hearing sound has material being in the air, and spiritual being through echo (*reflexio*). Odour on the other hand has intentional being in the case of a distant object (*in remoto*) and some (*de*) material being in the case of a near one (*in propinquo*).

Text 20. Albert, *De anima*, 2. 3. 25. v. 278ᵇ Borgnet

Since vapour is spiritual, just like a medium, sometimes it serves in place of a medium, and in the case of smell is carried up to the organ of smell. (The matter of odour is a smoky vapour only in the medium, not in the odoriferous object.) When it [the odour] reaches our smell, it does not act on it by way of material being, but by way of the intentional being which it has in it [the medium], thanks to its being a medium, and not thanks to its being the subject that has the odour by way of material being.

Text 21. Albert, *De anima*, 2. 3. 19, in *Opera Omnia* (Cologne edn.), vii/1. 127. 28–128. 1 Stroick

So it seems that we must say that broad circles coming from opposite directions touch each other in a part which is virtually a point, and there one compresses the other. But in other parts the arcs do not touch or compress each other, and in those parts the shape (*configuratio*) of the sound survives, and from them it is reconstituted in the adjacent air where the circle was broken by the opposing circle meeting it. For the air becomes resonant not by repetition, but by echo (*reflexio*), as we said above. For the production of sound is made easy by the fact that sound exists in some of the air only by way of intention (*per intentionem*), as we said above.

Text 22. Thomas Aquinas, *In De anima*, sects. 418, 493.

The greater spirituality of the sense of sight is made evident secondly by the type of change involved in it. For in no other sense is there a spiritual change

IV

without a natural one too. By a natural change I mean the way in which quality is received with natural being in something acted on, as when something is cooled, or warmed, or moved. A spiritual change by contrast is of the kind in which a species is received in the sense-organ or medium in the manner of an intention, and not of a natural form. For the perceptible species is not received in the sense with the same being as it has in the perceptible object. It is evident that in touch and in taste, which is a kind of touch, a natural change is produced. For something is heated or cooled by contact with the hot or cold, and it is not a spiritual change alone that is produced. Similarly the change induced by odour is accompanied by (*fit cum*) a certain smoky vapour, and the change induced by sound is accompanied by motion. But in the change of sight there is only a spiritual change. It is evident from this that sight is the most spiritual of all the senses and next after that hearing.

The reason for this difference of opinion seems to be that the early thinkers had no theory or observation concerning the spiritual change of a medium, but only concerning its natural change. For the other senses a certain natural change is evident in the medium, but not for sight. For it is clear that sounds or odours are brought to us by the wind or impeded, but colours not at all. It is also clear that the species of contrary colours are brought to our sight through the same part of the air, as when two people use the same air as a medium and one sees white, the other black, existing together in the same air. That does not happen in the case of smell, for contrary odours are found to impede each other even in the medium.

Text 23. Thomas Aquinas, *In De anima*, sect. 494

But it is clear that this cannot happen in smell, for when the odour of a corpse is sensed by vultures up to fifty miles or further it would be impossible for any bodily vapour from the corpse to be diffused such a long distance, especially as the object of sense changes the medium for an equal distance on all sides, unless it is prevented. It would not be enough to fill so great a space, even if the whole corpse were resolved into smoky vapour, since there is a fixed limit to the rarefaction to which a natural body can attain, namely that of fire. Still less when the corpse does not appear to be sensibly changed by odour of this type.

Text 24. Thomas Aquinas, *In De anima*, sect. 495

So we must say that a smoky vapour can indeed be released from the object of smell. But it does not reach as far as the terminus where odour is perceived. Rather, the medium is changed spiritually beyond the point where the said vapour can reach.

Text 25. Roger Bacon, *Opus maius*, ii. 409–10 Bridges

And when a beam passes through the medium of strongly coloured glass, or crystal, or fabric, there appears to us in the darkness next to the ray a colour like that of the well-coloured body. That colour on the opaque surface is called a likeness (*similitudo*) and *species* of the colour in the strongly coloured body through which the beam passes. It is called a likeness and image (*imago*) with reference to the thing that generates it, to which it is assimilated and which it copies. It is called a *species* with reference to sense and intellect, in accordance with the usage of Aristotle and the physicists, because Aristotle says in the second book of the *De anima* that sense in every case receives the *species* of perceptible things, and in the third book he says that intellect is the place of *species*. It is called a reflexion (*idolum*) with reference to mirrors, because we often have to do with it in that way. It is called a phantasm (*phantasma*) and replica (*simulacrum*) in dream-appearances, because those *species* penetrate the senses as far as the inner parts of the soul and appear in dreams as if they were the things of which they are *species*, because they are assimilated to those things, and the soul is not so capable of discriminating in sleep as when we are awake, and so is deceived and judges on account of the likeness that the *species* are the things themselves of which they are *species*. It is called a form (*forma*) in the usage of Alhazen, the author of the popular *Perspective*. It is called an intention (*intentio*) in the common usage of physicists, because of the weakness of its being with reference to the thing itself which declares that it is not truly a thing, but rather the intention of a thing, that is, a likeness.

Text 26. William of Ockham, *Reportatio* or *Quaestiones in Sent.*, in *Theological Works* (St Bonaventure, NY), vi. 59–60; 61; 141–2

First it is proved that the visible, that is, colour, causes something not of a different nature, but of the same nature; that is, colour in the object causes *colour* in the medium, even if less perfect colour (*licet imperfectior*). For multiplicity is not to be postulated unnecessarily, and there is no evident necessity to postulate 'species' of the kind mentioned above in the medium differing in nature from the objects that cause them.

Secondly, I say that something of the same nature as the object is produced in the medium. This is proved by observation of a beam passing through red or green glass. As was evident above, the beam passing through the glass produces a true colour on the wall opposite, with the colour in the glass mediating as a mediating partial cause. And that colour is of the same kind as the red colour in the glass.

Similarly it should be noted that colour is assumed to be caused in the medium not on account of vision, that is, on the supposition that it is a partial cause of the act of seeing—and that when it exists in a lower degree (*in gradu remisso*)—but on the basis of experience, because it is plain to the senses that when a beam travels through a transparent body, colour is produced on the side facing it, and that colour, like colour in a solid body, can partially cause an act of seeing. But that colour is not postulated to permit the seeing of some other colour, since it impedes the seeing of any other colour, as is plain to the senses.

*Addenda

Note 2: Gül Russell, 'The emergence of physiological optics', in R. Rashed and R. Morelon, eds, *The Encyclopedia of the History of Arabic Sciences*, Routledge, London 1996, pp. 672-716.

Note 58: Victor Caston has now interestingly argued that the Stoic *ennoêma* was already an intentional object, and that the use of *intentio* goes back, via Augustine, to Stoic *enteinein* (stretch out) in the theory of vision: 'Connecting traditions: Augustine and the Greeks on intentionality', in Dominic Perler, ed., *Ancient and Medieval Theories of Intentionality*, Brill, Leiden 2001, pp. 26–8, 44–5.

V

Aristotle on Sensory Processes and Intentionality.
A Reply to Myles Burnyeat*

On the Soul II, 5

I appreciate Myles Burnyeat's courtesy in expressing his disagreement with my idea that the material cause of seeing is the coloration of the eye jelly and that there are corresponding physiological occurrences as material cause for the exercise of the other four senses. He has now written not only his original paper "Is an Aristotelian philosophy of mind still credible? A draft",[1] but also two fresh explanations of his view.[2]

The case for my view was based on two different chapters, II, 11–12, starting towards the end of II, 11 and I will stand by everything I said about those chapters. So I am only considering here the question whether II, 5 and II, 7–8 express a different view. But I want to finish with a point about the whole perspective within which Aristotle writes *On the Soul*. This point will address Burnyeat's interpretation of *On the Soul* I, 1 in his first two papers and I believe it makes a positive difference to the case I earlier put about what Aristotle thinks.

My reaction to Burnyeat's two papers is different. On II, 7–8, I think the most crucial piece of evidence has not yet been brought into the discussion. On II, 5, however, I think his exposition is of the greatest value quite independently of what may be thought about our little debate. Let me mention one additional value. Suzanne Mansion thought the exposition of Aristotle's predecessors in *On the Soul*, Book 1, lacked the usual connexion with dilemmas and solutions to dilemmas found in other treatises of Aristotle.[3] Burnyeat's work on II, 5 shows that the connexion exists at least in II, 5. **[50]**

---

* Reply to Burnyeat [1992] and [1995]. This article was originally published in Dominik Perler, ed., *Ancient and Medieval Theories of Intentionality*, Leiden: Brill, 2001, pp. 49-61. The original page numbers are shown in square brackets within the text.

[1]   Burnyeat [1992].

[2]   One concerning Aristotle's *On the Soul* II, 7 and 8 appeared in its English version as "How much happens when Aristotle sees red and hears middle C? Remarks on *De Anima* 2.7–8", in Nussbaum & Rorty [1995]; the other is now published as "Aquinas on 'spiritual change' in perception," in Perler [2001].

[3]   Mansion [1961].

Much of the valuable material concerning II, 5, I believe, does not concern our debate. The crucial idea for that debate is that Aristotle holds that change is from opposite to opposite, with the proviso that intermediates can serve as opposites. The switch from possessing the perceptual faculty to using it is not a switch between opposites. That is why Aristotle says that the switch is not an ordinary kind of change.

This seems to me a very good idea. I think this reason might have motivated Aristotle in addition to the other reasons I had previously supposed to be motivating him. I shall come to these shortly. But let us for a moment go even further and suppose that it is the only reason motivating him. Even in that case, I would draw a different conclusion, that *On the Soul* II, 5 is neutral as regards our debate. For I take the clearly stated point that in discussing the idea that perception is some sort of change or qualitative change, Aristotle is on Burnyeat's interpretation discussing how perception is to be classified, not how it is constituted.

What follows from this point, I believe, is that for purposes of classifying perception, Aristotle has simply ignored physiology *pro tempore*. This in turn implies that perception might still stand in need of a physiological process as its material cause. And that physiological process might involve a change between opposites (e.g. between colourless and coloured in the eye jelly or between medium and warm temperature in the touch organ). The possibility is, on the interpretation in question, merely ignored, not denied.

In fact, we know Aristotle is not ruling out there being other necessary descriptions of what is going on and that they may involve opposites and may be descriptions of physical processes. An excellent example of the first is given by Burnyeat, in connexion with an earlier switch, the switch from being capable of acquiring knowledge to acquiring it. As is well pointed out, this switch can instead be characterised as a switch between opposites, from ignorance to knowledge.

The builder of II, 5, 417b9 provides an example of the other fact. Although the switch from possessing to using knowledge of house-building does not explicitly mention physical activity, we know that in Aristotle's view (I, 1, 403b3–7) it must involve the physical activity of arranging or causing to be arranged stones, bricks and timber to form a shelter.

There is another relevant fact. In concluding that perception is not an ordinary change of quality or undergoing of an effect, Aristotle **[51]** concentrates on only one aspect of perception, namely the switch to exercising perception. To perceive, of course, is not merely to switch to perceiving. But his point is that, if the switching is different, then perceiving will be different at least in respect of the initial switching and he does not need to show more. This confirms that Aristotle is simply looking for some relevant difference in perceiving. He is not examining every aspect and description of perceiving in the hope of showing that it does not need at any point to involve more familiar kinds of change or state, including physiological ones. If I am right, I can afford to welcome Burnyeat's interpretation. Let me now outline what mine has hitherto been.

I previously took it that in II, 5 Aristotle was referring to the physiological process that is involved in two switches, the switch from not having to acquiring the power to perceive and know, and the switch to exercising those powers. The physiological processes could be called changes of quality or undergoings of effects, if you liked, but only ones of a different kind from the normal. The differences mentioned at II, 5, 417b2–16 apply some to one switch some to the other. There is nothing original about my interpretation of their meaning. So far as I know, I am merely collecting what I thought were the best suggestions from the previous secondary literature before Burnyeat's paper. Thus the switch is a switch towards the thing's own nature (*physis*). It preserves, rather than destroys what was there before (*sôtêria* versus *phthora*). In saying it is a development into its own self (*eis hauto*), Aristotle may be contrasting the etymological root of his word for qualitative change, *alloiôsis*, which etymologically derives from the idea of becoming other (*allo*) with the idea of remaining the selfsame (*hauto*). The *hexis* arrived at is contrasted not only with *diathesis* as a stable rather than a temporary phenomenon, but also with *sterêsis*, and although *sterêsis* sometimes means no more than privation, as in the relevant discussion in Aristotle's *Physics* I, 9, it here reminds you that an ordinary change could legitimately be seen as depriving you of what you had before, whereas the switch now in question is the reverse of a deprivation.

Burnyeat and I might even combine our ideas. Perhaps Aristotle has in mind both my points and his. But even if he had in mind only Burnyeat's excellent point, I still think that result is neutral. I now want to return to II, 7, where I do prefer an interpretation different from Burnyeat's. **[52]**

On the Soul II, 7

The crucial passage for our purposes, I believe, is in Aristotle *De Sensu*, 3 at 439a18–b18.[4] There Aristotle explains the difference between alien colour

---

[4]   I am drawing on an unpublished translation and commentary I wrote in 1968–1969 on most of *De Sensu*, chs. 3–7. The most interesting findings, as I thought, have already appeared in articles, but not this one.

received by the transparent and a thing's own colour (*idion*, 439b13). His example is of the apparent colours taken on by the sea. The eye jelly is certainly not going to work in exactly the same way, much less the medium of vision. Nonetheless, I believe we can learn from this example the parameters within which the eye jelly is likely to work.

A body's own colour, Aristotle here says, is a boundary, but not the boundary of the body. Rather, every body is a blend of four elements, of which air and water at least are transparent. So every body contains transparency, albeit in too low a proportion for us normally to see through the body. The body's own colour is the boundary of the transparent within it, a boundary coincident with its own boundary. Moreover the shade of colour is a function of the proportion of earth at that boundary, which makes it tend towards dark or black, and of fire, which makes it tend towards bright or white. To the acclaim of Goethe, who saw Aristotle as the painter's poet as against the physicist Newton, Aristotle makes intermediate colours to be ratios of dark and bright.[5] This is explained in the sequel, 439b18 to the end of the chapter, esp. 440a31–b23.

The apparent colours taken on by the sea do not have the same material basis, yet they look the same. They are not, for example mere encodings or recipes for colour. In Aristotle's terms, they share the formal cause of colour because they can excite the actually transparent medium in the relevant way, a way which leads eventually to our seeing them. But they do not fully share the material cause of a body's own colour. For although resident in the body's transparency (and Aristotle insists on this in order to argue that transparency is the seat of colour in the standard cases too), they are not functions of the proportion of fire and earth within that transparency at its boundary, but depend on the colour of something else. **[53]**

This throws light on what I meant by my interpretation according to which the eye jelly takes on colour patches for Aristotle in the course of perception quite literally. It does not do so by the same mechanism as that by which the sea takes on colour, which depends on distance of viewing. But it has this much in common. It lacks the material basis of a body's own colour, but it looks the way a body's own colour looks, as opposed to being, for example, a mere encodement, and it could excite the transparent medium in such a way as to permit an ophthalmologist to see it. It thus fits the formal cause definition of colour. This is the sense in which the coloration is literal. I should like to claim the advantage of drawing on the example and doctrine

---

[5]   As explained in my [1972].

provided by Aristotle himself rather than supplying one of my own. At the same time, like Burnyeat in his paper on *On the Soul* II, 5, I look for it not in the chapter we started with, but in another work explicitly said by Aristotle to be connected. Of course the medium in the case of vision obviously does not undergo even this coloration, if we set aside curious views about menstruation in *On Dreams*, 2.

The *De Sensu* passage explains several further points, I believe, in Aristotle's *On the Soul*. It explains, I think, the remark discussed by Burnyeat in 1995 (on p. 425) from *On the Soul*, 418b4–6, that the transparent is visible not strictly speaking in itself but because of the colour of something else. Water is colourless. The sea borrows its colours and that is why we see it, rather than merely seeing through it.

I think the passage also helps to explain why Aristotle says at *On the Soul* III, 2, 425b22–23 merely that there is a way in which that which sees (I take him to mean the eye) is coloured. The main reason for this cautious formulation is that he has been telling us in II, 7, 418b26–30 that the organ of sight is colourless. But this is, on my interpretation, so that it may take on alien colours during perception. The other reason will not be revealed to us until we read *De Sensu*, 3, but it is that the colours taken on are indeed alien.

I have one caveat about the meaning of the doctrine in *On the Soul* III, 2, 425b26–426a6 that colour and sound in their full actuality are identical with seeing and hearing respectively. I take this to be another doctrine that makes no comment on physiology and is therefore neutral. A different impression could be created if it said that the *effect* (p. 428) of colour on the eye is seeing. This would be too obvious to need saying at such length, unless it were the doctrine that the *only* effect of colour on the eye is seeing, with the further [54] implication that that seeing includes no necessary physiological process. But in fact the analogy is, as rightly said, with Aristotle's idea in *Physics* III, 3. There he argues that although teaching does not have the same definition as learning, if you are counting how many processes are going on when someone is learning from someone who is actively teaching, you should only count one. By parity of reasoning, Aristotle is talking in our passage about colour which is fully active, not about the *effect* of colour, being identical with active seeing.

On the Soul II, 8

I should be content if the physical process in the case of sound were a wave motion in both the ear and the intervening medium. In fact, I think the evidence is rather different. But first let me ask why Burnyeat should want it to be a wave motion. Referring back to the 1995 paper he explains he has taken it that what happens in the organ is the same as what happens in the medium between organ and thing sensed. I do not believe Aristotle ever says this and I do not think he believes it in the case of vision, in which I take the eye jelly to go coloured, but the medium not. However, if sameness were required, then the possibility of dispensing with an ordinary change in the eye would imply the same possibility for the medium. And the apparent advantage of a wave motion in the medium is that it is not an ordinary change. But is it for reasons relevant to II, 5 that it is not an ordinary change?

It is not an ordinary change, because elsewhere, in the *Physics*, Aristotle recognises as movement properly so called only the movement of a body and does not consider the movement of a wave, III, 1, 200b3–201a3; V, 2, 226a32–b1. Still, the process might be an ordinary one by all the criteria we have identified as relevant in *On the Soul* II, 5. It involves a shift between opposite termini as much, or as little, as ordinary movement does. It may destroy the previous state of the air and deprive air of that, without bringing air to a more stable and natural state more representative of its true self. On my view of II, 5, none of this matters, because what is required in II, 5 to be different from ordinary change is not the process in the ear, but the switch from that process being potential to its being actual.

As I say, I believe that if Burnyeat allows that a wave motion **[55]** might be required not only in the medium of hearing, but also in the ear, he would grant everything I had previously asked for, since I did not explicitly address this particular issue. But as it happens, I think that Aristotle asks for more, at any rate as regards the medium.

On the one hand, Aristotle does seem to speak, not in the context of sound, of a wave motion passing through air or water in his treatment of dreams and prophecy through dreams, *On Dreams*, 2, 459a28–b5; *Div.*, 464a6–11. But in his treatment of echo at *On the Soul* II, 8, 419b25–7, he says it is the air which is pushed away again like a ball, which reads as if the air does the travelling, not a wave through it. Similarly at *De Sensu*, 6, 446b9, speaking of the distortion of utterances en route to listeners, he speaks of the air itself travelling towards us. *Pheresthai* is the verb for travelling. He could perfectly well have said that the air merely vibrated if he had wanted to describe instead a wave (*seiesthai*).

The discussion is very explicit. At 446b28, Aristotle repeats the reference to travel (*phora*), and refuses to allow us to treat sound, which is an example of *phora*, as like the case of light or other cases of qualitative change such as a pond's freezing over. The discussion of the instantaneous spreading of light or ice does not help. Among qualities defining the senses, only light can spread instantaneously, not half before whole (447a9–10). He admits parenthetically, although it is not his main point, that the instantaneous freezing of the water in a pond may occur part by part, if the pond is large. I do not see any clear sign that such a possibility is also canvassed for odour or any other sensible quality. If it were canvassed, it would not provide a standard example of wave motion, since that does not involve instantaneity. And in any case it is denied for sound.

My conclusion is that Aristotle has not thought of extending the idea of wave motion to sound.

The case of hearing is unlike the case of seeing, because the motions of air Aristotle describes in the two passages mentioned clearly take place in the intervening medium, whether or not they also take place in the ear. But in any case it would be hard to deny that the medium becomes noisy before we hear and smelly before we exercise smell, since it is obvious that it does so. If so, we have the phenomenon I mentioned in connexion with II, 5. For even if it had been possible to show that Aristotle postulated for the medium of sound something that was not an ordinary change, we should still **[56]** have found it accompanied by the ordinary change of going noisy (cf. smelly). In terms of *De Sensu*, 6, 446b22, Aristotle denies that fragments of the bell or incense have to reach you, not that the noise has to.

On the Soul, I, 1

Although I shall not repeat my positive evidence from II, 11–12 for the physiological process taking the form, for example, of coloration of the eye jelly, Burnyeat has kindly drawn my attention to footnote 38 of his 1995 paper, in which he says something important about the evidence on whether there is any physiological process at all. I had taken the concluding part of I, 1, at 403a3–b19, as evidence for that.

His point turns on a distinction between acting (*erga, poiein*) and undergoing (*pathê, pathêmata, paskhein*). It is only what the soul undergoes, Burnyeat suggests, that is said to have a physiological process as its material cause, and we need not take this to include sense perception. I will give my reasons for not taking I, 1 this way.

Acting versus undergoing does not play any big theoretical role in Aristotle's account of sense perception, as it does, for example in that of the Neoplatonists, who make sense perception active. It is not the same distinction as that in II, 5 between undergoing and what is not an ordinary undergoing.[6] Admittedly, at I, 1, 402b12–13, perceiving is treated as an act (*ergon*), in contrast to the perception faculty, which is treated as part of the soul. But that contrast, act versus part, is different, and shows very little, since as Victor Caston points out to me, even the assimilating of food can be treated as an activity (*energeia, praxis*) in contrast to a capacity of the soul at II, 4, 418a18–22. As Burnyeat shows in his paper on II, 5, Aristotle takes the most obvious classification of perception at *On the Soul* I, 5, 410a25–26; II, 5, 416b33–35, to be as an undergoing, until he explains, as something not obvious, and certainly not yet obvious in I, 1, that it is not the ordinary kind of undergoing. Our contrast in **[57]** I, 1 between acting and undergoing on the part of the soul seems to be used very casually. Most of the time in the concluding section of I, 1, Aristotle talks simply about what the soul undergoes (*pathê*). The most obvious reason for introducing the disjunction and including *acts* at 403a7 and 10 is that Aristotle is making a special point there about thinking, not perceiving, and thinking might plausibly be thought of as an acting more than an undergoing.

Perception is here treated on a par with the emotions. It is listed alongside anger, daring and desiring at 403a7 and, unlike thinking, is not signalled as being any kind of possible exception. Aristotle speaks of perceiving in general (*holôs*). Why "in general"? The most obvious reason would be to include all the functions of perception, including the common sense, imagination, memory and dreams. Even pleasure (*hêdesthai*) is treated later in *On the Soul* as a form of perception, III, 7, 431a10, so the same may well apply to joy (*khara*), one of the acknowledged *pathê* in our passage at I, 1, 403a18. The other emotions listed along with perception are sometimes (not always) treated as centrally involving *phantasia*, having things appear a certain way, and appearance is a function of sense perception, so it is not difficult for Aristotle to associate them with sense perception.

The discussion at 403a8–16 is about whether anything the soul does or undergoes could happen without any body at all. This is, incidentally, one of the signs that the discussion is not too closely related to II, 5, which does not consider this question. The only candidate considered for such separation from body is thinking. Perceiving never is. But the discussion which follows 403a16 is on the same subject, whether everything that happens with the soul is with a body (*meta sômatos*, 403a15 and 16–17). Some signs (*sêmeia*) are given of bodily involvement from the case of various emotions, 403a19–24.

---

[6]   When certain switches are described in II, 5 as not ordinary *pathê*, this is not on the grounds of their being cases of acting. Conversely, the switch to undergoing one of the *pathê* described in I, 1 such as loving or desiring could (in II, 5) well be denied the title *pathos*.

The emotions are a narrower group of *pathê*, selected as signs because their physiological connexions are apparent without special scientific knowledge. But the conclusion drawn in 403a24 is applied not just to the narrower group, but to *pathê* of the soul in general, that they are enmattered. If *pathê* had now to be taken in a narrower sense as applying only to emotions, such a restriction would be unannounced and, as we shall see, worse than unannounced. For the inference is drawn immediately, 403a25–b12, that the definitions of *pathê* of the soul must include the matter. The matter for anger is at first specified as 'such and such a body'. But this is then spelled out as a physiological process. We might speak of the **[58]** release of adrenalin, but Aristotle speaks of the boiling of the blood around the heart. We know that at least the more general functions of perception will turn out to stand in need of physiological processes, memory (*mnêmê*) at *On Memory*, 1, 450a32–b11, reminding oneself (*anamnêsis*) at *On Memory*, 2, 453a14–26, dreaming at *On Dreams*, throughout chapter 3. It would be amazing if Aristotle wanted to make an exception for the operation of the five senses and such an exception would have had to be announced and explained.

This may seem to leave in play the earlier suggestion about I, 1 made by Burnyeat in the first of his papers (1992). That suggestion was that the matter consists not in a physiological process, but merely in sense perception having to exist within an eye. Aristotle is telling us not that seeing requires the eye jelly to become coloured, but that it is simply a becoming aware of colour, but with a proviso, and this is the point about matter. It has to occur in, that is be dependent on, an eye.

But I think the same difficulty applies to this, so I should spell it out more. This is my point about perspective. The treatises of the *Parva Naturalia*, which include *On Memory* and *On Dreams*, are very closely connected with *On the Soul* and all these psychological works, as Burnyeat rightly stresses for *On the Soul*, are treated as part of the biological works. *On the Motion of Animals* also belongs in this group as part of the Biology. In these works, Aristotle finds that not only memory, reminding oneself, and dreaming stand in need of physiological processes, but also (*On the Motion of Animals*, chapters 6–10) desiring. Not only are the first three at least of these four classified as functions of sense perception, but all four are causally based on sense perception. In dreams, sense perception produces shaped eddies in the blood, which go down to the central sense organ in the heart. Incidentally, these eddies presumably do not display different colours as well as different shapes, so here there is room for the conjecture that some interpreters have made about the eye jelly, that colours are recorded only in coded form.

When we reach the central organ, we find that memory involves stamping an imprint of the previous *aisthêma* into bodily substances (blood or *pneuma*?), which risk being too fluid, so that they either fail to take the imprint well, or cause agitation when the effort to remind oneself and find the imprint stirs up the fluid.

The whole of *On Dreams*, chapter 1, and a substantial section of *On Memory*, chapter 1 (449b30–450a23), are devoted to showing that **[59]** these functions belong to the perceptual, not to the rational, part of the soul.

In the voluntary motion of animals, sense perception, on reporting attractive or dangerous things in the environment, causes a heating or cooling and hence an expansion or contraction of *pneuma*, which leads to limb movements towards or away.

Burnyeat and I are believers in the importance of the biological context of *On the Soul*. But I want to draw attention to one aspect of this, that the work fits into a whole programme of giving physiological processes as the material causes of mental *pathê*. Those of outlying sense functions are reserved for biological works other than *On the Soul*. In *On the Soul* itself, it is the physiological processes only for the five senses that we should expect to find. I would be astonished if Aristotle there suddenly dropped his interest in physiological process and even more astonished if he thought there were none, given that related sense functions have a physiological process and that sense perception provides the causal origin of the physiological processes he so lengthily describes in other biological works.

Fortunately, I believe there is no need to worry. For of course in my own view Aristotle's conception of the physiological processes required for sight and touch becomes inescapably clear, if not earlier, at least by *On the Soul* II, 11–12.

Intentionality

What has the foregoing to do with intentionality? Franz Brentano thought that the reception of form without matter in Aristotle's theory of perception expresses the idea that perception is directed to an intentional object.[7] And Burnyeat's interpretation opens the way to Brentano's view. I have instead understood the reception of form without matter in perception as a physiological process, for example that of the eye jelly taking on colour patches. And I have argued[8] that the people who converted the colour patches

---

[7]   Brentano [1973].
[8]   Sorabji [1991].

into intentional objects were the commentators on Aristotle who ran into problems about physical interference with the transmission of forms, if the transmission was construed in too physical a way. They thus slowly **[60]** transmuted Aristotle's colour patches into intentional objects in a tradition that eventually came to the attention of Brentano.

In *thinking*, as well as perceiving, the reception of form without matter has been construed in an intentionalist way.[9] But this is not made explicit by Aristotle. There is in any case a problem about Aristotle's thesis of the numerical identity of thinking with the intelligible. For the identity thesis is a general thesis about the activity of every agent and patient which is laid down in *Physics* III, 3, and applied in *On the Soul* to perceiving and perceptible qua acting on the perceiver at III, 2, and to thinking and intelligible qua active at III, 8. The thesis seems to presuppose that the intelligible, like the perceptible, is an agent acting on the cognitive faculties, in which case the question arises how such an agent can be an intentional object. The perceptible, acting as *efficient* cause could not be an intentional object, whereas the object of desire, acting as *final* cause, could be. But is the intelligible an agent as final or as efficient cause? Or does Aristotle change the direction of agency when he makes the active intellect the agent in *On the Soul* III, 5, so that intelligibles are after all not agents like perceptibles or objects of desire?

The commentators raised these questions. Already Theophrastus asked whether the active intellect or the intelligible is agent, *ap.* Themistium *in DA* 108,3–4. Alexander firmly replied, *DA* 88,24–89,8, that it is only qua intelligible that the active intellect can be described as agent. Ps–Alexander adds, *in Metaph.*, fr. 29, Freudenthal, that some intelligibles cannot be objects of desire, viz. evils. I agree with the commentators that intelligibles are best seen as efficient causes. For the identity with intellect in *On the Soul* III.8 is patterned on what is said about other efficient causes, the perceptibles of *On the Soul* III.2 and the teachers of *Physics* III.3.

I am more persuaded by Victor Caston's suggestion that Aristotle is alive to some of the problems which theories of intentionality address, and seeks to solve them by reference to a faculty of *phantasia* which avoids depending like the five senses on direct stimulation by existent objects.[10] Aristotle thus gets as far as treating *phantasia* as an intentional state, but not as far as treating its objects as intentional objects. I would conclude from the evidence that

[9]   E.g. Shields [1995].
[10]   Caston [1998].

Caston assembles **[61]** elsewhere[11] that it is above all the Stoics in the century after Aristotle who articulate the idea of intentional objects.

Bibliography

Brentano, F., *Psychology From an Empirical Standpoint*, London: Routledge 1973, translated from the German of 1924, first edition 1874.

Burnyeat, M., "Is an Aristotelian philosophy of mind still credible? A draft", in: Nussbaum & Rorty [1992 and 1995].

—, "How much happens when Aristotle sees red and hears middle C?" Remarks on *De Anima* 2.7–8", in: Nussbaum & Rorty [1995].

—, "Aquinas on 'spiritual change' in perception," in: Perler [2001].

Caston, V., "Towards a history of the problem of intentionality among the Greeks", *Proceedings of the Boston Area Colloquium in Ancient Philosophy* 9 (1993), 213–65.

—, "Aristotle on intentionality", *Philosophy and Phenomenological Research* 58 (1998), 249–98.

—, "Something and nothing: the Stoics on concepts and universals", in: *Oxford Studies in Ancient Philosophy* 17, Oxford: Clarendon Press 1999, 145–213.

Mansion, S., "Le role de l'exposé et de la critique des philosophies antérieurs chez Aristote", in: S. Mansion (ed.), *Aristote et les problèmes de méthode*, Paris: Nauwelaerts 1961.

Nussbaum, M. & A. Rorty (eds), *Essays on Aristotle's De Anima*, Oxford: Clarendon Press 1992 and 1995 (second edition).

Perler, D. (ed.), *Ancient and Medieval Theories of Intentionality*, Leiden: Brill 2001, pp. 129–53.

Shields, Ch., "Intentionality and isomorphism in Aristotle", *Proceedings of the Boston Area Colloquium in Ancient Philosophy* 11 (1995), 307–30.

Sorabji, R., "Aristotle, mathematics, and colour", *Classical Quarterly* NS 22 (1972), 293–308.

—, "From Aristotle to Brentano: the development of the concept of intentionality", in: *Oxford Studies in Ancient Philosophy*, suppl. vol., Oxford: Clarendon Press 1991, 227–59.

---

[11] Caston [1993]; cf. Caston [1999].

ARISTOTLE ON DEMARCATING
THE FIVE SENSES

I. Senses and Their Objects

IN THE *De Anima*, Book II, Chapter 6, Aristotle tells us that sensible qualities are related to the senses as *kath hauta*. In other words, one is defined by reference to the other.[1] I believe that Aristotle has no special interest in defining sense objects by reference to senses.[2] If he has not, then his point must be rather

---

[1] *D. A.* 418a8-25. For this sense of *Kath Hauta*, see *An. Post.* 73a34-b24. There are admittedly other senses. The following abbreviations are used in this paper:

An. Post.	*Posterior Analytics*
Phys.	*Physics*
G. & C.	*De Generatione et Corruptione*
D.A.	*De Anima*
D.S.	*De Sensu*
Som.	*De Somno*
Insom.	*De Insomniis*
Resp.	*De Respiratione*
H.A.	*Historia Animalium*
P.A.	*De Partibus Animalium*
Metaph.	*Metaphysics*

[2] If one looks at his definitions of color, light, sound, odor, flavor, hot, cold, fluid, dry, one will find that they very seldom mention the senses. (*D.A.* 418b9-10; 418b16-17, b20, 419a9-11, 420a8-9, a21-23, b11; *D.S.* 439a19-20, b11-12, 441b19-21, 443a7; *G. & C.* 329b26-32; *P.A.* 648a20-650a3.) Much less do the so-called common objects, properties perceptible by more than one sense, get defined by reference to the senses (e.g., unity: *Metaph.* 1015b16-1017a3, 1052a15-1053b8; change: *Phys.* 201a9-15). This is the more surprising, in view of the theory of actually functioning color at *D.A.* 425b26-426a26, which links color closely to sight.

Admittedly, the definitions of color and light bring in the notion of transparency. But the connection between transparency and sight is stressed only in the definition of light (not strictly a sense object at all) at 418b9-10. Here light is defined by reference to the idea that when the air or water around us is dark, it is only potentially seeable-through whereas when it is light, we can actually see through it.

Allowance should be made, of course, for Aristotle's purposes, which vary considerably in these different passages and which can influence the content of his definitions. But, nonetheless, it should not be supposed that he thinks the best or most scientific definition of sense objects, or the one that gives their essence, will mention the senses. The essence of color is stated at *D.A.* 419a9-11, without any very direct reference to sight.

VI

that the senses should be defined by reference to their objects. But the interpretation of *kath hauta* here may be controversial.[3] And we have no need to rest our case upon it, if we want to establish Aristotle's interest in defining senses by reference to sense objects.

That he wants to define (and in general to get clear about) the senses by reference to their objects is evident, if we consider the structure of the *De Anima*. Here Aristotle sets out to give an account of the soul. It emerges by Book II, Chapter 3,[4] that if one wants to give an account of the soul suitable for a specialized treatise, and not merely an account in very general terms, one should describe one by one the powers of which the soul consists; the power to think, the power to perceive, the power to absorb nutrition, and so on. And in the next chapter,[5] it turns out that in order to say what one of these powers is—for example, the power to perceive— one should first say what the corresponding activity is—the act of perceiving. That in turn requires that one should first study the object of the activity—for example, the objects of the senses. This point is made in Chapter 4, and in Chapter 6 of Book II.[6] It is this latter chapter which contains the statement that sensible qualities are related to the senses as *kath hauta*. And though this statement, taken on its own, may be ambiguous, the closing sentence of the chapter is not. It says that qualities like color, which are perceived by only one sense, the so-called *proper* objects of the senses, are the things to which the very being of each sense is naturally related.[7] It is already clear that Aristotle means to analyze the senses by reference to their objects, and the next five

---

[3] In a valuable series of publications, Professor Hamlyn has argued that the point is that sense objects must be defined by reference to senses, either instead of, or as well as, the other way round. ("Aristotle's account of Aesthesis in the *De Anima*," *Classical Quarterly* [1959], *passim;* "*Koine Aesthesis*," *Monist* [1968], esp. p. 205; "Seeing Things as They Are," Inaugural Lecture, Birkbeck College, 1965, esp. p. 12; *Aristotle's De Anima, Books II and III*, Clarendon Aristotle Series (Oxford, 1968), esp. pp. 105, 108, 117.

[4] 415a12-13.

[5] II.4, 415a14-20.

[6] 415a20-22; 418a7-8. It had already been mentioned as a possibility in I.1, 402b14-16.

[7] 418a24-25. Compare the statement at *Metaph.* 1021a29-b3, that sight is a relative term, related to color or to something like color.

56

chapters (II, 7-11) carry out the analysis, each chapter being devoted to one of the five senses. The analysis gives prominence to the sense objects throughout. The account of vision, for example, begins with an investigation of its object.[8] And when the account of the five senses is complete, and we move on to Book III, we there get our first, and on some views our only, conception of what the so-called *common* sense is, from hearing about its objects, motion, rest, shape, magnitude, number, unity.[9]

We should expect this pattern to be continued in the other psychological treatises. For whatever the date at which they were first drafted, the treatises included in the so-called *Parva Naturalia* are, in their final form, so presented that they will read as a continuation of the *De Anima*. Sure enough, we do find there the same tendency to define, distinguish, and identify sensory powers by reference to their objects. Thus, for example, in the *De Sensu* and *De Somno* Aristotle speaks of a central sense faculty which is responsible for various functions that a single sense could not perform on its own. This central sense faculty has a certain unity because it is dependent on a single bodily organ, the heart. But it differs in its being and in its definition, says Aristotle, according to the different *objects* that it perceives.[10]

Another example of the importance of sense objects for identifying senses is to be found in Aristotle's insistence that since fish and other animals perceive odor, we must allow that they exercise smell.[11] Evidently, the perception of odor is to be counted as smell, in spite of considerable differences in the mechanism involved. For the medium through which water animals perceive odor is not air, as it is for us, but water.[12] Correspondingly, the organ they use for perceiving odor contains water, in Aristotle's view, not air.[13] Nor is the organ used at all like our nostrils in structure. Fish use their gills, dolphins their blowhole, and insects the middle part of their body, according to Aristotle.[14] And neither fish nor insects,

---

[8] 418*a*26.
[9] 425*a*14-30.
[10] *D.S.* 449*a*16-20; *Som.* 455*a*21-22.
[11] *D.S.* 444*b*10, *b*15, *b*16; *D.A.* 421*b*21.
[12] *D.S.* 442*b*29-443*a*3; *D.A.* 421*b*9-13.
[13] *D.A.* 425*a*5.
[14] *P.A.* 659*b*14-19.

he says, inhale when perceiving odor.[15] In spite of these differences, their perception of odor is to be counted as smelling.[16] Similarly, the perception of sound is to be counted as hearing, and the perception of flavor as tasting, in spite of large differences in the mechanism involved.[17]

We have been arguing that Aristotle puts considerable stress on the sense objects in defining, distinguishing, and identifying the senses. In this, he shows himself faithful to a claim that Plato makes in the *Republic*.[18] For before asserting that knowledge and opinion have different objects, Plato maintains that in general different capacities have different objects, and different objects imply different capacities. Sight and hearing are adduced as examples of capacities.

We must not, however, exaggerate the unity of the passages cited from Aristotle. We should distinguish several different things he wants to do. (*i*) Firstly, he wants to get clear about what sight is, what hearing is, and so on, by means of a protracted discussion. For this purpose, the sense objects are important. And one needs to consider them in detail, not merely to mention them. However, it is not only the sense objects that one needs to investigate. One should also know, for example, how the sense objects interact with the environment, so as to affect the sense organs, and what the process in the sense organs is (*D.A.* II, 7-12).

(*ii*) Different from a protracted discussion is a definition. Assuming Aristotle had not abandoned the scientific method described in the *Posterior Analytics*, he would have hoped eventually

---

[15] *D.S.* 443a4-6, 444b15-28; *D.A.* 421b13-422a6.

[16] The differences of mechanism must not be exaggerated. For gills and the middle part of insects' bodies, though different in structure from nostrils, are analogous in function, according to Aristotle, who thinks they serve to cool the body. Again, the fact that we need to inhale in order to smell is due merely to the need to open a certain lid, which in some animals is not present. Inhalation is clearly then only an incidental feature of our smelling. Nor will every difference of mechanism be permissible. For all smelling must involve an organ becoming smelly. And all smelling must be done at a distance from the object smelled.

[17] *H.A.* IV, 8. And for differences of mechanism: *P.A.* 656a35-37, 657a17-24, 658b27-659b19, 660a14-661a30, 678b6-13; *H.A.*492a23-29, 503a2-6, 504a20-23, 505a33-35, 532a5-14; *G.A.* 781b23-24; *Resp.* 473a25-27.

[18] 477c-478b.

THE FIVE SENSES

to obtain a definition of sight, of hearing, and so on. The definition would mention only some of the facts about sight and hearing, but it could be used in deducing and explaining other facts about them. Evidently, his definition of sight and hearing would mention their objects, color and sound. But we know it would not be confined to this. For in the *De Anima*,[19] he says that one should refer to the physiological process involved, when one defines any mental *pathos*. Thus in the definition of sight, he would mention not only the sense objects, but also the coloration of the eye-jelly, which is, in his opinion, the physiological process involved.[20] His reason for including mention of the physiological process is probably not so much to help in distinguishing sight from other things, as to produce a definition fitted for scientific purposes, one which can be used in generating deductions and explanations.

(*iii*) Different again from giving a scientific definition of sight is the process of simply distinguishing sight from other things, and of showing what cases are to be counted as cases of sight. For this purpose, Aristotle puts a very heavy stress on the sense objects and attaches much less importance to other criteria. We should, however, make a disclaimer on his behalf. For he is not particularly interested in giving us logically necessary and sufficient conditions for something's counting as a case of sight. And so he is not suggesting that reference to the sense objects would supply such conditions. He is interested in demarcating the sensory powers that a zoologist can expect to find in this world, rather than ones which could exist in logically possible worlds. So in assessing the criteria by which he demarcates the senses, we ought to consider whether they are adequate for this zoological purpose.

Enough of exegesis, for the present. I want now to raise a

---

[19] 403*a*25-*b*9.

[20] Notice that reference to the physiological process will reimport reference to the sense objects. For according to Aristotle, the physiological process involved in sense perception is one in which the sense organ takes on the sense object. For example, the eye-jelly takes on color.

His theory is not the silly one, commonly attributed to him, that the whole eye, or the pupil, goes colored. What goes colored is merely the *Korê* (*D.A.* 431*a*17-18; *H.A.* 491*b*21; *P.A.* 653*b*25), which is the eye-jelly (*D.S.*438*a*16, *b*5-16; *H.A.* 491*b*21; *D.A.* 425*a*4; *G.A.* 780*b*23).

philosophical question, which may appear to take us away from Aristotle. Is it good advice, that we should stress the sense objects in defining the senses? The question may appear to take us away from Aristotle, because obviously our concept of definition is not his. But I should want of a definition some of the things that he wants. A definition of sight should include and exclude the right cases. And it should also bring out what, if anything, unites the various cases of sight. To answer the question, I propose to see how far one could get toward defining the senses, if one took things to an extreme and sought to define the senses solely by reference to their objects. Let us try defining hearing simply as the perception of sound, taste simply as the perception of flavor, smell simply as the perception of odor, and sight simply as the perception of color and other properties.[21] We need not expect that these definitions will prove adequate. But in seeing where they do and where they do not fail, we may learn what value there is in stressing the sense objects. And this in turn may help us to see whether Aristotle is well advised to emphasize the sense objects, as he does.

Concentrating on the case of sight, I shall consider three objections to this kind of definition. The first objection is that there is such a large variety of objects that can be perceived by sight. Consequently, it would be laborious to define sight by reference to its objects. Moreover, it would conceal what unity there is in the concept, and make it a mystery that the single name "sight" should be used to cover such a heterogeneous list. Certainly, sight has many more objects than the two which Aristotle lists as its proper objects—namely, color and the brightness of things that can be seen in the dark.[22] (By calling these proper objects he means that they can be perceived by no other sense.) In addition to these two properties, one can also see other kinds of brightness. One can see size and shape, motion or rest, texture, depth, or the location

---

[21] This is a more promising kind of formula, I think, than the kind studied by Grice in "Some Remarks about the Senses" (*Analytical Philosophy*, ed. by R. J. Butler, Series 1 [Oxford, 1962]). The latter kind is couched in terms of perceiving a material object to have such and such properties.

[22] *D.A.* 418a26-29, 419a1-9.

of things. One might be said to see darkness or light,[23] the warmth of a fire or, somewhat less naturally, the sweetness of a ripe fruit.[24] How could an Aristotelian reply to this objection, that the objects of sight are too many and various?

One line of reply would be to say that the objects of sight just listed fall into two, possibly overlapping, groups. Firstly, there is a group that includes such properties as color, brightness, and darkness. This group is small, and its members are somewhat akin to each other, both phenomenologically and, as is now known, in their physical basis, since they are all effects of the behavior of light. Secondly, there are objects of sight like size and shape, some of which are not at all like color, but which are perceived *by* perceiving color or what is like it. If this is so, then sight, as it operates in the everyday world, will be firstly the perception of color and of things like color,[25] and secondly the perception of other things by means of perceiving these.[26]

The expression "by" or "by means of" here covers a variety of different relations.[27] If anyone objects that the words are being

---

[23] I am here following Aristotle's distinction between brightness and light. By light he means that state of the air or water around us in which we can actually see through to colors at a distance from us. His idea is that when it's dark, we cannot actually see colors through the air or water. So the air and water are only potentially transparent. Light is the state in which they are actually transparent. This is all he means by the formidable-sounding definition of light as the actualized state of the transparent (*D.A.* 418*b*9-10, 419*a*11). It should be clear from this that light, a state of the surrounding medium, is quite different from brightness.

[24] Somewhat less naturally. These cases are not very like each other. For warmth consists of such powers as the power to melt things or make them red hot. And the fact that something is melting or red hot is something I can be said to see. Sweetness does not in the same way consist of powers whose exercise can be seen.

[25] Under "color" I include the three aspects of color: hue, saturation, and brightness. Under "hue" I include black and white along with the other hues. Under "things like color" I include brightness and darkness.

[26] When I say that one sees shape (etc.) by *perceiving* color (etc.), I do not mean that one has to *notice what colors are present*, in order to see the shape.

[27] Thus, in the case of three-dimensional shape, often colors, highlights, and shadows serve merely as clues to the shape of something. But in the case of two-dimensional shape, the relation between color and shape is often closer than this. For example, if there is a sharp boundary between an area of one color

stretched too far, we can drop them from our account of sight altogether. And we can simply say that one sees, if and only if one perceives color, brightness, or darkness. The idea that one cannot see shape and so forth without perceiving color, brightness, or darkness is put forward as applying at least to any cases that Aristotle was likely to encounter in his zoological enquiries. Whether it is a logically necessary truth is something that the reader may decide for himself.

This account of sight, if correct, will meet the present objection. For the list of objects of sight will be a short one. One probably need not mention more than color, brightness, and darkness. Moreover, the account reveals what unity there is in the concept of sight. For color and brightness or darkness have a certain kinship with each other.

The materials for such a reply can be found in Aristotle himself. Brightness he mentions as being like color (*D.S.* 439*b*2). By light, as distinct from brightness, he means that state of the air or water around us which permits us actually to see through it (*D.A.* 418*b*9-10, 419*a*11), and this could be treated in either of the two ways proposed. For on the one hand, he insists that light is very like color (*D.A.* 418*b*11; *D.S.* 439*a*18); indeed, like white color; darkness, like black (*D.S.* 439*b*14-18). But on the other hand, he would prefer to deal with the present question by saying that we perceive light by perceiving that we are successfully perceiving color through the air or water around us. And we perceive darkness by perceiving that we are unsuccessful (*D.A.* 422*a*20-21, 425*b*20-22). He might wish to add that it is better not to talk of *seeing* light and darkness, but more noncommittally of perceiving them by means of sight (*D.A.* 425*b*20-22). As for the use of sight to perceive size and shape, he explicitly says that size and shape are perceived through the perception of other properties such as color. And in general the common objects are perceived by

---

(hue, saturation, or brilliance) and an area of another, and if we see where the boundary runs, this *is* to see (part of) the shape of the areas.

Seeing sweetness is more like the first case, in that color and shine serve merely as clues to sweetness. Seeing warmth is, in some instances, more like the second case. For the relation between red (hot) and warmth is a much closer relation than that between a clue and what the clue points to.

THE FIVE SENSES

perceiving the proper objects (*D.S.* 437*a*5-9, perhaps *D.A.* 425*a*19). The same point is made about the use of sight to perceive sweetness (*D.A.* 425*a*22-24, *a*30-*b*4). In these cases, we see a color and know from past experience that sweetness is associated with it. All this suggests the view that to see is to perceive color or properties akin to color, and other things only through the perception of these.

I have said that the *materials* for this view are present in Aristotle. But I must add it is not clear that it is quite the view he states. For he seems to think he can get clear about what sight is without referring to sense objects other than color (which is seen in the light) and the brightness of phosphorescent things (which is seen in the dark). Why does he not mention other kinds of brightness? Surely he would have to do so if he took the view just outlined. One possible (though far from certain) answer is that he includes the brightness of things that shine in the light under the heading of color and therefore does not need to mention it separately. This would not be a normal way to use the English word "color." But Greek color words often did double duty, and were used as much to denote degrees of darkness and brightness as to denote hues.[28] So it is just possible that under the heading of color Aristotle means to include cetain kinds of brightness.

Before we leave the present objection, we should notice one further point. The suggested solution claimed to be able to exhibit the concept of sight as having a certain unity. It did so by insisting on the kinship between color and brightness or darkness. But part of this kinship was a phenomenological one. And to appeal to phenomenology is to appeal to the kind of experience to which these sense objects give rise. It becomes a question, then, whether the suggested definition of sight in terms of color, brightness, or darkness appeals only to sense objects. Is it not also appealing to something other than sense objects—namely, to the kind of experience to which these sense objects give rise?

I now turn to a second objection that may be raised to the idea of relying on sense objects in defining the senses. For may not senses other than sight sometimes perceive color? If so, we cannot

---

[28] See Platnauer, "Greek Colour Perception," *Classical Quarterly* (1921). Also Cornford, *Plato's Cosmology*, p. 277.

define sight simply as the power to perceive color and so forth, for other senses will fall under the description. An unfanciful example is provided by the ability of some people to tell the colors of flowers by smell. In the typical case, however, what happens here is most naturally described by saying that an odor is smelled and is known to be correlated with a certain color, not that a color is smelled.[29] Aristotle discusses such cases in the *De Anima* at 425a22-24 and a30-b4. He calls such perception a merely incidental perception of color. And with a view to meeting the present objection he could rule that such incidental perception of color does not count as seeing.

But what if we turn to the more unusual kind of case reported by psychologists, or resort to imaginary examples? Cannot we then expect to find cases in which there is non-incidental perception of color without there being an exercise of sight? A case that excited some interest recently was that of Rosa Kuleshova, reported in *Time* (January 25, 1963, p. 58). She allegedly distinguished colors and read ordinary print with her fingertips, without relying on the texture of the paper. Later the case was declared by T.A.S.S. to be a fraud. She peeped. But meanwhile other psychologists had reported that similar capacities were known in man and in other animals. May not cases such as this supply counterexamples to the claim that the non-incidental perception of color is always an exercise of sight?

---

[29] No doubt, this description would be preferred in fact. But is there good reason for preferring it? A partial answer can be gained by comparing the relation between odor and color with that between, say, being red (hot) and warmth, or between the shape things look and the shape they feel. Different as these latter two cases are from each other, they both involve a relationship such that we do not feel obliged to say merely that one property is seen and the other is known to be correlated with it. The first case has been mentioned in notes 24 and 27. Excellent discussions bearing on the second case can be found in H.P. Grice, *loc. cit.*, and in Jonathan Bennett, "Substance, Reality and Primary Qualities," *American Philosophical Quarterly* (1965). The point is that we do not have to talk of seeing visual shape and knowing that tactual shape is correlated with it. We can talk more boldly of seeing shape. For the shape things look and the shape they feel do not vary independently of each other. Nor is this a mere accident that could easily have been otherwise. If we try to imagine it otherwise, we will find we can no longer speak of there being physical objects and of these objects having a definite location in the imagined situation. For details, see the two articles mentioned.

It is by no means so easy to find counterexamples as one might at first suppose. Had the case of Rosa Kuleshova been genuine, we should have needed a lot of information about her before we could decide whether to say she was feeling color, or seeing color with an unusual part of the body, or feeling some such property as warmth and inferring to color. Only if she was feeling color would she supply a counterexample. To establish that she was feeling color, we should have to show (*a*) that hers was a case of feeling, not of seeing with an unusual part of the body. (It would help to show this, if she could distinguish colors with any part of her body surface.) But we should also have to show (*b*) that her perception of color was nonetheless non-incidental, in other words that she was not simply inferring to color. And the trouble is that the performance of one of these tasks is liable to impede the performance of the other.[30]

We may add that if a case of feeling color can be described at all, it will very likely not be a case that a scientist can expect to meet in the real world. And if not, it will not be a case of a kind that Aristotle is particularly concerned to classify.

Finally, we should raise a third objection against the appeal to

---

[30] Particularly important would be the question of what kind of experience she had. If the experience were too like that involved in seeing, we should be inclined to say she was seeing. If the experience were too like that involved in, say, feeling warmth, we might be inclined to say she was feeling, but that the perception of color was merely incidental. The solution might seem to be to look for a case in which the experience involved was neutral—i.e., neither too like that involved in recognized cases of seeing, nor too like that involved in recognized cases of feeling. But it is not clear that even this would enable us to classify the case as one of feeling color. For could we say her perception of color was non-incidental if the color did not give rise to the kind of experience normally associated with color? The answer to this will no doubt depend in part on one's conception of color, and on how closely one supposes the notion of color to be linked to a certain kind of experience. One might argue that the notion of color is connected not only with a certain kind of experience, but also with the behavior of light. So if we can show she is reacting to the behavior of light, and not to some by-product of light, such as temperature, we shall have reason to say her perception of color is non-incidental. (For experiments ruling out reaction to temperature, see *Nature*, August 29, 1964, p. 993.) But this suggestion in its turn creates a difficulty. For if she perceives by means of light receptors, this will make her unable to perceive by direct contact, and so cast doubt again on the idea that she is feeling. This is perhaps enough to indicate some of the difficulties.

sense objects. May not people be said to see when they are subject to total hallucination, or when they have afterimages, or when their eyes are closed and there is some stimulation of the optic nerve, or in other cases where there is no real color, brightness, or darkness in the objective world which they are perceiving? If so, it is not true that all seeing involves the perception of color, brightness, or darkness. Aristotle's own response would be to allow that in these cases no objective color is perceived, but to deny that they are cases of seeing. Rather, they are exercises of *phantasia*, the faculty of imagination. At least, this is the usual trend in Aristotle, though there are faint traces of a different trend.[31]

The Aristotelian answer is not satisfactory, for surely the examples in question are cases of seeing in the ordinary sense. Is there any other way of meeting the present objection, so as to preserve the idea that all seeing involves the perception of color, brightness, or darkness? It may be urged that when one sees with closed eyes, one is at least perceiving subjective color, even if there is no objective color in the external world that one is seeing. But one who thus appeals to subjective color should notice what he is doing. He is in effect appealing to something which initially we might have been inclined to distinguish from color itself—namely, the kind of experience to which color gives rise. He is saying that the experience is like that of perceiving objective color. He is not wrong, for the character of the experience is part of the reason why seeing with one's eyes closed is counted as a kind of seeing. But on the other hand, it is not clear whether the definition can still be said to confine itself to the mention of sense objects only.

What conclusions can we now draw from our attempt to define sight as the perception of color, brightness, or darkness? The definition goes a long way toward picking out the right cases, though, as the third objection shows, it does not, without special interpretation, cover quite all the standard cases of sight.

A more interesting point that has emerged en route is the im-

---

[31] For the predominant trend see, e.g., *D.A.* 428a16 and *Insom.* 458b7-9, 459a1-21. For traces of a different trend see *D.A.* 425b22-25, which is tempted by the idea that when one has an afterimage, one does perceive real, objective color—namely, the color taken on by one's eye-jelly, as a result of looking at the bright object.

portance of the kind of experience that is involved in sight. We found ourselves appealing to the character of this experience, firstly when we talked of the phenomenological kinship between color and brightness or darkness, secondly when (in note 30) we argued against the possibility of feeling color, and thirdly when we spoke of subjective color. It looks as if the character of the experience is an important element in the concept of sight. And part of the reason why it is helpful to mention the sense objects in a definition of sight is that reference to the sense objects implies in turn a reference to the kind of experience to which the sense objects give rise.[32]

A further conclusion is that we should be cautious in claiming that the attempted definition confines itself to the sense objects. For not only does the mention of color, brightness, and darkness import a reference to the kind of experience involved, but also there was an appeal to the notion of perception. Sight was treated as one species of the genus, perception. Now, if we were to analyze the generic notion of perception in its turn, we might well have to refer to the kind of physical mechanisms that distinguish sense perception from other forms of cognition. And if so, the attempted definition of sight in its turn involves an implicit appeal to these mechanisms.

Finally, we have been laying stress on two criteria, the sense objects and the kind of experience involved. But we should remember that it may be necessary to appeal to other criteria as well, at least when we leave the standard cases of sense perception and consider how to classify imaginary and logically possible cases. Here we may need to take into account the behavior involved, the mechanisms within the perceiver's body, and the mechanisms in the surrounding environment.[33]

Where does this discussion leave Aristotle? It suggests that his stress on the sense objects is helpful. For reference to these does pick out most of the standard cases of sight and does bring out the unity of the concept. But reference to the objects alone, we have seen, will not suffice. And so we may be glad that in his protracted discussion of the senses, the emphasis on sense objects does

---

[32] Grice arrives at a similar conclusion, traveling by a somewhat different route, in his valuable paper, *loc. cit.*

[33] These possibilities are discussed in detail by Grice, *loc. cit.*

VI

not lead to the exclusion of other aspects of each sense. With some qualifications, then, the verdict so far is in favor of Aristotle. But I have hitherto excluded from discussion a certain one of the five senses—namely, the sense of touch. To this I shall now have to turn.

II. The Sense of Touch

There is an exception to what we have been saying about the importance of sense objects. This exception is the sense of touch. I have in mind the layman's conception of touch, rather than the refined concept of psychologists, which has been influenced by neurophysiological discoveries. The layman's concept includes, roughly speaking, those perceptual powers which are called powers of *feeling* sensible properties, but only sensible properties of a kind that can belong to non-sentient bodies and not, for example, such properties as hunger or pain. In speaking of touch, I am using the noun "touch," not the verb. The verb that goes with it is not the verb "to touch," but the verb "to feel."

It would be unsatisfactory to rely heavily on the objects of touch in defining the sense. For one thing, the objects of touch are extremely varied.[34] Not only would it be laborious to define touch by reference to its many objects, but also knowledge of what these objects are would give no indication of what unites the varieties of touch, nor of why some kinds of sense perception are excluded. Again, given the diversity that already exists, one

---

[34] Aristotle might be able to shorten the list of objects somewhat, thanks to his view that coarse and fine, viscous and brittle, hard and soft, come from dry and fluid (*G. & C.* 329b32-34). In fact, he says all the other objects of touch are reducible to the basic four, dry and fluid, hot and cold (*G. & C.* 329b34, 330a24-26). If this is so, might he not be able to specify the objects of touch as dry and fluid, hot and cold, and other properties reducible to these? Such a specification runs two opposite risks. It would let in the objects of other senses, if any of these are reducible to dry, fluid, hot, or cold. At the same time, it is not clear how it would accommodate heavy and light, rough and smooth. For he does not show how these are reducible to dry and fluid, hot and cold, though he does bring out some causal connections between them. In any event, he can at best shorten the list of objects of touch. He cannot eliminate the irreducible difference between the pair, hot and cold, and the pair, dry and fluid.

would meet less difficulty than in corresponding cases with other senses, in classifying under touch new perceptual powers which have quite different objects from any of those currently recognized as objects of touch. So one does not want a definition that restricts too much the list of objects. A further inconvenience (though a surmountable one) for someone who lays stress on the objects of touch is that so many of the objects apprehended by touch are apprehended by other senses too, as, for example, are size and shape, rough and smooth, sharp and blunt, and perhaps hot and cold.

In view of these difficulties, it is not surprising to find people defining touch by reference to something other than its objects. We shall encounter two criteria that were canvassed in ancient times.

(*a*) *The contact criterion.* The criterion that impresses Aristotle is that touch, in his view, operates by direct contact with the body.[35] In saying this, he may be influenced by the etymology of the word for touch—namely, *haphê*, a word which was still often used with its original meaning of contact. At any rate, he says in the *De Anima* (435*a*17-18) that the sense of touch gets its name from the fact that it operates through direct contact.

Aristotle's appeals to the contact criterion are fairly numerous. Thus when perception occurs through direct contact, we quite often find him treating this as reason enough for classifying a perceptual power as a form of touch. In the *De Sensu*, for example (442*a*29-*b*3), he accuses Democritus of reducing all the senses to touch, apparently on the grounds that Democritus makes all the senses operate through direct contact between the body and the atoms that stream off the object perceived. Again, in the *De Anima*, at least on one interpretation of lines 434*b*11-18, he argues from the fact that an animal needs to perceive a thing when in direct contact with it, to the conclusion that it needs the sense of touch. In the immediately following lines, 434*b*18-19, again on one interpretation, he argues from the fact that taste apprehends

---

[35] This is not to say that touch operates through direct contact with the sense organ. For the organ of touch is within, according to Aristotle, in the region of the heart (*D.S.* 439*a*1).

something with which we are in direct contact—namely food—
to the conclusion that taste is a variety of touch. Elsewhere in the
De Anima, at 424*b*27-28, we find the statement "And all things
that we perceive when in contact with them are perceived by
touch."

An argument in the opposite direction is offered at *De Anima*
422*a*8-16. Not only does perception by direct contact indicate
the sense of touch, but all exercises of taste (a form of touch, in
Aristotle's view) are through contact. This is in spite of appearances to the contrary, which might suggest that fish taste food
thrown into the water at a distance from them, or that we taste
through the intervening liquid the sugar at the bottom of our
drink. Aristotle's argument travels in the same direction when he
says, "What is perceived by touch is directly contacted" (*D.A.*
434*b*12-13).

In these remarks, Aristotle has not abandoned the idea of
distinguishing the other four senses by reference to their objects.
On the contrary, he is presupposing it. And he thinks this way
of distinguishing them fits in with the definition of touch by
reference to direct contact. His idea is that sight, hearing, and
smell (where these are defined as the power to perceive color
[and so forth], sound and odor) are *never* exercised through
direct contact (*D.A.* 419*a*11-21, 419*a*25-30, 421*b*16-18, 422*a*14-15,
423*b*20-25). Taste, however (where this is defined as the power
to perceive flavor and is regarded as a form of touch), is
always so exercised (*D.A.* 422*a*8-16). It is given these facts that
we can, in his opinion, safely distinguish touch (including taste)
as operating through direct contact with the body. He does
not say how things would need to be classified, if some acts of
perceiving flavor were performed at a distance or some acts of
perceiving color were through direct contact.

Though Aristotle is wise to lay stress on something other than
the *objects* of touch, his choice of the direct contact mechanism
is difficult to work with. And this applies whether with him we
take touch as including taste, or not. To bring this out, let us
first notice which perceptual powers he lists under touch. He
includes the power to perceive hot and cold, fluid and dry, hard
and soft, heavy and light, viscous and brittle, rough and smooth,

coarse and fine, as well as the power to perceive flavor. These lists are taken from the *De Anima*[36] and from the *De Generatione et Corruptione*.[37] Elsewhere, rough and smooth are distinguished from the others, as being objects of sight as well as of touch—in other words, as being common objects.[38] Other common objects are size, shape, sharp and blunt, motion and rest, number and unity.[39] It is only when these common objects are perceived by direct contact that Aristotle thinks of them as being perceived by touch.

There are several difficulties to be mentioned in applying the contact criterion. Firstly, one can by the sense of touch feel the heat of a stove while at a distance from it. Again, though one sometimes tastes by direct contact, one can sometimes also taste the olive at the bottom of the martini without being in direct contact with it. Aristotle might wish to reply to the first example that one is really feeling the heat of the air that intervenes between the stove and oneself. Certainly, he says that fire warms a distant body by warming the intervening air.[40] As for the second example, he discusses a case of this kind and protests that the flavored object which is at a distance from one dissolves and gets mixed with the intervening fluid. So one really is in direct contact with the flavored object after all.[41] But if these are legitimate ways of showing that touch and taste always operate by direct contact, could they not have been used with equal plausibility to show that smell operates by direct contact? What makes Aristotle so sure that one does not smell the air intervening between oneself and the rose, or that one does not smell as a result of bits of rose dissolving and becoming mixed with the air?

This difficulty may suggest an alternative way of applying the contact criterion. Why did not Aristotle seek to distinguish touch (including taste) from the other senses by saying that touch is that group of perceptual powers that *can* operate by direct contact? Not every exercise of touch will involve direct contact, but those

---

[36] 422*b*25-27.
[37] 329*b*18-20.
[38] *D.S.* 422*b*5-7.
[39] *D.S.* 442*b*5-7; *D.A.* 425*a*16.
[40] *G. & C.* 327*a*3.
[41] *D.A.* 422*a*8-16.

exercises which do not will be similar to those which do, in ways which justify our counting them as exercises of the same sense, touch. Unfortunately, this way of applying the contact criterion runs into an immediate difficulty. For hearing and smell would seem to be powers which *can* operate through direct contact,[42] even if they seldom do so in fact.

Finally, there is a difficulty of another sort in relying on a contact criterion. It is that taste will have to be counted as a form of touch. Aristotle is quite happy so to count it. But our own concept of touch does not include taste. Nor did the concept that Aristotle inherited. At any rate, when we discuss the main rival to the contact criterion, we shall notice that a number of Aristotle's predecessors did not group taste along with the tactual powers.[43] So the contact criterion does not pick out existing concepts of touch. It seems more that Aristotle is making a recommendation— namely, that we should follow the contact criterion to its logical conclusion and include taste under touch. But the recommendation does not seem a very good one, given the way in which, as we have seen, this criterion cuts across other criteria for distinguishing senses.

Apart from the above difficulties involved in using the contact criterion, there was another reason why it could not be employed by certain of Aristotle's predecessors. For Empedocles, Democritus, and, according to Aristotle,[44] most of the other early philosophers of nature had made *all* sense perception operate by direct contact. The contact, in the case of some forms of sense perception, was with particles that streamed off the thing perceived and into the sense organs. Contact could not therefore be used as a criterion for distinguishing one sense from others. It characterized all forms of sense perception alike. Aristotle avoided this obstacle to using the contact criterion.[45] For on his theory, the sense organs did not receive particles of matter from the thing perceived.

---

[42] One can smell the snuff lodged in one's nostrils, and hear the bath water trapped in one's ears, though Aristotle seeks to deny this in the passage mentioned on p. 70.

[43] See pp. 74-75.

[44] *D.S.* 442a29-30.

[45] On this subject, see the useful article by Solmsen, "αἴσθησις in Aristotelian and Epicurean Thought," in *Mededelingen der Koninklijke Nederlandse Akademie van Wetenschappen Afd. Letterkunde* (1961).

Rather, they received form without matter.[46] The eye-jelly, for example, took on the colors of the thing perceived but did not come into contact with material particles from it.[47] It may be urged that the early philosophers of nature still could have used a contact criterion for drawing distinctions between senses. For there is a difference between being in contact with the main mass of the thing perceived, and being in contact with particles that have streamed from it. So why should not touch be distinguished as involving contact with the main mass? This new criterion no longer turns on the question of whether contact is employed, but rather on the question of what it is that is contacted. Assuming that it still deserves to be called a contact criterion, it does meet the latest objection to contact criteria. But it is not the contact criterion that Aristotle himself uses for touch, since he does not require contact with the main mass.[48] Nor, of course, would it escape the objections raised earlier against contact criteria.

(b) *The non-localization criterion.* There is evidence that some of Aristotle's predecessors had used another criterion instead of the contact criterion. The clearest example of this comes in Plato's *Timaeus*, 61D-65B. Here Plato groups together various properties that we should count as objects of touch—namely, hot, cold, hard, soft, heavy, light, smooth, and rough. But he does not use a contact criterion for grouping them, nor does he use one of the names for the sense of touch that is etymologically connected with contact—namely, *haphê* or *psausis*. Rather, he groups these properties together because, in his words, they are affections "common to the body as a whole" (64A, 65B). What he means is that they are perceived without the use of a localized organ, such as eyes, nose, ears, or tongue. Rather they can be perceived through any part of the body.[49]

---

[46] *D.A.* 424a18, 424b2, 425b22, 427a8, 429a15, 434a29, 435a22.

[47] In another sense, Aristotle did accept that all sense perception involved contact. The object seen must be in contact with the air, and the air in turn with the eye (*Phys.* 245a2-9).

[48] Thus, he allows that fish exercise taste, a form of touch, when in contact not with the main mass of their food, but with that part of their food that has dissolved in the water.

[49] Aristotle would not agree that touch lacks a localized organ. The organ is in the region of the heart (*D.S.* 439a1). He could still have distinguished the

VI

Plato does not always avoid the names that are connected with contact. Thus in the *Republic* (523*E*) we find him using for the sense of touch the name *haphê*. This time he is talking of the perception of thick and thin, hard and soft. He uses a related word for the sense of touch at *Phaedo* 75*A*, and perhaps at *Theaetetus* 186*B*, 189*A*, 195 *D-E*.

There is another author who combines the non-localization criterion with the use of terminology that is connected with contact. In *Regimen* I. 23, a treatise which was written perhaps around 400 *B.C.*, and which belongs to the Hippocratic collection of medical writings, there is reference to a sense called *psausis*, a name which is connected with contact. But the author goes on to add a reference to the non-localization criterion, saying that the whole body is its organ.

For a use of the non-localization criterion without terminology suggesting contact, we may refer to Theophrastus' report (*De Sensibus* 38) on Cleidemus, a pre-Socratic who was perhaps contemporary with Democritus. According to this report, Cleidemus distinguished between perception through the tongue and perception through the rest of the body.

This last example is important for an additional reason. Not only does it use the non-localization criterion for distinguishing a sense. But also by its treatment of what we should call taste, it implies a rejection of the contact criterion. For both perception through the tongue and perception through the rest of the body operate by direct contact. Yet for all that, they are not grouped together as forming a single sense.

The same is true in the passage cited from the Hippocratic treatise, *Regimen*. Even though this passage uses the name *psausis*, which is connected with contact, it does not include taste as falling under *psausis*. On the contrary, it distinguishes between perception through the tongue and perception through the whole body. And it is the latter that is called *psausis*. In spite, then, of using a name connected with contact, the author does not treat contact as a sufficient ground for including a form of perception under the

recognized tactual powers, if he had chosen, however, by saying that the other senses have either a localized organ at the surface of the body (ears, eyes, nose) or at least a localized channel at the surface (tongue).

74

heading of *psausis*. He seems to have preferred the non-localization criterion to the contact one.

The same seems to be true of other authors. At any rate, on the most natural interpretation, Democritus lists five senses in fragment 11—namely, sight, hearing, smell, taste, and touch. Though he uses a contact word, *psausis*, for touch, he agrees with Cleidemus and with the author of *Regimen* I, in refusing to subsume taste under the heading of touch. And he thereby implies rejection of the contact criterion. Admittedly, an alternative interpretation has been suggested for the passage. Solmsen[50] remarks that the word *psausis* might be being used not to refer to the sense of touch, but to emphasize that the other four senses named operate, in Democritus' opinion, by contact. This interpretation is very much less natural. But even if it be correct, we still get a result of some interest. For if contact characterizes the other four senses, then Democritus is not free to distinguish a fifth sense, touch, as the sense which employs contact. So, as was remarked before, if he wished to use the contact criterion, he would have to use a version of it different from Aristotle's.

Aristotle himself seems to have been influenced by the tradition which treats taste as distinct from touch, in so far as he devotes separate discussions in the *De Anima* to sight, hearing, smell, taste, and touch. He does not treat taste and touch together, in spite of his recommendation that we should subsume taste under touch.

Let us summarize these findings. On the one hand, we do encounter among Aristotle's predecessors the names *psausis* and *haphê*, which are connected with contact. On the other hand, a good many authors, including ones who used these names, seem to have rejected the contact criterion as a way of distinguishing the sense of touch. This rejection comes out in their insistence on treating taste as distinct from touch. (Moreover, their view that all the senses operate by direct contact commits them to rejecting Aristotle's own version of the contact criterion.) In place of the contact criterion for distinguishing touch, a number of them used the non-localization criterion. It looks as if, in spite of their choice of

---

[50] *Loc. cit.*

VI

nomenclature, the non-localization criterion answered more faithfully to the conception which they actually had.

Certainly, the non-localization criterion is the one that corresponds most closely to the present-day concept of touch, at least if we take the layman's conception, which I referred to before. The powers that the layman groups under touch (and here the power of taste is not included) are distinguished by the fact that they operate without any obvious localized organ. If modern research has discovered localized organs, these were not apparent at the time the concept was being formed. The absence of an obvious localized organ is the only feature that is common and peculiar to the very diverse powers that are grouped under the heading of touch. This is not to say that the feature is logically necessary or logically sufficient for making a perceptual power count as a variety of touch. But at least it has served as a principle of collection for the familiar varieties. And newly encountered or imaginary perceptual powers will be classified on the basis of their similarity to these familiar ones (even though the similarity will not necessarily be in respect of non-localization).

We get a strong indication of the influence that the non-localization criterion has had, if we ask ourselves the following question. What else has led to taste being excluded, and to the perception of temperature being included, under the heading of touch? It looks, then, as if the non-localization criterion, to be found in Plato and others, has retained its influence to the present day.

Two related points of clarification need to be introduced, however. The non-localization criterion does not on its own enable us to classify individual acts of perception. For one can, for example, feel the texture of something with one's tongue or ear. So we must not suggest that each individual exercise of touch will be carried out without the aid of a localized organ. Rather, the point is that the same quality, texture, can be apprehended by the same kind of mechanism and the same kind of experience, through a quite different part of the body, at least in the case of a healthy human being. And these considerations warrant our saying that, even if a given exercise of the power is confined to a localized organ, the power itself is not so confined.

The point could be put like this. The non-localization criterion

THE FIVE SENSES

is used to classify not individual acts of perception, but perceptual powers. And in deciding which individual acts fall under a given power, we may have to appeal to criteria other than the non-localization one.

This brings us to the second point of clarification. We have been saying that under touch we include at present those perceptual powers which operate without any obvious localized organ. But the truth of this statement depends on what counts as a distinct perceptual power. Is the power to perceive shape, for example, whether visually or tactually, to be counted as a single power? If so, we will get an unfortunate result. For when we ask whether or not this single power is confined to a localized organ, either answer will be unsatisfactory. Suppose, for example, it is said that the power to perceive shape is not confined to a localized organ, on the grounds that tactual exercises of the power are not so confined. Then the entire power of perceiving shape, even the power to perceive it visually, will have to be classified under touch, which is not the result we want. The moral is that the non-localization criterion can only be used to classify powers under the heading of touch, if we have adopted the right kind of procedure for individuating powers in the first place.

Now that we have introduced the non-localization criterion, we are in a better position to evaluate two arguments of Aristotle's. In *De Anima*, Book II, Chapter 11, he introduces several imaginary situations. One of these situations involves people being able to perceive flavor with any part of the body.[51] In this situation, he says, people would identify taste with touch. Taken in one sense, Aristotle's claim is perfectly correct, as our discussion of the non-localization criterion will show. For in the envisaged situation, the perception of flavor would not be through a localized organ. Taste in that case would have at least as good a claim as the perception of temperature to be classified under touch. Admittedly, this is not the kind of point that Aristotle himself is intending to make in the passage.[52] So all we should say is that our discussion of

---

[51] 423a17-21.

[52] Aristotle's own point is that in the imaginary situation described, we would fail to notice that taste is a distinct kind of perception in its own right, distinct from, say, the power of perceiving fluid and dry. For there would be no differ-

the non-localization criterion reveals one sense in which his remark is correct.

The second Aristotelian argument which we can now profitably recall is his objection to Democritus, that Democritus reduces all the senses to touch.[53] The ground of this charge is apparently that Democritus makes all the senses operate through contact. Aristotle is right about one thing. The name *haphê* originally meant, and still often meant, contact. Consequently, if all the senses operate through contact, the name *haphê* is not a very appropriate one to reserve for one of them. Rather, it should be applied to all. This point is only one about nomenclature, however. There is a much more important point on which Aristotle cannot fault Democritus. He cannot say that Democritus is debarred from distinguishing between the sense that is called touch and the other four senses. For Democritus is free to draw this distinction by reference to the non-localization criterion.

RETROSPECT

We have argued that Aristotle emphasizes the sense objects in his account of four of the senses. And we found some good reasons for following such a policy. But we argued that the policy would not be a good one in connection with the sense of touch, and that Aristotle wisely stresses a different criterion in speaking of this sense. He goes wrong, however, in choosing the contact criterion for touch, rather than the non-localization criterion that had been used by several of his predecessors. Although the name *haphê*, like

---

ence of organ or medium to attract our attention to its distinctness. Aristotle does think, however, that taste is a distinct kind of perception, and that it would remain so in the imaginary situation. This is not to retract his view that taste is a kind of touch, and would remain so in the imaginary situation. It is to insist that taste is, and would be, only one kind of touch. Aristotle suggests that just as in the imaginary situation we would fail to notice the distinctness of taste, so now perhaps we fail to distinguish different kinds of perception that are lumped together under the heading of touch.

[53] *D.S.* 442a29-b3.

our word "touch," was often used to mean contact, it is in fact the non-localization criterion that corresponds most closely to the conception of touch that people have actually had.[54]

[54] Earlier drafts were read at Cornell, Princeton, and London Universities, and at a weekend meeting of Birkbeck College. I benefited from many helpful comments at these meetings. But I should like to acknowledge in particular Hidé Ishiguro, Alan Lacey, and David Hamlyn, who prepared for me on these occasions valuable comments which have led to many improvements. Some of the work for this paper was done on leave, while I held a Howard Foundation Fellowship from Brown University, and a project grant, No. H68-0-95, from the National Endowment for the Humanities. I acknowledge these sources gratefully.

VII

ARISTOTLE, MATHEMATICS, AND COLOUR

Intermediate Colours as Mixtures of Black and White

Aristotle says in the *De Sensu* that other colours are produced through the mixture of black bodies with white (440[a]31–[b]23). The obvious mixture for him to be referring to is the mixture of the four elements, earth, air, fire, and water, which he describes at such length in the *De Generatione et Corruptione*. All compound bodies are produced ultimately through the mixture of these elements. The way in which the elements mix is described in 1. 10 and 2. 7. They mix in such a way as to produce an entirely new substance, in which the characteristics of the original earth, air, fire, and water survive only in modified form.

We can guess that elemental fire would be counted by Aristotle as white, and elemental earth as black. For he thinks that it is the presence of fieriness in a body that makes it white, and the absence of fieriness that makes it black.[1] The other two elements, water and air, are usually treated as having no colour of their own[2] (though they can contribute to the colour of a body into which they enter, air making it whiter, and water making it darker).[3]

To our ears, one of the strangest parts of this theory may be the idea that mixtures of black matter with white should produce anything other than grey. Yet Aristotle was not the first to suppose that black and white could produce the other colours. It can be understood why Aristotle and others might *want* to think this. In the simpler case of temperature, many of Aristotle's predecessors had thought of intermediate degrees of temperature as being blends of hot with cold. But why did this conception not appear absurd when it was extended to colours?

---

[1] *D.S.* 439[b]14–18, with 439[a]18–21 and *D.A.* 418[b]9–20. The fact that fire (especially pure, elemental fire) is to a certain degree transparent may also contribute to its whiteness, in Aristotle's opinion. And the non-transparency of earth may contribute to its blackness. At any rate, on one interpretation *D.S.* 439[b]6–12 implies that a total lack of transparency would yield black, while a certain degree of transparency increases the whiteness (though, as the next note indicates, too high a degree of transparency will instead make something colourless). Cf. also *G.A.* 779[b]27–33; 780[a]27–36 for a connection between non-transparency and blackness.

[2] Thus fieriness in air produces light, not white (*D.S.* 439[b]14–18). In general, Aristotle (forgetting the case of wine or coloured gems) speaks as if transparent things (like air or water) have no colour of their own, but only borrowed colour, due to reflection or other causes. This is the best interpretation

of *D.A.* 418[b]4–6: 'by *transparent* I mean what is visible, yet not in itself visible speaking without qualification, but visible through borrowed colour.' Cf. also *D.S.* 439[b]10–14, which, on one interpretation, speaks of 'transparent things themselves, like water and anything else there may be of this kind, I mean those ones which appear to [sc. merely appear to, but do not really] have a colour of their own'.

On the other hand, water and air can have *borrowed* colour due to reflection (*Meteor.* 1. 5 and 3. 2–6; *D.S.* 439[b]3–6), or other causes (the water of the eye-jelly takes on colour during the act of vision, and this is not due to reflection). Water displays a colour which gets darker, according as the water gets deeper and less transparent (*G.A.* 779[b]27–33; 780[b]8).

[3] Air bubbles give whiteness to foam, semen, oil, hair, and other stuffs. What is more watery, and less full of air, is darker (*G.A.* 735[a]30–736[a]22; 784[b]15; 786[a]7–13).

As a first step towards an answer, we may point to a certain fact about Greek colour words that is documented by Platnauer in his article 'Greek Colour Perception' (*C.Q.*xv [1921], 153). It is that a number of Greek colour words did double duty. They were used as much to denote the brilliance of a colour as to denote its hue. *Leukon* means bright, or light-coloured, as much as it means white. And *melan* means dark-coloured, as much as it means black.[1] Now Aristotle's theory will not seem quite so bizarre if we think of red as a bright colour, and if we think of him as saying that it is produced by mixing a lot of the brightest colour with a little of the darkest.

This is both similar to and different from what is said in modern colour theory. In the systems of Munsell and of Ostwald, coloured chips are placed in a three-dimensional arrangement. In one dimension, the chips vary in respect of brilliance, ranging between black at one extreme and white at the other. Intermediate brilliances can be specified in terms of such and such a percentage of white and such and such a percentage of black. So much is reminiscent of Aristotle. But it is not, of course, the case that red has only one brilliance, nor that there is any brilliance that attaches only to red.

In our search for an explanation, we ought to make use of a second consideration, and observe how Aristotle reaches his theory of the mixture of black with white, or at least how he tries to lead us to the theory. In *De Sensu* 3, he starts from two theories which he rejects, the theories that black and white produce the other colours by being juxtaposed with, or superimposed upon, each other. Aristotle leads us to his theory by substituting for juxtaposition and superimposition his pet notion of chemical mixture. This substitution is presented as enabling us to avoid the difficulties in the other two theories.[2] So it is made to look as if the Aristotelian theory has grown out of the other two. But why had the other two theories appealed to anyone? Aristotle speaks as if the grounds for them were *a priori*. A combination of black and white can't appear exclusively black, or exclusively white, but must have some colour; so it has an intermediate colour (*D.S.* 439^{b}22–5; 440^{a}24–6). We may wonder why not grey. But there is a piece of empirical evidence which Aristotle mentions in connection with the theory of superimposition. The sun is white (*leukos*), but if we look at it through a cloudy or a sooty medium, its appearance is darkened to red.[3] In this example, a reduction in brilliance goes hand in hand with a change of hue. And both are produced by superimposing black, sooty particles over a white light. Perhaps this phenomenon encouraged adherents of the superimposition theory. It certainly encouraged Goethe many centuries later, when, in the section on physical colours in *Zur Farbenlehre*, he described physical colour as involving a relationship between light and darkness. The case of the sun obscured by atmospheric conditions is one of the cases he cites. His theory is

---

[1] For symptoms of these facts in the *De Sensu*, see 439^{a}18–19 'light [i.e. illumination] is the colour of the transparent'; 439^{b}2 'sheen is a sort of colour'; 440^{a}11 'the sun appears *leukos*'.

[2] Both theories appeal to an illusion. When close up, one would see that there were two colours, black and white, instead of one. The theory of juxtaposition tries to avoid this by making the black and white specks too small to see, but this is a further impossibility. Also against the juxtaposition theory is that it is linked with the untenable idea that effluxes stream from the seen object into one's eyes, and misguidedly postulates a time-lag too short to perceive between the arrival of the black and the white particles (*D.S.* 440^{a}15–31, ^{b}16–18).

[3] *D.S.* 440^{a}7–12. Aristotle mentions similar phenomena in the *Meteorology* (374^{a}3; ^{a}27; ^{b}10).

often compared to Aristotle's, but it is, in this respect, more like the super-imposition theory, which Aristotle rejects.[1]

No empirical support is mentioned in connection with the theory of juxta-position. And it is not particularly likely that any would have been available to the inventors of the theory, though there is a phenomenon which they might have used for support, if only they had known of it. The English painter, Bridget Riley, has produced pictures in which black and white are juxtaposed, in long ribbons, not in imperceptible specks. When people look at these black and white ribbons, many are able to see all sorts of colours appearing. A similar use was made of black and white dots in early attempts to produce colour tele-vision. And the principle is exploited in an optical instrument known as a reflection grating. Whether the effect is sufficiently common in nature to have influenced the juxtaposition theorists is extremely doubtful.

THE MATHEMATICAL DISTINCTION OF SHADES

It is in connection with the mixture of black and white that Aristotle introduces mathematics into his theory. He hopes to apply to colours and flavours the mathematical treatment that had recently proved so successful in acoustical theory. Consonant notes in music, according to the definition most commonly given by Greek writers, are ones which blend together when played simul-taneously.[2] They were also considered the most pleasant combinations. Dissonant notes, on the other hand, compete with each other, so that each is heard separately. Notes separated by an interval of a fourth, a fifth, and an octave were the first to be recognized as consonant. But Aristotle is aware that there are other consonant pairs as well (*Metaph.* 1093^{a}26). To produce two notes an octave apart, one can pluck a string, halve its length, and pluck it again. Thus the string-length ratio corresponding to the interval of an octave is 2:1. Other consonant pairs also turned out to have uncomplicated ratios, namely 4:3 (fourth), 3:2 (fifth), 3:1 (octave+fifth), 4:1 (double octave). All these ratios are expressible by the numbers 1 to 4. Three of them are of the form n:1 (4:1, 3:1, 2:1). And three are of the form n+1:n (4:3, 3:2, 2:1). Aristotle never mentions the awkward exception, the octave+fourth, whose ratio is 8:3.

The extension of these mathematical ideas to colour and flavour is made in the *De Sensu* 3, 4, and 7. The treatise *De Coloribus* expresses a quite different theory, and I follow the normal view in taking it to be un-Aristotelian. The theory of the *De Sensu* is that colours intermediate between the darkest (black) and the lightest (white) consist of a mixture of black with white. And the most

---

[1] Goethe (*Zur Farbenlehre*, 1810, translated with notes by Eastlake as *Goethe's Theory of Colours*, John Murray, 1840), knew, and wrote about, Aristotle's theory, but he mistakenly counted as Aristotelian the *De Coloribus*, which talks in ch. 2 of mixing lights, not stuffs.
For details of modern colour theory, consult Ralph M. Evans, *An Introduction to Colour*, John Wiley and Sons, 1948, esp. pp. 65-6, 68-9.

[2] Archytas' followers, *ap.* Porphyry's commentary on Ptolemy's *Harmonics*, ed.

Wallis, p. 277; Plato, *Timaeus* 80A-B; Aristotle, *D.A.* 426^{b}3-6, *Metaph.* 1043^{a}10 (cf. *D.S.* 447^{a}12-448^{a}19); pseudo-Aristotle, *Problems* 19. 27, 38; Euclid, *Sectio Canonis*, introd., ed. Meibom, p. 24; pseudo-Euclid, *Isagoge* § 5, ed. Meibom, p. 8; Nicomachus, *Enchiridion* § 12, ed. Meibom, p. 25; Gauden-tius, *Isagoge* § 8, ed. Meibom, p. 11; Aelian, *ap.* Porphyry, loc. cit., pp. 218, 265, 270; Boethius, *De Institutione Musica*, 1. 3, 1. 8, 1. 28.—In general, see F. A. Gevaert, *Histoire et Théorie de la Musique de l'Antiquité*, Ghent, 1875.

pleasant colours are produced by ratios of black to white which are uncomplicated,[1] and (439^{b}32) expressible in numbers easy to calculate with. They are thus parallel to consonant combinations in music. The other colours are not *logoi*, or uncomplicated ratios (439^{b}29-30; 440^{a}14-15). Indeed, they are not expressible in (rational) numbers at all (440^{a}2-3; 440^{b}20; 442^{a}15-17), but stand in an incommensurable (439^{b}30) relation of predominance and subordination only (439^{b}30; 440^{b}20).

Aristotle does at 440^{a}3-6 mention an alternative distinction, according to which all colours are expressible in (rational) numbers, but some are regular and some irregular.[2] He does not, however, refer to this alternative again, except perhaps at 442^{a}14-16.[3] Otherwise he mentions it only in connection with an idea he rejects, that the mixture of black and white takes the form of a juxtaposition of tiny particles of black and white. When he goes on to give his own view that the mixture of colours is due to genuine chemical mixture of coloured bodies, not to a mere juxtaposition, he repeats only the original distinction between the rational and the irrational combination.

We may guess that this mathematical idea in *De Sensu* 3 fits in with Aristotle's division of colours into three main groups in chapter 4. First of all, there are black and white, the primary colours. And with these, he says, either yellow or grey should be counted in (442^{a}21-3; 448^{a}6).

[1] The word *logos* sometimes implies uncomplicated ratios (*An. Post.* 90^{a}19; 20; *D.S.* 439^{b}27-440^{a}3; 440^{a}14-15; *Probl.* 19. 41). But sometimes it has a wider sense, covering all sorts of mathematical relations (*An. Post.* 90^{a}22; *D.S.* 440^{b}19; 442^{a}15; 448^{a}8; ^{a}10), even incommensurable ones.

[2] A major problem about 440^{a}3-6 is that it starts off by suggesting that all colours are (expressible) in (rational) numbers, but appears to finish up by talking of a sub-class which are not in numbers. If we retain the traditional text, the best way to remove this appearance of contradiction is probably that of J. I. Beare, in the Oxford translation. Instead of 'not in numbers', we must understand Aristotle to mean 'not such (i.e. not pure) in their numbers'. I would translate: 'Or one can also suppose that all colours are in numbers, but some are regular, others irregular, and these latter are produced when the colours are not pure through not being pure in their numbers.' This, admittedly, is a strain on the Greek word order. In this translation, I take it that the impure colours are not a sub-class of, but are identical with, the irregular colours. It is for one and the same reason that they are called 'irregular' and 'impure'. For the meaning of 'impure', see below, p. 297.

[3] 442^{a}14-16 says 'according to a *logos* [or?] in a relation of more and less, whether according to certain numbers in the mixture and interaction, or also in an indefinite way'. I prefer to stick to the MSS. reading, which omits 'or'. In that case, the opening phrase,

'according to a *logos* in a relation of more and less', will be a perfectly non-committal one, which does not specify the particular relationships available. It need mean no more than 'in a quantitative relationship'. The insertion of 'or' has appealed to those who over-hastily connected the word *logos* with the *logoi*, or *uncomplicated* ratios, of chapter 3 (439^{b}29-30; 440^{a}14-15), and the words 'more and less' (*mallon kai hētton*) with what in chapter 3 is described as *merely* (*monon*) an *incommensurable* (*asummetron*) relation of predominance and subordination (*huperochē kai elleipsis*, 439^{b}30; 440^{b}20).

On our interpretation, it is left to the following words to specify what the possible relationships are. And the following words can be taken in either of two ways. Perhaps the phrase 'whether according to certain numbers in the mixture and interaction' introduces the second and less usual alternative of 440^{a}3-6, according to which all the relationships are commensurable and rational. The last phrase ('or also in an indefinite way') will then revert to the more usual alternative, according to which some relationships are commensurable, but there are 'also' incommensurable ones.

Alternatively, the remaining words confine themselves to the more usual alternative, and simply spell out the choice it offers between being in rational numbers and not being in rational numbers. In that case, the less usual alternative is never alluded to again after its original mention.

The second group consists of the secondary colours, red, purple, green, and blue, and possibly yellow (442ᵃ20–5; 448ᵃ8). These are the result of direct mixture of black with white. But the mixture is naturally, not artificially, produced. In fact, these colours, or the first three of them, are listed in the *Meteorology* (372ᵃ2–9) as the ones that painters cannot get by mixing. We may guess that these secondaries are the colours that are compared with consonant combinations of sound. At any rate, *De Sensu* 3 specifies purple, red, and a few like these as corresponding to the consonances, and as having a ratio expressible in rational numbers easy to calculate with (440ᵃ1).

The third group consists of the tertiary colours, which are mixed out of these (442ᵃ25), i.e. presumably out of the secondary colours, instead of being mixed directly out of black and white.¹ Of their original ingredients, therefore, one, e.g. blue, will exemplify one ratio, another, e.g. red, will exemplify another. It seems just possible that this is what Aristotle means when he alludes briefly to the alternative method for distinguishing colours, according to which some colours are irregular and impure (440ᵃ3–6). Perhaps 'impure' means that the original ingredients exemplify more than one ratio, and not, as Alexander of Aphrodisias says, that the final product exemplifies more than one.

Be that as it may, we can guess that the tertiary colours are the ones which correspond to dissonant notes, and which Aristotle normally classifies not as irregular and impure, but rather as having irrational ratios. His usual view of tertiary colours is that, like secondaries, they have a single ratio of black to white (see especially 448ᵃ10, 'in this way the ratio of the extremes becomes single').

How much of the foregoing scheme is Aristotle's and how much did he inherit? Oskar Becker² has suggested that the rational/irrational division stems from Archytas and Eudoxus, while the alternative regular/irregular division is due to Philolaos, Plato, and the Old Academy. Konrad Gaiser³ thinks that such precision is impossible, but that the mathematical ideas were already being worked on in the Academy before Aristotle wrote about them. A. E. Taylor⁴ detects a Pythagorean source. In fact, it is hard to say how much is due to Aristotle. He certainly learnt from others the theories that the remaining colours are produced from black and white by juxtaposition or by superimposition, while the substitution of chemical mixture for juxtaposition and superimposition is his own. But what about the introduction of a threefold division of colours in place of the twofold division of Empedocles, Democritus,

¹ One would suppose, however, that a tertiary colour, such as pink, could be produced not only by mixing two secondary colours, but also by mixing one secondary colour (red) with white, or with colourless water, or again by mixing two tertiary colours.
² 'Eudoxos-Studien V', in *Quellen und Studien zur Geschichte der Mathematik*, Abt. B. 3, 1936, p. 403.
³ 'Platons Farbenlehre', in *Synusia*, Festgabe für Wolfgang Schadewaldt, edd. Hellmut Flashar and Konrad Gaiser, Pfullingen, 1965.
⁴ *A Commentary on Plato's Timaeus*, Oxford,

1928, pp. 485, 489, 491. More extravagantly, J. Zürcher claims that the theory is not Aristotle's, but was added later by Theophrastus, under the influence of Aristoxenus (*Aristoteles' Werk und Geist*, Paderborn, 1952, pp. 302–5). A comparatively extensive contribution by Aristotle seems to be allowed in the account of P. Kucharski, 'Sur la théorie des couleurs et des saveurs dans le "De Sensu" aristotélicien', *Revue des études grecques* lxvii (1954), 355, and F. M. Cornford, 'Mysticism and Science in the Pythagorean Tradition', *Classical Quarterly* xvi (1922), 144.

and Plato?[1] What about the idea that the ratios will correspond to certain acoustical ones? What about the idea that the relevant distinction is that between uncomplicated ratios and irrational ones? What about the alternative idea that, if all the ratios are rational, then the distinction must be in terms of regular and irregular? Fortunately, we need not decide how much of this Aristotle is inventing and how much he is merely endorsing. For it will make no difference to our subsequent discussion of his responsibility for errors and miscalculations. Nor will it affect our discussion of whether he thinks it appropriate to apply mathematics to natural science.

APPARENT OVERSIGHTS

We must now observe that unfortunately Aristotle's exposition contains a number of apparent oversights. I shall bring forward five of them for discussion. The first is a minor one, since it involves no error on Aristotle's part, but only an omission. It concerns the question of why painters can't obtain secondary colours by mixing. Mathematically speaking, this ought to be possible. For given three vats of paint, each vat containing black and white in a different ratio, one should be able, as far as mathematics is concerned, to mix a suitable amount from the darkest vat with a suitable amount from the lightest, and obtain the ratio that yields the intermediate shade. Why, then, cannot one obtain a secondary colour by mixing together a darker one and a lighter one in suitable quantities? Indeed, why cannot one obtain any shade by mixing together any darker one and any lighter one in the right amounts? The answer cannot lie in mathematics.

Presumably, the material pigments are recalcitrant in some way. But in what way? It is a matter for regret that Aristotle does not discuss the divergence between the mathematical, and the real, possibilities. One explanation would be that certain pigments, just like oil and water, will not mix. Or at least, the techniques we have so far tried, such as stirring, will not make them mix. Alternatively, perhaps some pigments mix in such a way that, instead of getting a single colour, green, at the end of the mixing process, we get two colours, some brown and some orange. Another explanation would be that the pigments available as ingredients for our mixture are never perfectly homogeneous, and do not display a single ratio throughout.

There is yet another suggestion that we should mention, if only to get it out of the way. It is that when the material pigments are recalcitrant, this is because the ratio in the final mixture is not a function of the ratio in the original ingredients. In the De Sensu at 440[b]19, Aristotle seems to be thinking about the ratio of black to white in the original ingredients, in the original earth and fire, for example, before they were mixed together. But the De Generatione et Corruptione[2] suggests a sense in which black and white not only attach to the original ingredients, but also persist in modified form in the resulting compound colour. For the resulting purple or brown has a certain degree of darkness (or black) about it, and a certain degree of brightness (or white). So instead of talking of the ratio of the original black to the original white, one could talk of the ratio of the resulting modified black to the resulting modified white. This

---

[1] Empedocles, in Aëtius 1. 15. 3; Democritus in Theophrastus, De Sensibus 73–82, and in Aëtius 1. 15. 8; Plato in the Timaeus 67c–68d.

[2] See 327[b]22–31; 328[a]29–31; 334[b]8–30, with Harold H. Joachim's useful commentary, Aristotle on Coming-to-be and Passing-away, Oxford, 1922.

way of talking is used, in connection with hot and cold, not black and white, at
G. et C. 334ᵇ14–16. And on the present suggestion, what happens when the
material pigments are recalcitrant is that the ratio of modified black to
modified white in the compound colour is not a function of the ratio of
black to white in the original ingredients. Fortunately, we need not pin this
idea on Aristotle, since he never expresses it. It would make his theory less
attractive in several ways. We started with one unexplained piece of terminology, the ratio of black to white in the original ingredients. But now we should
have a second piece, the ratio of modified black to modified white. How would
these ratios be measured? Secondly, we should have a very large gap in our
explanation of how a given shade is produced, if the final ratio were not
a function of the original ratio.

The second apparent oversight in Aristotle's mathematical theory is this: he
seems to ignore the middle ground between the very simplest ratios and those
which cannot be expressed in rational numbers at all. Within this middle
ground there fall, for example, 9:8 and 256:243, the non-consonant intervals of
a tone and a semitone. Both are discussed by Plato at *Timaeus* 36B, where Plato
points out that the ratio of 256:243 is in rational numbers (*arithmos pros arith-
mon*). In fact, there must be an infinity of string-length ratios which fall within
the middle ground (even though Aristotle would not allow that, in any but
a very weak sense, one could perceive the difference between one ratio and
another that was exceedingly close to it).[1] We shall be very surprised, then,
when we read *Posterior Analytics* 90ᵃ21–2, and find that Aristotle equates the
question 'Is it possible for the high and the low note to be consonant?' with
the question 'Is their ratio expressible in (rational) numbers?' This equation
implies that any ratio which can be expressed in rational numbers at all will
yield a pair of consonant notes. And this is not correct. It is only certain
rational ratios, in most cases very simple ones, that yield consonant pairs. The
ratio 256:243 does not. We can hardly believe that a member of Plato's
Academy was unaware of these facts. What then, is the explanation of Aristotle's overlooking them? We get the same omission in the account of colour in
the *De Sensu* (439ᵇ27–440ᵃ3). After describing the simplest ratios, and assigning
them to the few pleasantest colours, Aristotle says at 440ᵃ2, 'The colours which
are not in numbers,[2] one may suppose, are the other ones.' This again implies
that the only alternatives are having very simple ratios, or having ratios that
cannot be expressed in (rational) numbers at all.

There are various reflections that ought to have saved Aristotle from this
apparent oversight. One, of course, would be to think about non-consonant
intervals in music, like 256:243. But in addition to this, mathematics makes it
unlikely that all tertiary colours will have irrational ratios. For mathematics
suggests that certain quantities of blue, with its uncomplicated ratio, mixed
into certain quantities of red, with its uncomplicated ratio, will yield a product whose ratio of black to white is itself uncomplicated, and expressible in

[1] *D.S.* 445ᵇ31–446ᵃ20. Tiny variations
cannot be perceived on their own, but are
perceived only through being part of, and
through contributing to, a larger variation.

[2] 'Not in numbers' (440ᵃ2–3) must mean
'not expressible in (rational) numbers at all'.
We cannot rescue Aristotle by taking it to

mean 'not in *simple* numbers'. The next line
(440ᵃ3–4) rules out this interpretation, by
putting forward the alternative that *all*
colours are 'in numbers'. This cannot mean
'in *simple* numbers', for there are not enough
simple ratios to go round *all* the colours.

rational numbers. At least, this will be so if we set aside the various ways in which the actual material pigments may be recalcitrant. Another warning is supplied by considering further the rather imperfect analogy between colour and sound. If a mixture of red and blue corresponds to anything in music, it corresponds to a combination of two different consonant pairs played simultaneously. Now the latter may be such that all four of its notes are consonant with each other, and bear to each other uncomplicated string-length ratios, expressible in rational numbers. Why then should a mixture of red and blue inevitably result in an irrational ratio?

Our third complaint is this. Aristotle has failed to observe that there will be twice as many simple ratios available for colours as for sounds. This can be seen from the following table.

Shorter string		Longer string	White		Black
1	:	4	1	:	4
1	:	3	1	:	3
1	:	2	1	:	2
2	:	3	2	:	3
3	:	4	3	:	4
			4	:	3
			3	:	2
			2	:	1
			3	:	1
			4	:	1

The reason is that in acoustics, the lower number in a ratio, such as 1:2, must always correspond to the shorter string. But in colour theory, the lower number may correspond *either* to white *or* to black. This has serious consequences for Aristotle's theory. For he says that pleasant colours and consonances are few in number, and that this is for the same reason, namely that there are only a few simple mathematical ratios available.[1] This claim is now spoilt by the fact that there are at least ten simple ratios available for colours, twice as many as for sounds. We may wonder why he does not recognize ten pleasant colours, corresponding to the ten simple ratios we have listed in the table above. But if the pleasant colours, described as 'purple, red, and a few like these' (440a1), are the secondary colours, there will be only five of them. Indeed, there are only seven colours altogether, according to chapter 4, though this statement ignores the tertiary ones. If there are five pleasant colours, the number of mathematical ratios (ten) cannot after all account for their scarcity. In addition, we are left with an unresolved question: which of the ten simple ratios enter into the five pleasant colours?

For our fourth and fifth complaints, we move on to a passage in *De Sensu* 7. But we must treat this passage with more caution, because Aristotle is not endorsing the argument which he propounds. Indeed, he thinks its conclusion mistaken. This is not to say that he is describing the argument merely for polemical purposes, or trying to make it sound silly. On the contrary, the argument is one of a set of three which he thinks plausible enough to create a genuine *aporia*, and worth propounding at length. But his main concern is to press on to his own view (449a5-20). He does not trouble to point out errors in any of the

[1] 440a1-2.

VII

ARISTOTLE, MATHEMATICS, AND COLOUR   301

three arguments on the other side. We can hardly suppose that he is unaware of any. We should not therefore attach significance to oversights in the present argument, unless either they have been gratuitously introduced, or they entirely remove the argument's plausibility. With these warnings, we may now look to see how the argument at 448^{a}1–13 goes.

The argument is trying to establish a conclusion that Aristotle will ultimately reject, namely that one cannot perceive two sense-objects simultaneously. One cannot perceive black and white simultaneously, so the argument alleges, because, being contraries, black and white set up contrary processes in a perceiver, and contrary processes cannot exist in a single place at a single time (448^{a}1–5). The same applies to grey and yellow, for grey is a kind of black and yellow a kind of white (448^{a}5–8; cf. 442^{a}20–3). The same applies to red and purple ('mixed' colours, 448^{a}8),[1] for these two are opposed to each other in a way. For one contains much black and little white, the other the opposite. Or one contains an odd number of units of black to an even number of white, the other the opposite. The only case in which one can perceive red and purple simultaneously is when they are mixed with each other to form a single intermediate colour which one sees as single. Then there is a single ratio of black to white, and so no opposition (448^{a}8–13), and so no barrier to one's perceiving the red and purple simultaneously.

I have stated the argument in terms of the colours, red and purple, because it is true of these, on Aristotle's theory, that if one mixes them with each other to obtain an intermediate colour, the resulting intermediate colour will have a single ratio of black to white. But the example actually given is drawn from the field of sound. And our fourth complaint is that the argument has failed to notice that there is no corresponding possibility here. For if we play simultaneously the two notes that constitute an octave and the two notes that constitute a fifth, we shall not thereby obtain a single string-length ratio. There will still be two ratios. This oversight seems rather elementary. But is it the fault of Aristotle or of the argument? The argument cannot afford to admit that there is ever simultaneous perception, when there are two opposed ratios. It can avoid admitting this, by denying that we ever hear an octave and a fifth with perfect simultaneity. There is no need, then, for Aristotle to make the argument take the alternative way out, of claiming that there will be a single string-length ratio. Aristotle appears to have introduced the error gratuitously.

[1] 'Mixed' is a confusing word to use, since in one sense, black and white are mixed colours, i.e. colours that mix *with each other* to form other colours. But Aristotle clearly means to refer to colours like red and purple, which are mixed in the sense that each is composed of black and white.

'Mixed things' cannot refer to black and white. For (a) The case of black and white has already been dealt with in 448^{a}1–5. (b) Lines 11–13 mention not two terms, but four (much: little and little: much). These four terms must correspond to the black and white that enters into a purple and the black and white that enters into a red. (c) If it were black and white that Aristotle was describing as 'mixed', he would be implying that they were already mixed with each other to form a single intermediate colour. He could not then go on to say (448^{a}8) that it would be impossible to perceive them simultaneously.

I believe there will be no obstacle to giving 'mixed' the required reference, provided we make a small emendation of the text at 448^{a}8–9 from λόγοι ἀντικειμένων to λόγοι ἀντικείμενοι. With this emendation, the argument will be using the opposition *between* red (which is one ratio) and purple (which is an opposed ratio), to explain why one can't perceive red and purple simultaneously. Without the emendation, Aristotle will be irrelevantly emphasizing the opposition *within* red and *within* purple.

VII

302

The fifth and last oversight on our list enters into the same argument. It has not been gratuitously introduced, however, and we cannot attach equal significance to it. But we may mention it, for the sake of completeness. The argument asks us to suppose that purple contains much black and little white, and red the opposite; or that one contains an odd number of units of black to an even number of white, the other the opposite. But this neglects the fact that many combinations (whether in the field of colour or of sound) will exhibit neither kind of arrangement. Indeed, the first kind of arrangement (much to little and little to much) is impossible in the case of sound, from which the argument draws its illustration. For here the higher number (or, in other words, the much) always corresponds to the greater string-length, and so to the lower pitch. It is not like the case of colour, where the higher number may correspond either to black or to white. Consequently, we shall never get instances of much high pitch to little low pitch. For this would mean, *per impossibile*, that the higher number (the much) corresponded to the higher pitch. The example actually given is that of the octave and the fifth. The ratios here are 2:1 and 3:2. And presumably, the argument would say that this exhibits the second kind of arrangement, even to odd, and odd to even. This assumes that 1 can be counted as an odd number. Certainly, Plato so counts it, at *Phaedo* 105c and *Hippias Major* 302a. So it will not be altogether surprising if the present argument does the same. But there is something a little unsatisfactory about its counting 1 as an odd number. For 1 lacks some of the properties by which odd numbers were commonly defined, such as having a middle, or being divisible into two unequal sets of integers. Moreover, Aristotle himself does not count 1 as a number (*Metaph.* 1088^{a}6), whereas he does treat oddness as a property peculiar to numbers (*Metaph.* 1004^{b}10–11; 1031^{a}1–6).

Aristotle's Willingness to Apply Mathematics to Nature

We have now finished expounding the mathematical aspect of Aristotle's theory. And I should like to raise, in relation to this aspect of his theory, three questions about his method in natural science. The first question concerns his willingness to use mathematics. It is tempting to contrast Plato as one who applies mathematics to natural science with Aristotle who does not. Indeed, some such contrast is a commonplace. Étienne Gilson, for example, writes as follows.[1] 'There are virtually only two great roads open to metaphysical speculation: that of Plato and that of Aristotle. One can have a metaphysics of the intelligible, suspicious with regard to the sensible, whose method is mathematical, which branches out into a science of measurement; or one can have a metaphysics of the concrete, suspicious with regard to the intelligible, whose method is biological, which branches out into a science of classification.' This contrast between Plato and Aristotle seems too simple, in light of the *De Sensu*'s application of mathematics to colour. So let us look more closely at what recent commentators have said about Aristotle's antipathy to a mathematical approach.

Augustin Mansion has maintained that Aristotle neglects the use of mathematical formulae in nature, except in connection with insignificant points of

[1] Translated from *Études sur le rôle de la pensée médiévale dans la formation du système cartésien*, Paris, 1930, p. 199.

detail.[1] And Léon Robin says that mathematics is used merely as a source of examples, or to present the results of empirical analysis with an outward appearance of simplicity.[2] Neither statement seems to fit the *De Sensu*'s treatment of colour.

Other commentators go further. Not only did Aristotle omit to apply mathematics to nature. He thought it quite inappropriate to do so. Friedrich Solmsen,[3] for example, puts great stress on a passage in the *De Caelo*. At 306ª1–21, Aristotle is attacking Plato's construction of matter out of triangles. Plato has used mathematical first principles in dealing with nature. But perhaps, says Aristotle, the first principles of perceptible things should be perceptible, of eternal things eternal, of perishable things perishable, and in general the first principles should be of the same kind as what falls under them. If this last statement is taken seriously, it seems to mean that the natural scientist may not take his first principles from mathematics. But can the statement be taken seriously? As early as Simplicius, we find doubts raised.[4] Simplicius points out that Aristotle says only 'perhaps', and suggests he is forced into this by the fact that matter, as Aristotle conceives it, is not an object of perception, but is none the less one of the first principles of perceptible objects. Maybe Aristotle's tentative 'perhaps' is due to an unresolved problem he raises in the *Metaphysics*, at 1000ᵇ23–9. If the first principles of perishable things were themselves perishable, he says, they would not be genuine first principles, for, being perishable, they would themselves stand in need of first principles, out of which they would arise, and into which they would perish. At any rate, whatever the reason for Aristotle's 'perhaps', the *De Caelo* statement is too tentative for us to be able to rest much weight on it.

It may, in any case, be that Aristotle has only a very limited point in mind. If one is giving an explanation of sensible phenomena, one's premises must be subject to the test of whether they are consistent with the sensible phenomena. Plato's *Timaeus* has not observed this rule, because, so Aristotle alleges, it uses premises which are inconsistent with the observable fact that solids made of earth can be transformed into fluids. It treats its mathematical premises as unassailable by reference to such observable facts. If this is the burden of Aristotle's complaint, he has left himself quite free to apply mathematics to nature, just so long as his hypotheses, about (say) the mathematical ratios of black to white, are not treated as ultimate, but are checked for consistency with the observable facts.

The passage just cited from the *De Caelo* comes from a long attack on Plato's treatment of matter in the *Timaeus*. Harold Cherniss[5] has said of this attack that Aristotle's fundamental objection to Platonic matter is that it is too

[1] In *Introduction à la physique aristotélicienne*, Louvain and Paris [1st edition, 1913], 2nd edition, 1946, esp. pp. 188, 225; and in 'La physique aristotélicienne et la philosophie', printed in *Philosophie et Sciences*, Journées d'études de la Société thomiste, 1936.
[2] *La Pensée grecque*, Paris, 1923, p. 332.
[3] *Aristotle's System of the Physical World*, Ithaca, New York, 1960, pp. 259–62.
[4] Commentary on Aristotle's *De Caelo*, p. 642.
[5] *Aristotle's Criticism of Plato and the Academy*, Baltimore, 1944, e.g. pp. 123, 124,

130, 161, 164. According to Cherniss, Aristotle also believes that different sounds are irreducible qualities, not to be explained as quantitative relations (p. 158 note). Because of this belief, says Cherniss, Aristotle denies in the *De Anima* that high notes are identical with swift movements (420ª31–3). But in fact, the *De Anima* passage is very guarded. And whatever it says, it does not disagree with the view of the *De Generatione Animalium* (786ᵇ25–787ᵇ20) that pitch varies with variation in speed.

mathematical. Plato wrongly reduces quality to quantity. None the less, whatever Aristotle's objections may be to certain uses of mathematics, these passages do not seek to condemn any and every application of mathematics to nature.

More striking perhaps is Aristotle's statement in *Metaphysics* 995ᵃ14–17. We should not demand mathematical precision in natural science, because the matter of which natural objects consist interferes, in such a way as to make precision impossible. Once again, I do not believe that this statement rules out the application of mathematics to nature. It implies only that there will be some restrictions. For example, because of the recalcitrance of the material pigments, painters cannot obtain certain colours by mixing, even though, mathematically speaking, this should have been possible. Again, though we may say that red has a ratio of 2:1, there are in fact several shades of red, and only one shade can have *precisely* the ratio of 2:1. In both ways, the application of mathematics to colour must be restricted, but the application of mathematics does not for that reason become impossible.

If we now turn to the evidence on the other side, we find that Aristotle repeatedly links four sciences, astronomy, optics, acoustics, and mechanics, with mathematics. His view of the exact nature of the link changes from time to time.[1] But one way or another he has to admit that mathematics has a large part to play in these sciences.

In the *De Sensu* we find him going further. Alongside acoustics, one of the four sciences just named, we must place colour theory. For this can be given a similar mathematical treatment. And there are hints that the same might be done in other fields too. Just as black and white can be mixed in various ratios, so too hot and cold can be mixed in a ratio of 2:1 or 3:1 (*G. et C.* 334ᵇ14–16). And again Aristotle in some ways approves of Empedocles[2] for saying that bone differs from flesh because of its numerical ratio, four parts of fire to two of water.[3]

In the *De Sensu* Aristotle actually seems to be more willing than Plato to apply mathematics to colour theory. In a much-discussed passage, *Timaeus* 68B, Plato appears to be saying that one should not try to state the mathematical ratios which produce various colours. Aristotle, however, has implied that the ratios are those of the consonant intervals, namely 1:4, 1:3, 1:2, 2:3, and 3:4. Moreover, he has roughly correlated these ratios with purple, red, and (we may guess) green and blue, and yellow, though he has not committed himself to any particular ratio for any particular colour.[4] In spite of Gaiser's attempt[5] to find a measure of agreement between Plato and Aristotle, it looks as if Aristotle has here gone beyond Plato in his willingness to apply mathematics to natural science. We cannot accept as it stands the stereotype of Plato as one who favours the application of mathematics and of Aristotle as one who opposes it.

---

[1] The stages in his thought are traced out by A. Mansion, *Introduction à la physique aristotélicienne*, 2nd edition, Louvain and Paris, 1946, pp. 190–5.

[2] See *Metaph.* 993ᵃ17-22; 1092ᵇ17; *D.A.* 408ᵃ14; 410ᵃ1–6; 429ᵇ16; *P.A.* 642ᵃ18–23; *G.A.* 734ᵇ33.

[3] For further evidence of Aristotle's willingness to use mathematics, see G. E. L. Owen, 'Aristotle', in the *Dictionary of Scientific Biography*, ed. C. C. Gillispie, vol. i (1970).

[4] See p. 300, where it is pointed out that there are perhaps ten simple ratios available, and that Aristotle has not told us which of the ten correspond to the four or five pleasantest colours.

[5] Op. cit., esp. pp. 193–5.

TESTABILITY OF ARISTOTLE'S THEORY

This brings me to my second question about Aristotle's method. To modern ears, the use of mathematical formulae will seem worthless, unless the mathematical suggestions can be empirically tested. Vlastos[1] has supplied a valuable analysis of early Greek theories of nature, in which he emphasizes that on the whole these theories were not formulated with sufficient precision to admit of empirical testing. Plato, in his treatment of colour, appears to go further still, claiming that it would be entirely inappropriate to subject to empirical test his explanation of how the various colours are produced (*Timaeus* 68D). There is nothing like this in Aristotle. But we should not go to the other extreme. For Aristotle shows no particular awareness of the need to formulate his theory so that it will admit of empirical testing.[2] Let us ask then, not whether he has stated the theory with a view to making it empirically testable, but whether it happens to be empirically testable.

It may seem that the theory provides us with no way of discovering what the ratios for particular colours are. Aristotle has not told us what they are in any one case. One barrier to testing will arise if the material pigments are recalcitrant in any of the ways we described earlier, on pp. 298–9. Another barrier to testing is the fact that we have not been told what it means to talk of the ratio of black to white in the original ingredients. Perhaps the black in a volume of earth and the white in the same volume of fire are to be counted as the same quantity of black and of white. But this will not enable us to discover the ratios of other colours, if we cannot obtain specimens of pure earth and pure fire, know when we have got them, and set about mixing them. In fact, it is implied in the *De Generatione et Corruptione* that the earth and fire available to us are not pure (330ᵇ21).

In spite of this, it may seem that more indirect methods of testing could be used. To give an example, suppose one takes a pint each of red, purple, green, and blue paint, and hypothesizes the exact number of units of black and of white in each. Such a hypothesis would facilitate predictions to the effect that so much of one pint, mixed with so much of another, should yield the same shade as so much of a third mixed with so much of a fourth, provided that the materials are not recalcitrant. Suppose the original hypothesis about the number of units were corroborated by the confirmation of these predictions. One might then infer that any pint of red paint would contain, not indeed exactly the same number of units of black and white, but units of black and white in the same ratio, let us say in the ratio of three whites to one black. But how much would one then have confirmed? Not surely the historical hypothesis that at some time in the past white bodies had been mixed with black, fire for example with earth, in a proportion of 3 to 1. One's result would be compatible with quite different theories, such as that red paint reflected three units of light for every one unit it absorbed. One might continue to speak of this as being composed of three units of white to one of black. But the sense of so speaking would no longer have anything to do with the historical hypothesis of mixture.

Moreover, even if such a method could be used for confirming part of Aristotle's theory, it could hardly be used for disconfirming it. For if one's

[1] Review of Cornford's *Principium Sapientiae* in *Gnomon* xxvii (1955), 65.
[2] He thinks theories about the observable world must be rejected if they are not consistent with the observable facts (see above, p. 303), but this is not yet to think of framing theories so as to fit them for empirical testing.

predictions never came out right, this could be put down to the recalcitrance of the materials. How seriously one takes this last difficulty will depend on one's view of the nature of science. Some would say that many theories of modern science have lacked the falsifiability which Karl Popper[1] considers the hallmark of scientific theory.

EXPLANATION OF ARISTOTLE'S OVERSIGHTS

I now come to my third and last question about method. We earlier discovered a series of oversights in Aristotle's mathematical treatment of colour. How are these oversights to be explained?

One explanation would be that Aristotle lacked the required mathematical competence. Gaston Milhaud wrote an influential article in 1903[2] in which he argued that Aristotle was insufficiently influenced by recent developments in mathematics, and retained the most naïve conceptions, conceptions which show him to be no true mathematician. Milhaud cites, for example, Aristotle's view of number as a discontinuous plurality of units. Such a notion ignores numbers other than the integers. The only time that Aristotle shows himself aware of recent advances is when he discusses the squaring of circles or lunules. And even then he is committed to coming out on the wrong side, and to denying the possibility of squaring lunules. For he thinks a straight line is incommensurable with a circle (*Phys.* 248ᵇ4), or curve. In discussing what we should call the laws of motion, he assumes that the relations that hold between speed, force, and density of the medium will be simple proportionalities, or inverse proportionalities. He is not alive to the existence of other mathematical relations. In denying the actualization of infinity, Aristotle cuts himself off from the infinitesimal methods that were being elaborated. Such are Milhaud's charges, and many leading scholars since have endorsed his conclusion, for example Werner Jaeger, Léon Robin, and Jean-Marie Le Blond.[3] The last of these simply refers to Milhaud for his support. W. D. Ross uses one of Milhaud's arguments when he says, 'A better mathematician might even in the absence of evidence have noticed the possibility.' (Ross is referring to the possibility that velocity and density of medium might bear a relation to each other more complex than that of inverse proportion.[4])

Henri Carteron and Augustin Mansion use a further argument for Aristotle's unfamiliarity with mathematics, namely that he appeals to specialists for the mathematical details of his celestial system, instead of working out the details

[1] *The Logic of Scientific Discovery*, Hutchinson, 1959.
[2] 'Aristote et les mathématiques', *Archiv für Geschichte der Philosophie* 1903. Also *Les Philosophes-Géomètres de la Grèce*, Paris, 1900, pp. 358–365.
[3] Jaeger, *Aristotle, Fundamentals of the History of his Development*, Oxford, 2nd edition (translated from the German of 1923): 'Aristotle lacked the temperament and the ability for anything more than an elementary acquaintance with the Academy's chief preoccupation, mathematics' (p. 21). Robin, *La Pensée grecque*, Paris, 1923, says

(p. 332) that it does not seem that Aristotle had the same mastery of mathematics as Plato. Le Blond, *Logique et méthode chez Aristote*, Paris, 1939, p. 192, calls Aristotle a mediocre mathematician. In contrast to Plato, he was not fundamentally a mathematician.
[4] Aristotle, *Physics*, a revised text with introduction and commentary, Oxford, 1936, p. 29. Cf. p. 31: the need for more complexity should have been apparent also from the fact that Aristotle is forced to admit a certain exception to his proportionalities.

himself (*Metaph.* 1073^{b}10–17; cf. *Cael.* 291^{a}29–32; ^{b}10).[1] The celestial system, with its 55 spheres, yields a fund of evidence. For it appears to be full of miscalculations. Aristotle has been defended on some charges more convincingly than on others. But at least when he says that the number 55 could be reduced to 47, few commentators deny that he has made an error in elementary arithmetic.

This evidence might suggest that Aristotle's oversights in the treatment of colour are due to mathematical incompetence. But caution is needed. For Aristotle's oversights in the treatment of motion a quite different, and to my mind, convincing, explanation emerges from the studies of H. Carteron and of G. E. L. Owen.[2] I do not think this explanation can be transferred in order to explain the oversights in Aristotle's colour theory. But it does modify the picture of mathematical incompetence that many writers have drawn.

Combining the arguments of Carteron and Owen, we may say that, when Aristotle postulates certain proportional relations as holding between speed and the density of the medium, his interest is in the limiting case, where density is zero. He is not especially concerned with cases that fall short of the limit. He wants to show (*Phys.* 215^{a}24–^{b}22) that a vacuum is impossible. For if the medium offered no resistance to motion, the speed of moving objects would *per impossibile* bear no ratio to other speeds, but would be infinite. So long as he can show that zero density involves infinite speed, he will not worry about getting other speeds exactly right. His method in connection with other speeds is to appeal to *endoxa*, that is to opinions that are commonly accepted. For it is the method of dialectic[3] to base one's conclusion (that zero density involves infinite speed) on *endoxa*. The *endoxa* may be facts of everyday observation, for example facts about the powers of ship haulers.[4] Another *endoxon* may be the simple idea that things do stand in proportion to each other.[5] The suggestion, then, that speed varies in inverse proportion to the density of the medium is entertained because it corresponds to *endoxa*, not because Aristotle is too naïve a mathematician to think of other relations. If he had introduced exact observations concerning intermediate densities and intermediate speeds, these observations would not have been *endoxa*. And this would have gone against his whole conception of the proper method of argument. One can see how unconcerned he is with finding a precise mathematical formula to cover all the cases, and how much more interested he is in *endoxa*. For he is perfectly willing to admit an exception (*Phys.* 250^{a}9–19) to the rules of proportion, when everyday observation suggests that there is one.

This explanation of Aristotle's oversights in the theory of motion is a good one. But we should not expect it to account for oversights elsewhere, for example in the celestial system, or in the theory of colour. No single explanation seems to fit all these cases. And even within the theory of colour, we should perhaps

[1] Carteron concludes that Aristotle was little versed in the mathematical sciences (Budé edition of Aristotle's *Physics*, 1926, vol. i, p. 16), Mansion that he neglected them ('La physique aristotélicienne et la philosophie', op. cit. (1936), pp. 26–7; cf. *Introduction à la physique aristotélicienne*, 2nd edition, 1946, p. 188).
[2] H. Carteron, *La Notion de force dans le système d'Aristote*, Paris, 1924; G. E. L.

Owen, 'Aristotle', in *Dictionary of Scientific Biography*, ed. C. C. Gillispie, vol. i (1970).
[3] See the definition of dialectic, at *Top.* 100^{a}29–30, as reasoning that starts from *endoxa*.
[4] For appeal to these facts, but as providing an exception, not confirmation, see *Phys.* 250^{a}17–19.
[5] See *Phys.* 250^{a}3–4, 'for in this way there will be a proportion.'

308

not expect a single explanation for the five oversights we have catalogued. Some of these oversights (the first and fifth) scarcely require explanation, the first because it is a mere omission, the fifth because it is not of Aristotle's own making. The fourth oversight, whereby he postulates a single string-length ratio for the octave and the fifth, could be a carelessness, fostered by his lack of interest in an argument which he rejects. This leaves us with two oversights which are harder to explain.

When he fails to notice that there are ten simple ratios, too many to explain the scarcity of pleasant colours, he has perhaps fallen victim to his willingness to leave mathematical details to people more expert than himself. Just as he says that he will leave to specialists the mathematical details of his celestial system (*Metaph.* 1073^{b}10–17, cited above), so here there are signs that he is leaving to others the details of his colour theory. For three times he gives us alternative hypotheses, without firmly deciding between them.[1]

But this will not account for what seems to be the worst oversight, the neglect of the middle ground between the simplest ratios and the irrational ones. Followers of Milhaud will be quick to conclude that Aristotle was unfamiliar with the facts of acoustical theory. It seems hard to believe that he could have been unfamiliar with facts so elementary, and yet it is also hard to avoid this conclusion.

RETROSPECT

There has been a stereotype of Aristotle as differing from Plato in being unwilling to apply mathematics to science. What we find in his theory of colour is not an unwillingness at all, but instead a great deal of oversight in the details of the application. These oversights have not one explanation, but a variety of different ones.[2]

[1] 440^{a}3; 442^{a}22; see p. 296 n. 3 on 442^{a}14–16.

[2] I read earlier drafts of this paper in three places, and received many helpful comments. I have responded to, or made use of, those by Professor J. L. Ackrill, by Jonathan Barnes, by Willie Charlton, and by Professor H. Post and his colleagues at the Chelsea College of Science and Technology. The donkey-work on Aristotle's *De Sensu* was done while I held a Howard Foundation Fellowship from Brown University, and a project grant (no. H68–0–95) from the National Endowment for the Humanities.

I have used the following abbreviations:

An. Post.	*Analytica Posteriora*
Top.	*Topica*
Phys.	*Physica*
Cael.	*De Caelo*
G. et C.	*De Generatione et Corruptione*
Meteor.	*Meteorologica*
D.A.	*De Anima*
D.S.	*De Sensu*
G.A.	*De Generatione Animalium*
Probl.	*Problemata*
Metaph.	*Metaphysica*

VIII

ARISTOTLE ON COLOUR,
LIGHT AND IMPERCEPTIBLES[1]

Abstract. Aristotle *On Sense Perception* 3, 6, and 7 explains the nature of light and of the borrowed colour of the sea. These need distinguishing from each other and from non-borrowed colour. Aristotle also allows imperceptible sounds and changes of pitch, yet denies imperceptible times. Why? I suggest that the discussion of imperceptible change of pitch is the target attacked in Theophrastus' account of singing. The theory of imperceptible times attacked seems unexpectedly elaborate, and I suggest it is a version of one found in the pseudo-Aristotelian *de Audibilibus.*

I shall try to explain the main concepts of what I find the three most interesting chapters of Aristotle's *On Sense Perception*, Chapters 3, 6 and 7, chapters which influenced his successor Theophrastus. Aristotle describes borrowed colour, such as the colour of the sea and air in *On Sense Perception* 3, 439b1-14. An example of air taking on colour is that of clouds to be mentioned below, but I shall concentrate on the sea as the clearer case. He contrasts its colour with the colour that is a thing's own (ἴδιον, b13). The terms 'other's' (ἀλλότριον) and 'own' (οἰκεῖον) are used of colour in *On the Soul* 2.7, 418b6; 419a2 and 6, and I think it fits best to take the ἀλλότριον colour to be borrowed colour. I want to consider how the two kinds of colour differ from light, but first how they differ from each other. It will be easiest to start with a thing's own colour.

Own colour

Colour is defined in terms of its function in *On the Soul*, but the contrast with borrowed colour comes out more clearly in *On Sense Perception* 3, where its material cause is given. Colour in *On the Soul* is what acts on the light in the medium intervening between itself and the observer. More exactly, it acts on the transparency of the medium, when that transparency is in its illuminated state of being actually seeable through, 418a31-b2; 419a9-11. Another

1 I first got to know Bill Fortenbaugh when we gave a seminar together on Aristotle's Ethics in King's College, London, in 1973. I learnt an enormous amount from our discussions, which were attended by Jim Dybikowski and David Sedley. Since then, he has moved a long way and founded the Theophrastus project, which has successfully made available to the world the fragments of Theophrastus and the ideas of the other early Aristotelians. Connie Fortenbaugh has repeatedly offered hospitality to the scholars from many countries who were drawn into the project, and who were well represented at the conference held in Bill's honour at the Institute of Classical Studies in June 2003. I have decided to substitute for the paper I delivered there one more closely related to Bill's work on Theophrastus and the early Aristotelians.

description of colour is that it is the object of sight, but this is used to define sight, not colour.[2] Phosphorescence is distinguished from colour at 419a1-6 on the ground that it is seen in the dark, not in the light. Like other shiny things, *On Sense Perception* 2, 432a32, it does not produce light. It might seem to be a problem here that the colour of a fire can be seen in the dark, but that is answered by the point that fire always illuminates the medium to some extent, so that it is not wholly dark, 2.7, 419a23-5, and that will distinguish phosphorescence.

In *On Sense Perception* 3, a thing's own colour is said to be a boundary or surface, but not the boundary of the body, rather the boundary of the transparency within the body, 439b11-12. Moreover, the particular shade of colour depends on the ratio of the darkest to the brightest ingredients, in the mixture of ingredients at that surface, 440a31 - b23. The reference to mixture shows how to make sense of this, namely in terms of Aristotle's idea that every body beneath the moon is a mixture of earth air, fire and water. The last three of these ingredients are transparent in varying degrees, which is why there is some transparency in every part of every body. Fire provides the brightest colour, earth the darkest. Aristotle's words μέλαν and λευκόν are inevitably translated as black and white, but hue was not sharply distinguished by the Greeks from brightness and darkness. The resulting theory of other shades as due to a mixture of the brightest and darkest ingredients was praised by Goethe in his *Farbenlehre*, as greatly superior, from the painter's point of view, to Newton's theory. Aristotle's surprisingly Pythagorean idea that the ingredients are mixed in mathematical ratios is extended to flavours in the next chapter, 4. I have explained the application of mathematics to colour theory elsewhere.[3]

Borrowed Colour

The borrowed colour of transparent bodies like the sea is introduced to make clear that transparency, and more precisely its surface, is indeed the seat of colour. The sea has such a predominance of the transparent elements, that its transparency is obvious, but the seat of colour is the same in bodies which contain so much earth as to be in effect opaque to us.

Where does the borrowed colour of the sea come from? Aristotle points out that with rigid bodies - and he is thinking of opaque ones - the *appearance* of colour, though not its own colour, can be changed by the surroundings (τὸ περιέχον). Presumably, then, the sea, which is treated as having no colour of its own, could have its borrowed colour changed by the surroundings, such as the sun and the sea bed. In *Meteorology* 1.5 and 3.2-6 Aristotle cites reflection as the cause of various colours in the clouds as well as of such other optical effects as rainbows, haloes, mock suns, and rods. Reflection would make it easy to explain the fact which he points out at *On Sense Perception* 3, 439b3-5, that the colour of the sea depends on the distance of the viewer. This fits very well with the point he makes explicitly about reflection in *On Sense Perception* 2, 438a8, when dismissing the relevance to your vision of the reflection in your eye. He there makes the very good point that that reflection is in the *observer* of your eye, by which I take him to mean that what is reflected depends on the

---

2 So Richard Sorabji, 'Aristotle on demarcating the five senses', *Philosophical Review* 80 (1971) 55-71, reprinted in *Articles on Aristotle*, eds Jonathan Barnes, Malcolm Schofield, Richard Sorabji, vol. 4 (London 1979).

3 Richard Sorabji, 'Aristotle, mathematics and colour', *Classical Quarterly* 22 (1972) 293-308.

observer's angle of viewing. The same applies to the angle of viewing of the observer of the sea. The angle of viewing would also affect which portion of sea bed was showing through to the observer, and showing through is something he discusses for quite different purposes at 3, 440a6-15.

Unexpectedly, though, Aristotle says that the variability of sea colour with distance of viewing is because of the colour being in an unstable, not a rigid, body (διὰ τὸ ἐν ἀορίστῳ, 439b3). I think rigidity might be better introduced as the reason why rigid bodies do not undergo changes in their own colour. They would, if different proportions of earth, air, fire and water, were for ever being tumbled to the surface of the transparency within them. Instability or tumbling, however, does not explain the effects of *distance* on borrowed colour. Surface instability could at best cause different parts of the sky to be reflected, but this would be independent of the *distance* of viewing. Another factor, but again independent of *distance* of viewing, would be that surface instability could lead to different *depths* of transparency, and in *On the Generation of Animals* Aristotle says that the more easily the total volume of a thing can be seen through, and – a different claim, but one not very clearly distinguished – the more transparent stuff, such as air, a thing contains per unit volume, the lighter or whiter its colour, 735a30 - 736a22; 779b27-33; 780a27-33; b8; 784b15; 786a7-13. Is this because there is less contaminating earth in these transparent bodies (a fact which should make them lighter in weight as well as colour), or is it that transparency is not merely the *seat* of colour, but also an independent influence on colour shade? I do not think that Aristotle emphasizes the independent influence of transparency on shade in *On Sense Perception*, and in any case rigidity is better understood as protecting rigid bodies from colour change, rather than as explaining the effects on sea colour of distance viewing.

Aristotle is a little inaccurate in making rigidity the differentiating mark between bodies with borrowed colour and bodies with their own colour, since fluid milk has white as its own colour, and modern diamonds and glass, though rigid, have borrowed colour. Precious stones and glass would in Aristotle's day, however, have been less refined and less receptive of borrowed colour. At *On the Soul* 2.7, 418b6-7, he remembers to take account of the fact that many rigid bodies are transparent.

Sea and air are not the only examples of borrowed colour, but some of the mechanisms in other cases will be entirely different. As I interpret *On the Soul*, above all 2.11, 424a2-10, but also 425b22-4; 427a8-9; 435a22-4, the organ of sight, the eye jelly, takes on borrowed colour patches, when it switches to seeing. That is why the second of these passages at 425a22 says that it is only *in a way* that what sees is coloured.[4] This is because the coloration is borrowed, not on my view because the coloration is not literal. The mechanism is considered entirely different from reflection, because Aristotle, we have seen, rejects the idea that seeing is due to reflection, *On Sense Perception* 2, 438a5-10.

Light

Light, like colour, receives a functional definition, which is straightforward, and a material definition, which is problematic. It is defined by reference to its function, at *On the Soul* 2.7,

---

4 Richard Sorabji, 'Aristotle on sensory processes and intentionality. A reply to Myles Burnyeat', in *Ancient and Medieval Theories of Intentionality*, ed. Dominik Perler (Leiden 2001) 49-61.

418b9-10 and 419a11, as the state in which the transparent is actually, not just potentially seeable through. That commonsensical idea is all that is meant by the sonorous phrase 'actualization of the transparent'. It would be sensible to understand that light is the state of the transparent in which one can see *colour* through it, not just phosphorescence, which Aristotle acknowledges can be seen in the dark.

The material definition of light, that is of illumination, not of brightness, at *On the Soul* 2.7, 418b16-7 and 20, *On Sense Perception* 3, 439a19-20, is that it is the presence of fire or something like fire in the transparent, that is, in what is seeable through. Phosphorescence does not count as firelike for this purpose, but merely *appears* firelike, *On the Soul* 2.7, 419a3. But besides ordinary fires, there are many things that are firelike. The fifth element that makes up the celestial bodies will also serve to create light throughout the celestial region, *On the Soul* 2.7, 419a11-13. Fire itself is of different kinds. The fires familiar to us on the earth are a kind of extreme or boiling of the transparent smokelike exhalation, which constitutes the sphere of much purer fire beneath the moon, *On Generation and Corruption* 2.3, 330b29; *Meteorology* 1.3 and 4, 340b23; 341b21-2. Our fires are treated as something that is not transparent and cannot contain light at *On Sense Perception* 2, 438b5-11. But elemental fire, which is most fully concentrated in the sphere of purer fire above, is merely *like* these fires, *On Generation and Corruption* 2.3, 330b24, and we do see through it to the celestial bodies beyond. Sometimes it erupts into flames at various places, *Meteorology* 1.3 and 4. And when Aristotle wants to avoid the celestial bodies possessing self-destructive qualities like heat, he suggests an awkward theory that they too ignite the lower atmosphere by friction and transmit heat, *Meteorology* 1.3, 341a12-36, and even light, *On the Heavens* 2.7, 289a20, to us by that method. Whichever of Aristotle's theories we pursue, there seem to be plenty of sources of light in the universe.

But so far Aristotle has spoken of light as the mere *presence* in a transparent region of such things as fire or the sun. Mere presence is not enough to explain the directionality of light. Why, for example, are there any shadows at all, including the shadows that constitute night, and lunar eclipse? For the sun and other firelike stuff is *present* in the universe surrounding the earth, a surrounding all of which is transparent. The requirement of presence does not explain why there is not light round the corners. The awkward theory of daylight as due to celestial friction in every direction makes the question of shadows even more intractable, but the theory of light as presence creates difficulty enough on its own.

The problem would be solved if Aristotle replaced the idea of light as a mere presence by the idea that light travels in straight lines. But, consistently with his theory that light is a presence, he refuses to agree with Empedocles that it travels, *On the Soul* 418b18-26; *On Sense Perception* 7, 446b27-447a11. In the latter place, he distinguishes the travel of sounds and odours from the instantaneous existence over a region of light, and of the effect of colour, which he takes to be different from light but equally travel-free. He further allows, here and at *Physics* 8.3, 253b13-31, that certain changes of quality, such as freezing, can occur all at once over a whole region without spreading part before whole. Even though the effect of colour does not travel, it raises for Aristotle the same question as sounds and odours, namely whether differently stationed observers are perceiving the same thing. Or are they perceiving the same physical object, but each a different instance (*idion*) of the same sense quality, 6, 446b17-27?

Nonetheless, Aristotle recognizes that light would not go round any corners, if it were not being constantly reflected, in unobtrusive ways, without necessarily casting a shadow, *On the Soul* 2.8, 419b29-33. The facts of geometrical optics put him under great pressure to think in terms of directionality and of something travelling after all, whether or not it is light. He talks of the sun's rays, *Meteorology* 3.4, 374b4, and of the reflection of rays or light, *Meteorology* 1.3, 340a28; *On the Soul* 2.8,419b29-33. But light, for Aristotle, is only a prerequisite for seeing, and the process of actually seeing involves the directionality of something else. Throughout the *Meteorology*, and once in *On the Heavens*,[5] he speaks of sight travelling out from the eyes. But this theory is rejected in *On Sense Perception* 2, 438a25-7; *On Memory* 2, 452b10-11; *On the Soul* 3.12, 435a5-10. In *On Generation of Animals* 5.1, 780b35, Aristotle says that it does not matter for his purposes whether one thinks of sight as travelling outwards or of an effect coming from the thing seen. It is unclear whether this is a change of mind, or whether he was all along only catering to the more popular view as geometrically equivalent to his. In any case he now prefers the latter view, which still involves the language of travel. He speaks of a change as *arriving, from outside, from a distant object* and as *taking a straight course*, or *being scattered*, 5.1, 780a29; 780b35-781a12. The theory that he adopts here and in *On Sense Perception* 2, 438b4-5; 3, 440a18-20; *On the Soul* 2.8,419a9-21; 2.11, 423b12-17; 3.7, 431a17-18; 3.12, 434b27-435a10, and *Physics* 7.2,245a2-9, is that colour acts on the light in the medium, and the medium in turn acts on the organ of sight. The influence of colour can be reflected at a mirroring surface in between the coloured object and the eye, *On the Soul* 3.12, 435a5-10. In these texts too, the language sometimes might suggest travel, as when Aristotle uses the phrase '*in turn* 'at *On the Soul* 3.12, 435a10, of the action of air at the reflecting surface, or twice insists that the medium and observer are not affected '*together* ' by the action of colours, as they are by the action of tangibles. But 'together' may mean 'both passively', rather than 'simultaneously', and in general what Aristotle needs is the idea of a direction of influence, not the idea of travelling part before whole.

The situation is, then, that his definition of light as the mere *presence* of something like fire or the sun in a transparent medium leaves the fire-like stuff too inert to explain geometrical optics. What needs to be added to *presence* is the idea of a direction of influence. On the other hand when he explains the actual process of vision, for which light is merely a prerequisite, he goes too far when he speaks in terms of travel, whether the travel of sight outwards, a theory he at least eventually rejects, or the travel of the influence of colour inwards. What he needs both for light and for the influence of colour, in order to explain geometrical optics, is the idea of a direction of influence, not the idea of travel part before whole. In fact, in the psychological works, this is probably what he intends. It is hard for anyone not to slip into talk suggesting travel, even when all they want is directionality.

It has been said that Aristotle's commentator, Philoponus, completely rejects Aristotle, turning light from a static to a kinetic phenomenon, better suited to the needs of geometrical optics. I have argued elsewhere that Philoponus need not be introducing travel rather than the

---

5 *Meteorology* 1.6,343a13-19; 1.8,345b11; 2.9, 370a19; 3.2, 372a29-32; 3.3, 372b16-373a18; 3.4, 373a35-b7; 374a23-375a3; 3.6, 377b18-378a11; *On the Heavens* 2.8, 290a17-21.

directionality of light.[6] What Philoponus does is to give to *light* the same directionality as we have found in Aristotle's psychological works applied to the action of *colour*. Philoponus has replaced mere presence with something more directional, but Aristotle's later treatment of colour showed the way.

Relation of light to colour

Light and colour have both turned out to involve transparency and fire-like stuff for Aristotle. How, then, are they related? Bodies with their *own* colour are opaque and have their colour confined to a surface. It is the transparent bodies with *borrowed* colour that are harder for Aristotle to distinguish from bodies filled with light. But they too are said to have their colour only at the surface, 439b12-14, and I think that there will be a further major difference if at *On the Soul* 2.7, 418b4-6, Aristotle means that it is only borrowed colour, not light, that makes transparent bodies seeable. What light does is not to make them seeable, but seeable *through*. Light is not seen, so much as recognized by using one's sight and finding that one can see not it, but colours, *On the Soul* 3.2, 425b20-2. And one cannot see a body filled with light when it is in direct contact with one's eye, *On the Soul* 2.7 and 11, 419a11-23; 423b12-17. Light is not, therefore, listed as an object of sight at *On the Soul* 2.7, 418a26-8.

Imperceptible quantities and times

After explaining colour, flavour and odour in *On Sense Perception* chapters 3, 4 and 5, Aristotle goes on to raise puzzles about sense objects in chapters 6 and 7, most of the puzzles having to do with continuity and discontinuity. I want to address an apparent conflict between his readiness in *On Sense Perception* Chapter 6, 445b30 - 446a20, to allow that small enough quantities and variations of degree are in a sense imperceptible, and his hostility in the next chapter, 7, 440a21 - 448b16, as well as in Chapter 3, 440a20-3, to imperceptible times. I will first try first to bring out the apparent conflict and then to explain it.

Imperceptible sizes, variations and intervals allowed with qualification

In Chapter 6, 445b27 - 446a20, Aristotle distinguishes between actual and potential imperceptibility of colour patches and shade variations, and similarly for notes and pitches and other perceptible qualities. But perceptibility also has different meanings. There seem to be three levels. First a very small patch, if separated, is either dissolved (446a8), or at best potentially perceptible. Secondly, if joined to a larger whole it becomes actually perceptible, but in a weak sense of perceptible, namely because it is in the perceptible whole (ὅτι ἐν τῷ ὅλῳ, 446a18). Since even a sizeless point can be in a perceptible whole, but is implied not to be perceptible by the argument of 7, 449a 20-31, Aristotle probably means something stronger, perhaps that it contributes to the perceptibility of the larger whole. At 446a1, he says more modestly that sight has covered it (ἐπελήλυθεν). But there is, thirdly, a stronger

6 Richard Sorabji, in his, ed., *Philoponus and the Rejection of Aristotelian Science* (London and Ithaca, New York 1987) ch.1, 'John Philoponus', 1-40 (26-30), commenting on Shmuel Sambursky, 'Philoponus' interpretation of Aristotle's theory of light', *Osiris* 13 (1958) 114-26.

sense of perceptibility in which something is perceptible separately (χωρίς, 446a18), and not merely because it is in the whole.

In this strong sense of perceptibility, there is only a finite number of perceptible colour patches in an area and variations of shade in a spectrum, or pitch in a glissando (446a16-20). In the weaker sense of perceptibility, perceptible because in the whole, there is an infinite number of colour patches and variations of shade or pitch. But separately perceptible variations of shade or pitch are not continuous or infinitely variable in their own right (μὴ καθ' αὐτὸ συνεχές), 445b28, but only, I take him to mean, in respect of the continuous tightening or relaxing of the vocal cords, or the continuous rearrangement of coloured ingredients which underlies them.

(Ch. 6, 445b30-446a15) And for this reason, the ten thousandth part of a grain of millet that is seen is undetected, even though sight has covered it, and the sound within the quarter-tone (δίεσις) is undetected, even though one hears the whole change of pitch (μέλος), which is continuous. But the distance from what is intermediate to the boundaries [of the δίεσις] is undetected. It is similar with what is very small in other perceptibles, for it is potentially visible, but not actually, when it is not separate. For one foot exists potentially in two feet, but exists actually, once separated. However, it stands to reason that such small increments on being separated would be dissolved into their surroundings, as is also the tiny drop of flavour, once poured into the sea. Be that as it may, because the increment exists potentially in the more exact perception, so also it will not be possible actually to perceive so small a perceptible, if separated. But it will nonetheless be perceptible, for it is already potentially so, and it will be actually so, when added to the whole.

(446a15-20) So it has been stated that some magnitudes and affective qualities are undetected and why, and in what way they are perceptible and in what way not. When therefore there are present the maximum number that are perceptible actually, and not merely in virtue of being in the whole but separately, it is necessary that these should be limited in number, whether they are colours, flavours, or sounds.

Theophrastus

I think this passage could be the target which Andrew Barker seeks[7] of Theophrastus' attack in his fragment 716 FHS&G, 64-5, lines 108-124, a passage from Porphyry *On Ptolemy's Harmonics*. Theophrastus, Aristotle's successor, is talking about singing and is attacking a view that the minimal perceptible musical intervals (διέσεις) cause differences of pitch, by not being audibly sounded. Aristotle could well be taken as committed to this view by our passage. He is not thinking of the discontinuous notes produced on the αὐλός, but, like Theophrastus, is thinking of singing. He is assuming that when singing, you tighten or loosen your vocal cords continuously, but the slide between the separately audible notes on either side of the δίεσις is not itself separately audible. It is audible only in Aristotle's very weak sense of *contributing* to the separate audibility of the notes that bound it on either side. The smallest recognized gap between these notes, at first a semi-tone, later a quarter-tone, is by Aristotle given its normal name, δίεσις, but it is also correlated with a μέλος, or change of

7 Andrew Barker, 'Theophrastus and Aristoxenus: confusions in musical metaphysics', in the present volume.

pitch, so named by Aristotle because it is the smallest possible part of a tune, smallest in variation and number of notes. When Aristotle says that the change of pitch (μέλος) is continuous, he does not mean that anything continuous is perceptible in the strong sense of being heard as a glissando. But he does think that there is a continuous change of vocal tension that is perceptible in the weak sense of contributing to the separate perceptibility of something else, of the difference in notes to either side of it. This is just what Theophrastus is objecting to: the idea that the gap, δίεσις, though not heard as a slide, could cause the separate audibility of the notes at either boundary. Theophrastus would have known Aristotle's discussion in Chapter Six, given that, as we shall see, he addresses Aristotle's next chapter, Seven, with its discussion of the instantaneous spread of light.[8] An implication, incidentally, of Aristotle's account is that each note has a certain latitude or breadth, because if the vocal tension is altered by an amount less than that corresponding to a *diesis*, no different note will be heard.

Imperceptible times denied

Aristotle's recognition of items that are in a sense imperceptible ought, one would think, to make room for very small times not being perceptible in a strong sense. Nonetheless, a theory of imperceptible times is attacked in *On Sense Perception* first at 3, 440a20-3, where it had been used to defend a pointilliste theory of other colours arising out of tiny juxtaposed dots of black and white. An alternative theory that the dots are superimposed on top of each other is said at 3, 440a23-5, not to require imperceptible times, because here the dots underneath do not directly affect the eye, but only indirectly by affecting the superimposed colour. Evidently, on the theory of juxtaposition, all dots affect the eye directly, but avoid affecting it simultaneously. The most obvious reason would be that, as in the theory of high and low notes attacked by Aristotle at 7, 448a19-20, the effects of black and white not only travel to us, but travel at different speeds, contrary to Aristotle's own view at 6, 446b27 - 447a11, according to which vision involves no travel at all. The theory's difference of speed would protect the eye from having to respond to opposite qualities at the same time, at least from a surface whose points were all equidistant from it.

Imperceptible times are attacked again at 7, 448a19-b16. At 448a19-22, Aristotle refers to a certain theory about consonant pairs of notes. In a consonant pair, one note is higher and one lower. Evidently some people thought that higher notes travel towards us faster. This theory is found in Plato, *Timaeus* 67B and 80AB, in Plato's Pythagorean friend, Archytas, ap.Porphyry *On Ptolemy's Harmonics*, ed. Düring, p. 56, and it seems to be accepted by Aristotle himself at *On Generation of Animals* 5.7, 786b7-788b2. On the other hand, Aristotle's reference to speed at *On the Soul* 2.8, 420a29-b4 seems to be different. He is talking of moving the sense, not the sound, the high note being experienced as a quick stab, the low as a slow push, and speed and slowness are treated as incidental. In general, it is not easy to tell in musical contexts whether references to speed concern a swift motion of the string or other instrument, or a swift process in the hearer, or a swift transmission of sound from source to hearer. See Theon of Smyrna, *Expositio rerum mathematicarum ad legendum Platonem utilium*, ed. Hiller, pp 50 and 61. Some people, according to Aristotle, said that

---

8 Theophrastus ap. Themistium and Simplicium, fragments 155B and C FHS&G.

consonant notes merely *appear* to arrive simultaneously, because the difference in arrival time is imperceptible. This might very well be taken to be Plato's theory in *Timaeus* 80B, where the slower movement fits its beginning onto the similar faster movement, as the latter ends, and mingles a single experience (μία πάθη) of high and low.

One might have thought that Aristotle himself would, in the context of sounds, favour the idea of time lags that were not in a strong sense perceptible. For even if he gives up the idea of *On Generation of Animals* that high notes travel faster, he does in *On Sense Perception* think that sounds travel, 6, 446a20-b27, and the notes can presumably travel from distances that differ by amounts too small to be perceptible in a strong sense. If the *distances* can differ by amounts that are in that sense imperceptible, why should not the differences of *arrival time* be in the same sense imperceptible?

Aristotle goes on, after mentioning the imperceptible times of consonance theory, to say, 448a22-24, that this theory of imperceptible times might be extended by his opponents, who throughout Chapter 7 are those who claim that one cannot perceive more than one sense object simultaneously. They might defend the idea that one cannot, for example, see and hear at the same time, by postulating a succession of seeing and hearing so rapid that the time differences are imperceptible.

One would think that, as with Plato, all such people need postulate is two successive times, (i) a time in which the first perceptible arrives and is perceived, and (ii) a time in which the second perceptible arrives and is perceived. All that is undetected, in that case, is the difference between these two times. The proponents of imperceptible times need not agree, as Aristotle alleges at 448a26-30, that their own perceiving is also undetected, nor, as Aristotle alleges at 448b1-11, that there is a time *in* which notes are undetected, or that there are notes which are undetected. Why, then, does Aristotle charge them with maintaining these extra assumptions?

The opponents do not require the extra assumptions, but perhaps historically there happened to be a more complex theory.[9] In fact there may be a version, perhaps a later version, of the theory here attacked in the pseudo-Aristotelian *De Audibilibus* 803b29 - 804a8. But its chief emphasis is on frequency or speed of *vibration*, and it is less clear whether there is also a reference to speed of *travel*. The claim is that the higher note corresponds to more frequent vibration, and that we do not notice the gaps (διαλείψεις) between the blows, so that the sound appears continuous and joined up. Similarly with consonant pairs of notes, we do not hear the more frequent blows of the higher note insofar as they fall between the less frequent blows of the lower note, because we do not hear the pauses (καταπαύσεις) in either note, but hear the repeated blows as a continuous sound, and the two notes as simultaneous.

This more complex theory gives us much of what Aristotle complains about. There are gaps in which no blow is reaching our hearing, and we perceive nothing during these gaps, but the gaps are too short for us to notice. It is even possible that at 803b38, the idea about colour perception is that it too involves imperceptible times, and this could be a version of the theory of colour vision attacked by Aristotle in his Chapter 3, 440a20-23. On the other hand, it may mean no more than that colour is seen as existing continuously.

9 I am grateful to Catherine Osborne for insisting quite rightly that Aristotle must have a more complex theory in mind.

138

Though the pseudo-Aristotelian theory is complex, modern psychological studies recognize even more radical reinterpretations of temporal sequence. In the colour-phi phenomenon, instead of seeing two separately located lights, one flashing red and another flashing green shortly afterwards, one seems to see a single light moving from the first location to the second and turning green at a half-way point *before* any illumination at the second location. In the cutaneous rabbit phenomenon, one experiences taps at irregular distances up the arm as if a small animal were running continuously all the way up one's arm, even though some sequences of taps stop short of the upper arm.[10]

> (*De Audibilibus* 803b29-804a8) For as one bit of air moves another, it makes the whole sound (φωνή) alike, as happens in the case of high and low pitch. For the frequency (τάχος) of the blow keeps the sounds like their source. The blows imposed on the air by strings are many and separated, but since hearing cannot be conscious of (συναισθάνεσθαι) the gaps (διαλείψεις), because of the smallness of the time interval (ὁ μεταξὺ χρόνος) between blows, the sound appears to us one and continuous, just as in the case of colours [the appearance is one and continuous? or the gaps are unnoticed?]. For with these [which?], what is spaced out often appears to us to be joined up (συνάπτειν ἀλλήλοις), when it travels quickly [or in quick succession?]. And this same thing happens with consonant pairs of notes. Because some of the sounds (ἦχοι) are included in others and the pauses (καταπαύσεις) in the two notes happen at the same time, we fail to notice (λανθάνειν) the [more frequent] sounds that occur between the others. For in all consonant pairs of notes, the blows on the air of the higher sound (φθόγγος) are more frequent (πλεονάκις), because of the speed of vibration (τάχος τῆς κινήσεως). But the last of the [more frequent] sounds falls on our hearing at the same time as the sound from the slower [vibration]. So since hearing, as has been said, cannot perceive the [more frequent] sounds that intervene [between the less frequent], we seem to hear both sounds simultaneously and continuously.

This is unlike Aristotle's treatment of sound in another way, that it envisages not a movement *of* air, but a movement of a wave *through* the air, as one bit of air moves another, as at pseudo-Aristotle *Problems* 11.6, 899a32-b17. Aristotle recognizes wave motion in a completely different context at *On Divination through Sleep* 2, 464a6-11, but in the context of sound appears to think it is the *air* that travels, *On Sense Perception* 6, 446b9; *On the Soul* 2.8, 419b25-7.

Aristotle's criticisms are relevant only to a complex theory of imperceptible times like this one, not to imperceptible times in general. At 7, 448a26-30, he complains that during the imperceptible times that he has in mind (those of the complex theory) one would not be conscious of one's perceiving, and so not of one's existence. At 448a30-b12, he claims that we need to subtract the imperceptible times in which, on the complex theory, one perceives nothing, in order to reach the remainder in which one does perceive. But he objects that there would be no remainder. This objection muddles two different conceptions of imperceptible time. On the complex theory, there would be a remainder. On the simple view, it is true that subtracting segments too small to be perceived in a strong sense would leave no remainder. But subtraction would be the wrong process. This is especially clear, if the small segments

10 See Daniel C. Dennett, *Consciousness explained* (Boston 1991), 114-44.

are perceptible in the weak sense that they contribute to the perceptibility of the whole. The whole is perceptible in a strong sense only so long as the small segments that contribute to its perceptibility have *not* been subtracted.

Smallest perceptible sizes denied

The complex theory which Aristotle attacks includes the idea that there are sounds too small to perceive. So in summarising his reply, Aristotle says at 448b12 that all [sizes] are perceptible, and, equivalently, at 448b14-15 that what one perceives is never indivisible, even if it appears so. This last way of putting the point in terms of divisibility takes us back to the opening of the previous chapter, 6, where he asks at 445b3-6 whether sensible qualities, including sound, are infinitely divisible. But the point is the same, whichever way it is put, because, as he immediately explains in 445b6-11, if sounds are infinitely divisible, then indefinitely small magnitudes will be perceptible. What is surprising in chapter 7 is that Aristotle does not remind us of the restriction in chapter 6, that it is only in a weak sense that indefinitely small sounds are perceptible, the sense of contributing to the perceptibility of a larger whole.

The qualifications of chapter 6 are not mentioned either when Aristotle returns to the subject in 7, 449a20-31, and says that a perceptible cannot be an indivisible. His argument could equally be used to exclude perception of indivisible points or to exclude smallest perceptible sizes. But it is the second that is relevant, for he is adding an end note on 448b14, where he allowed that a perceptible magnitude can *appear* the smallest possible, and he is saying that it cannot *in fact* be indivisible. In this final attack, he makes use of a type of puzzle that he treats very brilliantly in the *Physics*,[11] a problem of first and last points in a transition. In this example Aristotle's use of the puzzle would, however, prove too much.

Aristotle's argument seeks to reduce to absurdity the idea that there is an indivisible that is perceptible. If there were, imagine it approaching an observer until it comes into view. There will be a last point at which it cannot be seen and a first point at which it can. But these points cannot be separated by a gap in which the indivisible is neither seen nor not seen, nor by a gap in which it is both seen and not seen. And Aristotle rightly emphasizes (*Physics* 6.1, 231a21-b10) that points in a continuum cannot be adjacent to each other, but are rather always separated by other points. All that remains is that the last point of indivisibility and the first of visibility are the same point, but that itself commits the absurdity of making the indivisible both perceptible and imperceptible at that point. We can escape only by denying that an indivisible is perceptible at all.

The argument proves too much, because, if sound, it would prove the imperceptibility not only of indivisibles, but also of the large surface of a large object approaching from afar. Imagine this approaching surface slightly curved, so that all the points on it are equidistant from one's eye. There will be a last point of invisibility and a first of visibility, and the argument will proceed as before to the conclusion about its imperceptibility.

11 See Richard Sorabji, 'Aristotle on the instant of change', *Proceedings of the Aristotelian Society*, supp. vol. 50 (1976) 69-89, reprinted with revisions in *Articles on Aristotle*, eds Jonathan Barnes, Malcolm Schofield, Richard Sorabji, vol. 3 (London 1979). A third version is in Richard Sorabji, *Time, Creation and the Continuum* (London and Ithaca, New York 1983) ch. 26, 'Stopping and starting'. All versions are discussed by Niko Strobach, *The Moment of Change* (Dordrecht 1998).

VIII

The right way to tackle this kind of problem, I believe, is to find context by context a non-arbitrary reason for preferring a first position, or a last, but not both. In the present example, one might prefer a first position of visibility on approach, and a last position of visibility on retreat. If there was a third option of indeterminacy as regards perceptibility, this would not alter the general principles, but would merely call for non-arbitrary decisions as regards the new boundaries separating the indeterminate from the visible on one side and invisible on the other.

Theophrastus again

Aristotle's successor, Theophrastus, is described by the commentators Themistius, *in Phys* 191,23-198,2, and Simplicius, *in Phys* 982,1-987,8, as having, in the first book of his *On Motion*, drawn a connexion between some of the points made in Aristotle's *On Sense Perception* and in the *Physics*.[12] If some change does not take time, and Themistius suggests this is a reference to light leaping in Chapter 6 of Aristotle's *On Sense Perception*, then there *can* be a first instant of having changed from dark to light, whereas, according to Aristotle, there is *no* first instant of having changed to being in motion, nor a first instant of black spreading over a white surface. This objection is said by Themistius to have caused trouble for the commentators. The Theophrastus fragments are translated at FHS&G 155-6.

The objection is used by Theophrastus in querying the asymmetry that Aristotle allows in his discussion of the instant of change, for example in *On Sense Perception* 7, the instant of change from being visible to being invisible, or elsewhere from rest to motion. At that instant, is a thing resting or moving? Neither, because Aristotle allows nothing to *be* moving or resting at a sizeless instant, *Phys.* 6.3; 6.6; 6.8. But we can ask if there is a first instant of *having* left the starting point (cf Themistius *in Phys* 196, 9-13). Aristotle allows an asymmetry, which is what Theophrastus questions. Aristotle's asymmetry allows a first instant of having completed a change, but not a first instant of having started one, *Phys.* 6.5 and 8.8, 263b15-264a6. Themistius tries out the possibility that Aristotle means only to deny a first *length* of time, but then why not deny a last length, 195,13-28? In other words, the asymmetry seems arbitrary, whether applied to a sizeless instant or to a length of time, if it is taken as a general asymmetry between beginning and ending. But Aristotle's examples may be justified[13] if we reflect that in a continuum there is no first position away from the starting point, but can be a point of termination. So in a continuous movement there can be a first instant of having reached the terminus, but not a first instant of having left the starting point. The observation ascribed to Theophrastus that this will not apply to discontinuous movement like the leaping of light can simply be accepted.

12 Theophrastus, fragments 155A-C; 156A-B FHS&G.
13 Richard Sorabji, *Time, Creation and the Continuum* (above n.11), ch. 26; Niko Strobach, *The Moment of Change* (above n.11).

IX

Aristotle on the Instant of Change

The problem

'The train leaves at noon', says the announcer. But can it? If so, when is the **69**
last instant of rest, and when the first instant of motion? If these are the
same instant, or if the first instant of motion precedes the last instant of rest,
the train seems to be both in motion and at rest at the same time, and is not
this a contradiction? On the other hand, if the last instant of rest precedes
the first instant of motion, the train seems to be in neither state during the
intervening period, and how can this be? Finally, to say there is a last
instant of rest, but not a first instant of motion, or *vice-versa*, appears
arbitrary. What are we to do?

This is not only an intriguing puzzle. It has some further importance,
because I think we must decide how to handle it *before* we can decide how
best to define motion or rest at an instant. Aristotle's answer also has some
historical significance. One of his solutions, a denial of motion or rest at an
instant, has been picked on for impeding the progress of science. Here I
want to suggest a solution to the puzzle, which turns on treating motion
differently from rest. I want then to argue that Aristotle was attracted by a
second solution very close to the one I shall advocate, and that his treatment
of dynamics can to this extent be reassessed. In an appendix, I shall suggest
that some versions of the puzzle also bear on recently revived problems
about vague concepts. The puzzle has had a long history. It is to be found
already in Plato's *Parmenides* (156C-157A), and it had a great revival in
mediaeval times.[1]

Does it apply to the real world?

First we need to consider whether the problem could apply to the real
world. It may be doubted whether it could , for the statement of the problem
involved a number of assumptions. First, I assumed (what Aristotle argues
in the *Physics*)[2] that time is continuous. This has many implications. It

1. This revival has been discussed by Curtis Wilson in *William Heytesbury*,
Madison, Wisconsin 1956, and now in an illuminating paper by Norman Kretzmann,
'Incipit/Desinit', in Machamer and Turnbull (eds), *Motion and Time, Space and Matter*,
Columbus, Ohio 1976, pp.101-36. This should be read by anyone interested in the
continuing history of the subject. Professor and Mrs Kretzmann plan further
publication on the mediaeval treatments.

2. Aristotle argues in the *Physics* that time and space are both continuous. The
point in space is like the instant in time, in not being a very short line, or having any
size. It is the boundary of a line, and (*Phys.* VI 1, 232a6-11) it cannot be next to

70   means that time will be infinitely divisible, and there will be no such thing as a time-atom, that is, an indivisible period with an indivisible duration. An instant will be not a time-atom, nor any kind of period, but rather the *boundary* of a period, itself having no duration. Instants, unlike time-atoms, cannot be next to each other. Rather, between any two instants, there will be another, indeed, an infinity of others. This is what is involved in time being continuous, and our problem will apply to the real world only if time is so. If there were time-atoms, so that time was not continuous, the train would be in its old position at one time-atom, and in a new position at the next. The earlier time-atom would be the last time-atom in the period of the train's resting; the later time-atom would be the first time-atom in the period of the train's moving,[3] and our problem would not arise. The problem does arise, however, if Adolf Grünbaum is right[4] that neither quantum theory, nor anything else in modern physics, has given us reason to deny that time is continuous.

Another reason why someone might question whether our problem applies to the real world is that a train consists of a mass of moving atoms, and so does the railway track. Can the train have any *first* instant of motion, or last of rest, if its atoms are moving all the time, and how would these instants be defined? Yet another doubt concerns the fact that a train is not perfectly rigid. When some parts of the train, or of the engine, have started to move, other parts will be lagging behind, so that there is not a single first instant of motion or last of rest for the train as a whole. Both these doubts can be met by raising our problem not about the train as a whole but about some point within the train, such as the centre of mass, and its first instant of motion and last of rest, in relation to some point on the railway track.[5] In talking of points, rather than of trains, we will be moving beyond the range of observable entities.

So far as I can see, then, our problem does apply to the real world, in as much as it applies to unobservable points on a real train. But two further things need to be said. First, the problem would still be of interest, even if it applied only to a world different from ours. Second, we have so far

---

another point. Aristotle is well aware that other views had been taken. Some people had believed in atomic spatial magnitudes, and Aristotle spends a lot of time attacking them (*Phys.* VI 1, 2, 4, 10, VIII 8).

3. Its motion would be discontinuous; for continuity of motion involves occupying intervening positions between any two; and even if we imagine space to be continuous, so that there are intervening positions between any two, we are imagining time to be discontinuous, so that between adjacent times there will not be intervening times at which intervening positions can be occupied. Aristotle makes related points in his attack on atomism. Discontinuous motion would result, he argues, if there were atomic motions or distances (*Phys.* VI 1, 232a6-11), or if the moving object were of an atomic length (*Phys.* VI 10, 240b31-241a6).

4. Adolf Grünbaum, *Modern Science and Zeno's Paradoxes*, Middletown, Connecticut 1967.

5. It may be objected that if the atoms of a body are forever joggling, and if their motions are not equal and opposite so that they cancel each other out, then the centre of mass will also be for ever moving, so that it will have no *first* instant of motion. We may reply that, even if this is so, we can still ask about the first instant of motion (and last of non-motion) of the centre of mass in a *given* direction, or in response to a *given* force. I shall neglect this complication in what follows.

considered only one version of the problem, and if this version were **71**
inapplicable to the real world, it might still be the case that other versions
were applicable. Thus far I have considered only the transition between rest
and motion. But our problem can be raised, and was raised by Aristotle, in
connexion with other kinds of transition. He discusses the transition from
being one colour to being another colour, from being non-existent to being
existent, and from being invisible to being visible. (The last will be
discussed in the appendix). In each case, the question can be asked: when is
the last instant of the old state, and when the first instant of the new? Or
moving from time to space, we may be able to ask where is the last point of
the one state, and the first point of the other? In some of these new forms,
the question may well apply to our world.

Proposed solution for cases of continuous change

With the problem now stated and generalised to apply to all kinds of
transition, we can start making some suggestions about how to handle it.
But first we should be clear how much we need to ask of a solution. The
original question was about when the last instant of the old state occurs,
and when the first instant of the new. One of the difficulties about
answering was that if we said that one of these instants existed, but not the
other, we seemed to be being arbitrary. It would be a sufficient solution, if
we could show that it would not be arbitrary to prefer one instant to the
other. For this purpose, we need only show that there is a reason for
preferring one to the other; we need not show that it is mandatory to do so.
On this basis, I would suggest that there is a solution available for those
cases where the earlier state, or the later state, or both, consists in a
continuous change. We can illustrate by considering a transition from rest
to motion and back again to rest, provided that the motion is construed as
continuous, not jerky. By this I mean that the motion involves passing
through an infinity of points, between any two of which there are other
points, which are also passed through. Ordinary usage is not precise, but
leaves it indeterminate whether we should regard the instant of transition
between rest and continuous motion as an instant of motion or not. We **72**
must therefore make a recommendation about how to regard it, if we want
to solve our problem. Fortunately, there are at least two considerations
which would justify the decision to call it an instant of rest.

First, there is an asymmetry between the series of positions away from the
position of rest and the position of rest itself. There can be no first *position*
away from the starting point, or last *position* away from the finishing point in
a continuous motion, or in any other continuous change. Hence there can
be no first *instant* of being away from the starting point or last *instant* of being
away from the finishing point. No such considerations apply to being at the
position of rest. This already supplies us with a solution to our paradox, in
some of its applications. For if someone were to ask, 'when is the last instant
of being at the position of rest, and when the first of being away from it?', we
could safely reply that the latter instant does not exist. But we can go
further. The asymmetry between the position of rest and the positions *away*
from it can provide us with the excuse we want for treating rest differently
from *motion*. It would be perfectly reasonable to mark the asymmetry by

162

saying that just as there is no first or last instant of being *away* from the position of rest, so equally there is no first or last instant of *motion*. It would be reasonable, but not mandatory. Reasonableness is all we need in order to escape the charge of arbitrariness.

In more detail, my idea is this. If we are going to introduce an asymmetry between motion and rest, it is not arbitrary to introduce it by denying first and last instants of motion, rather than the other way about. This is not arbitrary because we must in any case admit that there can be no first or last instants of being away from the position of rest. And the period of motion is in *other* respects a period of being away from the position of rest, if we ignore for a moment the problematic instant of transition.[6] Thus if we introduce the asymmetry between motion and rest in the direction I recommend, we will be aligning the asymmetry between motion and rest with an already existing asymmetry, and this is not arbitrary. Contrast the opposite decision, according to which it is rest that lacks first and last instants. Certainly, that decision is theoretically possible, but it would be an arbitrary one, because the asymmetry introduced would not be aligned with an already existing asymmetry. Indeed, it would fly in the face of one, for when something started moving, the state of motion on which it was embarking would be assigned a first instant, while the state of being away, on which it was also embarking, would not be. In other words, of the two theoretically possible ways of introducing an asymmetry, one is not arbitrary because it has the backing of an asymmetry which is always there, while the other does not.

My second consideration is this. Let us suppose that not only change of place is continuous, but also change of velocity. In other words, in passing from one velocity to another, an object passes through all the infinitely many intervening velocities. Once again, quantum theory has nothing to say against this assumption. If it is made, then there cannot be a first or last instant of having a velocity greater than zero, for there is no first or last velocity above zero. There is, however, no corresponding objection to there being a first or last instant of having velocity zero. Now it seems more natural, though again it is not mandatory, to connect zero velocity with rest, and velocities above zero with motion. If we do, we get the result that there is no first or last instant of motion, but that there may be first or last instants of rest.

73   These two arguments are based on slightly different strategies. The argument about an already existing asymmetry is only meant to show that it would be *permissible*, not that it would be *desirable*, to deny first and last instants of motion. It shows that *if* we deny this, we shall not be open to the threatened objection of arbitrariness in preferring this asymmetry to the opposite one. This is not yet to say that the decision is positively *desirable*. To show that, in the absence of obstacles, the decision is *desirable*, I appeal to the existence of the paradox I begin with, the paradox about whether the train can start. The asymmetry I recommend would solve the paradox; that

6. We must also ignore the special case in which the object moves back through its position of rest, as Norman Kretzmann has pointed out to me. Even so, for each instant of moving back through the position of rest, there will be an infinity of instants of being away from it. So this exception seems too minor to upset my claim that the asymmetry I recommend is aligned with an already existing asymmetry.

is what makes it *desirable*. It would be in line with an already existing asymmetry; that is what makes it *permissible*. The status of the second argument, the one about velocity, is different. For I there try to show that the asymmetry I advocate is not merely permissible, but positively desirable, on the basis of considerations *other* than the existence of our paradox. I appeal instead to the naturalness of associating motion with velocities above zero.

In arguing for the non-arbitrariness of the decision to deny first and last instants of continuous motion, I am not saying that the period of motion has no boundary. It will have an instant bounding it on either side, and my only question has been whether that instant should be regarded as one at which there is motion, or rest.

I do not deny that there are considerations which point to the opposite decision, that the instant of transition is after all one of motion, and it will be as well to bring one of them into the open. A doubt which might be raised is whether change of acceleration always behaves in the same way as change of velocity. We have supposed that velocity always changes continuously. But does acceleration, the rate of change of velocity, always in its turn 74 change continuously, or can it jump discontinuously from zero to, say, one foot per second per second? A similar question could be raised about yet higher derivatives, such as the rate of change of acceleration. Nonetheless, I do not think our solution is seriously threatened. On the one hand, if acceleration does change continuously, there will be no first instant of acceleration above zero, and so we will have yet further incentive to deny a first instant of motion. On the other hand, if acceleration were sometimes to jump discontinuously from zero to something higher, we should admittedly have no obvious general reason for choosing between talk of a last instant when acceleration is zero and a first instant when acceleration is above zero. But even if on some of these occasions we were to talk of a first instant of acceleration above zero, the considerations we rehearsed earlier would still be strong enough to make us hesitate before calling that first instant of positive acceleration an instant of motion.

In spite of this defence, our proposal must be understood in a flexible spirit. We should recognise that for everyday purposes, and for many scientific purposes, it simply does not matter which way one talks. One's choice can legitimately be based on the most transient of reasons, or on no reason at all, while the reasons we have given can without penalty be ignored. The point of our reasons is simply that they are available to rebut the charge of arbitrariness in case of need. If a discontinuous jump from zero acceleration were to occur, and if in the context our whole interest were in the acceleration to the exclusion of position and velocity, and in the positive acceleration, rather than in the zero acceleration, then our reasons for denying a first instant of motion might be overridden in that particular context; and this would not matter. The point is that we would still not be forced to be arbitrary.

The solution suggested does not in any way preclude physicists' talk of initial velocity. For the initial velocity of a projectile is not a first velocity in its entire motion, but merely the first velocity which it is convenient to consider for the purposes of a given calculation. We should also recognise that the last instant of rest in relation to one point may, of course, be an

164

instant of motion in relation to a different point. Throughout we must be understood as talking of rest or motion in relation to a *given* point.

75   The solution will apply not only to continuous motion, but to all changes which are continuous in the same sort of way. It will apply to changes of size, of temperature, or of colour, if these involve a continuous progress through a series of points between any two of which others are traversed. It will not apply to *discontinuous* changes, or to other processes or states which lack this kind of continuity. If, for example, we considered the transition from not singing to singing, we should not have the same reasons to deny a first instant of singing. Clearly, arguments based on direction or velocity would be inapplicable. It might be thought that something like our first argument would still be applicable, for the singing lasts through a continuous series of instants, and there can be no first instant after the instant of transition. But our first argument cannot in fact be applied, for it depended on the *asymmetry* between the single position occupied during a period of rest and the continuous series of positions occupied during a period of motion. In the case of singing, there is no asymmetry, for there is a continuous series of instants traversed during the period of non-singing, just as much as during the period of singing.

One might expect the proposed solution to appeal to Aristotle, for in his attack on the atomists he is at great pains to insist that motion, time and space are all alike continuous.[7] He argues hard against the atomists that what has moved must previously have been moving (*Phys*. VI 1, 232a6-18; VI 6, 237a17-b22; VI 10, 240b31-241a6); it cannot simply have *jerked* into its new position (232a6-11; 240b31-241a6). It was his successors Diodorus Cronus and Epicurus (or his followers)[8] who were willing to accept jerky motion. Nonetheless, we shall later see that Aristotle's solution is somewhat more complicated.

Treatment of other cases

Our solution leaves a very large range of cases unsolved. For often neither the earlier state nor the later state is a process of continuous change, as we have remarked. The transition may be from one colour to a different colour,

76   from non-existence to existence, or from invisibility to visibility. In these cases, what considerations are there, to help us to a decision? If we are watching a receding aeroplane, or looking for an approaching one, we cannot normally tell at the time what will prove to be the last instant of visibility as it recedes, or the last instant of invisibility as it approaches. If we want to register this instant as it arrives, we shall normally have to wait until the new state is upon us, before we can do so, and it may then reasonably be held that we are not registering the end of the old state, but, at best, the beginning of the new. This means that, in many contexts, we have a good reason for not talking of the last instant of the old state, but (if it has one) of the first instant of the new. This solution seems to have appealed

7. For the continuity of motion in *Phys*. VI, see VI 1, 231b18-232a18; VI 4, 235a9-37; VI 5, 236a7-27; VI 6 throughout; VI 10, 240b31-241a6.

8. Diodorus Cronus, according to Sextus Empiricus *Adv. Math*. X.48; 85-6; 91-2; 97, 102, 143, cf. 120. Epicurus or his followers, according to Themistius, *Phys*. 184.9, and Simplicius, *Phys*. 934.24.

to Peter of Spain, for certain kinds of case.[9] But it needs to be noticed that our interest is not always in registering the instant as it arrives. We may instead want to discuss the instant of transition prospectively or retrospectively. So the present consideration does not provide a solution for all cases, or even for all the cases Peter of Spain applies it to.

Aristotle himself may have another consideration relevant to the particular example of visibility. For he classifies seeing as an *energeia*, and on one interpretation, an *energeia* has no first instant. This is how J.L. Ackrill[10] interprets Aristotle's idea (e.g. *Sens.* 446b2) that 'he is seeing' entails 'he has seen'. Ackrill treats the perfect tense 'he has seen', like 'he has *been* seeing', as implying an earlier period of seeing. This interpretation has been disputed,[11] but if it is correct, it implies that there will not be a first instant of seeing, and therefore not a first instant of seeing the approaching object in Aristotle's problematic example, to be discussed in the appendix below.

The various considerations we have mentioned do not begin to cover all the cases there are. There may well be unique considerations attaching to particular occasions of discussion. And we must add that there may well be cases in which there are no adequate considerations to guide us. In these last cases, we shall not be able to answer the question, 'what is the last **77** instant (or point) of the one state and the first of the other?' The most we shall then be able to do is this. If our questioner happens to assume (without reason) that one of the instants (or points) exists, we shall always be able to tell him that in that case the other does not exist.

Two rival solutions

An entirely different way of trying to cope with our problem has been advocated by Brian Medlin in his paper 'The origin of motion' (*Mind* 1963). Medlin says, in effect, that a thing can be both in motion and at rest at an instant, and equally neither in motion nor at rest at that instant. The first may sound as if it violates the law of contradiction, the second as if it violates the law of excluded middle. But Medlin avoids this, by simply defining motion at an instant, and rest at an instant, in such a way that they are neither contradictories nor contraries of each other.[12] Given his definitions, all four statements can be true together, namely, that a thing is in motion at an instant, not at rest at that instant, and that it is at rest at

9. According to Kretzmann, *op. cit.* It looks as if Peter of Spain failed to see that whether one's interest is in identifying the instant as it arrives is quite independent of whether one is discussing what he calls 'permanent' states, or 'successive' states, or the beginnings or endings of either.

10. J.L. Ackrill, 'Aristotle's distinction between *energeia* and *kinesis*', in *New Essays on Plato and Aristotle*, ed. R. Bambrough, London 1965, esp. pp. 126-7.

11. Disputed by L.A. Kosman, 'Aristotle's definition of motion', *Phronesis* 1969, and Terry Penner, 'Verbs and identity of actions', in *Ryle*, ed. Oscar Wood and George Pitcher, New York 1970.

12. In effect, he defines 'it was in motion (not at rest) at instant t' by saying something like 't was either followed, or preceded, or both, by a period throughout which it moved'. And he defines 'it was at rest (not in motion) at instant t' roughly as 't was either followed, or preceded, or both, by a period throughout which it did not move'.

166

that instant, not in motion at it.

My objection to this is not so much that it runs the risk of causing confusion, but that it is not sufficient to solve the problem that interests us. Medlin is free to define motion at an instant and rest at an instant in such a way that they are not contradictories or contraries of each other. But he cannot, and does not, deny that there *is* a contradictory of the claim that something is in motion at an instant. He himself suggests a way in which we might formulate the contradictory. We could talk of its *being the case that* something is in motion at that instant. Once we have found a formula for picking out the contradictory, we can pose our original problem all over again in terms of the new formula. We shall simply ask what is the last instant when it is *not* the case that our object is in motion, and what the first instant when it *is* the case that it is in motion. To this question Medlin himself would agree that we cannot say it is the same instant. When the problem is posed this way, we see that we shall have to fall back on a different solution from Medlin's, such as the one we have advocated, according to which there can be a last instant when it is *not* the case that our object is in motion, but not a first instant when it *is* the case that it is in motion.

A second rival solution has been called by Norman Kretzmann the neutral-instant analysis, and ascribed to Aristotle. I do not find it in Aristotle myself,[13] although there is something more like it in Plato, *Parmenides* (156C-157A). It differs from the two solutions I shall ascribe to Aristotle, even from the first one, because that first one will deny that there is motion or rest at *any* instant, and will thereby fall foul of modern dynamics. The neutral-instant analysis avoids this; it allows that there can be rest or motion at an instant, and denies rest or motion only at the instant of transition between motion and rest. In thus avoiding Aristotle's difficulties, however, it pays a price. For it assumes that at most instants a body *must* be in motion or at rest. The question then arises how it can *avoid* being in motion or at rest at the instant of transition. It would not be enough simply to *stipulate* that it avoids this, on the grounds that in this way we can

13. The first difficulty about finding the neutral-instant analysis in Aristotle is that he seems in his first solution to deny motion or rest at *any* instant. It might be replied that he only means that an instant has no duration within which a thing could get any distance – and indeed some of his arguments do seem to suggest only this. This would leave him free to go on to say (a) that at an instant a thing can nonetheless be *in course of* moving or resting, and (b) that it is so at all instants, except the instant of transition between motion and rest. This would amount to the neutral-instant analysis. But, first, I do not find statements (a) and (b) spelled out by Aristotle. And, second, there are three places at which Aristotle's argument would actually suffer if he allowed (a), without more ado. These three passages are VI 3, 234a34-b5; VI 6, 237a11-17; VI 8, 239a3-6. In the first passage, Aristotle cites our paradox in order to show that nothing can move at an instant. If it could, then at the instant of transition it would both move and rest. If, in spite of this denial, Aristotle were prepared to allow (a), then his remark here would leave us wondering how he escapes saying that at the instant of transition a body is both in course of moving and in course of resting. This would surely be the place for him to add, if he really held (a) and (b), that although he concedes (a), that a body can at an instant be in course of moving or resting, he still escapes the paradox, because (b) withholds this concession from the instant of transition.

win free of the paradox. It needs to be shown *how* it can avoid this, given that at *other* instants a thing has to be either in motion or at rest. To show this, we need some consideration, independent of the existence of the paradox, to show us that it is right, or at least permissible, to say that it avoids being in motion or at rest at the instant of transition. I do not rule out such a consideration being found, and if it is, the neutral-instant solution might either replace mine, or be put alongside it, depending on the nature of the consideration. But I think the consideration has yet to be given. And it would not do simply to define motion or rest at an instant, so as to make the instant of transition neutral. This would only raise the question what consideration made it right or permissible to define motion or rest at an instant in this way rather than in one of the other ways.

There is one special instant for which the neutral-instant analysis may well be a good one, and that is the instant of reversing direction. We can imagine the centre of mass of a ball travelling vertically upwards and slowing down until it reverses direction at an instant, without pausing for any period of time at the apex of its journey. We will now have an extra incentive for denying that the centre of mass is in motion at the instant at which it is at the end of its upward journey. For not only will its velocity be zero at that instant, but we could not say that its motion had one direction rather than the opposite direction at that instant.[14] This favours our saying that at the instant of reversal the centre of mass is not in motion. But there is a consideration, which I acknowledged in my original paper, but whose import I perhaps failed to consider sufficiently, which could make it reasonable to say that the centre of mass is not at rest either. This is that at the instant of reversing direction, the centre of mass is (as in all cases of coming to a halt) at a different position from that occupied at preceding instants, and also (differently from ordinary cases of coming to a halt) at a different position from those occupied at succeeding instants. There is thus no sameness of position at all, and since sameness of position is important to the concept of rest, this may make it reasonable to say that the instant of reversing direction is not one of rest. In that case, since it is not an instant of motion either, it will be a neutral instant, an instant of non-motion.[15]

It would take a further argument, however, to show that the neutral-instant analysis is viable for ordinary cases of coming to a halt or starting off.[16] In case a suitable argument is found, I would simply make two points.

14. Someone may object that we are in any case committed to motion without any particular direction. For imagine that the centre of mass of a ball is deflected only slightly, so that it does not stop moving, but at the same time is deflected at an angle rather than in a curve. In that case, we shall be unable to assign the earlier direction rather than the later at the instant of deflection, in spite of wanting to describe the ball as moving. It can be replied, however, that if deflection, in cases where there is no stopping, is always in a curve (since otherwise there would be a discontinuity in the velocity in some direction), it will be possible to assign a direction to the motion at any instant, by taking a tangent to the curve. And in that case, we are not committed to motion without a particular direction.

15. I am grateful to Colin Strang for pointing out to me the implications of my acknowledgement.

16. One argument that might be urged is that even if, on starting off, a thing is at the same position as it occupied at arbitrarily close *preceding* instants, it is at a *different* position from those occupied at arbitrarily close *succeeding* instants. This *difference* of

IX

168

First, the neutral-instant analysis shares my view that the instant of starting is not one of motion, and should therefore welcome my argument that the velocity is zero. Second, if the paradox were put in terms of a choice not between motion and rest, but between motion and non-motion, then the neutral-instant analysis would make an asymmetrical choice parallel to my own, and reject motion.

Aristotle's treatment. Preliminaries (i): The four main kinds of change and the thesis that they all involve a gradual transition

I shall now turn to Aristotle's solutions of the problem. He is well aware that different kinds of case need different solutions, but, not surprisingly, he looks for solutions of some generality, and does not acknowledge that the matter might ever be decided by the unique interests of a particular context. We shall suggest that in the case we are going to discuss, Aristotle is attracted by two solutions. Sometimes, like us, he denies that certain continuous changes can have a *first* or *last* instant, without, however, making it very clear that it is the continuity which precludes this. At other times, he goes further, and denies that there can be change or stability at *any* instant.

Before expounding his two solutions, we shall have to make some preliminary points clear. A first thing to notice is that Aristotle recognises only four kinds of change as being changes in the full sense of the word. There is change of quality (as when something changes colour), change of place (in other words, motion), change of size (in growth and diminution), and finally the creation or destruction of substances (*Phys.* III 1, 200b32-201a16; cf. V 2; *Meta.* XI 12).

A second point is that in all four kinds of change, he thinks there is a gradual process of transition (*Phys.* VI 6, 237a17-b3; b9-21). Qualitative change, such as change of colour, is said to take time. Change to a new place or size involves passing through intervening points. The creation of something like a house takes time, and occurs part by part, the foundation before the whole.

Aristotle does not by any means think that changes other than the four genuine ones must all involve a gradual process of transition. Indeed, he sees that an infinite regress would be involved, if the gradual process by which something came into being had itself to come into being by a gradual process (*Phys.* V 2, 225b33-226a6). In the very passage where he explains that a house comes into being only part by part, he points out that this cannot be true of things that have no parts (VI 6, 237b11; b15), points and instants, for example.

---

position might be thought to make it, if not desirable, at least permissible to avoid talk of rest, while the *sameness* of position made it permissible to avoid talk of motion. In that case, calling the instant of starting a *neutral* instant would be at least *as* allowable as my decision of calling it an instant of rest. I think the argument is weak, however. Certainly, if there is *no sameness* of position, this makes a case for avoiding talk of rest, but it is less clear that *some difference* of position gives us much pretext for avoiding it, when there is also some sameness. Admittedly, the difference of position makes it less than a paradigmatic case of rest; but does that prove enough? Ordinary thought connects rest with sameness of position, and hence with the absence of difference, so long as difference *excludes* sameness. But in the present case, difference of position is *combined* with sameness.

Preliminaries (ii): How can change of colour be gradual?   **79**

It may be wondered how change of colour can be gradual, given the view stated in the *De Sensu* (6, 445b21-9; 446a16-20) that there is only a finite number of discriminable shades. In that case, a change to a new colour would be gradual when it involved passing through a number of intervening shades. But within this process, how could the change from one shade to the *next* be treated as gradual?

Aristotle seems to have two incompatible answers. One answer is implied in *Physics* V 6 (230b32-231a1), VI 4 (234b10-20), VI 9 (240a19-29), VI 10 (240b21-31), when he says that certain changes occur part by part.[17] While a surface is changing from white to the next shade, grey, he says, part of the surface must still be white, and part already grey. The greyness spreads gradually over the surface. This claim, that certain changes occur part by part, is used in combating the view that a partless atom could undergo change or motion. In its turn, the claim has as its ground that, while a thing is actually changing or moving, it cannot yet be in its terminal state, nor can it still be in its initial state. It must therefore be partly in one state, partly in the other, and so must have parts. In the case of motion, it must move part by part into the adjacent area. Diodorus Cronus and certain Epicureans were later to get round this objection to the motion of partless atoms, by denying that an atom actually *is* moving at any time; rather, at any given time it *has* moved with a jerk.[18]

But Aristotle seems not always to keep in mind the view that these changes occur part by part. For in the *De Sensu* (6, 447a1-3) he actually denies that qualitative change has to occur part by part, and illustrates how it can happen with the case of a whole pond freezing over at once. In one of the *Physics* passages where he says that qualitative change (*en tois enantiois*, 237b1) is gradual, he speaks as if he must prove this on the basis of time taken, but cannot prove it on the basis of space covered (237a19-28; a29; b2; b21). Why not, if he remembers his view that a surface changes colour part by part? He seems to be forgetting that view, and he probably forgets it again in VIII 8, where he declares that while something is becoming white, it is not yet white (263b27; b30). This way of putting things seems to neglect   **80** the idea that there will be a stage of being partly white. How then can the transition from one shade to the next be represented as gradual?

A second way of arguing that the transition is gradual serves to refute the idea that part by part changing is indispensible for this purpose. The second way is suggested by what Aristotle says in *De Sensu* 6. Admittedly, there is only a finite number of discriminable shades, so that discriminable colours form a discontinuous series (445b21-9; 446a16-20). But nonetheless colours, musical pitches, and other ranges of sensible qualities have a kind of *derivative* continuity (445b28; b30, *to mê kath' hauto suneches*). The sort of thing Aristotle seems to have in mind is that a change to the next discriminable

17. Aristotle probably has this answer in mind also in VI 5, 236b5-8, where he stresses that, even if colour is not in itself divisible, the surface to which it attaches is divisible.

18. References in note 8 above. See esp. Sextus *Adv. Math.* X 143 where the idea that bodies can only *have* moved is connected with the idea that bodies and places are indivisible.

IX

170

pitch, in the *discontinuous* series of discriminable pitches, may be produced by a *continuous* movement of a stopper along a vibrating string. Or in the case of colour, a change to the next discriminable shade, in the *discontinuous* series of discriminable shades, may be produced by a *continuous* change in the proportions of earth, air, fire and water in a body. As the stopper moves along the vibrating string, we hear the sound all the time, but do not hear a change of pitch, until the stopper has moved the distance that corresponds to a quarter tone (446a1-4). Variations of pitch less than a quarter tone are not perceptible except by being part of the whole variation (446a18, *hoti en tōi holōi*), by which Aristotle probably means that they only *contribute* to the perceptibility of the whole variation. This suggests a way in which Aristotle can maintain that a change to the next discriminable colour or pitch can be continuous. A body is changing to the next discriminable shade all the time that the continuous change in its elemental ingredients is going on, which will eventually lead to its displaying that next discriminable shade.

In what follows, we shall only consider Aristotle's treatment of the four genuine kinds of change. This will leave open how he might have treated the many other cases of (non-genuine) change.[19] In connexion with the four genuine kinds, and the transitions involved in them, we find two rather different kinds of treatment.

81 *Aristotle's first solution*

The better known one is less satisfactory. It is most fully expressed in connexion with rest and motion in *Phys.* VI 3 (234a24-b9) and 8 (239a10-b4). Here Aristotle says that there can be neither rest nor motion at an instant. He explicitly cites our problem as one ground for his conclusion (VI 3, 234a34-b5), saying that if something stops moving, the instant of transition between motion and rest is an instant neither of motion nor of rest, since otherwise we could not avoid the contradiction of saying that it is an instant of both motion and rest. At VI 6, 237a14-15, Aristotle extends his treatment of motion to all change, saying that a thing cannot be changing (*metaballein*) at an instant. An extension is also attempted in VI 8, 239a3-6, where Aristotle denies that there is a first instant of slowing to a halt, by arguing that slowing to a halt implies moving, and that there is no moving at an instant. (To make the argument valid, he ought to show that slowing to a halt at an instant would imply not just moving, but moving at an instant).

Aristotle gives several grounds for denying rest or motion at an instant, besides the need to avoid difficulties about the instant of transition between rest and motion. In VI 3 (234a24-b9), one argument is that to rest is to be in the same state now as then, but an instant does not contain a then. Another argument is that differences of speed would be impossible at an instant, because such differences would imply that the faster body had traversed in *less* than an instant what the slower body traversed in an instant. Finally, if we cannot speak of motion at an instant, we cannot speak of rest at an

---

19. We earlier made a suggestion about one of the non-genuine cases, the transition from not seeing to seeing, when we pointed out that, on one interpretation, Aristotle is committed to denying a first instant of any *energeia* such as seeing.

instant, since we can only talk of rest where there would have been the possibility of motion.

Aristotle allows that, when something stops moving, there is a single instant which is both the last of the period during which the object is moving, and the first of the period during which it is resting (VI 3, 234a34-b5). And something parallel is true when a thing *starts* moving. But this does not in the least commit him, as he makes very clear, to saying that this is an instant at which the object is moving or resting.

Since Aristotle thinks his view holds not only for motion and rest, but for change and stability in general, we can apply his remarks, for example, to a change of colour, in which a surface starts off wholly of one shade, and by a gradual process of transition, finishes up wholly of another shade. If we raise problems about the first and last instants of its changing colour, Aristotle will say, for reasons similar to those already quoted from VI 3, that there is no first or last instant, nor indeed any instant, at which it is *changing* colour, or *remaining* the same colour.

Aristotle sees, however, that this solution is not a complete one. For although he denies that things can *change* or *remain* in the same state at an instant, he concedes that there are many other things that can be true of them at an instant. He is quite prepared to allow that what is moving can be at a point (VIII 8, 262a30; b20), or level with something (VI 8, 239a35-b3) at an instant. As regards other kinds of change, the object that is changing colour can be white at an instant (VIII 8, 263b20; 23), or the white have perished and non-white have come into being at an instant (263b22). In general, a change can have been completed, and the new state of affairs can have come into being at an instant (VI 5, 235b32-236a7; VI 6, 237a14-15). In allowing something to *be* white at an instant, he is not allowing that it could *remain* white, or *rest* in the white state, at an instant.[20] Since he allows something to *be* of a certain colour at an instant, he cannot finally dispose of our problem by ruling out of order questions about a first or last instant at which a surface is *changing* colour. For this still leaves us free to ask about a first instant at which the surface is no longer grey, or wholly grey, and a last instant at which it is not yet white, or wholly white. Aristotle recognises the need to deal separately with this further question, and this brings us on to the second kind of treatment that we find in his work.

Aristotle's second solution

In *Phys*. VIII 8, 263b15-264a6, Aristotle discusses a change from not-white to white (or *vice versa*), and a change from not existing to existing. He thinks of the final state (e.g. white) as being reached by a gradual process of transition, but this is one of the passages where he does not construe the process as one of white spreading part by part over the surface. Instead, he implies that throughout the process of transition the surface will remain non-white (263b27; b30). He distinguishes an earlier state, by which he means the state when the surface is still not-white but is changing to white, from a later state, by which he means the final state of being white. Or rather, since he switches his example in mid-discussion, the earlier state is

20. All he is committed to is the view expressed elsewhere (*Phys*. VIII 8, 264b1), that what is white must remain white *over a period*.

172

one of being white while changing to not-white, and the later state is one of being not-white, but for simplicity I shall stick to the one example. He then says that there is no last instant of being in the earlier state, but there is a first instant of being in the later. I take it that it is crucial to understanding the passage to notice that the earlier state, of which there is no last instant, is one which involves changing[21] while the later state does not. His view is generalised in an earlier chapter (VI 5, 235b6-32),[22] where it is said in connexion with all genuine change that there is a first instant of being in the terminal state after a process of transition. One ground Aristotle gives for his verdict is again the existence of the very problem that interests us. He says that the verdict provides a way (he fails to consider whether it is the only way) of avoiding the contradiction of something being in its old state and in its new state at the same instant (263b11; b17-21). He concedes that there is an instant which is equally the end of the period during which white was coming into being and the beginning of the period during which the surface is white, but he insists that at that instant the surface is already in its later state, white (263b9-15; 264a2-3).

84   Aristotle's treatment of the problem here is by and large very much in line with the solution which we have advocated. For we should agree with him that there is no last instant of being not yet white, *if* changing to white is a continuous process. However, we must to some extent qualify our claim to be in agreement. For when Aristotle gives his reasons for denying a last instant of the earlier state, he does not give our reason, the *continuity* of the process of becoming white. This continuity may well be what influenced him, but if so, he has not managed to identify it explicitly as the reason.[23]

There are further passages, besides the pair we have mentioned, where Aristotle is attracted to a view close to our own. We have so far considered his denial of a *last* instant at which something is non-white while becoming

21. That he thinks the process of change is going on is clear e.g. from 263b21-2, 'non-white *was coming into* being, and white *was ceasing to be*'. 263b26-7, 'If what exists now, having been previously non-existent, *must have been coming into being*, and did not exist *while it was coming into being* ...'. 264a2, 'The time in which *it was coming to be*'. 264a5, '*It was coming to be*'.

22. There is such a thing as the time 'when first a thing has changed' (VI 5, 235b7-8; b31; b32), i.e. has completed its change. This is an indivisible time (235b32-236a7). And at that instant the thing is already in its new state (235b8; b31-2).

23. Aristotle's solution is only appropriate, given his two assumptions that the discriminable shades form a discontinuous series, and that nonetheless the change from one discriminable shade to the next is a continuous one. A quite different treatment of colour changes would be called for, if he took the view (i) that colours form a continuous series. In that case, the possibility would arise of producing a continuous alternation of shade along the spectrum. In a continuous change of shade such as this, there could not be a last instant of one shade, nor a first of another. The situation would be different again, if (ii) he took colours as forming a discontinuous series, and also took the change from one colour to the next as being discontinuous. In that case, nothing we have so far said would enable us to decide which colour to speak of at the instant of transition from one colour to the next. As for (iii) a discontinuous transition through several intervening shades to a distant one, such a transition might be thought of (though it need not be) as having a first instant (namely, the first instant at which a colour other than the original one existed), and a last instant (namely, the last instant at which the penultimate colour was in existence).

white. But he also discusses whether there can be a *first* instant at which something is changing. At VI 5, 236a7-27, he wants to show that there is no earliest time at which something was changing (236a15, reading: *meteballen*), whether that earliest time is construed as a divisible period, or as indivisible. If indivisible, it might be construed either as an instant, i.e. as a boundary with no duration, or as an atom of time with an indivisible duration. In 236a17-20 (whatever may be true of a16-17), he is construing the putative earliest time as a durationless instant. And he takes the view which we have advocated in connexion with continuous changes, that there is not a first instant at which something is changing. Moreover, for the first time he actually contradicts his other solution by saying that there is a last instant at which something is resting (contrary to the doctrine of VI 3 and 8, which denies rest at an instant). His ground for denying a first instant at which it is changing is yet again the existence of the kind of problem we are discussing. Once we assume that there is a last instant at which it is resting, there cannot be a first instant[24] at which it is changing. For at such an instant, the object would already have changed to some extent,[25] and it cannot have changed to any extent at the very instant at which it is still resting. Aristotle does not give as his ground for denying a first instant at which something is changing the view he takes in VI 3 and 8 that there are *no* instants at which something is changing. He may instead be influenced by our kind of consideration; for just as we associated moving with being away from the starting point, so he associates changing with having changed to some extent. And he may be influenced by the fact that in a *continuous* change there is no first instant of having changed to some extent. But if this is what has influenced him, he has again not articulated the reason.

There is one more place where Aristotle comes close to our view. The theme of *Physics* VI 6 is that what has changed must have been changing earlier (237a17-b22), and what was changing earlier must before that have accomplished some change (236b32-237a17), so that it has already changed an infinite (237a11; a16) number of times, and you will never get a first in the series of changing and having changed (237b6-7). This implies that there cannot be a first *instant* of having to some extent changed, not, for example, a first instant of having ceased to be wholly grey, or of having started to be partly white. This implication, which is admittedly not explicitly spelled out by Aristotle in so many words, is precisely what we considered to be true of continuous changes.[26]

85

24. It is confusing that this putative instant is referred to by *two* letters, *AΔ*, and not just one. The reason is that *AΔ* stands for the putative earliest time of changing, which is later treated as a period with *A* and *Δ* as its terminal instants. Here, however, it is treated as a durationless instant, so that *Δ* is not separate from *A*.

25. Or 'have begun to change'. At 236a7-10 'has changed' (*metabeblēke*) is said to be ambiguous between 'has completed its change' and 'has begun to change'. The latter sense is relevant in the present lines (236a19-20); the former is not.

26. There is another way in which this passage diverges from Aristotle's first solution. Though there is no first instant of having to some extent changed, there is an instant which divides the period of stability from the period of change. This instant is the last instant of the period during which the object is not changing, and Aristotle's view elsewhere (234a34-b5; 263b9-15) suggests that it can also be called the first

174

There are then two strands of thought in Aristotle about the process of transition involved in the four genuine kinds of change. Sometimes he argues or implies, in conformity with our view about continuous changes, that there cannot be a first instant at which a thing is changing, nor a first instant at which it has left its initial state, nor a last instant of not having reached its terminal state. Unfortunately, he does not seem to have a firm grasp of the latter point of view. For in *Phys.* VIII 8, 262a31-b3; b21-263a3, he appears to contradict it, by assuming that when a moving object reverses direction, there is a first instant of having left the point of reversal. At least, this is the assumption which he seems to require for his conclusion, which is that the reversing object must spend a period of time at the point of reversal. The assumptions seem to be that there is a first instant of having reached the point of reversal, and a first instant of having left it, and that these cannot be adjacent or identical instants, so must be separated by a pause during which the reversing body rests.

Assessment of Aristotle's first solution

Let us return briefly to the first strand of thought, according to which a thing cannot be changing or resting at an instant. This view may have appealed to recent philosophers,[27] and is not to be lightly dismissed, but it does have severe disadvantages. For it ignores that it is possible, and very useful, to give sense to the idea of changing at an instant. It is possible, so long as we acknowledge that change at an instant is a *function* of change over a period. It is useful because the velocity of a body in a given direction at an instant is one of several factors from which we can calculate in detail its future behaviour. Much of modern dynamics depends on the possibility of talking of acceleration at an instant, whereas Aristotle would rob us of this possibility.

86

Relevance of our problem to the definition of motion at an instant

Nonetheless, the task of defining motion at an instant is by no means easy. And the kind of problem we have been discussing, about last and first instants of rest or motion, gains importance from the fact that it needs to be resolved, if we are to obtain a satisfactory definition of motion at an instant. What definition will be satisfactory depends in part on our purposes. But if motion is continuous, then at least for some purposes, our discussion suggests that motion at an instant ought to be defined so as to exclude a first or last instant of motion. For a start, we may suggest that an instant of motion will be one that falls *within* a period of motion, while an instant of

instant of the period during which the object is changing. But at one point in the present chapter, VI 6, wittingly or not, he casts doubt on the latter description. For he says (237a15) that at any instant of the period during which a thing is changing, it has already changed. This would seem to rule out not only a first instant of having to some extent changed, but also the applicability of the description 'first instant of the period during which a thing is changing'. Aristotle thereby contradicts for a second time an aspect of his other solution.

27. I am not sure whether this is the intention of Vere Chappell in 'Time and Zeno's arrow', *Journal of Philosophy* 1962.

rest will be one that falls within *or bounds* a period of rest. But this definition may need revision in the light of other difficult examples, such as that of the ball thrown vertically upwards, and slowing down until it changes direction at an instant. We found reason to regard this instant either as an instant of rest or as a neutral instant, whereas the definition just proposed would make it an instant of motion, and may need to be revised, for this and other reasons. But however the definition may eventually be formulated, our discussion suggests that for some purposes it should be formulated so as to exclude first and last instants of continuous motion, and so as to avoid, if possible, our problems about the relation to first and last instants of rest. The necessity of getting clear about these things may not always be appreciated. Bertrand Russell gives a definition of motion at a moment in § 446 of *The Principles of Mathematics* (London 1903, 2nd edition 1937) and denies, unlike us, that the instant of transition between rest and motion can be an instant of rest. He does not, however, make it so clear whether or not it can be an instant of motion.

General assessment of Aristotle's position

I should like to finish with a general assessment of Aristotle's treatment of our problem. He has earned notoriety for his refusal to allow motion at an   **87** instant. G.E.L. Owen remarks that this refusal not only 'spoilt his reply to Zeno' on the paradox of the flying arrow, but also 'bedevilled the course of dynamics'.[28] In more detail, Owen explains: 'Unable to talk of speed at an instant, Aristotle has no room in his system for any such concept as that of initial velocity or, what is equally important, of the force required to start a body moving. Since he cannot recognise a moment in which the body first moves, his idea of force is restricted to the causing of motions that are completed in a given period of time. And, since he cannot consider any motion as caused by an initial application of force, he does not entertain the Newtonian corollary of this, that if some force F is sufficient to start a motion, the continued application of F must produce not just the continuance of the motion but a constant change in it, namely acceleration. It is the clumsy tools of Aristotelian dynamics, if I am right, that mark Zeno's major influence on the mathematics of science.'[29]

   With the first part of this I entirely agree. Aristotle cannot accommodate the useful concept of initial velocity, by which is meant, of course, not some first velocity in the entire motion, but the first velocity which it is convenient to consider in a given calculation. But what about the second part? A reader might take 'a moment in which the body first moves' to be a first instant at which the body is moving. We have argued that it is precisely Aristotle's merit that he denies that there is such an instant; I would not regard this denial as a defect.

28. 'The Platonism of Aristotle', *Proceedings of the British Academy* 1965, p.148. Similarly 'Aristotle' pp.225-6 in vol. I of *The Dictionary of Scientific Biography*, ed. C.C. Gillespie, New York. Owen's papers on the continuum are required reading for students of this subject.
   29. 'Zeno and the mathematicians', *Proceedings of the Aristotelian Society* 1957-8, pp.220-2.

I would accept, then, some charges against Aristotle, but not others, and at the same time I would draw attention to two merits of his discussion. First, it is a merit that he recognises that not all cases call for the same treatment. The treatments we have been discussing apply only to those processes of gradual transition which he believes to be involved in the four genuine kinds of change. Second, Aristotle does express the view which we believe to be reasonable for continuous change, namely that there is no first instant at which a thing is changing, or at which it has begun to abandon its original state, and no last instant at which it has not yet achieved its final state.

Appendix: another version of the problem

By way of appendix, I will draw attention to an interesting version in *De Sensu* 7 (449a21-31) of the problem with which we began. Here Aristotle has an unsatisfactory argument, which is intended to prove that an indivisible thing is not perceptible. If it were perceptible, he says, then we could imagine some particular occasion on which an indivisible point approached a particular observer, until it came into view. But there are difficulties about imagining this. For there would have to be a last point at which it was still invisible, and a first point at which it was visible. Now where would these points be? Points cannot be adjacent, he maintains. If the points are the same, or if the last point of invisibility is closer than the first point of visibility, the approaching object will be still invisible, but already visible, at the same time. On the other hand, if the first point of visibility is closer than the last point of invisibility, the approaching object will be in neither state when at the intervening distance. The moral that Aristotle draws is that we were wrong to suppose an indivisible point would ever become visible.

This inference is unwarranted, because the problem which Aristotle has raised will apply not only to an approaching point, but also to something which he admits to be in principle visible, namely an extended surface that is approaching an observer on some particular occasion, until it comes into view. We can ask, as before: what is the nearest distance at which the surface is still invisible, and what the furthest at which it is visible? If we were to copy the solution that Aristotle proffers for the case of the approaching point, we should have to say (absurdly) that it is wrong to suppose that a surface which started off invisible would ever become visible. Aristotle is not entitled to his inference; the problem he seeks to raise merely for the case of an approaching point has wider implications than he bargains for.

It may be thought (wrongly) that there is a very easy solution for this version of the problem along the following lines. Aristotle has made a false assumption, it may be said, in supposing that there is no third state between being invisible and being visible. Why should there not be an intermediate distance at which there is no straightforward answer to the question whether the approaching object is visible or invisible? For one thing, it is not entirely clear what conditions must be met in order for an object to count as visible. Must it, for example, stand out from its surroundings? For another thing, it may be difficult to be sure with regard to some conditions whether they have been met, or not. Does the object really stand out from its surroundings? What conditions must be met may vary according to one's purposes in different contexts. Is one being asked to identify the approaching object by vision, or simply to shoot at it regardless of its identity? One may be uncertain what one's task is supposed to be, so that one is also uncertain what it is reasonable to count as visible. The intended conclusion is that we should not join Aristotle in expecting a sudden switch from invisible to visible. There will be an intermediate distance at which neither predicate is straightforwardly applicable.

This suggestion does not dispose of the problem, however. Even if we do not revise our terms, so as to provide a clear-cut test of visibility, the problem can still be stated. We are talking about a *particular* observer on a *particular* occasion. Of course, there is no *general* rule about the distance at which things are visible, any more than there is a general rule about how many grains make a heap, or how many hairs are needed to save a man from baldness. But on a particular occasion, given a particular context, and a particular observer, there may be a first time at which he ceases to be confident whether an object is invisible. Now we can state the problem not as one about the transition from invisibility to visibility, but as one about the transition from being indisputably invisible to being problematic. The question will be about the nearest distance at which an approaching object on some particular occasion is *indisputably* invisible, and the first position at which there is *not a straightforward answer* to the question whether it is invisible. Thus formulated, the problem cannot be so quickly brushed aside.[30]

Some of these remarks should help in solving the ancient Megarian paradox of the heap or bald man, which has been revived in recent discussions of vague predicates.[31] The Megarian paradox starts with no grains or hairs, and declares that you can never obtain a heap or a non-bald man. As each grain or hair is added, it is argued that the addition of *one* could never make a difference. If we take a *particular* occasion, however, and supply some context and point to the discussion, it could well be that for a particular man the addition of one hair did make a difference at some stage. He might for the first time *hesitate* as to whether he was still bald.[32]

30. There is a somewhat similar version of it in the 3rd century A.D. commentary by Alexander of Aphrodisias on Aristotle's *De Sensu* (p. 122 in the Berlin edition). Referring to the claim that Aristotle makes in an earlier chapter (ch.6), that some magnitudes are too small to be perceptible on their own, Alexander argues that nonetheless we cannot have both a largest imperceptible magnitude and a smallest perceptible one. Without further argument, he concludes that we have neither.
31. Max Black, 'Reasoning with loose concepts', *Dialogue* 2, 1963, pp.1-12; Crispin Wright, 'Language mastery and the Sorites paradox' in *Truth and Meaning*, ed. G. Evans and J. McDowell, Oxford 1976; Hans Kamp, 'Two theories about adjectives', in *Formal Semantics of Natural Languages*, ed. E. Keenan, Cambridge 1975.
32. I have had many helpful discussions on this topic, but I am particularly indebted to Geoffrey Lloyd for a thorough correspondence about some of the texts, to my student Marcus Cohen and to Malcolm Schofield for some very helpful discussions on the philosophical issues, and to Professor Clive Kilmister for patient advice on Newtonian mechanics. The present version has been revised not only by the addition of an appendix, but also in light of the excellent comments I received, especially from Norman Kretzmann and Colin Strang, when the first version was delivered at the Joint Session of the Aristotelian Society and Mind Association in 1976.

X

Aristotle's Perceptual Functions Permeated by Platonist Reason

Aristotle drew a sharp distinction between rational functions of the mind, which non-human animals lack, and perceptual functions. These functions had been mixed together in Plato, and slowly over the next thousand years, Platonist commentators on Aristotle came to permeate with reason the functions which Aristotle had treated as merely perceptual. I shall illustrate this in three areas, first, briefly, in that of concept formation, then in that of perception, and finally in that of self-awareness.[1] In connexion with the last two areas, I shall assess the philosophical merits of certain positions.

1. Concept Formation

Aristotle seeks, in *Anal. Post.* II 19, to give an alternative to Plato's account of concept formation as the recollection of concepts known by the soul before birth. Universal concepts are here called by Aristotle "universals". A rudimentary universal concept, to supply an example, the rudimentary concept of an ox, is based on nothing more than many memories of perceived oxen, which he calls

---

[1] Translations of the texts cited, with discussion, can be found in Sorabji (2004), 1(a), 4(c), 5(b), (c), (d). The aim of this paper is to bring together and develop as a theme what was there presented in scattered form. Fuller discussion of concept formation can be found in SORABJI, R., "Universals Transformed", in CHAKRABARTI, A. - STRAWSON, P. (eds), *Universals, Qualities, Concepts*, Aldershot (Ashgate), 2006, pp.105-125, and of perception in Plato and Aristotle in Sorabji (1993), Ch. 1-2.

"experience" of oxen. My own preference is to take the word "or" in "experience *or* the whole universal stabilised in the soul" at 100 a 6-7 to mean that the rudimentary universal concept just *is* the many memories. For otherwise it is left unexplained how we reach the rudimentary universal concept. But "Philoponus" (436.2) and Eustratius (264.12), commenting on the *Posterior Analytics*, avoid this interpretation in different ways.

In a fresh attempt at explaining, Aristotle says something not said elsewhere, that even though, as he always insists, one perceives a particular, e.g. the man Callias, perception is of the universal, i.e. of human, not of human Callias. The commentators on the passage regard this as a dim or confused universal, not fully separated from the particular, and Themistius and Eustratius compare Aristotle's account of how children at first have a confused concept and call all men "daddy".[2] "Philoponus" explains that it is not only the individual's distinctive characteristics that leave a mark in our sense image (αἴσθημα), but also, in a dim way, such universal characteristics as being a human and a mortal, rational animal.[3]

Reason is, however, given a role soon after this by the ancient commentators. Perception transmits the information to the imagination, and onwards, Eustratius adds, to reason (λόγος) as a prerequisite of the process of conglomerating a separated universal concept from the particular perceptions.[4] Hermias and Philoponus make our reason responsible for the conglomerating.[5] Aristotle himself implies that reasoning plays a role, when he says at 100 b 2-4 that in concept formation we pass by induction (ἐπαγωγή) from a type of animal (ox would be an example) to animal in general.

Reason (λόγος) was thought of by Aristotle[6] and by the Neoplatonists as different from intellect (νοῦς), even though both faculties are for Aristotle rational faculties. Reason is a faculty for step-by-step reasoning, different from intellect (νοῦς), which contemplates without moving step-by-step. What happens when Aristotle gives a role to intellect (νοῦς) at 100 b 12-15, where I take him to be talking of the formation not of rudimentary concepts, but of fully scientific ones? My own preference has been to think that

---

[2] Arist., *Phys.* I 1, 184 a 22 – b 14.

[3] "Philop"., *In Anal. Post.* 437.15-438.2.

[4] Eustrat., *In Anal. Post.* 266.14-29.

[5] Hermias, *In Phaedr.* 171.8-25, and Philoponus, *In Phys.* 12.24-28.

[6] Arist., *Eth. Nic.* VI 8, 1142 a 25-26; VI 11, 1143 a 35 – b 5.

Aristotle means no more than intellectual "spotting", which would be true to real life and to how scientists actually work. To take Aristotle's example from *Analytica Posteriora* II-8, when the scientist spots that lunar eclipse is that special lunar loss of light that is due to the earth's shadow, the intellectual spotting is called νοῦς. But the commentators build up a much more intellectual theory.

Starting with the Aristotelian Alexander, and using slightly different nomenclature from each other, they build up a theory of three types of intellect on the basis of Aristotle's *De Anima* III 5. This intellectualisation of Aristotle's process of concept formation is qualified only insofar as the lowest of the three types of intellect is identified with the imagination, in contrast to Aristotle's view that imagination is a function of perception, not intellect. Thus Themistius identifies what he calls potential intellect with imagination as a storehouse of imprints that can be turned into concepts.[7] And Philoponus says that passive intellect, being the same as imagination, takes imprints from perceptible objects and possesses them within itself.[8]

The idea that Aristotle distinguishes three types of intellect is already found before any of these Neoplatonist commentators in *De Anima* by Alexander, head of Aristotle's school around 200 AD, and in Alexander (?) *Mantissa*, much of which is likely to be by him. According to Alexander *De Anima*, there are three intellects.[9] We are born with a material intellect; the active intellect gives the material intellect its proper disposition (ἕξις),[10] so producing, thirdly, the dispositional intellect and enabling us to form concepts which we store (ἀποκεῖσθαι)[11] in the dispositional intellect. But there are different accounts in Alexander *De Anima* and in Alexander (?) *Mantissa* II (= *De Intellectu*). According to *De Anima*,[12] the material intellect can already separate concepts (νοήματα) from enmattered objects presented in sense perception, although only the dispositional intellect, produced by active intellect, can deploy concepts in the absence of sense perception. In *Mantissa* 108.19-24, it is only active intellect that enables our material intellect to separate

---

[7] Themist., *In De An.* 98.35-99.10.

[8] "Philop"., *In De An.* 5.38-6.4, 11.7-11.

[9] Cf. also Alexander (?), *Mantissa* 107.21-34.

[10] Alex., *De An.* 88.23-24; *Mantissa* 107.31-34; 111.29-32.

[11] Alex., *De An.* 86.5.

[12] Alex., *De Anima* 84.19-21; 85.20-86.6; 87.24-25.

102

forms from matter, and it does so by constituting an example of matterless form to refer to (ἀναφορά). Alexander(?) applies to active intellect the term from Aristotle *De Gen. anim.* 736 b 28, "intellect from outside", which, unlike Philoponus, he takes to be a non-human intellect.

Themistius and the so-called "Philoponus" give a role in concept formation to active intellect, but regard it as *human*. For Themistius, active (= productive) intellect turns into universal concepts the imprints derived from perception which are stored in potential intellect.[13] "Philoponus" makes active intellect inscribe imprints like the painter of Plato's *Philebus*.[14]

There were at least three approaches among later Platonists to the sharp contrast between Aristotelian and Platonist concepts. Some considered that both types of concept co-existed in us,[15] although the Aristotelian empirically gained concepts were inferior. Some, though listing Aristotelian concepts as one type of universal, argued that Aristotelian concepts could not do the work required of them and we needed only Platonic ones.[16] Some argued that Aristotle himself had accepted Plato's recollected concepts alongside his own empirically gained ones.[17]

The net result of all these changes, if I am right in my reading of Aristotle, is that his balance between empiricism and intellectualism in the account of concept formation has been tilted in the direction of intellectualism.

2. Perception

The intellectualisation of Aristotle's account of perception is even more striking. Plato's *Theaetetus* in the 4th century BC made perception dependent on supplementation by reason. I have argued elsewhere that his pupil, Aristotle, made them independent.[18] As a

---

[13] Themist., *In De An.* 98.33-99.10.

[14] "Philop"., *In De An.* 538,4-10; Plato, *Phil.* 39 b-c.

[15] Alcinous, *Didasc.* IV; Hermias, *In Phaedr.* 171.8-25, and Philoponus: see *In De An.* 4.30-32 for acceptance of Platonic concepts.

[16] Syr., *In Metaph.* 12.28-13.3, 95.13-17, and 95.29-36; Proclus, *In Eucl.* 12.9-13.27; Simpl., *In Phys.* 1075.4-20; Olymp., *In Phaed.* 12, 1.9-25.

[17] Iamblichus, according to "Philop"., *In De An.* 4, 533.25-35; Plutarch of Athens, judging from the report of "Philop". *In De An.* 3, 520.1-12; Philop., *In De Intellectu* 38.99-40.43 (ed. Verbeke).

[18] Sorabji (1993), Ch. 1-2. But for another view, see Kahn (1992), 367 -372.

biologist, he wanted a taxonomy that would distinguish animals, who all perceive, from humans who have reason as well. It is interesting to see how over a thousand years Platonism managed to impose its view.

In *Theaetetus* 186 a – 187 a, Plato says that perception can grasp, for example, whiteness, but not being or truth. Being (οὐσία) may include the idea that something *is* white. It requires reasoning (συλλογισμός: 186 d) and opinion (δοξάζειν: 187 a). But reflections (ἀναλογίσματα) about being are not available to the newborn (186 b-c). Nonetheless, opinion is available to animals, because it is found in the lower parts of the soul, which are active in animals.[19] Aristotle, by contrast, classes opinion, like reasoning, as belonging to the faculty of reason (λόγος), which he *denies* to animals.[20] He therefore uses a different method to enable animals to cope with the world, viz. compensatingly expanding the content of perception far beyond the whiteness and suchlike to which Plato had confined it. The lion, according to Aristotle, can perceive that the ox is near and rejoice that he will have a meal.[21] In addition, in the text cited where Aristotle treats opinion as belonging to the faculty of reason, he explicitly says that opinion does *not* belong to animals, but distinguishes in this respect appearance (φαντασία), for example the appearance that something has a certain size, as *not* involving reason. Plato by contrast had made appearance *include* opinion.[22]

Aristotle would have rejected not only Plato's account of *appearance* here, but also the account of *opinion* which Plato canvasses in *Theaetetus* 190 e – 196 c. Admittedly, Plato himself rejects this as an account of *false* opinion. But Aristotle would not have thought the account a candidate for describing any kind of opinion, because it runs together what he distinguishes as rational and as perceptual faculties. Opinion for Aristotle, is rational, but it is treated by Plato here as a kind of recognition (ἀναγνώρισις), and recognition is a fitting together of perception with memory imprints. Aristotle regards perception and memory as both perceptual faculties, as we shall see. Plato further interchanges talk of fitting perception to thought (διάνοια), which Aristotle classes as rational. Plato again describes perception and memory as both giving us knowledge,

[19] Plato, *Resp.* 430 b; 442 b-d; 574 d; 603 a; *Phaedrus* 255 e – 256 a; *Legg.* 644 c-d; 645 a.

[20] Arist., *De An.* III 3, 428 a 22-24.

[21] Arist., *Eth. Nic.* III 10, 1118 a 20-23.

[22] Plato, *Soph.* 263 e - 264 d.

using the whole gamut of words for knowledge, at least some of which Aristotle reserved for the rational: ἐπίστασθαι, εἰδέναι, γιγνώσκειν.

We are now in a good position to move beyond Plato and Aristotle, and see what happens to these differences later. Plato's successor Speusippus talks of perception that is scientific (ἐπιστημονικός).[23] But much more detailed is Alcinous' Middle Platonist handbook of Platonism from the 1st or 2nd century AD, the *Didascalicus*. Aristotle is well represented in Chapter 4 of this handbook. Reason (λόγος) had been treated by the Stoics as a collection of concepts,[24] and here in this syncretist work we find a kind of reason that reminds us of Aristotle's anti-Platonic treatment of concepts, because, like Aristotle's concepts, this kind of reason is derived from sense perceptions,[25] and is not in Plato's manner innate or pre-nate. The *Didascalicus* calls its empirically based reason "reason involving opinion" (δοξαστικὸς λόγος), as opposed to the more Platonising reason involving understanding (ἐπιστημονικὸς λόγος).[26]

But here similarities to Aristotle begin to come to an end, because Alcinous says that perceptual recognition involves a kind of *reason*, the empirical kind. There is no vicious circle here with empirical reason deriving from perception, and perception from empirical reason, for empirical reason is needed not for basic perception, but for perceptual *recognition*.[27] Alcinous is entirely faithful to Plato *Theaetetus* 190 e – 196 c, in treating opinion as a combination of memory and perception which requires us to connect, συντιθέναι, the perceived with the remembered.[28] Aristotle would have disagreed. He treats memory as a perceptual faculty belonging to animals, opinion as rational.[29]

According to Alcinous, empirical reason can be more or less involved in perceptual recognition. Perceptual recognition of colour or the coloured is by perception not without empirical reason. But

---

[23] Speusippus, fr. 75.2-11 (ed. Taran). I thank John Dillon and Bob Sharples for the reference.

[24] Galenus, *PHP* 5.3 (= *SVF* 2.841).

[25] Alcin., *Didasc.* 4, 154.40-155.5.

[26] *Didasc.* 4, 154,25-29.

[27] I owe this helpful point to Sedley (1996).

[28] *Didasc.* 154.40-155.5.

[29] *De Mem.* 449 b 30 – 450 a 15.

honey is a bundle (ἄθροισμα), to borrow an idea from Plato's *Theaetetus* 156 d – 157 c, that includes also, e.g., sweetness and the sweet,[30] and so requires us to make more connexions. Hence perceptual recognition of honey is by empirical reason, not without perception.[31]

The later Neoplatonists accepted this Platonising account, but took it much further. Proclus agrees in the fifth century AD that perceptibles are objects of opinion, which knows their being (οὐσία), because it has prior concepts (λόγοι) of them. Perception can recognise the qualities of an apple, but only opinion can recognise it as an apple.[32] Priscian in the 6th century agrees that bodies are known not by perception alone, but also by δοξαστικὸς λόγος, for it is opinion (δόξα) that grasps their being (οὐσία).[33]

The idea that perception needs to be *supplemented* by reason is standard in Platonism.[34] But, starting with Iamblichus in the 3rd to 4th centuries, and continuing with Proclus, the later Neoplatonists go further and make reason *permeate* sense perception. According to Proclus, perception, though irrational in itself, is seated in the opinionative part of the soul (δοξαστικόν), and is illuminated by that and becomes like reason.[35] Non-human animals that have perception also partake of intellect (νοῦς).[36] Iamblichus had, I believe, denied reason to animals, and so he says that humans have a power of perception in a different sense from the irrational power, of sense perception.[37]

The late Neoplatonists next go well beyond Plato, in postulating that the concepts (λόγοι) needed in sense perception are mentally projected by us (προβάλλεσθαι). The theory of mental projection in geometrical thinking is ascribed to the Pythagoreans by "Simplicius",[38] so it may have been introduced by Iamblichus, who

---

[30] *Didasc.* 154.40-155.5.

[31] *Didasc.* 156.1-11.

[32] Proclus, *In Tim.* I 249.13-27.

[33] Prisc., *In Theophrastum* 19.9-13.

[34] Plato, *Theaet.* 184-187; Alcinous, *Didasc.* 4, 156.8-11; 154.40-155.5; Plotinus V 3 [49], 3.1-9; IV 3 [2], 23.21-24; 33-34); Proclus, *In Tim.* I 249.13-27; I 292.27-293.5; (cf. *Theol. plat.* III 6, 23.25-24.2; Prisc., *In Theophrastum* 19.9-13).

[35] Proclus, *In Tim.* I 248.25-29.

[36] Proclus, *Theol. plat.* III 6, 23.25-24.2.

[37] Iambl., *ap.* "Simpl"., *In De An.* 187.36-188.3.

[38] "Simplicius", *In De Anima* 233.17-19 and 277.1-6.

X

sought in the 3rd to 4th centuries to integrate Pythagorean philosophy with Platonic. The projection in perception will not be entirely like that of *geometrical* concepts in doing geometry. The latter is a projection into the imagination and Proclus treats it as like the projection in a modern cinema. He compares the screen of imagination with a mirror,[39] and contrasts the indivisible concepts in the projector with the extended representation on the screen.[40] Priscian in the 6th century ascribes the perceptual version of the theory to Iamblichus.[41] But ideas about projection and the imagination are already found in Iamblichus' probable teacher, Porphyry.[42]

Priscian says that in perception the concepts are projected to fit onto the form (εἶδος) which is derived from the thing perceived. The derivation may not be direct, since the form is said to be a perfection of the likeness in the sense organ of the thing perceived, a likeness displayed (ἔμφασις) in the sense organ.[43] The form is not the likeness itself. The question has been much debated in ancient and modern commentators whether the form (εἶδος) which is received on Aristotle's theory of perception is literally a likeness in the organ, or something more spiritual.[44] Iamblichus seems to have distinguished the likeness in the organ of the *external* form received from the *perfected* form, and then further distinguished the concept projected to fit the form.[45] This view is pretty much followed also by someone who has been considered to be possibly identical with Priscian,[46] "Simplicius", the author of *In De Anima*,[47] except at two places where he speaks as if it was not the λόγος, but the perfected *form* that was projected (166.6-8), by the λόγος (126.6). Boethius

[39] Proclus, *In Eucl.* 1, 121.2-7; 141.2-19.

[40] Proclus, *In Eucl.* 1, 53.18-55.13.

[41] Prisc., *In Theophrastum* 7.11-20.

[42] Porph., *Sent.* 15, 7.1-2; 18.9-19.8 (ed. Lamberz).

[43] Iambl., *ap.* Prisc., *In Theophrastum* 7.11-20.

[44] Sorabji (1991). For an overview, see CASTON, V. (forthcoming),"The Spirit and the Letter: Aristotle on Perception", in SALLES, R. (ed.), *Metaphysics, Soul and Ethics. Themes from the Work of Richard Sorabji*, Oxford (Oxford University Press).

[45] Prisc., *In Theophrastum* 2.26-3.17.

[46] This view of Carlos Steel and Fernand Bossier, disputed by Ilsetraut Hadot, has been updated by Steel in his introduction to *"Simplicius" On Aristotle's On the Soul 2.5-12* (Steel - Huby [1997]).

[47] "Simpl"., *In De An.* 124.34-125.2; 126.1-16; 128.22-29; 166.3-29.

writing in Latin earlier in the 6th century, speaks of the mind applying (*applicare*) the forms (*formae, species*) that it holds within to the marks (*notae*) from outside and images (*imagines*).[48]

In the two earliest Neoplatonists, Plotinus and Porphyry in the 2nd to early 3rd century, the appeal to concepts is still limited. In perceiving fire, Plotinus says,[49] one fits the data one receives to Fire in the world of Forms. More generally, discursive reason uses forms (εἴδη) which it has in itself, in order to pass judgement (ἐπίκρισις) on images provided by sense perception.[50] But for recognising Socrates, although discursive reason is needed, it relies only on memory and on analysing the data stored in images.[51] Porphyry adds that because reason (λόγος) possesses and preconceives the form (εἶδος) of what is perceived, it can correct the inaccuracies of sense perception.[52]

Modern studies of infant psychology stemming from J.J. Gibson seem to support Aristotle's side in this debate.[53] The infant is geared not for perceiving patches of whiteness and instances of sweetness, but for seeing motion in relation to itself and objects as within reach or out of reach and as allowing or disallowing interactions with itself, just as Aristotle's lion perceives that the ox is near and rejoices that it will have a meal. As Aristotle says, the lion does not rejoice at the lowing of the ox, but rather perceives that the ox is near through the lowing, and rejoices at the meal. In other words, animals are geared to respond to situations, not merely to sense qualities. And yet it is implausible to ascribe to infants or most animals such sophisticated possessions as *concepts* of these things or inferences about them. Admittedly, Aristotle does grant a little *experience* to animals in *Metaphysics* I 1, 980 b 26-7, and, on my interpretation, rudimentary concepts are equated with experience at *Posterior Analytics* II 19, 100 a 6-7, so that, on this view, Aristotle allows to animals a little conceptual competence at a level below rationality. But with young infants and lower animals, I think it more plausible to say that they can perceive quite complicated facts without having anything that deserves to be called a concept. Christopher Peacocke has introduced the idea of non-conceptual content. In his example,

---

[48] Boethius, *Cons. Phil.* 5, metr. 4.30-40; prose 1.1-10.

[49] Plot., VI 7 [38], 6.1-7.

[50] Plot., I 1 [53], 9.18-20.

[51] Plot., V 3 [49], 3.

[52] *Commentary on Ptolemy's Harmonics* 14.32-15.6

[53] See, e.g., Neisser (1993), quoting the work of J.J. Gibson.

X

108

one can see a mountain top as having a certain complex shape, without having the *concept* of that shape.[54] Why should not infants too see things as variously positioned in relation to themselves, without having the *concept* of such positions.

There is still more that an infant has to do, and again before, as far as I can see, it can be said to possess concepts or powers of inference. It has not only to see how a ball, for example, is positioned in relation to itself, but also to see which of the two is moving, the ball, or itself, or both. A common view is that self-motion is detected by the feeding in of information about one's intentions to move and kinaesthetic sensations of moving.[55] This might seem to bring in computation and hence ratiocination. But the computations are effected physically by the nervous system, not by the infant itself. They simply result in the visual scene appearing to the infant as one in which the ball is moving. The infant does not reason that the ball is moving.

So far, then, I prefer Aristotle's view that perception can have a rich content of its own, even without the aid of anything we should want to call reason, although reason can certainly enrich that content very much further.

3. Self-Awareness

The question of perception being permeated by reason returns in the context of self awareness. There was felt to be a need for unity in what apprehends our psychological states. Aristotle gives a certain unity to self-perception when he makes the "common sense" responsible for it. But he takes up the question of the unity of perception more explicitly when he raises the question, what discriminates sweet from white, a question which comes from Plato's *Theaetetus* 184 b – 186 e. Plato answers that the senses must converge (συντείνειν) on something unitary (μία), the soul (184 d), and at 186 a – 187 a, he stresses the soul's reasoning activities as needed for these discriminations. Aristotle substitutes for soul one particular capacity of the soul, the common sense, and he repeatedly stresses that its role of comparing different types of sensible requires it to be

[54] Sorabji (1993), ch. 3, more fully developed in Bermudez (1998).

[55] Grusser (1986) refers to Arist., *De Somn.* 459 b 7-20, and its influence on Jan Evangelista Pukyne. I am grateful for the reference to Thomas Campbell, who tells me that theories on the subject go back at least as far as Franciscus Aguilonius in 1613.

unitary.[56] Otherwise it would be as if I perceived sweet and you perceived white.[57] The point is repeated by the commentators *ad loc.*, and, e.g., by Alexander, Plotinus, and "Philoponus".[58]

There are different kinds of unity. If perception is to compare sweet and white, to take the example of Plato and Aristotle, there must be something unitary other than taste and sight, which can be aware of the objects of both senses. Aristotle does not here, unless tacitly, apply the requirement of unity to awareness of tasting and seeing, but only to awareness of sweet and white. But elsewhere he looked for a single faculty to account for awareness of our seeing.[59] Indeed, we shall see that the Neoplatonists all looked for a unitary faculty to be aware not just of our seeing, but of our varied psychological operations, and "Philoponus" made it explicit that there ought to be one thing apprehending all, if we are to avoid Aristotle's threat of its being as if I perceived one thing and you another.[60] They were looking for a single *faculty*. They did not consider the option I find more plausible, that what needs to be unitary is not the faculties, but the *owner* of the faculties, in other words, the person or self. Finally, beyond these requirements of unity, there is the *sense* of a unitary self. On the whole, the ancient texts were discussing not the *sense* of a unitary self, but the need for a unitary subject of awareness.

Aristotle made us aware of our own seeing not by sight, but by sense perception taken more generally in the form of the so-called common sense,[61] and his successor Theophrastus agrees.[62] Plotinus complicates the situation by addressing apprehension (ἀντίληψις) not only of our sensing, but also of our thinking, appetite and psychological acts generally. He is not discussing the automatic self-thinking of intellect, but rather *our* awareness of our psychological activities, and this is not something he thinks very valuable. It is a distraction, he points out, if we are aware of our reading when we

[56] Arist., *De An.* III 1, 425 a 30 – b 1; III 2, 427 a 9-12; *De Sensu* 7, 449 a 6-20; cf. *De An.* III 7, 431 a 14-20; *De Somn.* 2, 455 a 12-22.

[57] *De An.*III 2, 426 b 17-23.

[58] Alex., *In Sens.* 36.13-19; *De An.* 60.27-61.3; Plot., IV 7 [2], 6.18-19; "Philop"., *In De An.* 465.10.

[59] Arist., *De Anima* III 2, 425 b 12-25.

[60] "Philop"., *In De An.* 465.7-11.

[61] Arist., *De Somn.* 2, 455 a 12-22.

[62] Theophrastus, *ap.* Prisc., *In Theophrastum* 21.32-22.1 (= FHSG 296).

X

read I 4 [46], 10.6-29. He therefore tends to assign the double awareness of perceptions and thoughts to a lowly faculty, the imagination (φαντασία, φανταστικόν).[63] Presumably, Plotinus thinks imagination can perform this double job because of the point, made in the adjacent chapter (IV 3, 31), that there are two faculties of imagination, one concerned with intelligibles, one with sensibles. An earlier treatise refers apprehension of appetite to inner sense (ἡ αἰσθητικὴ ἡ ἔνδον δύναμις),[64] which is the probable origin of Augustine's use of the corresponding Latin phrase (*interior sensus*), or discursive reason, and of our mental activity generally to the perceptual faculty,[65] which is the faculty in which Aristotle had located φαντασία. In the two passages which invoke imagination, Plotinus compares mirroring, and speaks of thought bending back (ἀνακάμπτειν) and being thrust back again (ἀπωσθῆναι πάλιν).[66]

Proclus objects to this account on two grounds, without naming Plotinus. First, he says at *In Eucl.* 141.2-19, that mirroring in the imagination by projecting (προβάλλειν) patterns there merely shows you the outward form (μορφή). In order genuinely to see oneself (ἑαυτόν), one would need to stand in the relationship exemplified by the self-thinking intellect which is both thinker and thing thought: one would need to become both seer and seen. This would require a procedure of turning (στροφή) inwards.

Secondly, Proclus objects that there are not two or three, but many different types of mental activity and we need a single thing to exercise consciousness (παρακολουθεῖν) of all of them.[67] In cognition, there are the five senses, the common sense and reason. Among desires, there is appetite (ἐπιθυμία), anger (θυμός), deliberate choice (προαίρεσις), to which a unitary vital faculty can give the nod (συνεπινεύειν), having enabled us to say "I have appetite", "I am angry", "I exercise deliberate choice". But prior to (πρό) both cognitions and desires, there is another unitary faculty conscious (παρακολουθεῖν) of all these activities, which says, "I am perceiving", "I am reasoning (λογίζομαι)", "I have appetite", "I will (βούλομαι)". It both knows the activities and distinguishes among

[63] Plot., IV 3 [27], 30.5-16; I 4 [46], 10.6-21.
[64] Plot., IV 8 [6], 8.10-11.
[65] Plot., V 1 [10], 12.5-14.
[66] Cf. Plot., I 4 [46], 10.6-10.
[67] Proclus, *In Parm.* IV 957.28-958.11.

X

them. It is set over (ἐπί with dative) the common sense, and is prior to (πρό) opinion (δόξα), appetite and will (βούλησις).

In another passage, Proclus gives a unifying role to λόγος, reason, which can use faculties both higher and lower than itself, in order to judge about objects.[68]

From a report about Proclus' teacher, Plutarch of Athens (not of Chaeroneia), we learn even more, in the commentary on Aristotle *De Anima* Book III (464.20-465.31) ascribed to Philoponus, but thought by some to be by a pupil of Philoponus, and by others to be by the still later Stephanus. "Philoponus" starts by saying that in Plutarch's view it was the lowest faculty of the rational soul, namely opinion (δόξα), that was responsible for knowing the activities of the senses. But he finishes by saying that this was an interpretation of Plutarch by certain newer interpreters whom he rejects. For he has nowhere found Plutarch giving this view, but considers that Plutarch followed Alexander in holding the common sense responsible, a view which "Philoponus" considers wrong. Why the discrepancy?

I think the solution to this apparent contradiction may be relevant to the theme of permeation. Plutarch, unlike Aristotle, might have located the common sense wholly or partly in the rational soul as its lowest part. He could have done so, if he included the common sense within φαντασία. For he is reported by "Philoponus" at 515.12-15, as having been like Plotinus[69] in recognising a higher kind of φαντασία which is the lower boundary of discursive reason. Moreover, Plotinus, at least in the first of these two passages, equates the higher φαντασία with opinion (δόξα), so Plutarch might have done the same. The net result would be that both reports about Plutarch could be right: Plutarch might have made the common sense responsible, as "Philoponus" says, but also, in a passage unnoticed by "Philoponus", equated the common sense with δόξα, so that the newer interpreters were right as well. This would fit with the Platonist tradition, that includes Plutarch's pupil, Proclus, of treating human sense as imbued with rationality. This is an alternative to the suggestion that Plutarch changed his mind.[70]

The newer interpreters, we are told, had postulated an extra part of the rational soul which they called the "attentive" (προσεκτικόν). Because the human being is unitary, this part needs to apprehend all

[68] Proclus, *In Tim.* I 254.31-255.20.

[69] Plot., III 6 [26], 4.18-23; IV 3 [27], 31.1-20.

[70] Blumenthal (1975).

X

mental and even biological activities, or it would be, as Aristotle said,[71] as if you perceived one thing and I another. But the part gets different names, being called the προσεκτικόν insofar as it ranges over cognitive activities, and conscience (συνειδός) insofar as it ranges over the vital desires. Συνείδησις was a name for both conscience and consciousness. Opinion could not do this work, because it could not apprehend activities higher than itself.

On the next page (466.18-29), "Philoponus" endorses the role of the προσεκτικόν and explains that *sight* could not know what it sees, because it would have to turn back (ἐπιστρέφειν) on itself, and such turning back would require it to be separable from body. This last explanation goes back[72] at least as far as a commentator earlier than Proclus or "Philoponus". Porphyry[73] explains that sight, unlike intellect, cannot know itself, since by having its essence (οὐσιῶσθαι) in body, it is prevented from turning back (στρέφεσθαι) on itself. For bodies cannot penetrate themselves, a point which is further stressed by "Simplicius".[74]

There is a final twist to the story even more relevant to the theme of permeation, because Aristotle's appeal to the common sense comes to be reinstated, but in a form that Aristotle himself would entirely repudiate. Common sense is turned into a rational, instead of a perceptual, faculty. We have raised the question whether this development might have started in Plutarch of Athens. It is certainly found in Priscian and in "Simplicius" *On Aristotle On the Soul* 3, whose authorship is still disputed, but which is assigned, we have seen, by Carlos Steel and Fernand Bossier to Priscian. In *On Theophrastus' On Sense Perception* 21.32-22.23, Priscian says that Aristotle's successor, Theophrastus, agrees with Aristotle that it is the common sense which is conscious (συναισθάνεσθαι) that we see. Instead of repudiating the view, Priscian defends it, by saying that the common sense is more separable from bodies than are the individual senses, and so can turn back (ἐπιστρέφεσθαι) into itself.

"Simplicius" agrees.[75] Only humans can perceive that they perceive, because only the rational can turn back (ἐπιστρέφειν) on itself. And rationality, as already hinted by Iamblichus, penetrates

---

[71] *De Anima* III 2, 426 b 17-23.

[72] I am grateful to Carlos Steel for what follows.

[73] Porph., *Sent.* 41.

[74] "Simplicius, *In De Anima* 173.3-7.

[75] "Simplicius", *In De Anima* 187.27-188.35; 173.3-7.

human sense perception, so that what perceives is to some extent separable from bodies. This separability is especially true of the common sense, which therefore has consciousness (συναίσθησις) of our seeing. But it falls short of intellect and reason, in that it recognises not substance, nor power, but only activities, and in that it recognises individuals. Other things cannot turn back on themselves at all (ἀνεπίστροφον).

4. Modern Controversy: Higher Order Thought and Perception

The controversy continues today on how we are aware of our own perceptions, by perception or thought. David Rosenthal has suggested that in self awareness there are individual thoughts about one or more psychological states.[76] He calls these "higher-order thoughts" (or HOTs in his abbreviation), because they are about psychological states at a lower level. Against Rosenthal's view that self awareness involves *thoughts* of a higher order ("HOTs"), William Lycan has argued in a forthcoming paper that it involves higher-order *perceptions* (HOPs). The paper is appropriately called "The Superiority of *HOP* to *HOT*".[77]

5. Alternatives

Both these views are opposed to views which regard self-awareness as being due to something more *direct* than a higher-order awareness,[78] and among views maintaining directness we can again distinguish different versions. One instance of direct self-awareness is provided by Aristotle's view, endorsed by Plotinus, that thinking thinks itself.[79] In this self-thinking, there is no higher-order thought, because the acts of thinking involved are identical, and not at different levels. Another direct view is offered by Plotinus' pupil, Porphyry, late in the 3rd century AD, when he speaks of one being

---

[76] Rosenthal (2002-3).

[77] Lycan (2004).

[78] Although higher-order awareness is not considered direct, Lycan thinks that self-awareness gives an *illusion* of direct presence, and that it is an advantage of the appeal to higher order perception, that perception, like self-awareness gives this illusion, whereas thinking, in his view, does not. I do not know where Plotinus' candidate, the imagination, should be placed in this assessment.

[79] Arist., *De An.* III 4, 430 a 2-4; cf. 429 b 9; *Metaph.* XII 7, 1072 b 19-21; cf. XII 9, 1074 b 38 – 1075 a 5.

present to oneself,[80] and this is probably where Augustine got the idea of the soul being present to itself,[81] early in the 5th century, as a result of which the soul knows itself directly.[82] This Neoplatonist idea is compatible with yet another one recorded above in connexion with Proclus, *In Eucl. 1* 141.2-19 , but also found in Porphyry, e.g., *Sentences* 41, and reflected in the same work of Augustine (*De Trin.* XIV 6, 8). According to this view, one turns into oneself, so as to find oneself directly.

Thus HOT and HOP are only two views among many. Moreover, even among those who agree in postulating an *indirect* higher order awareness of one's own psychological activities, there are other alternatives besides the two canvassed in the recent literature, perception and thought. Plotinus, we saw, postulated imagination, and the "newer interpreters" postulated the faculty of attention, to which I shall return, as giving us awareness of our psychological activities.

Proclus created a problem for the idea that perception is what makes us aware of our psychological activities, when he pointed out that we need to be aware not just of perception, for which perception might seem an appropriate monitor, but of many types of desire and reasoning as well. For these other objects of awareness one would need special reasons if one is to retain perception, like Aristotle, or a perceptual faculty like imagination, as monitor. One strategy, we saw, was to impregnate perception with reason. Alternatively, Plotinus and Plutarch of Athens recognised a higher kind of imagination related to reason. Plotinus may have had an additional ground for thinking the mirror of imagination adequate for awareness of our thoughts and perceptions, given that he thought that such self-awareness was not necessarily required in ordinary mental functioning like reading.

Admittedly, Aristotle had sided with the HOP against the HOT view, but only for awareness of *perception*. His reason is partly in order to avoid certain infinite regresses.[83] He invokes in particular the so-called common sense, rather than one of the five particular senses,[84] as giving us awareness of *perception*. As regards awareness

---

[80] Porph., *Sent.* 40, 49.10-11 Lamberz.

[81] Aug., *De Trin.* X 3, 5; X 7, 10; X 9, 12; X 10, 16.

[82] Aug., *De Trin.* X 4, 6.

[83] Arist., *De An.* III 2, 425 b 12-28.

[84] Arist., *De Somn.* 2, 455 a 15-22.

of *thought*, he takes a very differently motivated view that thought is aware of *itself*. This is neither a HOP not a HOT view, because self - thinking is a direct awareness, for the reason explained above, that no act of thinking is considered to be at a higher level, but there is an identity between the acts of thinking mentioned.

If there is any threat of an infinite regress in awareness of perception (which I do not believe), Aristotle's HOP solution, which makes perception aware of seeing, is not very promising, because it could not be applied generally to other psychological states, for example to disgust. It is no more disgust at one's disgust than pleasure at one's disgust that makes one aware of one's disgust. Either attitude to the disgust already presupposes awareness of it.

6. The Importance of Attention

Before I give my own view, let me consider for a moment those late Greek interpreters who ascribed our self awareness to a general ability to *attend*, because I think attention does need to be taken into account. It is not unreasonable to think of attention as a single generic faculty, even though it will have very different mechanisms, according to the type of object to which it is directed. But one reason why it is valuable to pick out attention as a general faculty is that there are circumstances in which attention is heightened by an alarm, or impaired by damage, quite generally, and not in respect of just one type of cognition such as seeing or thinking. Indeed, attention is more general still, because attention to our own psychological states is only one instance of attention. Plotinus is right when he points out that we attend little, indeed we can attend only selectively, to *what* we are perceiving,[85] just as we attend little to the *fact* that we are perceiving.[86] The appeal to attention has the further advantage that, like the appeal to thought, but unlike the appeal to perception, it avoids Proclus' problem concerning the great variety of psychological states of which we may be aware, very different types of desire as well as of cognition. Attention is something that can be directed to a great variety of objects. I have found attention playing many roles in ancient Greek thought.[87] Inattention was cited by Aristotle to explain going against one's better judgement.

---

[85] Plot., IV 4 [28], 8.9-16.

[86] Plot., I 4 [46], 10.6-29.

[87] Some of these examples can be found in the index to Sorabji (2000).

Switching attention was recommended by Epicurus as a way of reducing emotional upset. But inattention can also heighten emotion, for example when one does not attend to the fact that one is only watching a play, not reality. The Stoics spoke of attending to themselves in moral self-interrogation. Strato may have thought that all perception required attention. But attention is often invoked only in passing, and so I think the "newer interpreters" approved by "Philoponus" did well to pick it out as sufficiently important to be separated out as a distinct capacity.

Attention to what one is perceiving or hearing is not an extra bit of perceiving or hearing. It is only because I have already heard the clock strike three times, without attending, that I can tell you, when asked a few moments later, that it struck three times. What I do in this case is either attend to what I perceived, or, on another view, attend to some representation lingering in the imagination of what I perceived. I do not do some extra perceiving, and it is not enough either that I should merely do some thinking.

We find further evidence that attending is not necessarily a piece of extra perceiving or thinking, when we consider attention not to the clock striking, but to our own hearing. Somebody whose ears have been blocked for a time, and then unblocked, may be aware both of the *fact* that they are hearing again and to the *quality* of their hearing. Those people reported by Plato, in *Republic* 531 a, who tried to discover the smallest change of pitch that could be detected were interested in the quality of their hearing. What they needed was not to do some extra hearing, but to attend to the sounds, and equally to their detection of the sounds, to find how many changes they could detect. They had to count the detectable changes and compare them with seen physical changes going on in the musical instrument or felt changes in the vocal cords, in order to tell what they might be missing. This did not involve extra hearing. It did involve some thinking, but the thinking was concerned with data acquired by attending to what was detectable. The story would be different again if we considered an impressionist painter attending to the quality of his or her experience of light and how it might be represented in the available materials.

7. Conclusion on Self-Awareness

What I now want to suggest, turning to my own view, is that we have asked a wrong question in asking what supplies awareness of our psychological states and of our perceiving in particular. It is a wrong question, because there is no single answer to it. If there is unity in one's self-awareness, the unity is supplied by the single owner of that awareness, not by the owner's using a single faculty.

Even if we confine ourselves to awareness of *perceiving*, that is not a single thing. It may be awareness of fact or quality. Further, there are different mechanisms in different contexts by which we have this awareness. In awareness of perceiving, extra perceiving is often not needed. Certain types of thinking may have a special relevance to awareness of perceiving. But thought, in the examples given, only comes in after attention has been directed to some particular experiences. That initial attention to experience is not very naturally called "thinking". This is not to say that "attending" would give us a complete account of what happens. Attending to how small a change you can detect involves some attention to experience, but it also involves some thinking. I am suggesting that the "newer interpreters" were right to insist on the central role of attending, but that whether thinking is also involved, and what thinking, will depend on exactly what we want to be aware of.

If we turn to awareness of our *thinking*, this too may be awareness of the *fact* of thinking or of its *character*. Here the need for extra perception may be still less, and the need for extra thinking greater. Attending will be required, but if one is to be aware of the *character* of one's thought, one may be required to ask oneself questions about one's thoughts, and recall how they happened. Admittedly, in this case, the term "thinking" is wide enough for this questioning and recalling to count as a form of thinking. But higher order thinking cannot serve, any more than can higher order perceiving, as the sole mechanism of self-awareness.

X

BIBLIOGRAPHY

BERMUDEZ, J.L. (1998), *The Paradox of Self-Conciousness* (*Representation in Mind*), Cambridge (Mass).

BLUMENTHAL, H.J. (1975), "Plutarch's Exposition of the *De Anima* and the Psychology of Proclus", in DÖRRIE, H. (ed.), *De Jamblique à Proclus* (Entretiens sur l'Antiquité classique, 21), Geneva, 123–47.

GRUSSER, O.-J. (1986), "Interaction of Efferent and Afferent Signals in Visual Perception. A History of Ideas and Experimental Paradigms", in *Acta Psychologica* 63, 2–21.

KAHN, C.H. (1992), "Aristotle on Thinking", in NUSSBAUM, M.C. – RORTY, A.O. (eds), *Essays on Aristotle's* De Anima, Oxford, 367–72.

LYCAN, W.G. (2004), "The Superiority of *HOP* to *HOT*", in GENNARO, R.W. (ed.), *Higher Order Theories of Consciousness* (*Advances in Consciousness Research*, 56), Amsterdam, 93–113.

NEISSER, U. (ed.) (1993), *The Perceived Self: Ecological and Interpersonal Sources of Self-Knowledge* (*Emory Symposia in Cognition*, 5), Cambridge.

ROSENTHAL, D. (2002–3), "Unity of Consciousness and the Self", in *Proceedings of the Aristotelian Society* 103, 325–52.

SEDLEY, D.N. (1996), "Alcinous' Epistemology", in ALGRA, K. – VAN DER HORST, P.W. – RUNIA, D.T. (eds), *Polyhistor: Studies in the History and Historiography of Ancient Philosophy Presented to Jaap Mansfeld* (*Philosophia antiqua*, 72), Leiden, 300–312.

SORABJI, R. (1991), "From Aristotle to Brentano: the Development of the Concept of Intentionality", in BLUMENTHAL, H. – ROBINSON, H. (eds), *Aristotle and the Later Tradition, Oxford Studies in Ancient Philosophy*, supp. vol., 226–59.

SORABJI, R. (1993), *Animal Minds & Human Morals. The Origins of the Western Debate*, Ithaca/New York.

SORABJI, R. (2000), *Emotion and Peace of Mind* (*Gifford Lectures*), Oxford.

SORABJI, R. (2004), *The Philosophy of the Commentators, 200–600 AD*, vol. 1: *Psychology*, London.

SORABJI, R. (2006), "Universals Transformed: The First Thousand Years after Plato", in CHAKRABARTI, A. – STRAWSON, P. (eds), *Universals, Qualities, Concepts*, Aldershot, 105–125.

STEEL, C. – HUBY, P. (transl.) (1997), Priscianus, *On Theophrastus on Sense-Perception*, with Simplicius, *On Aristotle on the Soul 2.5–12* (*The Ancient Commentators on Aristotle*), London.

XI

Self-awareness

It is a great pleasure to have an opportunity to honour Alan, from whom I have benefitted for over 35 years through his philosophical range, his unfailing contributions to innumerable seminars in Ancient Philosophy, his valued comments on translations of late Greek Philosophy, and his ever supportive and genial presence. Characteristically, he has by a quiet but decisive objection caused me to modify one of the points I am making in the present chapter.

When we talk of self-awareness, this can be awareness, among other things, of our activities, our motives, our character, or our true self. But these are inter-connected, so the idea of self-awareness is not just a random collection of ideas.

It has been argued at various times that self-awareness is impossible, or at any rate so difficult that it is better achieved through awareness of others, or on the other hand that it is quite the reverse: inevitable and infallible. Further, it has been asked what faculty gives us a unified awareness of all our psychological activities. I have discussed these topics in chapters 11 to 14 of *Self*, which has been published since the conference in honour of Alan Lacey that formed the origin of the present book. But I think it might be useful to offer a streamlined overview of most of the topics, though I shall omit the discussion of inevitability.

1. The impossibility of self-awareness

One argument for the impossibility of self-awareness is rehearsed by Plato in his *Charmides* at 167c-d; 168d-e. It is that sight cannot be sight of itself and not of colour. If sight is seen, it will have itself to be coloured. This is generalised to knowledge and belief not being just of themselves at 168a, and to other relations at 168d. On one interpretation, the argument is that sight that was just a perception of sight and of nothing else would have no content, for it is colour that gives sight its content. A further difficulty for self-awareness is discussed by Plato's pupil Aristotle at *On the Soul* 3.2, 425b12-28, and it adds on to Plato's difficulty of contentless sight the danger of an infinite regress. How are we aware that we are seeing (or, equivalently, of our seeing)? It must be by sight, for if we had to be aware of an act of awareness (e.g. that we are seeing) by an act of *another* type (other than sight), we should have embarked on an infinite regress of types.

There is another kind of regress that needs to be considered, but it is a regress of acts, not of *types* of act, and is exploited by the song about a lovers' quarrel, 'I thought you thought I was thinking'. If psychological activities are not self-luminous, but are known by further acts of awareness, then there has to be, for finite minds, at any given time, at least a temporary halt to a regress of acts of awareness of awareness. I can be aware that I am aware that I am seeing, but at any given moment the first awareness in any chain will always be something of which I am not currently aware. Of course, there is in principle no barrier, only the barrier of lack of concentration, to my becoming aware of it, and so adding an extra awareness to the beginning of the chain. But this new awareness will be something of which I am not yet aware. Whether Aristotle considers a regress of acts we shall consider shortly, but at present he is concerned with a regress of *types* of act.

Aristotle has another objection to allowing that I have to be aware that I am seeing through a type of faculty *other* than sight. If this supposed other faculty is not to be contentless, as Plato's argument threatened, it will have to be aware not only that I am seeing, but also of the colour seen. But in that case, there will be two faculties, sight and the supposed other faculty, directed to one type of object: colour. And it goes against a principle accepted by both Plato and Aristotle that there should be two faculties for the same type of object. For both philosophers distinguish faculties by the different objects they have.[1]

So far, it seems that I am aware that I am seeing by sight. But Aristotle considers a further difficulty. As Plato himself threatened, our seeing, or at least that which reveals our seeing, in other words the eye that sees, would have to be coloured. For sight by definition is aware of the coloured. Aristotle gives two answers. One is that the eye that sees *is* coloured in a way, and I take this to be because while it is seeing, it takes on colour patches, though not as intrinsic colours of its own, only as borrowed from the scene it is seeing. But the more important solution offered by Aristotle is that perceiving by sight is different from seeing. We do not see that we are seeing, but merely perceive it by the use of sight. He compares how we do not see darkness, because sight is defined as perception of colour or brightness. But we nonetheless perceive darkness by trying to use our sight (and failing), so we perceive darkness by sight. In the case that concerns

---

[1] Plato *Republic* 477 c-d; Aristotle *On the Soul* 2.4, 415a20-2.

us, we perceive that we are seeing by using the generic faculty of perception which includes all five senses and more besides. But it is important that the generic faculty of perception should be brought to bear on our seeing not on our hearing. So it is by sight that we perceive that we are seeing, even though we do not *see* that we are seeing. Aristotle here refuses to generalise Plato's suggestion about lack of content. He has agreed that seeing would lack content if it did not include colour among its objects, but perceiving, or perceiving by sight, is not treated as depending on colour for its content.

According to Aristotle's greatest ancient exponent, Alexander, if the passage is his,[2] Aristotle finishes his discussion at 425b26ff by removing a regress of *acts* of awareness. Aristotle here says that there is a sense in which an act of perceiving is identical with what it perceives. Aristotle does not explain why he makes this point here. But the point would acquire relevance if it is meant to stop a regress of acts of awareness.

So far, Plato has raised a doubt about whether self-awareness is possible and Aristotle has intensified the doubt, but sought to answer it. But the debate continued, for, around 200 A.D., more than 400 years after Aristotle, the sceptic Sextus Empiricus raised related, though slightly different, doubts, and 50 years later again Plotinus sought to answer them.

2. Is self-awareness so difficult that it is more easily achieved through awareness of another?

It has been observed in modern psychology that at around 9 months, normal human children, unlike any of the great apes and unlike certain types of damaged children, play with mother, father or carer the game of 'are we looking at the same thing?'. The desired state has been called one of shared attention. It has been argued that children get the idea of themselves as having a gaze only hand in hand with the idea of someone else having a possibly divergent gaze. They see themselves as having psychological characteristics only in connexion with seeing others as having possibly divergent characteristics.[3] If so, Descartes has things the wrong way round. It is not that I know my mind alright, but as regards others, I do not know if they are automatons. Instead, I only have the idea of my mind insofar as I have the idea of another's. I know myself through another.

---

[2] Alexander(?) *Quaestiones* 3.7, 92, 31.
[3] See e.g. Tomasello (1994) and (1999).

134

This view is put forward by Plato in the *First Alcibiades*,132c-133c, if it is by him, although he is talking about knowing one's *true* self as being one's reason. Just as one cannot see oneself just by looking, but does better to see oneself reflected in the eye of another, so one recognises one's true self by seeing reason at work in another. Augustine was to disagree 750 years later in *On the Trinity* 10.3.5. Incorporeal things are not known by mirroring. Nothing is more present to the soul than itself.

Aristotle accepts Plato's idea, though in a different connexion. He addresses the question what the value of friendship is, given the rather alien Greek idea that the ideal person would be self-sufficient. His answer turns on the idea that awareness of one's friend is connected with awareness of oneself. The friend, it is suggested, is another self, and easier to observe. There are at least four versions of his argument,[4] but in none is he, like Plato, discussing the true self. In some, he is talking about awareness of one's friend's activities as good and as one's own. At two points, I believe, he is referring to the phenomenon I have mentioned of shared attention to activities and is treating it as being particularly pleasurable, *Eudemian Ethics* 7.12, 1244b24-28; 1245b21-24.

The difficulty of direct self-awareness is evidenced by the Aristotelian author of pseudo-Aristotle *Magna Moralia* 2.15, 1213a13-26, through the point that it is much easier to recognise the faults of others than our own. The same point was to be made 500 years later by the doctor Galen,[5] who drew the conclusion that to correct our faults we should rely not on introspection, but on getting someone else to criticise us.

The Stoics introduced awareness of self through another in a quite different context to which Brad Inwood has drawn attention.[6] A surviving papyrus fragment from an author of the second century AD, the Stoic Hierocles, asks why the chick does not fear the leaping bull close to it, but scuttles away from the small, distant hawk, *Elements of Ethics* col.3, lines 39-45, A. A. Long.[7] His reply is that the chick has awareness of the liabilities and abilities of its physical self, and, as Inwood points out, this awareness about its physical self has to take into account the likely actions on it

---

[4] See Aristotle *Eudemian Ethics* 7.12, 1244b24-1245a12; 1245a30-b1; 1245b21-24; *Nicomachean Ethics* 9.9, 1169b33-1170a4; 1170a29-b14; and pseudo-Aristotle *Magna Moralia* 2.15, 1213a13-26.

[5] Galen *On the Errors and Passions of the Soul*, in Galen *Scripta Minora*, ed. Marquardt et al., Teubner edition, vol. 1, ch.2, p.4, line 11- p.5, line 2; ch.3, 6,17 – 7,1.

[6] Inwood (1984).

[7] Similar is Seneca *Letter* 121.19.

of other beings. Although these other beings do not have to be seen as having minds, they are seen as being safe or unsafe. This is how others come into the idea of self. Hierocles has an additional view that the chick's awareness is not to be classified as the work of reason – the Stoics hold that animals lack reason. But neither is it mere unconscious instinct – nature in Greek terms. It is something in between these two: self-perception. Alan Lacey has pointed out to me that reaction to the hawk shape does look suspiciously like an instinctual response, which would not have to be mediated by self-awareness, but it was self-perception for which Hierocles was arguing.

A final example has a rather different character. Plotinus at *Enneads* 5.1 [10] (1-17), is struck by the irony that the rebellious adolescent wants to belong to himself and to have self-determination, but by distancing himself from his parents becomes unaware who he is. This is used as a simile for describing the process by which inferior entities are formed in the universe, souls by apostasis from Intellect. Plotinus here sees knowledge of one's parentage, hence knowledge of others, as entering into one's very conception of who one is.

3. The infallibility of self-awareness

It is Augustine, possibly influenced by Plotinus, who makes the shift towards the point of view we find later in Descartes. The soul, according to his *On the Trinity*, is present to itself, so does not have to seek itself. The difficult question for Augustine is how it ever makes a mistake about itself, but his answer is that, although it has a continuous knowledge (*nosse*; *notitia*; cf. *nota*) of itself even in infancy, it can make mistakes when it starts thinking (*cogitare*) about itself, 14.5.7; 14.6.8-9. It makes mistakes when it forms extended images to imagine itself, because it is not something extended, 10.3.5; 10.3.7 – 10.6.8; 10.8.11; 10.10.16 (72-85) ed. Mountain, CCL 50.

Augustine gives one of his many versions of the Cogito argument that Descartes was to use later, according to which doubt is impossible about one's own psychological activities: it comes in *On the Trinity* 10.10.14:

But who will doubt that he lives, remembers, understands, wills, thinks, knows and judges? For even if he doubts, he lives. If he doubts where his doubts come from, he remembers. If he doubts, he understands that he doubts. If he doubts, he wants to be certain. If he doubts, he thinks. If he doubts, he knows that he does not know. If he doubts, he judges that he ought not rashly to give assent. So whoever acquires a doubt from any source ought not to doubt any of these things whose non-existence would mean that he could not entertain doubt about anything.

In some ways Augustine is more explanatory than Descartes was later to be in the second *Meditation*. He here shows very clearly the principle on which his Cogito rests. He is not relying on the supposed infallibility of introspection. Instead, he is confining himself to conditions which have to be met if there is to be any doubting at all. If he doubts the holding of such conditions, the doubt itself guarantees that they are met and that the doubt is untenable. He carefully avoids asserting anything unwarranted by putting everything in terms of an 'if': 'if there is doubt'. He also explains better than Descartes why he thinks wanting is undoubtable by arguing that doubting implies wanting. He cannot be accused of giving us a weak argument by failing to express it in the first person with an 'I' like Descartes, because if the argument gains anything from being cast in the first person, which is a controversial claim, Augustine does cast it in the first person in some of his other formulations: *si fallor, sum* – 'if I am mistaken, I exist'.

It has been suggested by Dominic O'Meara[8] that Augustine may have been influenced by a passage in Plotinus. Certainly Plotinus is looking for irrefutability and he uses an analogous strategy. Intellect is irrefutable because it confines itself to thinking what is identical with itself, 5.5 [32] 2 (18-21):

> So that the real truth, conforming with itself and not with something else, says nothing other besides itself, and what it is it also says, and what it says it also is. Who then could refute it? From where would he bring the refutation?

Augustine continues in *On the Trinity* 10.10.16 to argue, like Descartes, for the incorporeality of the mind (*mens*). It has just been shown that the mind is certain (*certus*) about itself and so knows (*nosse*) itself. And then a controversial premiss is used, that a thing cannot be said to be known (*sciri*) so long as its essence is not known. Aristotle had already given examples which show this principle to be wrong. One can know that the moon is

---

[8] O'Meara (2000).

eclipsed without knowing that the essence of lunar eclipse involves the earth's shadow. Nonetheless, Augustine continues by saying that the mind must therefore know (*nosse*) and be certain of its essence. But it is not at all certain whether it is air, fire, or anything bodily. So it is not anything bodily (presumably in its essence).

Descartes in the seventeenth century argues for this conclusion somewhat differently, because he completes the argument of the second *Meditation*, which initially sounds similar, only in the sixth, where he appeals to the further notion of clear and distinct ideas. But what does seem closer to Augustine's argument for incorporeality is the Flying Man argument produced by someone who could not have known of Augustine's Latin, the brilliant Islamic philosopher Avicenna, or Ibn Sina, in the eleventh century. A major presentation of the argument is given in *Al-Shifā* (*the Healing*): *Soul*, 1.1, (Rahman 15.18 – 16.17) in Arabic, translated into medieval Latin in *De Anima* 1.1, in Avicenna Latinus, ed. S. Van Riet. In a letter to a former pupil, Bahmanyâr, published by Jean (=Yahya) Michot in *Muséon* 2000, he explains his premises – one which we can see to be interestingly different from Augustine's, though equally unintuitive. Whoever knows something knows his *own* essence. Avicenna imagines a man who comes into existence floating through the air, feeling no contact even of one limb with another. Such a man would know directly that his essence existed. But he would not know that body existed, since he would have no evidence for its existence. Avicenna concludes that his essence, which he takes to be soul, is independent of body.

There are further similarities between Avicenna and Augustine. Both use the idea that the soul is present to itself. Both argue that what is imagined cannot be part of one's essence. Avicenna draws a distinction like that of Augustine between two kinds of awareness: the intellect has knowledge (*shu'ûr*) of existence, but there is no intelligising (*'aqala*) of intellect. If there is an explanation of the similarities in the argument for incorporeality, it must be a common Greek source of influence, and they did both know the work of Plotinus' pupil Porphyry. Porphyry, a little before Augustine, writes in *Sentences* 40-41 of being present to a self that is present to itself (*parôn paronti*). Further, speaking not of soul as a whole, but just of intellect, he writes that since intellect can turn away from the body and still both remain intact and know itself, it does not owe its essence to the body.

One element of Porphyry's argument was taken by the ancient Greek commentators to be contained already in Plato's *Phaedo*. When Plato there makes Socrates advocate withdrawing one's soul from the body, he reveals that body is not in the essence of soul.

4. What unifies our awareness of our psychological activities?

I come now to my final topic of the unification of self-awareness. Plato asks how we distinguish sweet from white, since no one sense can distinguish them. He infers that the five senses must converge (*sunteinein*) on something unitary (*mia*), the soul, *Theaetetus* 184d, and he stresses the soul's reasoning activities, 186a – 187a. Aristotle makes the same point very graphically. Without sweet and white being presented to something unitary, it would be as if *I* perceived sweet and *you* perceived white, *On the Soul* 3.2, 426b17-23. But for the task of distinguishing sweet from white, he holds, the unitary thing is not the reasoning faculty of soul, but something sensory, the common sense, or sense perception taken generically as opposed to one of the five senses.

Aristotle takes the subject further in *On Sense Perception* 7, 447b24 – 448a1. In order to tell whether we are perceiving qualities from the same range or (like sweet and white) from different ranges, we have to know whether we are using one sense or two. In order to tell which end of a range we are perceiving, we have to know whether we are perceiving a positive quality, or (like wet or cold) a privation. In order to tell whether the sweet and white belong to one thing, we have to know whether we are perceiving sweet and white simultaneously.

This last point of Aristotle's, which was drawn to my attention by Stephan Eberle, seems to me important. It implies that we get the idea of qualities belonging to the same object in the external world only through the idea of the same person perceiving them at the same time. Thus there will be no idea of a physical world of bodies possessing qualities without an idea of a single perceiver possessing simultaneous perceptions. This is an argument that we need the idea of a person possessing psychological states, not just the idea of streams of consciousness possessed by no one. I shall return at the end to another argument for a unitary self which possesses psychological states. This one has analogues in Kant and in Hindu thought (cited in my *Self*, p.293).

In the third and fifth centuries A.D., the subject is taken further by Plotinus and even more emphatically by Proclus, *Commentary on Plato's Parmenides* 957, 28 – 958, 11, Cousin, when they point out that the range of psychological activities of which we can be aware is far wider than the perception of sweet and white. In cognition, there are the five senses, the common sense and reason. Among desires there are appetite, anger and deliberate choice, to which a unitary vital faculty can give the nod, having enabled us to say, 'I have appetite', 'I am angry', 'I exercise deliberate choice'. But prior to both cognitions and desires there is another unitary faculty conscious of all these activities, which says, 'I am perceiving', 'I am reasoning', 'I have appetite', 'I will'.

The debate on whether it is Plato's reason or Aristotle's common sense that serves as the unifying faculty has continued into modern philosophy, with David Rosenthal backing higher-order thought (*HOT*) and William Lycan higher-order perception (*HOP*), that is respectively *thought* about psychological activities versus *perception* of psychological activities.[9]

But *HOT* and *HOP* are only two views among many. By postulating a higher order of awareness, that is, an awareness of awareness, both views reject the idea that self-awareness of psychological activity is *direct*, and does not need a further level of awareness. Moreover, there are several different ways in which ancient philosophers suggested that awareness of psychological activities might be direct. Augustine's idea of the soul being present to itself is only one. Another view was Aristotle's, mentioned above, that in some sense an act of perceiving or thinking is identical with its object, so that when the object is itself an act of awareness, we do not need to postulate that it constitutes a second, lower level of awareness. Then there is the Neoplatonist view that intellect is self-aware by turning in on itself (*epistrephesthai*), a thing that bodily entities cannot do.

But even if we accept that awareness of our psychological activities involves a higher level of awareness, the ancient philosophers offered more suggestions about the higher level than just perception or thought. Plotinus tended to suggest that the mirror of imagination was used for awareness of non-intellectual psychological activities. But by far the most interesting suggestion, recorded by pseudo-Philoponus, *Commentary on Aristotle On the Soul 3*, 464, 24 – 465, 31, is that we need to postulate a faculty of *attention* (*prosektikon*). This idea is ascribed to the 'Attic commentators', and he may have in mind the Athenian Proclus.

It does seem to me that this, though not the whole story, is an important step forward. Attention deserves to be singled out as a distinctive capacity. For one thing, our attention can be subject to a global alert or heightening, so that after a shock received through one sense modality or

---

[9] Rosenthal (2002-3); Lycan (2004).

through one piece of thinking, we remain for several hours or days on alert for further information through all our cognitive modalities, as if attention was something that could operate as a single unit, and furthermore as if it had the wide range that Proclus was looking for, because it can operate on all our modalities.

Pseudo-Philoponus offers at 466, 30-35, an elegant argument that awareness of perception is not itself a kind of perception. Suppose I am busy reasoning out a problem while I walk along the street and I pass my friend while thus absorbed. When I get home, and am no longer in a position to see my friend, I reflect for the first time that I did see him. Previously, I was aware of my friend and even perhaps of my friend as seen from a certain angle. But this awareness of a view of my friend is not yet an awareness of seeing him. In this case at least it is not perception that recognises that I saw my friend. Pseudo-Philoponus suggests that it is reason. This is not incompatible with the suggestion that it is attention, if attention is classified, as Proclus may have classified it, as a kind of reason.

This is an objection to *HOP*, but it can also be argued that sometimes awareness of psychological activity is not due to *HOT*. In the *Republic* Plato describes musical theorists who struck pairs of notes in order to see how small a difference in pitch could be detected. Thinking is involved in such a case, but only after attention has been directed to hearing. One first attends to one's hearing and only then thinks about what that implies for the size of interval.

These examples illustrate what I believe to be a general truth, that there is no single faculty by which we are aware of our own psychological activities. We use different faculties in different cases, even though it is a step forward to include attention on the list of faculties. So the unity which Aristotle rightly says is needed, if it is not to be as if you perceived one thing and I another, does not come from a unitary faculty, as both ancient Neoplatonists and modern philosophers suppose. It is the burden of my book on self that many problems remain insoluble until we recognise that there is such a thing as Self. In this case, I believe, it is not a unitary faculty, but the unity due to the faculties belonging to the same self, that gives unity to our awareness of diverse psychological activities.

References

Inwood, Brad 1984: 'Hierocles: theory and argument in the second century AD',
Oxford Studies in Ancient Philosophy, 2, pp.151-83.
Lycan, William G. 2004: 'The superiority of *HOP* to *HOT*'. In: Gennaro, Rocco W.
(ed.): *Higher Order Theories of Consciousness: An Anthology*. Amsterdam:
John Benjamins, pp. 93-113
O'Meara, Dominic J. 2000: 'Scepticism and ineffability in Plotinus'. *Phronesis,* 45,
pp. 240-51.
Rosenthal, David 2002-3: 'Unity of consciousness and the self'. *Proceedings of the
Aristotelian Society* 103, pp. 325-52.
Sorabji, Richard 2006: *Self: Ancient and Modern Insights about Individuality, Life,
and Death*. Chicago and Oxford: Chicago and Oxford University Presses.
Tomasello, Michael 1994: 'On the interpersonal origins of self-concept'. In:
Neisser, Ulrich (ed.): *The Perceived Self*. Cambridge: Cambridge University
Press.
Tomasello, Michael 1999: *The Cultural Origins of Human Cognition*. Cambridge,
Mass: Harvard University Press.

XII

Moral Conscience: Contributions to the Idea in Plato and Platonism

It is a great pleasure to write in honor of Charles Kahn, from whom I first learnt when he wrote a seminal paper about Aristotle in 1966, and who invariably brings out the very general interest of whatever he discusses across a huge range of topics and authors, so that conversations with him are always of the highest value. In the present book, his work on the Presocratics and Plato has been chosen for celebration, so I shall select the Platonist aspects of some work I have been doing on the idea of moral conscience.[1]

I think that the Greeks and Romans played a vital role in the development of the concept of conscience which Christianity took over and developed differently for its own purposes. Although the Hebrew Old Testament provides thrilling examples of what *we* should call conscience, notably in King David's remorse for acquiring Bathsheba by arranging the death of her husband, these use for conscience only the general word for heart, the seat of many different emotions. The few references to conscience in English versions of the Old Testament come from the ancient Greek translation of the Hebrew. This is not necessarily to say that the Hebrew writers lacked the concept. They could have had it without the word, but it was the Greek word that stimulated Paul's discussions of conscience in the New Testament. It has been suggested that it may have been the

---

[1]   I am drawing on Richard Sorabji, "Graeco-Roman Origins of the Idea of Moral Conscience," delivered to the Oxford Patristics Conference of 2007, and published in *Studia Patristica* 44–49 (Leuven: Peeters, 2010), 361–384. My next book will be *Moral Conscience through the Ages* (Oxford and Chicago University Presses, 2014).

Greek-speaking Corinthians, not Paul, who first raised the question of conscience in their correspondence.[2]

INTRODUCTION: SHARING KNOWLEDGE WITH ONESELF OF A DEFECT

I believe that the Greek expression which came to be the standard term for conscience began to appear with some of its eventual meaning in the playwrights of the fifth century BCE, Aristophanes and Euripides. When we have a particular form of the verb for knowing, *suneidenai*, coupled with the reflexive pronoun in the dative, e.g., *heautôi* (oneself), it means to share (*sun-*) knowledge with oneself of a defect, not at first necessarily a moral defect. The image of *sharing* treats us as if we were each composed of two people. One of them knows of the defect and the other is ignoring it, but the knowledge ought to be shared between the two. If the reflexive pronoun is absent, as it is bound to be when the noun is used, *suneidêsis*, instead of the verb, then one can tell only from the context whether the meaning is to share knowledge with oneself of a defect; for the root term, *suneid-*, can have quite a range of other meanings. But in the particular grammatical construction specified, I believe the meaning is clear.

It is usually thought that the original meaning of *suneidenai* must have been to share knowledge with *another* person. After all, the idea of sharing knowledge with oneself is not an obvious one. But I think that the sense of sharing knowledge with *another* person becomes common only later. It becomes common among lawyers, above all in Cicero in the 1st century BCE, because lawyers have often to talk about accomplices, witnesses and confidants, who share the guilty knowledge of someone *else*. There is one such use, we shall see, already in Plato in the fourth century. But this use often presupposes the idea of sharing knowledge with oneself. The guilty person shares knowledge with himself, and the second person shares the first person's guilty knowledge.

In Christian texts, the legal interest recedes, and the emphasis turns to an idea already prominent in the Stoic Seneca in the

---

2   C. A. Pierce, *Conscience in the New Testament* (London: SPCK Press, 1955).

first century CE.³ In fact Seneca is congratulated by the Christian Lactantius for expressing the idea that one may try to avoid sharing one's guilty knowledge with one's fellow humans, but one cannot keep it hidden from God. From this perspective, there is not much occasion for Christians to talk of one human sharing another human's guilty knowledge. The concern was that that would not be shared, which left God as the only one who could share the knowledge.

By strange good fortune, the special Greek idiom went over easily into Latin through the use of the adjective *conscius*, sharing-knowl-edge-with, a direct Latinization of the Greek participle *suneidôs*. One can say in Latin that a person is *sharing-knowledge-with* himself. Very early on, the Roman comic playwrights, Plautus in the third century BCE and Terence in the second, speak in Latin of sharing knowledge. Terence has a character say, "I am sharing knowledge with myself that this fault (*culpa*) is far from me." Plautus speaks of sharing knowledge of guilt with *another* person picked out by the reflexive pronoun: "Beware that they do not share knowledge with yourself (*ipsi*) of your wrongdoing." The Latin tradition is continued by Cicero in the first century BCE and by the Stoic Seneca in the first century CE. Each speaks of sharing knowledge with oneself of a fault or of its absence, although the reflexive pronoun is not always explicit. Each also speaks of sharing knowledge of guilt with *another* party, and here they do not use the reflexive pronoun, except insofar as they are discussing the original guilty party. The sharers of guilty knowledge may be gods or humans, and even inanimate room walls are imagined as being witnesses.⁴

A new element in the Roman writers, Cicero and Seneca, is the interest in a conscience that is not merely clear of wrongdoing. The idea of a clear conscience, we shall see, is already found in Plato's *Republic*. But the Romans had the idea of sharing knowledge of one's own or another's *merit*. Seneca had particular occasion to refer to this in discussing the ethics of benefactors in his treatise *On Benefits*.⁵

---

³ Lactantius, *Divine Institutes*, 6:25.12–17.

⁴ Cicero, *Pro Caelio* 60.

⁵ See Cicero, *Tusculan Disputations* 2.64; Seneca, *On Benefits* 2.33.2–3, 4.11.3, 4.12.4, *Letters* 71.76, and on his wife's approval of his interrogating himself on his conduct at the end of the day, *On Anger*, 3.36.

The Stoic Roman Emperor Marcus Aurelius has a special word, *eusuneidêtos*, for having a good conscience.[6] But the idea of sharing awareness of merit was dropped by Christianity. At most, the idea of a joyful Christian conscience can be used in John Chrysostom (347–407 CE) in connexion with the martyr, whose conscience makes him joyful in adversity. However, a joyful conscience was the very antithesis of the repentance for which the Christian Church often called and of the despairing conscience of Luther from which he sought a merciful redemption in the promise of Christ's Gospel.

Reference to *oneself* is already explicit, or clearly understood, in certain uses of *suneidenai* in plays of the fifth century BCE. It is used by the comic playwright Aristophanes three times, with the reference to oneself explicit, and by the tragedian Euripides twice, with the reference to self understood.[7] In Aristophanes, people share knowledge with themselves of infidelity after three days of marriage, and of having set a defendant free by giving the wrong vote, and an ironical suggestion is made that someone will not succeed in politics if he shares knowledge with himself of having done anything good. In Euripides the knowledge shared with self is Orestes' self-knowledge (described as a sickness) of murder and Jason's (insisted on by Medea) of his breaking his marriage oath to her. The examples of sharing knowledge with oneself given by these playwrights, unlike many of those in Plato, all involve a moral failing.

It has often been said that early Greek culture is a culture of shame, not of guilt, and that is entirely compatible with the failing being a moral one, since shame can be a moral sentiment. As a matter of fact, although my case does not depend upon it, I do not think that shame can be separated off from guilt so easily in all these examples given by the dramatists. Even in the guilt culture, which Christianity is said to be, shame and guilt can very well accompany each other. The difference between shame and guilt has been explained in one account by saying[8] that the person who is ashamed is thinking

---

[6]   Marcus Aurelius, *Meditations* VI 30.

[7]   Aristophanes, *Wasps* 999–1002; *Thesmophoriazousae* 477; *Knights* 184 (where "good" is ironical for "bad"; Euripides, *Medea* 495; *Orestes* 395–396.

[8]   B. Williams, *Shame and Necessity* (Berkeley: University of California Press, 1993), 88–94 and Appendix 1.

about what sort of person he is, typically in relation to the imagined contempt of others concerning his deficiencies, but sometimes, as I think the account would agree, in relation to his own self-image. The deficiencies include non-moral ones like poverty. The person who feels guilt, by contrast, is typically thinking more narrowly about a victim and justified recrimination.

So far this account in terms of a victim omits the idea of violating the requirements of an authority such as God. But another source of guilt, I believe, is thought about violation of the requirements of an accepted, possibly divine, authority and about that authority's disapproval, whether or not there is a victim. I agree with a further claim in this account that, although the Greeks do not distinguish guilt from shame, the situations which provoke shame in the Greek portrayals in some cases provoke also the attitudes which *we* distinguish as guilt, even though the Greeks and Romans did not make the distinction. This sort of phenomenon is very common—with regard to the different idea of conscience, the Hebrew Old Testament describes the existence of tormented conscience, without having a distinctive word, or otherwise drawing attention to differences from other kinds of torment. May not moral guilt be included along with shame in the idea of Jason's breaking his marital oath, of Orestes murdering his mother, and of Aristophanes' case of marital infidelity after three days? For these all involve a victim, and one at least invites divine disapproval. Jason has violated his oath to the gods, who side with Medea. There are complications about assigning feelings of guilt. Orestes' feelings are bound up with ideas of pollution, but E. R. Dodds has argued that this does not prevent him from feeling guilt rather than shame.[9] Another complication is that the divine Furies that pursue Orestes are presented by Euripides as mere delusions of a man sick with knowledge of his misdeed. But what matters is that Orestes himself believes he has violated divine authority.

Whether or not there is a sense of guilt, the knowledge shared with self is of a moral defect, whereas the defect is not necessarily moral in Plato's examples, to which I shall now turn.

---

[9]   E. R. Dodds, *The Greeks and the Irrational* (Berkeley: University of California Press, 1956), ch. 2, "From shame culture to guilt culture."

PART 1: THE CONTRIBUTION OF PLATONISM

Plato's examples of sharing with oneself knowledge of a defect

In all nine cases where Plato uses the full expression "to share knowledge with oneself," he is referring to knowledge of one's own defect or weakness, or once of its absence.[10] Socrates shares knowledge with himself of his own ignorance, Alcibiades of self-neglect and unjustifiably disobeying Socrates, Cephalus of faultless-ness—of *not* having committed injustice—others of being seduced by poetry, of being unduly hasty or precipitate, of speaking well only of Homer and so lacking any art of literary criticism, and of their feeble attempts in childhood to distinguish letters from each other (admittedly a trivial defect in this case). In one last case in the *Laws*, Plato speaks of sharing someone else's guilty knowledge of their cowardice or injustice, and uses the reflexive pronoun "themselves" (*sphisin*), evidently to emphasize that the person with whom one shares guilty knowledge shares it also with himself. These nine cases make it particularly clear what is meant when the verb is used with the reflexive pronoun. That leaves four cases in which Plato speaks of sharing knowledge with *another* person, *without* using the reflexive pronoun. In these cases the knowledge is usually about their bad actions, but once about their talents, and once about whether they will take the course of action that has just been praised as the only acceptable one.[11]

---

[10] Plato, *Apology* 21b4 and 22d1 (Socrates' claim to know nothing in the second passage supports my interpretation of the first as expressing awareness of not being wise, rather than mere non-awareness of being wise. I thank Christopher Taylor for the query); *Phaedrus* 235c7 (aware of own ignorance in all three passages so far); *Symposium* 216a3; b3 (aware of self-neglect and mistaken disobedience to Socrates); *Republic* 331a2 (aware of no injustice in self); *Republic* 607c6 (aware that seduced by poetry [reading: *hautois*]); *Laws* 773b1 (aware that unduly hasty and precipitate); *Ion* 553c5 (aware that others say I speak well only about Homer, in which case I may lack the art of literary criticism); *Theaetetus* 206a2 (aware of youthful attempts to distinguish letters [a weakness, not a fault]); *Laws* 870d2 (sharing someone else's guilty knowledge, which he also shares with himself, of cowardice or injustice).

[11] Plato, *Apology* 34b5; *Euthyphro* 4c; *Symposium* 193e4; *Protagoras* 348b7.

A second Platonist contribution: Socrates' guardian spirit

Plato presents Socrates as frequently being warned by a daemon, acting as a guardian spirit. According to Plato, the daemon is a voice which opposes some of Socrates' intentions, but never proposes.[12] When Xenophon allows that the daemon may tell Socrates to do things as well as not to do them,[13] he need not be disagreeing, since whether a command to change one's intention is formulated in terms of staying or not going, it can equally be negative in the sense of forbidding an intention to leave. Socrates treats the warnings as indubitable, and it is made explicit by Xenophon that they are indubitable.[14] We shall see below that it was not the standard Christian view that the deliverances of conscience are indubitable. Nor was it a very common view in Graeco-Roman thought. Seneca and Olympiodorus are exceptional in calling conscience infallible.[15] Elsewhere the Stoic Epictetus stresses the difficulty of applying preconceptions of good and evil, Phaedra in Euripides' *Hippolytus* says that it is difficult to know the right time to heed shame, and Pseudo-Aristotle *Magna Moralia* and Galen both talk about the difficulty of knowing one's own faults.[16]

A connection was made among the Greeks between conscience and Socrates' daemon. Apuleius, the Platonist of the second century CE, said that the daemon resides in the very depths of the mind in place of conscience (*vice conscientiae*), and 400 years later, the last pagan Neoplatonist professor in the Philosophy school at Alexandria, Olympiodorus, speaking for the benefit of his Christian pupils,

---

[12] Plato, *Apology* 31d–32a (a voice, only opposes); *Apology* 40a–c; *Phaedrus* 242b–c (opposition).

[13] Xenophon, *Recollections of Socrates* 1.1.4 (orders to do or not to do). Vlastos sees Xenophon's account as differing in this from Plato's, in his *Socrates, Ironist and Moral Philosopher* (Ithaca, NY: Cornell University Press, 1991).

[14] Xenophon, *Recollections* 1.3.4.

[15] Seneca, *On the Shortness of Life* 10.3; Olympiodorus, *On Plato's* First Alcibiades 23, 2–7, ed. L. G. Westerink.

[16] Euripides, *Hippolytus* 380–387, as analyzed by B. Williams, *Shame and Necessity*, 95; Galen, *On the Errors and Passions of the Soul*, Scripta Minora, Vol. 1, ed. J. Marquardt, ch. 2, 4.11–5.2; ch. 3, 6.17–7.1; Pseudo-Aristotle, *Magna Moralia* 2.15, 1213a13–26.

actually identifies Socrates' daemon with conscience (*suneidos*).[17] Earlier than either of these, but four centuries later than Plato, another Platonist, Plutarch, wrote a treatise on Socrates' daemon, and included a speech ascribed to Socrates' friend the Pythagorean Simmias, which again reminds us of conscience. Simmias is made in turn to cite what he had heard from Timarchus. A daemon or guardian spirit is compared with a buoy in the water. It is identified with intellect (*nous*), just as in Plato's *Timaeus* the top part of the soul, which is intellectual (*katanooun*), is a daemon.[18] The daemon in Simmias' report of Timarchus is in contact with the head, but it holds up with a tether the irrational parts of the soul submerged in the water. Through this tether it inflicts on the irrational parts of the soul repentance and shame (*metameleia, aiskhunê*),[19] a function given by others to conscience. If Socrates' daemon is his intellect, this implies that what the daemon says is not entirely news to Socrates, but something that he himself knows, and that has been argued to be exactly Plato's view.[20] On the other hand, Plutarch diverges from Plato when he adds to the function of warning the further functions of causing repentance and shame. In Plato, Socrates' daemon does not shame him, nor for that matter is it described as refuting him—*elenkhein*, the word later used for one's conscience *convicting* one. It is Socrates and his intellect which do the refuting of *other* people.

Platonists and Augustine on how the voice communicates

Although Plato calls Socrates' daemon a voice, Plutarch ascribes to Simmias the interpretation that there is no speech, or voice, or striking of the air (*phthongos, phônê, plêgê*). Rather, as in sleep, the thought of the statement (*logou noêsis*) contacts one, and one grasps the beliefs and thoughts (*doxai, noêseis*) in the statements,

---

[17] Apuleius, *On Socrates' Daemon* 16; Olympiodorus, *On Plato's First Alcibiades* 23, 2–7, ed. L. G. Westerink.

[18] Plato, *Timaeus* 90a–d.

[19] Plutarch, *On the daemon of Socrates* 591e–592b.

[20] Roslyn Weiss, *Socrates Dissatisfied* (New York: Oxford University Press, 1998), 17–23.

merely thinking that one hears them. The statement contacts one simply through what is indicated (*to dêloumenon*) by the thinker and by what is thought (*to noêthen*). The air signals (*ensêmainetai*) the statement by means of what is thought (*to noêthen*). These thoughts do not need verbs or nouns. Rather, like light, they produce a reflection in the receiver.[21] Later Platonists agree. Calcidius in the fourth century CE says that in dreams, when we think we hear voice and speech, there is in fact only meaning (*significatio*) doing the duty of voice, and that is how, when awake, Socrates divined the presence of the daemon, by the token of a vivid sign.[22] Both authors suggest that the daemon communicates pure meaning (*to dêloumenon, to noêthen, significatio*), although the meaning is not yet said itself to be a language. Proclus in the fifth century returns to the analogy of light, saying that light is received in the tenuous material (not flesh) that provides a vehicle for our souls, and by that route reaches the fleshly sense organs and is recognized by self-perception (*sunaisthêsis*).[23]

Augustine, who could have had access to Calcidius' Latin, discussed how God speaks to us and denied that the process involves figures appearing (this is all he meant by denying the comparison with dreams). On the other hand, there is no ordinary hearing either. Rather, God speaks to those who can hear with the mind (*mens*) by means of the truth itself (*ipsa veritate*).[24] Truth here does the work of meaning in Plutarch and Calcidius.

Platonists on conscience as belonging to a special "attentive" faculty of the soul

There is a commentary doubtfully ascribed to the Neoplatonizing Christian Philoponus of the sixth century CE on Book 3 of Aristotle, *On the Soul*. It tells us of a new interpretation according to which all self-awareness of our own psychological activities needs to belong,

---

21 Plutarch, *On the daemon* 588b–589d.

22 Calcidius, *Commentary on Plato's* Timaeus, ch. 255, p. 288.

23 Proclus, *Commentary on Plato's* First Alcibiades 80.

24 Augustine, *City of God* 11.2. I thank David Robertson for first drawing my attention to this discussion.

for Aristotelian reasons, to a single faculty. A single faculty was postulated called the "attentive" faculty (*prosektikon*).[25] But the faculty had different names. When it was aware of our cognitive activities, it was called "attentive." But when it was aware of our vital (*zôtikai*) activities (our appetites) it was called conscience (*suneidos*), the same word for conscience that was mentioned above as being used a little later by Philoponus' fellow-Alexandrian Olympiodorus. The notion of the attentive faculty had also been used perhaps a little earlier by the head of the Athenian Neoplatonist school, Damascius, and he too says that one and the same faculty acts as attentive to the cognitive faculties and as conscience (*suneidos*) to the desiring faculties (*orektikai*).[26] But the probable source of the idea of the attentive faculty is the Athenian Neoplatonist of the previous century, the fifth CE, Proclus. For the "newer interpreters" are presented by "Philoponus" as correcting Proclus' teacher, Plutarch of Athens. The idea could then have been passed by Proclus to his pupil, Ammonius, head of the Alexandrian school, and it could there have passed again both to Damascius, during the latter's stay in Alexandria, and to Ammonius' pupil, Philoponus, or to whoever wrote the commentary ascribed to Philoponus.

Platonists on the value of conscience: not appeasement, forgiveness, or remission of sin

Iamblichus, a third to early fourth century CE Neoplatonist and devotee of Egyptian religion, addressed a probing question about divine impassivity posed by his teacher Porphyry. Porphyry had asked: do not invocations (*klêseis*) to the gods imply that they can be swayed by emotion (*empatheis*)? Iamblichus allows that the gods are benevolent, loving and solicitous (*eumeneis, philia, kêdemonia*), but he replies that invocations work by allowing priests to gain union with the gods and that the divine nature has so little to do with

---

[25] "Philoponus," *On Aristotle On the Soul*, Book 3, Commentaria in Aristotelem Graeca, Vol. 15, 465, 7–17. For Philoponus and Damascius on the attentive faculty, see Richard Sorabji, *The Philosophy of the Commentators, 200–600 AD, A Sourcebook*, Vol. 1, Psychology (London: Duckworth, 2005; Bloomsbury, 2013), ch. 4 (c).
[26] Damascius, *Lectures on Plato's* Phaedo I, para. 271, ed. L. G. Westerink, 162–163.

emotion that the union actually purifies the priests from emotion (*katharsis pathôn*). As regards our appeasing (*exhilasis*) God's wrath (*mênis*), Iamblichus uses the analogy of our stepping out of the light.[27] Appeasement is not to be seen in a conventional way. It is our stepping back into the light. Simplicius, the Neoplatonist of the sixth century CE, goes even further. He asks why it is thought that God is persuaded to change his mind (*metapeithesthai*) and to pardon those who go astray (*sunginôskein hamartanousin*) by means of gifts, votive offerings, prayers, benefactions, and supplications. Simplicius denies that this is what happens. God is not even angry (*orgizetai*), nor does he turn away from us when we go astray, or turn back when we repent (*metamelomenôn*). Rather it is we who have turned away. The analogy is with a man who allows his boat to slip away from the rock to which it had been tethered. Acts of repentance help to bring him back again to the rock, and assimilation to God (ideally even union) was the Platonist ideal. But the rock is meanwhile unmoved. The goal of our repentance is to be purified (*katharsis*) and embrace virtue. Those who are genuinely repentant are corrected more quickly because of the sharp wounds of *conscience* (*to suneidos*).[28]

An earlier Christian view had gone only some of the way in this direction. Lactantius in the fourth century CE had said in *On the Anger of God* that God's anger is not an emotional disturbance like ours, but he can be angry (*irascitur*), and we can give him satisfaction (*satisfactio*). He can be appeased (*placabilis, placatur*), but "he is appeased not by incense, not by a sacrificial victim, not by precious gifts, which are all perishable things, but by a reformed way of life (*morum emendatione*)." In his *Divine Institutes*, Lactantius sees reform as one of two benefits deriving from repentance. The other benefit is God's remission of sins, where remission is unlike forgiveness, in that it erases sins from the ledger, instead of continuing to acknowledge them. This is more suitable to an unemotional

---

[27] Iamblichus, *Mysteries of the Egyptians* 1.12–13, pp. 40, 16–43, 15, ed. E. Des Places, replying to Porphyry's fragmentary *Letter to Anebo* (quoted here and edited by A. R. Sodano).

[28] Simplicius, *Commentary on Epictetus' Handbook*, ch. 38, lines 674–703, in I. Hadot = ch. 31, 107, 15–22, ed. F. Dübner.

XII

God, and it calls only for the Stoic virtue of mercy or clemency, which is not an emotion. God, he says, with his great indulgence (*indulgentissimus*) and mercy (*clementia*), will remit, obliterate, and condone sins and abolish the stain (*remittere, obliterare, condonare, labem abolere*). Hence we should purify our conscience (*conscientia*) by opening it to God.[29] The Platonists would not think that Lactantius went far enough with his idea that God's anger involves no emotional disturbance. God for Simplicius is free from anger, and it is up to us to re-assimilate ourselves to God.

PART 2: NON-PLATONIST CONTRIBUTIONS

Conscience, being watched and confession

The evolving idea of conscience was indebted to many thinkers and schools, and I shall finish by outlining briefly some of the non-Platonist contributions. The Epicureans connected conscience with confession and with being watched. This is in spite of the fact that Cicero and the Stoic Seneca ascribe to Epicurus a conception of conscience that they find inadequate as mere fear of detection and punishment. And indeed, the Epicurean Lucretius stresses that one who shares knowledge with himself (*conscius sibi*) of bad deeds torments himself with fears about punishment after death.[30]

But Epicurus stressed a more fruitful idea, that of being *watched*. People believe (wrongly according to Epicurus) that even if they escape human eyes, they are watched by the gods, and so they are troubled in *conscience*, a total of three agencies.[31] We have seen the Stoic Seneca being praised by Lactantius for similar remarks. In Seneca, one's conscience is open to God, and one has God within as an observer of bad and good. In a single letter, Seneca asks us to live as if someone (presumably someone human) were observing us, then points out that in fact nothing is hidden from God, and as a result he determines that he will watch himself. Thus, like

---

[29] Lactantius, *On the Anger of God* 21; *Divine Institutes* 6:24 1–5 and 20–29.
[30] Cicero, *On Ends* 2.16.53, 2.22.71; Seneca, *Letters* 97, 15–16; Lucretius, *On the Nature of Things* 3.1010–1024.
[31] Cicero, *On Ends* 1.16.51.

Epicurus, Seneca brings in three different types of watcher.[32] His younger Stoic contemporary, Epictetus, says that God (Zeus) has installed a daemon within us to watch us and is within us himself.[33]

Seneca cites Epicurus as originator of the idea, when he repeatedly advises you to have a philosopher as companion and mentor,[34] or to imagine an admired philosopher simply watching you.[35] With Epictetus, Seneca also recommends imagining a past philosopher to serve as a model and example (*exemplum*).[36] The imagined philosophical watcher foreshadows the conscience as imagined impartial spectator in Adam Smith.[37]

But most interesting of all for its relevance to later developments in Christianity is the connection made by the Epicurean Philodemus around 100 BCE between conscience and the practice of confession. Philodemus' *Rhetoric* describes people who because of a guilty conscience (*suneidêsis*) engage in lawsuits until they are convicted and ruined.[38] His *On Death* provides the only use in Greek of another word for conscience, when it speaks of a (good) conscience (*sungnôsis*) and irreproachable life.[39] But most striking for our purposes is the treatise *On Frank Criticism* about the practices in the residential school in Athens two hundred years after Epicurus, which included confession by students and even teachers more than a hundred years before the birth of Christ.[40] One fragment declares: "Even the servants share his (guilty) knowledge (*sunoidasin*)."[41] Another fragment, on the standard reading, says that if the profes-

---

[32] Seneca, *On Benefits* 7.1.7; frg. 24 Haase (=Vottero 89) from Lactantius, *Divine Institutes* 6:24.12; *Letters* 41, 1–2; 83, 1–2.

[33] Epictetus, *Discourses* 1.14.11–15.

[34] Seneca, *Letters* 6.5–6; 52, 1–4.

[35] Seneca, *Letters* 11.8–10; 25.5–6; 32.1; 83.1–2.

[36] Seneca, *Letters* 95.72; 104.21–2; *On Leisure* 1.1, *On the Shortness of Life* 14.5; Epictetus, *Handbook* 33.12.

[37] Adam Smith, *The Theory of Moral Sentiments*, Part III, ch. 1.

[38] Philodemus, *Rhetoric* II, frg. 11, lines 1–9, (Sudhaus), 139–140.

[39] Philodemus, *De morte* 34. 35 (Kuyper). I thank David Armstrong and Benjamin Henry for showing me this text and the latest emendations of it.

[40] Philodemus, *On Frank Criticism*, frg. 41.

[41] Philodemus, *On Frank Criticism*, col. XIIa, line 5.

sor quickly turns away from assisting the student who is slipping up, the student's swelling (*sunoidêsis*) will subside.[42] Why should professorial neglect make a *swelling* subside? This makes no sense, and an emendation suggested a long time ago by C. J. Vooys should be accepted. *Suneidêsis* (conscience) differs from *sunoidêsis* (swelling) by only the one letter "e," which, in Greek as in English, looks very like an "o." Moreover, four short lines later the related verb *syneidenai* appears. It makes perfect sense that the student's conscience will become less intense, if the professor does not attend to criticism and help of the right sort, and this gives us a picture of the Epicurean school in Athens at the time of Philodemus' teacher, Zeno of Tarsus, in the second century BCE, wanting to develop the consciences of its students through a process of confession and carefully tailored, but frank, criticism.

Divine and natural law

There is another relevant idea which flourished as early as the idea of sharing knowledge with oneself of a defect, although the two ideas were not yet connected. The other idea was that of divine or natural law. Already in the fifth century BCE, the philosopher Heraclitus said that all human laws are fed by the one divine law.[43] Aristotle drew attention to two other examples from the same century. In Sophocles' play of that name, Antigone accepts that the king's law (*nomos*) forbids her to bury her brother. But she insists that there is a law (*nomimon*) not of today or yesterday but of all times which requires her to bury him.[44] Aristotle calls it a natural law (*nomos kata physin*) and naturally just (*physei*). His second example is from the philosopher Empedocles, who spoke in the same century of a law (*nomimon*) that, unlike human laws, obtained everywhere, that one should not kill sentient beings, animal or human.[45] Aristotle gives a third example from the next century, his own, of Alcidamas,

---

[42]   Philodemus, *On Frank Criticism*, frg. 67. I thank David Sider for showing me the emendation.

[43]   Heraclitus, frg. 114 (Diels-Kranz).

[44]   Sophocles, *Antigone* 450–457.

[45]   Aristotle, *Rhetoric* 1.13, 1373b4–17.

Moral Conscience: Contributions to the Idea in Plato and Platonism

who declared, contrary to Aristotle's own view, that no slavery is natural. Cicero ascribes to Zeno, who founded Stoicism in 300 BCE, the belief that natural law (*naturalis lex*) is divine and commands what is right and forbids the opposite.[46] Elsewhere he describes the law more fully.[47] God gave the law, but it also comes from nature, and it holds at all times and places. The bold step that is found in Cicero, whether or not he is following Zeno, is the internalization of natural law. Such law is the same as reason, that is, correct reason not wrong reason, in the human mind, and we all have right reason—even those who go against it.

Five times in Book 3 of *On Duties*, Cicero gives an example of a Stoic law, for which he uses four expressions: "law of nature" four times (*naturae lex*), "law of nativity" (to paraphrase "born with a law"—*lege natus*), "law of nations" twice (*ius gentium*) and "formula" three times (*formula* also in Latin). On each of these occasions he gives the same example of a law: There are common bonds of humanity and certain behavior would break them. In giving the formulation of the Stoic Antipater, Cicero puts the point more positively: the common interest of human society should be yours and vice versa.[48] The Stoic Seneca comes out with just the same example, when he looks for a *formula*. After describing the natural bonds of human society, he thinks the *formula* is best summed up in the verse of the comic playwright Terence: "I am a human; nothing human do I think to be alien from me."[49] The Christian Lactantius, writing in Latin like Cicero and Seneca whom he quotes, refers to Cicero's law, but distorts in an interesting way. He identifies Cicero's law not, like the Stoics, with preserving the bonds of human fellowship, but with making the sacrifice of a pure *conscience* (*conscientia*).[50]

It was in fact Saint Paul who first made explicit a close connection between the idea of divine law and the (Greek) word for

---

[46]   Cicero, *On the Nature of the Gods* 1.14.36.
[47]   Cicero, *On Laws* 1.6.18; 1.7.23; 1.12.33; 2.4.8. *On the Republic* 3.22.33.
[48]   Cicero, *On Duties* 3.19–21; 23; 27–28; 52–53; 69.
[49]   Seneca, *Letters* 95.51–53.
[50]   Lactantius, *Divine Institutes* 6.24.20–29.

XII

conscience. Subsequent Christians went on to build up the Christian idea of conscience by pooling together some of the other ideas we have found the Greeks and Romans keeping separate from the basic idea of sharing knowledge with oneself of a defect.

Saint Paul on conscience

In his Letter to the Romans, Paul has something new and important to say about conscience. He refers to the written law of God by which the Jews distinguished themselves, and which would include the Ten Commandments delivered by God to Moses, and he contrasts the written law with the law written in men's hearts. This latter law he connects closely with conscience:[51]

> When Gentiles who have not the law do by nature
> what the law requires, they are a law to themselves,
> even though they do not have the law. They show
> that what the law requires is written in their hearts,
> while their conscience also bears witness and their
> conflicting thoughts accuse or perhaps excuse them
> on that day when, according to my gospel, God
> judges the secrets of men by Christ Jesus.

The law written in men's hearts was already referred to in the Hebrew scriptures.[52] What is new is to connect it so closely with conscience. Paul describes it as something that co-witnesses (*symmarturei*). On one interpretation, the conscience of Gentiles on the Day of Judgement, even if ignorant of the Jewish *written* law, co-witnesses that they knew the *inner* law which they have violated. Paul does not say that conscience is *identical* with the law written in the hearts of men. But he licenses the Church Fathers to make extremely close connections between conscience and that inner law.

By connecting conscience more closely with law, Paul connects it with a very *general* knowledge of right and wrong, instead of merely with knowledge of *individual* wrongdoing. Moreover, he

---

[51] Romans 2:14–16.
[52] *Isaiah* 51:7a; *Jeremiah* 38:33 (LXX). I thank Josef Lössl for the references.

thereby adds an extra role to conscience, that of directing towards the *right* without having necessarily, like Socrates' guardian spirit, to oppose an intention toward the wrong. This is an expansion, but at the same time, in Christianity there is a contraction in the scope of the words for conscience. Discarded are the consciousness of one's own merit in Cicero and Seneca and the consciousness of non-moral faults and weaknesses in Plato and others. Further, one is said to have a conscience only about one's *own* faults.

Paul had earlier made another very important point in discussion with Greeks from Corinth, that one's conscience is not infallible. Of course the inner law is faultless, but one's reading of it is fallible. It is a great mercy that this became the main Christian tradition, since humans' claims of infallibility are dangerously wrong. Paul makes the point in his first letter to the Corinthians. This addresses Greek Christians who claim to have a clear conscience in eating meat sacrificed to idols, because they are sophisticated people who know that the belief in idols is a delusion. Paul replies that if they are seen eating sacrificed meat they may corrupt the conscience of their less sophisticated brethren.[53] The message is that a clear conscience is not a sure guide, and this is reaffirmed, without the word conscience, in the same letter when Paul says that his own unawareness of fault does not acquit him, since God is the judge.[54] In the Judaeo-Christian tradition, the Jewish thinker Philo, speaking, as I believe, not of the Stoics, but of the inner law implanted, as he thinks, in *Plato*'s immortal human souls, regards awareness of that inner law as fallible.[55] The Christian Origen thinks that Paul's law is sown by God into the hearts of men, but that when we are still growing up, we do not hear it.[56] The metaphor of sowing may suggest that the seed is there from birth. Augustine's remark may be ambiguous, that the natural law in our hearts only appears (*apparet*) at the age

---

[53]   1 Corinthians 8:7–13.

[54]   1 Corinthians 4:4.

[55]   Philo, *Every good man is free* 46. Von Arnim *Stoicorum Veterum Fragmenta* 3. 360 gives this as a Stoic fragment, but the Stoic human mind was not immortal.

[56]   Origen, *Against Celsus* I 4; *On Romans* VI 8 (PG 14, 1080A–81A).

of reason, but he certainly has the idea that people may have the law in their hearts and in their conscience but be unwilling to read it.[57]

Early Church Fathers pool together further Graeco-Roman ideas

Early Church Fathers pooled together further ideas from the Graeco-Roman tradition to build up the idea of conscience that they found in Paul. We have already seen Lactantius in the fourth century connecting the sacrifice of keeping a pure conscience with Cicero's divine inner law, and praising Seneca's appeal to God and our conscience as both watching us, without any possibility of our closing our conscience to God.

In the previous century CE, the third, the Christian Origen borrowed from the Pythagoreans the practice of interrogating himself every night and morning on whether he had spent the day aright.[58] The fullest surviving account of this practice, conducted at bedtime had been given by Seneca, who also took it from the Pythagoreans. But in Seneca the atmosphere is quite different from the Christian one. He is seeking moral progress and is on the whole rather pleased with himself. He finds the practice calming.[59] His younger Stoic contemporary Epictetus advocated the same practice conducted every morning as well as evening.[60] When Origen took the practice over, he connected it, unlike Seneca, with a shameful recital (*aoidêmon rhêseidion*), "bites" (*dakneisthai*) of *conscience* and compunction (*katanussein*). Origen and Epictetus cited the same questions to ask, drawn from the Pythagorean book, *Golden Verses*: "Where did I go astray? What have I done? What duty has been left undone?"[61]

[57] Augustine, *Letters* 157.15 (PL 33, 681); *Enarratio in Psalmos* 57.1 (PL 36, 673).

[58] Origen, *Commentary on Romans* VI 8 (PG 14, 1080A–81A).

[59] Seneca, *On Anger* 3.36, cf. *Letters* 28.9–10; 41,1–2; 83.1–2.

[60] Epictetus, *Discourses* 4.6.35.

[61] Origen, frg. On Psalms IV, from René Cadiou, *Commentaires inédits des Psaumes* (Paris: Société d'Edition "Les Belles Lettres," 1936), 74; Origen, Selections on the Psalms IV (PG 12, 1144B–45B), drawing on the Pythagorean *Golden Verses*, lines 40–44.

Origen also took the Stoic idea of common conceptions, among which some, the "Stoic 'preconceptions,'" are written into us (the same metaphor as in Paul) by nature without special thought on our part. According to the Stoic Epictetus, we have preconceptions of good and evil supplied by nature, but they are hard to apply (the theme of fallibility again).[62] Origen went on to compare with these Stoic common conceptions Paul's law written in our hearts.[63]

Multiple sources of the Christian idea of conscience

To return to Plato and Platonism, it supplied an important strand in the formation of the Christian concept of moral conscience. But some aspects of that strand were rejected, for example the voice's indubitability and the concern with non-moral defects; and the sources of the Christian concept were numerous. Among philosophers, contributions were made not only by Plato and Platonists, but especially also by Pythagoreans, Epicureans and Stoics. The Romans superimposed their own rather different values on the Greeks. Important too were the playwrights of the Greeks and Romans and their lawyers, even though the perspective of lawyers was not entirely relevant to Christianity. Here, then, in honour of Charles, I have been emphasizing one important strand, the Platonic, while putting it in the context of other Graeco-Roman strands of influence.

---

[62]   Epictetus, *Discourses* 2.11.1–15.

[63]   Origen, *Against Celsus* 1.4.

The concept of the will from Plato to Maximus the Confessor

The concept of the will evolved gradually and there have been many suggestions about who first formulated it. Suggestions have included Plato,[1] Aristotle,[2] the Stoics Chrysippus and Posidonius, followed by the Platonist Galen,[3] the Stoic Seneca,[4] the Stoic Epictetus,[5] Augustine[6] and Maximus the Confessor.[7]

Terminology

To start very briefly with the terminology of the will, it developed somewhat independently of the concept, and both developed only gradually until their full flowering in the Latin of Augustine, whose *On Free Choice of the Will* was written in AD 388–95. As regards terminology, Aristotle sometimes reflects the practice of Plato's Academy, which used *boulêsis* as a term for rational desire for the good, as opposed to *thumos* for the desire for honour, and *epithumia* for the desire for pleasure.[8] *Boulêsis*, both in this context and in others, is often translated 'will'.

It has been shown that in the Christian era forms of another word for willing, *thelein*, became more prominent.[9] *Thelein* and *thelêma* are often used in the New Testament, along with *thelêsis* in the Septuagint version of the Old Testament. When Christ asks for the cup to pass from him, but nevertheless for his Father's will, not his, to be done, the verb used is *thelein* more often than *boulesthai*, and the noun is *thelêma*.[10] Origen, discussing human self-determination (*autexousion*), asks if it is threatened by Paul's remarks that reward does not depend on the man who wills (*thelei*), but on God's mercy, or that it is God who wills (*thelei*).[11] Among the pagans, Epictetus uses the verb *thelein* often enough, but not the corresponding nouns, which are not common pagan usage, although we shall notice *thelêma* for the will of the One in Plotinus,[12] Porphyry speaks of the soul's *ethelousion*,[13] and *thelêsis* appears once as a species of *boulêsis* for the Stoics.[14] The Christian who made *thelêsis* the standard word for will, it has been said,[15] was Maximus the Confessor in the seventh century.

But the most important terminological developments were in Latin. The phrase 'free will', *libera voluntas*, appears in Latin in the first century BC in the Epicurean Lucretius, followed by Cicero.[16] But in Lucretius, although there is an important discussion of freedom due to the unpredictable swerve of atoms, the fact that this is connected with will does not prove to be very significant. The innovation, I believe, has more influence on terminology than on concepts.

As others have shown, the Christian Tertullian, writing in Latin shortly after AD 200, uses the phrase 'free power of choice' (*libera arbitrii potestas*) and 'freedom of choice' (*arbitrii libertas*).[17] These are, at least sometimes, translations of the completely different Greek term *to autexousion*, self-determination, which makes no reference to choice or will.[18] It has been suggested that the phrase 'free choice of the will' (*liberum arbitrium voluntatis*) originates with Augustine, who uses it extensively in his *On Free Choice of the Will*.[19] From this account of Latin terminology, it looks as if Boethius is reading Augustine's Latin expression back into an earlier Greek debate, when he talks of free choice of the will.[20]

The concept: a history of clustering

But that is enough on terminology. I want to focus instead on the development of the concept, and to reframe the central question. Instead of asking 'who invented the concept of will?', I think it is more profitable to ask something different, since there is no one concept, and much less is there an agreed concept nowadays. Rather, will is a desire with a special relation to reason and a number of functions associated with it. Some of these functions come in clusters. It is more illuminating to ask when these functions came together and who made the decisive difference.

The functions include two important clusters, freedom and responsibility on the one hand and will-power on the other. My claim will be that both these clusters can be found early in Greek philosophy, and even in the same philosophical treatise, but totally dissociated from each other, and often connected with reason rather than with rational desire. It is a long time before all the elements get associated together.

When they do get associated, yet other ideas previously instantiated in isolation join the group: the idea of perverted will and of will as ubiquitously present in all decisions. Once this history of clustering is clear, it will be the history that matters. As to when the concept of will was invented, we can say what we like, but we shall see the reasons for saying one thing rather than another.

In conclusion, I shall explain why I do not think the invention has to wait for Maximus the Confessor.

Reason versus rational desire for the good: Aristotle's restructuring of Plato

Aristotle gave a strong impetus to the idea of will as a desire, so distinct from reason, but none the less belonging with reason as rational. In two passages Aristotle treats *boulêsis* as belonging to the rational part of the Platonist soul.[21] At the same time, in one of the two passages he urges against Plato that if one is going to distinguish parts of the soul, one should bring *boulêsis* together with other types of desire, *thumos* and *epithumia*, to form a desiderative part of the soul (*orektikon*) quite distinct from reason.[22] Thus far this seems to encourage the view that *boulêsis* is not reason, but a rational desire. And I think this is close to Aristotle's view, but I must enter a caveat. For Aristotle qualified the Platonist view that *boulêsis* belongs to the rational part of the soul, as indeed Plato himself had done before him.[23] At the opposite extreme, Aristotle once says that *boulêsis* exists in children before reason or intellect (*logismos, nous*) and is irrational.[24] But elsewhere he calls it rational.[25] And his more considered view is that the part of the soul that desires, even if called irrational, does have a share in (*koinônein*) reason, and can even in a secondary sense be said to have reason (*logon ekhein*), because it listens to reason even if it does not reason things out for itself.[26] The general effect is to make *boulêsis* distinct from reason, though still related to it.[27]

With regard to *boulêsis* being directed to the good, Aristotle draws on an idea found in three passages of Plato,[28] where Plato was seen to use the verb *boulesthai* to say that what we really want is good. The contrast in each of the three passages is with mere appetite (*epithumia*), which is for pleasure, not for good. Plato added that no one is satisfied (*arkein*) with apparent good.[29] But in Aristotle's version *boulêsis* is directed to what is *or* appears good.[30] Later, as I will argue, the Stoics had more to say about whether the good willed in *boulêsis* is real or apparent. The term 'good' (*agathon*) in this context is used by Plato and Aristotle in a narrow sense, in contrast with honour and pleasure, which are the goals of the lower types of desire, *thumos* and *epithumia*.[31] In some sense, however, Plato and Aristotle are ready to say that all desire, not just *boulêsis*, sees its objective as good in some way or other.[32]

Plato: freedom and responsibility separated from will-power

Plato might seem an unpromising source for a concept of the will, since we have already seen Aristotle criticizing him for not distinguishing sharply enough between reason and rational desire. None the less, the good point has been made that something very like the function of will-power is assigned by Plato to another part of his soul, high spirit or the spirited part (*thumos, thumoeides*).[33] *Thumos* is like will in being distinct from reason, but a desire which, according to Plato, is always allied with reason and never opposes it in a struggle against appetites (*epithumiai*), although elsewhere it is sometimes shown opposing reason.[34] Plato thus foreshadows the debates that arose in AD 1270 as to whether will is free to oppose reason.[35] However, according to Plato's first-mentioned view, *thumos* shepherds the baser appetites, as if it were reason's sheepdog. So far it seems to play the role of will-power. What is missing is any particular connection with moral responsibility, or with freedom, so that only some of the criteria for a concept of will are satisfied.

In another part of Plato's *Republic*, however, choice (*haireisthai*) is connected both with freedom and with moral responsibility.[36] Souls are represented as choosing their next lives before reincarnation. Because of the choice, the responsibility will be theirs, not God's: 'Responsibility (*aitia*) is the chooser's; God is not responsible (*anaitios*)'. Moreover, they may choose virtuously, and virtue is free: it has no master (*adespoton*). This is the earliest use I have encountered of the metaphor of freedom. It is earlier than the use of the same word by Epicurus, to which Charles Kahn has drawn attention.[37] What is still missing is any cross-reference to the treatment of *thumos* as will-power elsewhere in the *Republic*.

Platonists: the separation continues

The separation of the two subjects continues in later Platonists, although they develop one of the subjects. They pick up Plato's term for freedom (*adespoton*),[38] and integrate it much more fully with the ideas of responsibility and will, and Christians follow. The Middle Platonist *Didaskalikos* says that if virtue has no master (*adespoton*), it must be voluntary (*hekousion*), and that since the soul chooses (*helesthai*) its next life and has no master, it is up to it (*ep' autêi*) whether it acts or not. Plotinus connects the term *adespoton* not only with choice (*helesthai*) and with what is up to us (*eph' hêmin*) and voluntary (*hekousion*), but also with *boulêsis*,[39] one of the words conventionally translated as 'will'. Virtue is up to us and without a master, if we will and choose. Plotinus has an extended discussion in the treatise which Porphyry calls *On the Voluntary and the Will [thelêma] of the One*.[40] We find extra terms not only for the will (*thelêma*) and willing (*thelein*) but also for freedom (*to eleutheron*), control (*kurios*) and purpose (*proairesis*). The Christian Gregory of Nyssa repeats that virtue and the soul have no master (*adespoton*), and adds that virtue is voluntary (*hekousion*). He connects this with the self-determination (*autexousion*) of the human will (*proairesis*) or soul, and with the soul being steered by its own willing (*thelêmata*).[41]

None the less, Plato's idea of *thumos* as will-power which is found in an earlier part of the *Republic*, is not integrated with these other ideas, either by him or by later Platonists. When the power of *thumos* is treated by a later Platonist, Galen, it is again dealt with separately from these other ideas. Galen discusses contests of strength between reason (*logismos*) and high spirit (*thumos*). The talk is of strength (*iskhuron, rhômê*), violence (*sphodroteron*), domination (*arkhein, kratein, epikratein*), carrying off (*sunapopherein*), dragging (*sunepispan*), defeat (*nikasthai*) and weakness (*arrhôstia*).[42] In another passage, it is all three elements of the Platonic soul that are involved, not only reason and high spirit, but also appetite (*epithumia*). Each of these can stir up or stop impulses (*hormai*). But already there is an important difference from the passage in Plato's *Republic* 440. *Thumos* in Galen is not always the ally of reason, but frequently opposes it. So if we want to find rational desire in Galen's account, we must look rather to his *boulêsis, boulêthênai*. But *boulêsis* is not treated in this context as having any special dominance over the other desires, *thumos* or *epithumia*. Any of the three elements will have more or less power at different times.[43] When Galen wants to give the highest element in the soul a special status, comparing it with a charioteer or a rider who ought to take control, he reverts to Plato's usage, calling it reason (*logismos*) rather than *boulêsis*.[44]

Galen's discussion of will-power, if it is one, is not connected by him with any discussion of freedom or responsibility. He does also discuss, as others have well shown,[45] the power exerted from the brain through the nerves. But this is a discussion of physiological power, and so takes us away from will-power.

Aristotle's *proairesis* distinct from responsibility and will-power

I have ascribed Aristotle a role in developing the concept of will in so far as he contrasted two concepts borrowed from Plato, those of reason and of *boulêsis*, or rational desire for the good. But it was *boulêsis* which I stressed. It is in Aristotle's other concept of *proairesis* that some interpreters have detected a concept of will.

Proairesis is generated from *boulêsis*, which, as Plato had already hinted,[46] is the desire for ends. *Proairesis* is the desire for the means which will lead towards those ends.[47] And *proairesis* is even more closely connected with reason, because it is a desire based on reasoning out what means would secure those ends.[48] An example of *proairesis*, as I understand it, would be the kind of dietary policy that Aristotle cites, like eating dry food.[49] This is something one might have reasoned would lead to the goal of health.

I do not think the concept of *proairesis*, as it features in Aristotle, is yet very close to a concept of will. Aristotle does not treat *proairesis* as a kind of will-power. When he discusses people who fail to abide by their *proairesis*,[50] he does not present this as due to their *proairesis* being weak. In his main account of this failure of control (*akrasia*), he insists that appetite makes us overlook the facts, for example the fact that the food we are taking is not of the right sort.[51] Furthermore, he follows Plato, and says that it is reason (*logos*) against which the appetites fight.[52] He does not say it is will. Conventionally, this discussion is spoken of as Aristotle's explanation of weakness of will. But this is a misnomer. His diagnosis is not in terms of *proairesis* being weak or strong. If he concedes anything to the idea of will-power, then I would agree with the point that has been put to me[53] that it is when he discusses the opposite phenomenon, that of maintaining control (*enkrateia*) and sticking by our *proairesis*, in the face of rival desires. I agree that this is described in terms of winning or losing (*nikan*, *hêttasthai*) against strong (*iskhuros*) desires.[54] But the discussion is extremely brief, because all the emphasis is given to failure of control. Moreover, it is never said what enables *proairesis* to win, when it does. But if Aristotle had addressed the question, at least part of his answer would surely have been in terms of intellect, rather than will. It must make a difference how carefully you have thought out your policy (*proairesis*) at the stage when you were deliberating about the best means to your goal. Aristotle's very silence is significant: a proponent of will-power would be likely to tell us how victory depends rather on the strength of the will.

12

Aristotle does not associate *proairesis* very closely with freedom, and he even dissociates it from moral responsibility. He is explicit that voluntariness, which links with moral responsibility,[55] extends much more widely to the doings of animals and children, who are not capable of anything as rational as *proairesis*.

> Although *proairesis* (deliberate choice) appears to be voluntary, then, it is not the same thing. The voluntary extends further. For children and animals both share in the voluntary, but not in deliberate choice.[56]

I have elsewhere resisted an alternative interpretation according to which Aristotle distinguishes 'up to us' (*eph' hêmin*) from voluntary (*hekousion*), at least in the *Nicomachean Ethics*, connects only the 'up to us' with moral responsibility, and confines the 'up to us' to what has been sanctioned by rational *proairesis*.[57] Against this, I think Aristotle implies that all that is voluntary is also up to us. He sometimes includes this requirement directly in the definition of voluntariness[58] and sometimes makes it an implication of the demand, which is itself included in the definition of voluntariness, for an internal origin of action.[59] Nor is it unreasonable of Aristotle to suppose that, despite lacking *proairesis*, the dog which bites you can be blamed. Animals were held morally responsible by other philosophers too, possibly by Democritus,[60] certainly by Clodius or Heracleides of Pontus,[61] and tame animals by Epicurus.[62]

Alexander and Aquinas: making *proairesis* ubiquitous in all action that is up to us

It is rather, I believe, the much later Aristotelian Alexander who makes the moves just described. In speaking of what is up to us, he ties it, unlike Aristotle, to *proairesis*. It is found only in beings capable of *proairesis*, and (I think he means) only when they are using their *proairesis*. In this he conforms, at least verbally, to the Stoic Epictetus, who had said that nothing is up to us except what falls under *proairesis*, in his rather different sense of the term.[63] Alexander is motivated to show that Aristotelianism can match the intellectualist presuppositions of Stoicism. He not only accepts the Stoic linkage of what is up to us with *proairesis*, but borrows the Stoics' own terminology in linking *proairesis* with rational impulse (*logikê hormê*).[64]

Thomas Aquinas compromises, but is closer to Alexander's intellectualist account in his discussion of *proairesis*, which he translates into Latin as *electio*.[65] He claims that voluntariness in the primary sense does depend on *electio*, so that animal behaviour is voluntary only in a secondary sense.[66] There is reason to think that Thomas may have known the treatise *On Fate* in which Alexander presented his interpretation.[67]

Alexander's new move has the significant effect of making *proairesis* ubiquitous in all action that is up to us. This gives it something in common with concepts of the will in Descartes and in modern philosophy as involved in every intentional action.[68]

In another passage, Alexander switches attention from *proairesis* to *boulêsis* and gives it a special role in preserving our freedom. Impulse and desire (*hormê, orexis*), he says, going along with the Stoics' intellectualist account, are cases of assenting that something is choiceworthy (*epi tisi sunkatathesis hôs hairetois*). But, he warns, *hormê* will not necessarily lead to action, if *boulêsis* does not concur (*sundramein*).[69]

The Stoics: will related to voluntariness but not distinct from reason

The Stoics, I believe, come closer than Aristotle to a full-blooded idea of the will, but there are still some very important differences. When Seneca describes anger as involving an act of will (*voluntas*) to the effect that (*tamquam*) we should be avenged,[70] he is using *voluntas* in a broad sense to refer to impulse. What is significant is that he does not contrast will, as a type of conation, with cognition. He intellectualizes it, treating it as merely one type of cognition: assent to a proposition about how it is appropriate to react. This fits perfectly with the view ascribed to the Stoics in general that impulse (*hormê*) is assent to a proposition[71] and in particular is assent to the appearance that it is appropriate (*kathêkei*) to act.[72] Assent to appearance, we know, is a judgement. Impulse is also described intellectualistically as reason (*logos*) commanding (*prostaktikos*) us to act.[73] It matters that the command is said to come from reason. I dissent from the view that Seneca innovates and dissociates will from intellect.[74]

It is important to see that the Stoics are going beyond Plato's Socrates in their intellectualism. Socrates' few restrictions in Plato's early dialogues on what beliefs are compatible with wanting fall far short of Chrysippus' bold idea that wanting simply is the intellectual judgement that a certain act is appropriate. I believe that will has traditionally been thought of as much more distinct from rational judgement than that.

Although Seneca treats wanting here as an intellectual judgement, in the same paragraph he takes a step in the direction of a fuller concept of the will, by connecting the will (*voluntas*) with the notion of voluntariness (*voluntarius*), and hence with moral responsibility. This connection, it has been pointed out, is one which comes out in Latin, but not in Greek,[75] since the Greek word for voluntariness, *hekousion*, has no connection with words for will. The link between the Latin terms is found already in Cicero.[76]

Seneca is using the word *voluntas* in a wide sense for any desire or *hormê*. But sometimes *voluntas* and *boulêsis* are used in a narrow sense for an attitude that only the sage achieves,[77] and then the Stoic usage has a further implication. Since the sage is supposed to be infallible, he knows what is really good, and so his will must be a desire not merely for the apparent good, but simply for what is good. A non-sage could presumably achieve a similar result by desiring what he believes to be good, only with the reservation, 'if God wills'. He can then set his heart on what he believes to be good only in so far as it actually is so. But a non-sage's desire will be called a *boulêsis* or *voluntas* only in a looser sense.

The Stoics: interrogation of appearances versus Posidonius's willpower

Although there were developments in the direction of a fuller concept of will, for most Stoics a big gap remains: no notion of will-power is at all prominent, because their account is more intellectualist. Great moral effort is required, but it is the intellectual effort of questioning appearances. Epictetus told his students to practise questioning the appearance that the beautiful or grand passer-by involves something good, or the bereaved or hungry person has encountered something bad.[78] Admittedly, Epictetus does refer to the questioning of appearances as a struggle (*agônisteon*),[79] but the process is described in intellectual terms.

Other references to strength, or domination, are also intellectualized by the Stoics. Although they talk of strength and weakness, connecting it with tension in the soul, which enables it to endure,[80] the weakness is the intellectual weakness of a weak assent: if you have not sufficiently questioned appearances, you will have a weak and changeable opinion about what is good, or bad.[81] There is a similar intellectualizing when the Stoics talk of the ruling (*hêgemonikon*) or dominating (*kratoun*, *kurieuon*) part of the soul, for it is standardly referred to as reason, not as will. And similarly, when the runner's momentum is greater than (*pleonazei*) his impulse to stop, we have to recall that the impulse thus overpowered is an intellectual judgement.

There is, Mansfeld points out (op. cit.), at least one exception to this lack of reference to will-power. But it is found in Posidonius, the Stoic who deliberately reverted to Plato's tripartite psychology. Posidonius takes up Chrysippus's concession that people sometimes weep without willing to (*mê boulomenoi*). But he makes an entirely different use of the notion of will. He says that the emotional movements press so hard (*sphodra enkeisthai*: a military metaphor) that they cannot be mastered (*krateisthai*) by the will (*boulêsis*).[82] Here the will is turned into something that tries (but fails) to exert power. Similarly, some people stop weeping in spite of willing (*boulesthai*) to continue, because the emotional movements can no longer be aroused (*epegeiresthai*) by the will. The will had not been treated in this dynamic way by Chrysippus. On his account, people who weep, or cease weeping, against their will are receiving conflicting appearances,[83] presumably appearances about whether things are bad. Theirs is a state of intellectual confusion, not a failure of will-power. It is Posidonius' Platonist sympathies which bring will-power into the Stoic account.

Elsewhere Posidonius tends to speak in terms of reason (*logismos*) rather than will (*boulêsis*), but, as noted above, at least he puts a premium on reason as opposed to high spirit and appetite, by following Plato's comparison of it to the charioteer who ought to take control.[84]

Even Posidonius' teacher, Panaetius, had moved a little way in this Platonic direction, when he suggested that there is a force (*vis*) called impulse (*hormê*) in the appetite (*appetitus*) and another force in reason (*ratio*), and that reason presides (*praesit*), while appetite submits (*obtemperet*). At least in the temperate person, the impulses are obedient (*oboedientes*) to reason. But the force in reason is not spoken of in this brief citation as a kind of will.[85]

Epictetus: *proairesis* connected with freedom and responsibility

Epictetus, as I have noted, does not follow Posidonius in speaking in terms of will-power. But he gives renewed prominence to Aristotle's term *proairesis*.[86] Zeno had continued to use this term in Aristotle's way,[87] but Epictetus changes its meaning in a way that brings it much closer to an idea of will, which is how I have translated it, in the passage in which he says: "I will fetter you."

> "What did you say, man? Fetter me? You will fetter my leg, but my will [*proairesis*] not even Zeus can conquer."

Here and repeatedly elsewhere, Epictetus is insisting that my *proairesis* is free from all constraint.[88]

16

Epictetus connects *proairesis* not only with freedom, but also with what is up to us (*eph' hêmin*). All that falls under *proairesis* is up to us.[89] Moreover, unlike Aristotle, he holds that nothing is up to us except what falls under our *proairesis*.[90] I have already suggested that this may have helped to motivate a parallel shift in Alexander.[91] The result is that only the mental is up to us. Epictetus specifies, following his teacher Musonius Rufus, that the evaluation of appearances is up to us,[92] and so is assent to those appearances,[93] and hence the shaping of our *proairesis*, but nothing else.

Had any earlier Stoic anticipated the idea that only the mental is up to us? Antipater, head of the Stoic school from about 152 to 129 BC, has been named as a possible candidate.[94] He described the goal of life as doing everything in one's power (*kath' hauton*) to achieve the natural objectives.[95] So it is probably he who made the comparison with an archer, and said that the goal is not hitting the target, but doing everything one can (*facere omnia quae possit*) to aim or align (*collineare*) the arrow right.[96] Evidently, hitting the target is not thought of as, or as necessarily, in one's power. What is, or is necessarily, in one's power is a step towards aiming right. But are these steps sometimes, or always, mental rather than physical? For all that we have been told, physical steps may be, at least often, in one's power, and it has not even been excluded that in favourable circumstances hitting the target may be in one's power. Thus, Epictetus is the first to make it clear that physical activity is never up to us, on the grounds that it always could be frustrated.

So far I have argued that Epictetus connects *proairesis* not exactly with will-power, but with freedom and with what is up to us. I assume the last means that he connects it with moral responsibility, that is, with what you can be praised or blamed for. But this inference has been challenged.[97] It would mean that someone could not be blamed directly for a physical activity, but only for the mental attitudes involved in a physical activity. Can we be sure that Epictetus intended this? For we have evidence that at least some late Stoics broke the connection between 'up to' and moral responsibility by allowing that animals' behaviour is up to them, without, however, holding them morally responsible.[98] However, I am persuaded that Epictetus does not break the connection.[99] For he is prepared to confine moral responsibility as narrowly as what is up to us, that is, confine it to mental attitudes. We should praise or blame (*epainein*, *psegein*) people only for their judgements (*dogmata*), not for indifferents (*koina*),[100] and you are accountable (*hupeuthunos*) only for the only thing that is up to you (*epi soi*), and that is the proper evaluation of appearances.[101]

Epicureans: freedom more important than will

The Stoics' Epicurean rivals were interested in freedom, but less so in the will. As others have pointed out,[102] Epicurus made a very early use of the metaphor of freedom. The text, as emended by Usener, says of the wise man:

> He laughs down that fate which is introduced by some as mistress (*despotis*) of all, and says instead that some things happen of necessity, some by chance, and some things are due to us (*par' hêmas*). For he sees that necessity is unaccountable, and chance unstable, but what is up to us has no master (*adespoton*) and it is to this last that blameworthiness and the reverse naturally belong.[103]

In fact, Epicurus' usage goes back still earlier to Plato, as we have seen.[104] But what is missing from the passage is any reference to will. Lucretius takes Epicureanism further.[105] He is the first to introduce the expression 'free will' (*libera voluntas*), though he is shortly followed by Cicero, who complains that the Stoics preclude free will.[106]

Lucretius bases its possibility on the unpredictable swerve of atoms. But what seems to do the work in Lucretius' explanation of freedom is the swerve rather than the will. He is perfectly happy to say that the mind (*animus*), when it wills (*velit*), strikes the force of the soul, rather than talking of the will acting.[107]

Perverted will, pride, and fall: Pythagoreans and Plotinus

I have mentioned Plotinus already as developing Plato's treatment of the choice of one's next incarnation, and as using *thelema* as a word for the will. But much more important were his views on pride and will as the beginning of evil. For souls that turn away, break loose, and become ignorant of the Father the beginning of the evil is pride (*tolma*) and willing (*boulêthênai*) to belong to themselves alone. They are pleased with their own self-determination (*autexousion*) and create the greatest possible distance (*apostasis*) from the Father.[108] The same happens at the level of intellect, when it becomes multiple by willing (*thelein*) to possess everything.[109] There is a restless nature originally at rest in eternity, which, however, wills (*boulesthai*) to govern itself and belong to itself, and chooses (*helesthai*) to seek more than the (timeless) present. This results in the creation of time out of timeless eternity.[110]

Tolma, or pride, had also played a role in earlier sources in the creation of lower levels of reality. Thus the neo-Pythagoreans' Dyad, which provided a model for Plotinus's intellect, was called by them *tolma*, because it separated itself from their version of the One.[111] Further, Irenaeus reports that among certain Gnostics it is *tolma* which leads to the creation of the physical world.[112] However, in Plotinus the connection of *tolma* with will makes closer the relation to Augustine, who alludes to Plotinus's treatise.[113]

Augustine's clustering

Augustine's treatment of the will is new in more than one way. Most relevantly, Augustine brings together all the criteria which we have seen occurring separately in others. I will illustrate this for each in turn. First, will (*voluntas*) belongs to the rational soul:

> To the irrational soul also He gave memory, sense, appetite, to the rational he gave in addition intellect, intelligence and will.[114]

Second, Augustine connects the will with freedom, for the choice (*arbitrium*) that the will makes is free, and one of his best-known treatises is called *On Free Choice of the Will* (*De libero arbitrio voluntatis*).

Third, Augustine connects the will (*voluntas*) with responsibility, as in the following passage, whose talk of perverted will (*perversa*) may remind us of the perverted reason (*aversa*) of Zeno and Chrysippus:

> It makes a difference what a person's will (*voluntas*) is like. If it is perverted (*perversa*), these movements [sc., appetite, fear, joy, grief] will be perverted in him. If it is upright (*recta*), they will be not just blameless, but praiseworthy. Indeed, the will is present in all these movements. Rather, they are all nothing other than acts of will (*voluntates*).[115]

Another relevant passage connects free choice of the will with responsibility:

> And I attended in order to understand what I heard, that free choice of the will is the cause of our doing wrong.[116]

Fourth, Augustine repeatedly speaks in terms of will-power and the failure of will-power. He sees his will as struggling against lust. He often speaks in terms of the will's command, while Julian insists against him that he should also recognize the will's different role of consent.[117]

Fifth, Augustine comes to make willing ubiquitous in all action:

> Yet, if we attend more subtly, even (*etiam*) what anyone is compelled to do unwillingly (*invitus*) he does by his will, if he does it. It is because he would prefer something else that he is said to do it unwillingly (*invitus*), that is, wanting not to (*nolens*). He is compelled to act by some evil, and he does what he is compelled to do through willing to avoid or remove from himself the evil. For suppose his will is so great that he prefers not doing this to not suffering that. Then indubitably he will resist the compulsion and not do it. Hence if he does it, it is not indeed with his full (*plena*) and free will. But because the effect follows his will, we cannot say control over his act was missing.[118]

Augustine reached this position gradually. First, he suggests in *Confessions* 7 that whatever we really do we do by will, but this leaves out the evils that one does unwillingly (*invitus*), because these one may undergo (*pati*), rather than doing.[119] But this exception is put in doubt in *Confessions* 8 by the view that one has two wills, neither of them complete (*tota*),[120] which suggests that reluctant misdeeds may be following the will, even if not the complete will. This is confirmed in our new passage, among others.[121] Unwilling acts follow the will, even if not the full (*plena*) will. That is why Augustine says even (*etiam*) unwilling acts are done by will. *A fortiori* all other acts are so done.

Sixth, Augustine develops the criterion of a perverted or bad will. In *City of God*[122] he quotes a version of Ecclesiasticus: 'The beginning of all sin is pride (*superbia*)'. He connects this with the will, saying: 'What could be the origin of evil will (*mala voluntas*) except pride?' Further, he applies this to the Fall of Man, saying that the effect on the will of being too pleased with oneself and falling away from God instead of loving him was what made Eve believe the serpent and Adam heed his wife, rather than obey God's command. Another fall, that of the fallen angels, is treated by Augustine,[123] as it had been earlier by Evagrius,[124] as due to pride (*huperêphania*). In addition, Plotinus had seen *tolma* as causing a descent. Augustine himself applies the message to his own case. Lust was the result and punishment of his own pride, when he failed to listen to God.[125]

A further great innovation of Augustine's is to expand enormously the functions of the will. In *On the Trinity*, for example, will performs some of the functions of directing attention. It unites perception with the perceptible,[126] memory with internal vision,[127] and intellect with objects taken from memory.[128] It is responsible for imagination.[129]

Faith depends on the assent of the will.[130] Emotions are acts of will,[132] and the will is the centrepiece of Augustine's objections to lust. The expansion of functions gave the will a greater importance than ever before.

We have seen how the different functions discussed here gradually became associated in clusters with each other and with a rational desire for the good distinct from reason itself. We can see that Augustine made the most decisive difference. But the associations had started long before him, and it will not matter if we talk of concepts of will in earlier philosophers, provided we see, as we now can, how they fall short of Augustine's.

Maximus's *thelêsis* and Stoic *oikeiôsis*

I do not think that the concept of the will had to wait until Maximus the Confessor in the seventh century added his contribution. So much had already been brought together by Augustine, and what Maximus added did not remain an uncontroversial piece of orthodoxy. I also want to suggest that Maximus's contribution was not so novel either. Instead, it was a borrowing from something that had gone before, but something from a completely different direction: the Stoic theory of *oikeiôsis*.

Maximus was defending the view that Christ had two wills, one human, one divine. But he wanted to explain why Christ's human will could not sin. Therefore, he distinguished Christ's human will as a natural will (*thelêma phusikon*) different from our gnomic will, since the latter can turn in either direction, towards good or bad, according to our opinion. This, to scholastics, came to be seen as the right view, and Maximus has been praised for defining the natural will as a faculty directed of its essence to the good, rather than as something one calls 'will' when it happens to be so directed. Another point considered important is that the will aims at this good quite independently of reason, although reason recognizes the same good.[133] This last point, however, is not a universally agreed feature of the will, since after 1270 it became a matter of debate whether and in what sense the will was independent of reason.[134] As for the first point, the idea of a naturally directed desire for the good does not seem particularly new. Even before the Stoics, Aristotle already holds that everybody naturally desires a happy life.[135]

In fact, it is the Stoics from whom Maximus's favoured definition of the will seems to derive. No less than five features of the definition he cites (and silently presupposes) proclaim this link. First, the good aimed at is self-preservation. Second, what is to be preserved is described by the Stoics' word *sustasis*, our 'constitution'. Third, will is said to depend only on nature, unlike *proairesis*. Fourth, the Stoic term *sunektikê, sunekhein* is used when it is said that will holds the substance together. Even more characteristically, what it holds together is the *idiômata*, the attributes which the Stoics postulated as lasting through an individual's life and distinguishing it from all other individuals.

My suggestion is that Maximus's will (*thelêsis*) is a variant of the Stoics' *oikeiôsis*, that attachment that is felt by newborn infants and animals to their own physical constitution (*sustasis*), and which the adult human can later extend to his entire rational constitution. This attachment drives infants and animals to preserve that constitution. The claim that it is natural is important to the Stoics, because they argue, against opponents who want to ascribe reason to animals, that this penchant for self-preservation is due to nature, not to reason.[136] The account of the will that Maximus turns out to favour, and for which he has been so much praised, is as follows:

> They say that natural *thelêsis* or *thelêma* is a capacity desirous (*orektikê*) of what is in accordance with nature, a capacity which holds together in being (*sunektikê*) all the distinctive attributes (*idiômata*) which belong essentially to a being's nature. The substance, being naturally held together by this, desires (*oregetai*) being and living and moving in accordance with perception and intellect, striving for (*ephiesthai*) its own natural and complete existence (*ontotês*). A thing's nature has a will (*thelêtikê*) for itself, and for all that is set to create its constitution (*sustasis*), and it is suspended in a desiderative way over the rational structure of its being, the structure in accordance with which it exists and has come into being. That is why others, in defining this natural *thelêma*, say that it is a rational and vital desire (*orexis*), whereas *proairesis* is a desire, based on deliberation, for things that are up to us. So *thelêsis* is not *proairesis*, if *thelêsis* is a simple rational and vital desire, whereas *proairesis* is a coming together of desire, deliberation, and judgement. For it is after first desiring that we deliberate, and after having deliberated that we judge, and after having judged that we deliberately choose (*proaireisthai*) what has been shown by judgement better in preference to the worse. And *thelêsis* depends only on what is natural, *proairesis* on what is up to us and capable of being brought about through us.[137]

22

The idea of the will as a desire for self-preservation continues in the fourteenth century.[138] My suggestion is that this, coming through Maximus, may be a Stoic legacy.[139] I shall not discuss here the immediately following lines of Maximus's text, in which he describes the stages by which will is converted into action, because, although I believe these stages are of greater interest, they are not the ground on which he has been presented as inventing the concept of the will.

Evaluation

I have ascribed to Augustine the originality of bringing all the criteria together. But it is a different question whether bringing them together is a good idea. I believe new reasons would need to be found, and indeed a recent work has offered a rationale to show that some such clustering round a concept of will is required in order to show what human action involves.[140] But without a new rationale, we have little incentive to accept the clustering.

The idea of perverted will involves a metaphysics that is not now widely shared. As for the idea of will as ubiquitously present in all action, people may nowadays be more sympathetic to Aristotle's idea that in voluntary action what is always present is an internal cause,[141] always, I believe, desire, sometimes negligence in addition,[142] but not always rational will. Aristotle's examples include such baser desires as anger[143] and appetite.[144]

The idea of freedom may be better treated without the idea of will. Certainly, Lucretius's idea of an uncaused swerve in the operation of the will seems to me unhelpful, leaving us caught in the dilemma as to whether our actions are inexplicable or necessitated. I have sought elsewhere to tackle this dilemma by arguing that actions can be fully explained, and indeed caused, without being necessitated.[145] But there are other treatments of freedom too, which feel no need to invoke the idea of will, and I shall mention another shortly.

As for moral responsibility, Aristotle's view is persuasive that it extends wider than just to actions and agents motivated by rational will.

For some idea of will-power there is a good use. We need to describe the effort to pursue what we think best against desires of which we approve less. But this phenomenon may be better analysed in the way just indicated, in terms of different layers of attitudes. Desires at the first level may be the subject of second-order approval or disapproval. The effort to act in accordance with the approved desires requires what we call will-power. But I doubt that anything is gained by thinking of this effort in terms of the exercise of a rational faculty, rather than in terms of the varied thoughts, imaginings and acts of attention involved.

One element in the notion of freedom has also been analysed, in recent years, in terms of first- and second-order attitudes. Freedom involves being able to give second-order approval to one's attitudes of the first order.[146] To this extent there may be some overlap between treatments of freedom and of will-power. But on the whole, we may think it was more reasonable of Plato, Posidonius and Galen to handle them quite separately.

Notes

A version of this chapter has appeared in my *Emotion and Peace of Mind: From Stoic Agitation to Christian Temptation*, Oxford University Press, 2000.

1 David Sedley, 'Commentary on Mansfeld', *The Boston Area Colloquium in Ancient Philosophy*, vol. 7, 1991, pp. 146–52. The idea that Plato invented the will had also been expressed in conversation to me by George Kerferd; and Jaap Mansfeld, ibid., p. 107, n. 1, cites a passing remark along the same lines by F. Dirlmeier in Aristoteles, *Nikomachische Ethik*, 3rd edn., Berlin, 1964, p. 327, n. 3.
2 Terence Irwin, 'Who Discovered the Will?', *Philosophical Perspectives*, vol. 6, *Ethics* 1992, pp. 453–73.
3 Jaap Mansfeld, 'The Idea of the Will in Chrysippus, Posidonius and Galen', *The Boston Area Colloquium in Ancient Philosophy*, vol. 7, 1991, pp. 107–45. On Chrysippus, see Pohlenz, *Die Stoa*, vol. 1, pp. 141–53; N. Gilbert, 'The Concept of Will in Early Latin Philosophy', *Journal of the History of Philosophy*, vol. 1, 1963, pp. 17–35, at p. 22.
4 Pohlenz, op. cit., p. 319; Gilbert, op. cit., pp. 25–7.
5 Charles Kahn, without committing himself, shows what is to be said in favour of this in 'Discovering the Will: From Aristotle to Augustine', in J. Dillon and A. Long (eds), *The Question of Eclecticism*, Berkeley, 1988, pp. 234–59.
6 Albrecht Dihle, *The Theory of Will in Classical Antiquity*, Berkeley, 1982.
7 R.A. Gauthier, *Aristote: l'Éthique à Nicomaque*, 2nd edn. (only), vol. 1, pt 1. Introduction, Louvain, 1970.
8 Plato, *Charmides*, 167 E and further references below; Aristotle, *Topics*, 126a12–14; *On the Soul*, 3.9, 432b5–6; *Politics*, 7.15, 1334b22; *Nicomachean Ethics*, 3.2, 1111b11; *On the Movement of Animals*, 6, 700b22.
9 See, for example, John D. Madden, 'The Authenticity of Early Definitions of Will (*thelêsis*)', in F. Heinzer and C. Schönborn (eds), *Maximus Confessor* , Fribourg, 1982, pp. 61–79.
10 Luke 22: 42; Matthew 26: 39; Mark 14: 36.
11 Origen, *On First Principles*, 3.1.8; 3.1.18; 3.1.20.
12 Plotinus, 6.8, entitled in Porphyry's edition *On the Voluntariness* [*hekousion*] and Will [*thelêma*] of the One.

13 Frag. 268, in A. Smith (ed.), *Porphyrius Fragmenta* (Leipzig, 1993), pp. 100–1.
14 Stobaeus, 2.87.22 Wachsmuth (= SVF 3.173), conjectured by some to be from Arius Didymus's *Epitome of Stoic Ethics* (translations in preparation by Brad Inwood and by Arthur Pomeroy).
15 R.A. Gauthier, 'Saint Maxime le Confesseur et la psychologie de l'acte humaine', *Recherches de Théologie Ancienne et Médiévale*, vol. 21, 1954, pp. 51–100, at p. 78; Madden, op. cit.
16 Lucretius, *On The Nature of Things* 2.251–93; Cicero, *On Fate*, 9.20.
17 Tertullian, *On the Soul*, 21.6 and 20.5, recorded by Kahn, op. cit., pp 250–1.
18 Tertullian, *On the Soul*, 21.6; Jerome, *Against the Pelagians*, 3.7.
19 Augustine, *On Free Choice of the Will*, 2.1.1 and passim.
20 Boethius, *On Aristotle's De Interpretatione* 9, 2nd comm., 195.2–197.10; 217.17–219.9 Meiser.
21 Aristotle, *Topics*, 126a12–13; *On the Soul*, 3.9,432b5–6; cf. ibid., 3.10, 433a24–5.
22 Aristotle, *On the Soul*, 3.9, 432a22–b7. I have not been persuaded by challenges to this conventional interpretation of Aristotle: see my *Animal Minds and Human Morals*, Duckworth and Cornell University Press, 1993, p. 70, n. 38.
23 Plato, *Laws*, 863 B; 904 B–C; Paul Vander Waerdt, 'Aristotle's Criticism of Soul Division', *American Journal of Philology*, vol. 108, 1987, pp. 627–43, at p. 641.
24 Aristotle, *Politics*, 7.15, 1334b22–5.
25 Aristotle, *Rhetoric*, 1.10, 1368b37–1369a4.
26 Aristotle, *Nicomachean Ethics*, 1.13, 1102b29–1103a3.
27 For different views, see Terence Irwin, *Aristotle's First Principles*, Oxford, 1988; Michael Frede, Introduction to M. Frede and G. Striker (eds), *Rationality in Greek Thought*, Oxford, 1996, p. 8 and pp. 25–6. Frede's Sather Lectures will be devoted to the subject of the will, but I have not had access to these at the time of writing.
28 Plato, *Gorgias*, 468 C; *Meno*, 77 E–78 B; *Charmides*, 167 E.
29 Plato, *Republic*, 505 D–E.
30 Aristotle, *Nicomachean Ethics*, 3.4, 1113a15–24; *Rhetoric*, 1.10, 1368b37ff.
31 Plato, *Charmides*, 167 E.
32 Plato, *Republic*, 505 E; Aristotle, *Nicomachean Ethics*, 1.1, 1094a1–3.
33 Plato, *Republic*, 440 B, D. So Sedley, Kerferd, and Dirlmeier (as in note 1, above).
34 For example, Plato, *Republic*, 9, 586 C7–D2. Thanks to Julius Tomin for this reference.
35 Bonnie Kent, *Virtues of the Will*, Washington, 1995, ch. 3, 'Voluntarism'.
36 Plato, *Republic*, 617 E.
37 Epicurus in Diogenes Laertius, *Lives of the Eminent Philosophers*, 10. 133, cited by Kahn, op. cit. Plato's use is also the subject of work in progress by Myles Burnyeat.
38 Alcinous, *Didaskalikos*, ch. 31, 184.37–40; ch. 26, 179.10–11. Thanks to David Sedley for the Platonist references.
39 Plotinus, 6.8.5 (30–2).
40 Plotinus, 6.8.1–6.
41 Gregory of Nyssa, *On the Making of Man*, 4; 16.11; cf. 16.14.

42 Galen, *On Hippocrates' and Plato's Doctrines*, 3.3.5–6, pp. 184–6 de Lacy.
43 Galen, op. cit., 4.2.36–8, pp. 244–6 de Lacy. Both passages are discussed by Mansfeld, op. cit., on whom this whole paragraph depends.
44 Galen, op. cit., 5.5.32–5; 5.6.31; 3.3.5–6, pp. 324, 332, 184–6 de Lacy.
45 Mansfeld, op. cit.
46 Plato, *Gorgias*, 467 C–E.
47 Aristotle, *Nicomachean Ethics*, 3.2, 1111b26–30; 3.4, 1113a15.
48 Ibid., 33, 1113a10–11; 6.2, 1139a32; b4–5.
49 Ibid., 7.3, 1146b35–1147a7; cf. 6.7, 1141b20; 6.8, 1142a22–3.
50 Ibid., 7.4, 1148a9–10; 7.8, 1151a7; 1150b29–1151a4; 7.9, 1151a29–35; 7.10, 1152a17.
51 Ibid., 7.3, 1146b31–1147b19, discussed above; cf. 6.8, 1142a23.
52 Ibid., 1.13, 1102b13–31, also discussed above; 7.3, 1147b2–3.
53 By David Sedley.
54 Aristotle, *Nicomachean Ethics*, 7.2, 1146a9–16; 7.7, 1150a12–13; 33–6.
55 Literally, praise and blame, ibid., 3.1, 1109b31.
56 *Nicomachean Ethics*, 3.2, 1111b6–9. Cf. *Eudemian Ethics*, 2.8, 1223b37–1224a4; 2.9, 1225a37; 2.10, 1226b30, for voluntariness distinguished from *proairesis*.
57 In my *Animal Minds and Human Morals*, ch. 9, pp. 111–12, referring to Walter Englert, Terence Irwin and Roderick Long.
58 Aristotle, *Nicomachean Ethics*, 5.8, 1135a24; *Eudemian Ethics*, 2.9, 1225b8–10 (cf. 2.10, 1226b30–2).
59 *Nicomachean Ethics*, 3.1, 1110a15–18; 3.5, 1113b19–23; 1114a18–19.
60 Democritus frags. 257–9 DK, from Stobaeus *Florilegium*, 4.2.13, Hense.
61 Ap. Pophyrium, *Abstinence*, 1.14.
62 Epicurus, *On Nature*, 34.25, lines 22–34, Arrighetti, 2nd edn, Turin, 1973.
63 Epictetus, *Discourses*, 1.22.10.
64 Alexander, *On Fate*, ch. 33, 205. 15–22 Bruns (CAG suppl., vol. 2, pt 2), discussed in my *Animal Minds and Human Morals*, p. 110.
65 R.A. Gauthier traces other uses of *electio*, first for the Stoic *selection* (*eklogê*) of preferred indifferents, and then, in William of Auxerre, for assent: 'Saint Maxime le Confesseur et la psychologie de l'acte humaine', pp. 86–7, n.127; p. 92.
66 Thomas Aquinas, *Summa Theologiae*, II-I, q.13, a.2, ad 3; II-I, q.6, a.2, in corp. See Terence Irwin, 'Who discovered the will?', *Philosophical Perspectives* 6, 1992, 453–473.
67 Alexander, *On Fate*, ch. 13. Bob Sharples has pointed out that P. Thillet's preface to his 1963 edition of the medieval Latin attributes the Latin to Thomas's associate, William of Moerbeke.
68 Descartes, *Fourth Meditation*.
69 Alexander, *On the Soul*, 72. 26–73. 2 Bruns (CAG suppl., vol. 2, pt 1), a passage discussed by Victor Caston at the Commentators Workshop, Institute of Classical Studies, London, 16 June 1997.
70 Seneca, *On Anger*, 2.4.1.
71 Stobaeus, 2.88. 1 Wachsmuth (= SVF 3.171).
72 Stobaeus, 2. 86.17–18 Wachsmuth (= SVF 3.169).
73 Plutarch, *On the Contradictions of the Stoics*, 1037 F (= SVF 3.175).
74 Pohlenz, *Die Stoa*, vol. 1, p. 319. This has been the dominant view. For replies see Rist, *Stoic Philosophy*, 224ff., and, decisively, Brad Inwood, 'The Will in Seneca the Younger', *Classical Philology*, 95 (2002): 44–60.

26

75 Kahn, 'Discovering the Will', Gauthier, 'Saint Maxime le Confesseur et la psychologie de l'acte humaine', p. 90.

76 Cicero, *On Fate*, 11.23.

77 Cicero, *Tusculan Disputations*, 4.12.

78 Epictetus, *Discourses*, 3.3.14–19.

79 The title of Epictetus, *Discourses*, 2.18 is, 'How one is to struggle [*agônis-teon*] against appearances'.

80 Galen, *On Hippocrates' and Plato's Doctrines*, 4.6.5–6; 5.2.26–7, p. 300 de Lacy.

81 Stobaeus, 2.111.18–112.8 (= SVF 3.548; LS 41G). The point is made by Sedley, 'Commentary on Mansfeld'.

82 Posidonius at Galen, *On Hippocrates' and Plato's Doctrines*, 4.7.37, p. 288 de Lacy, discussed by Mansfeld, op. cit.

83 Chrysippus at Galen, *On Hippocrates' and Plato's Doctrines*, 4.7.16, p. 284 de Lacy.

84 Galen, *On Hippocrates' and Plato's Doctrines*, 5.5.32–5; 5.6.3 1, pp. 324, 332 de Lacy.

85 Cicero, *On Duties*, 1.101; 2.18.

86 Robert Dobbin, '*Proairesis* in Epictetus', *Ancient Philosophy*, vol. 11, 1991, pp. 111–35, argues that Epictetus appropriates the term in order to answer criticism from the Aristotelian school, that the Stoics failed to make room for *proairesis* in their account of basic causal principles (*arkhai*).

87 The contrast of *proairesis* and nature as sources of nobility in Zeno's letter to King Antigonus contains some echo of Aristotle: Diogenes Laertius, *Lives of the Eminent Philosophers* 8. 7.

88 Epictetus, *Discourses*, 1.1.23; cf., for example, 1.17.21–8; 4.1.72–80; *Handbook* 9. I discuss this further in *Self: Ancient and Modern Insights about Individuality, Life and Death*, Oxford and Chicago University Presses, 2006, Chapter 10, 'Self as practical reason: Epictetus' inviolable self and Aristotle's deliberate choice.

89 Epictetus, *Discourses*, 2.13.10; 4.1.100.

90 Epictetus, *Discourses*, 1.22.10.

91 Alexander, *On Fate*, 33, 205. 19–20.

92 Musonius, frag. 38, Hense, from Stobaeus 2.8.30 Wachsmuth; Epictetus, *Discourses*, 1.1.7; 1.12.34; 2.19.32 and 39; 3.24.69; 4.1.74.

93 Epictetus, *Discourses*, 4.1.74.

94 Susanne Bobzien, 'Stoic Conceptions of Freedom and their Relation to Ethics', in Sorabji (ed.), *Aristotle and After*, pp. 71–89.

95 Stobaeus, 2.76. 13–15 Wachsmuth.

96 Cicero, *On Ends*, 3.22; with Plutarch, *On Common Notions*, 1071 B–C.

97 See the illuminating D.Phil. dissertation of Susanne Bobzien, 'Determinism and free will in Stoic philosophy', Oxford, 1992, revised version *Determinism and Freedom in Stoic Philosophy*, Oxford, 1999; overview provided in her article 'Stoic Conceptions of Freedom and their Relation to Ethics'.

98 Alexander, *On Fate*, ch. 13, 182.8–20; cf. Nemesius, *On the Nature of Man*, ch. 35, both discussed by Bobzien.

99 By Ricardo Salles, who supplied me with the first reference and plans to discuss the matter further. See his *The Stoics on Determinism and Compatibilism*, Ashgate, Aldershot 2006, based on his Ph.D. dissertation, London 1997.

100 Epictetus, *Discourses*, 4.4.44.
101 Ibid., 1.12.34.
102 Kahn, 'Discovering the Will'.
103 Epicurus, *Letter to Menoeceus*, in Diogenes Laertius, *Lives of the Eminent Philosophers*, 10.133.
104 Plato, *Republic*, 10, 617 E 3.
105 Lucretius, *On the Nature of Things*, 2.251–93.
106 Cicero, *On Fate*, 9.20.
107 Lucretius, *On the Nature of Things*, 4.886–7; Gilbert, 'The Concept of Will in Early Latin Philosophy', pp. 19–20.
108 Plotinus, 5.11.1 (1–22). The references are collected by John Rist, *Augustine*, Cambridge, 1996, p. 188.
109 Plotinus, 3.8.8 (32–6).
110 Plotinus, 3.7.11 (15–16).
111 Pseudo-Iamblichus (Nicomachus of Geresa), *Theologoumena Arithmeticae*, p. 9, lines 5–6 de Falco (Teubner edn.). See the note in A.H. Armstrong's translation of Plotinus (Loeb edn.), ad 5. 1. 1, and his discussion in the *Cambridge History of Later Greek and Early Mediaeval Philosophy*, Cambridge, 1970, pp. 242–5; see also Naguib Baladi, 'L'audace chez Plotin', in *Le Néoplatonisme*, Colloque CNRS at Royaumont, Paris, 1971, pp. 89–97.
112 Irenaeus, *Against Heresies*, 1.2.2ff.; 1.29.4.
113 Augustine, *City of God*, 10.23, alluding to 5.1.1.
114 Augustine, *City of God*, 5.11.
115 Ibid., 14.6. For perversion of reason in Zeno and Chrysippus see Galen *On Hippocrates' and Plato's Doctrines*, 4.2.12 and 24; 4.4.17; 4.4.20–1; 4.4.23; 5.5.14, pp. 240–2, 254–6, 318–20 de Lacy; Diogenes Laertius, *Lives of the Eminent Philosophers*, 7. 110; Themistius, *In DA* 107. 17–18 (= SVF 3. 412, 382); Calcidius, *In Tim.* ch. 165; Cicero, *Tusculan Disputations*, 4. 11 (= SVF 3.229 and 229a; 1. 205).
116 Augustine, *Confessions*, 7.3.5.
117 Augustine, *Against Julian*, 5.5.20.
118 Augustine, *On the Spirit and the Letter*, 31.53.
119 Augustine, *Confessions*, 7.3.5.
120 Ibid., 8.9.
121 Cf. also Augustine, *Literal Interpretation of Genesis*, 9.14.25.
122 Augustine, *City of God*, 14.13.
123 Augustine, *Confessions*, 7.3.5.
124 Evagrius, *On Eight Bad Thoughts*, 15 , col. 1217 A, *Patrologia Graeca*, vol. 79.
125 Augustine, *Confessions*, 7.7.11.
126 Augustine, *On the Trinity*, 11.2.2ff.; 11.2.5; 11.3.1.
127 Ibid., 11.3.6.
128 Ibid., 14.10.13.
129 Ibid., 11.17.
130 Augustine, *Exposition of Propositions in the Epistle to the Romans*, Ch. 60; *Sermons*, 43.4; *On the Spirit and the Letter*, 31.54; 34.60.
132 Augustine, *City of God*, 14.6.

XIII

28
133 Gauthier, 'Saint Maxime le Confesseur et la psychologie de l'acte humaine', 58, 79, endorsed by Madden, 'The Authenticity of Early Definitions of Will (*thelêsis*)'. I am grateful to Martin Stone for drawing my attention to this literature.
134 Kent, *Virtues of the Will*, ch. 3.
135 Aristotle, *Nicomachean Ethics*, 1.1, 1094a1–3.
136 Sorabji, *Animal Minds and Human Morals*, ch. 7. *Oikeiôsis* is explained in chapters 12 and 13.
137 Maximus, *Letter to Marinus*, cols. 12 C–13 A, Patrologia Graeca, vol. 91.
138 Kent, *Virtues of the Will*, ch. 3.
139 I am grateful for discussion with Malcolm Schofield, who has helped me to strengthen my case, and to B. Markesinis for letting me see his forthcoming edition of the text and for his valuable comments.
140 Thomas Pink, *The Psychology of Freedom*, Cambridge, 1996.
141 Aristotle, *Nicomachean Ethics*, 3.1, 1111a22–4.
142 Aristotle, *Nicomachean Ethics*, 5.8, 1135b17–19, as treated in my *Necessity, Cause and Blame*, pp. 275, 279.
143 Aristotle, *Nicomachean Ethics*, 3.1, 1110b25–7; 5.8, 1135b20–2 with 1135a23–33.
144 Aristotle, *Nicomachean Ethics*, 7.3, 1147a33–4, with 7.10, 1152a15–16.
145 Sorabji, *Necessity, Cause and Blame*, ch. 2, Duckworth, 1980.
146 Harry Frankfurt, 'Freedom of the Will and the Concept of a Person', *Journal of Philosophy*, vol. 68, 1970, pp. 5–20.

INDEX ON PERCEPTION

Chapter XII on Moral Conscience, and Chapter XIII on Will, have been indexed separately, and are printed after this index on Perception, which mostly covers Chapters I–XI. References to "Intro" refer to the sections of the Introduction at the front of the book.

used for ruling out smallest magnitudes:
VIII 139–40
in *discontinuous* spreading of light, first
instant of illumination: VIII 140
in *continuous* change, no first or last
velocity above zero: IX 162
no first or last instant or point of being
away from start or finish: IX 159,
161–2, 171–4
easier to register first instant of having,
than last instant of not having, come
into view: IX 164–5
no first or last velocity above zero:
IX 162
no first instant in Aristotle's *energeia*,
if to be engaging is to *have* been
engaging in *energeia*: IX 165
alternative of *no* motion or rest at an
instant: IX 159; 170–71, 174, 175
'impeded science': IX 159, 174, 175
applicable to instant of reversing
direction?: IX 167
but at an instant can be white, or at a
point, or *have* completed a change or
acquired a new state: IX 171
definition of motion at an instant:
IX 174–5
Continuum (3)
time continuous, so infinitely divisible,
not atomic: IX 160
instants sizeless boundaries, cannot be
adjacent: IX 160
discontinuous motion of partless atom,
which cannot occupy a new position
part by part: IX 164, 169
no process of coming into being of the
process of coming into being, nor of
sizeless points or instants: IX 168
paradox of heap, one grain cannot make a
difference: IX 177
Cook, John: 1.63
Cooper, John: III 195
Cornford, Maurice: VI 63
Crane, Timothy: III 199–201
Cyrenaics: III 199

Davidson, Donald: III 206
Democritus: I 44–5, 53, 55; VI 69, 72, 75, 78;
VII 297–8; Intro for Ch. VIII
Dennett, Daniel: III 206; VIII 138
Descartes: I 42, 44–51, 55, 59, 61–2, 64;
III 211, 224; IV 227; XI 133, 136,
137
Desire, its connexion with action: I 56–9
Dewan, Lawrence: IV 238, 243

Diels, Hermann: III 201
Diodorus Cronus: IX 164, 169
Diogenes of Oenoanda: III 207
Donini, Pierluigi: Intro for Chs I–II
Dreams: V 9
Dretske, F: III 207
Durandus: IV 245

Ebbesen, Sten: IV 246
Ebert, Theo: III 199
Echo: IV 230–31, 244; V 6
Ellis, John: III 225; IV 227, 233–4
Emilsson, Eyjólfur: IV 235
Emotions: I 47; II 155–6; V 8–9
Empedocles: I 44, 53, 55; VI 72; VII 297–8,
304, VIII 132
Energeia
vs. *dunamis*: I 43
vs. *kinêsis*: I 46
actualisation: I 46
Epicureans: III 199, 201, 206–7
Epicurus: III 201, 206, 207: IX 164, 169
Estimative faculty (Avicenna): IV 236
Eudoxus: VII 297
Eustratius: X 100
Evans, Gareth: III 200
Evans, Ralph, M. (colour theory): VII 295
Experience: III 201–2
dist. belief: III 202

Farabi, al-: IV 238
Fire, different purity of ordinary and
transparent elemental fire: VIII 132
Fodor, Jerry: III 199
Fortenbaugh, William: I 59; III 198;
VIII 129
Frank, Richard M.: IV 246
Frede, Michael: III 195, 203–4, 207
Freud, Sigmund: III 224; IV 247

Gaiser, Konrad: VII 297, 304
Galen: II 153–7, 161; III 209; IV 230, 231;
X 104; Intro for Chs I–II
Gauthier, René Antoine: IV 241, 246–7
Geach, Peter: III 200
Ghazâlî, al-: IV 238
Gibson, J.J.: X 107
Gill, Christopher: III 206
Gilson, Étienne: VII 302
Glidden, David: III 209, 210
Goethe, Wilhelm: V 4; VII 294–5; VIII 130
Gottschalk, Hans: Intro for Chs I–II
Grice, Paul: VI 60, 64, 67
Grünbaum, Adolf: IX 160
Grusser, O.-J.: X 108

INDEX ON MORAL CONSCIENCE

All page references in this index relate to Chapter XII, 'Moral conscience: contributions to the idea in Plato and Platonism', and the Introduction at the front of the book.

later, esp. in lawyers' stress on witness,
    accomplice, confidant, reference to
    self-knowledge no longer explicit:
    512; Intro for Ch. XII
but without explicit reference to *oneself*,
    the knowledge is not always of
    defect: 512; Intro for Ch. XII
Christian stress that God, if not others,
    shares one's guilty knowledge:
    512–13
Latin renders Greek as *conscius* with
    oneself: 513
besides the backward-looking role

of knowing a defect, the concept
developed forward-looking roles
of averting misconduct, reform, or
gaining forgiveness: Intro for Ch. XII

Terence: 513, 525
Testament, New: 511
Testament, Old: 511, 515

Xenophon: 517

Weiss, Rosslyn: 518
Williams, Bernard: 514–15

INDEX ON WILL

All page references in this index relate to Chapter XIII, 'The concept of the will from Plato to Maximus the Confessor', and the Introduction at the front of the book.